Making the March King

MUSIC IN AMERICAN LIFE

A list of books in the series appears at the end of this book.

Making the March King

John Philip Sousa's Washington Years, 1854–1893

Patrick Warfield

UNIVERSITY OF ILLINOIS PRESS
URBANA, CHICAGO, AND SPRINGFIELD

Publication supported by the Manfred E. Bukofzer Endowment
of the American Musicological Society

Manufactured in the United States of America
C 5 4 3 2 1

∞ This book is printed on acid-free paper.

Library of Congress Control Number: 2013950026

To Kirsten

Contents

Illustrations

FIGURES

MUSIC EXAMPLES

TABLES

Acknowledgments

I HAVE HAD THE PLEASURE of getting to know a large number of librarians, archivists, collectors, enthusiasts, and scholars since I first began work on the career of John Philip Sousa in 2001, and I thank them all. Most of the primary source materials directly related to this study are held by the Library of Congress, the University of Illinois, and the United States Marine Band. The staffs at each of these institutions gave generously of their time and expertise. I owe a special debt to Loras Schissel at the Library of Congress, who was kind enough to retrieve countless documents and carefully read an early draft of this study. At the University of Illinois, I am indebted to Scott Schwartz and Adriana Cuervo, who swiftly and generously responded to my many requests for materials. I cannot possibly show enough gratitude to the staff of the library of the United States Marine Band. Chief Librarian Master Gunnery Sergeant Jane Cross and Assistant Chief Librarian Gunnery Sergeant Kira Wharton provided almost unlimited access to that institution's rich collection of primary materials.

Archivists at many other libraries and collections were also quick to answer questions. The staffs of the National Archives and Records Administration, the New York Public Library, the Martin Luther King Jr. Memorial Library, the Charles Sumner School Museum and Archives, and the District of Columbia Office of Public Records were immensely helpful (my special thanks to the volunteers at the Historical Society of Washington, D.C.). The community of band scholars, Washington experts, and musical collectors has also proved gracious and invaluable. A number of people were kind enough to open their private collections, chat about the March King, or otherwise offer advice. These new friends and colleagues include Keith Brion, Carolyn Bryant, Shirley Cammack, Sarah Cole, Dianna Eiland, Jonathan Elkus, Lloyd Farrar, George Foreman, Barry Owen Furrer, Sandra Hussey, David Montgomery, Mary Moran, Kevin O'Brien, and Craig Parker. Several scholars were kind enough to read portions of this study (in various manifestations), and I especially thank Raoul Camus, Nicholas Cook, Richard Crawford, Annegret Fauser, Dorothea Gail, Louise Goldberg, John Graziano, Mark Katz, Jeffrey Magee, Leta Miller, Katherine Preston, Thomas Riis, John Spitzer, James Wierzbicki, and Bennett Zon. For their editorial advice and encouragement, I am pleased to thank the staff at the University of Illinois Press, especially Laurie Matheson, Dawn Durante, and Jane Zanichkowsky. Lance Ottman kindly helped with the setting of musical examples.

Portions of this book bring together revised versions of my earlier articles about John Philip Sousa, and I thank the generous scholars and editors who saw those articles to publication. Much of the information about John Esputa is drawn from an article that appeared in *19th-Century Music Review*; the material on Sousa's fight for composers' rights comes from an article in the *Journal of the Society for American Music*; the data on Washington orchestras is drawn from my article in *American Orchestras in the Nineteenth Century*; the story of David Blakely first appeared in *American Music*; the summary of Sousa's theatrical inclinations is drawn from the *Journal of the American Musicological Society*; and much of the material on march form and performance practice is taken from my volume in the series *Music of the United States of America*. Financial support for this project was generously provided by the Graduate School at the University of Maryland, the Society for American Music's Adrienne Fried Block Fellowship, and the American Musicological Society's Manfred E. Bukofzer Endowment.

There are three individuals without whom this study would have permanently stalled. No examination of Sousa can proceed without the aid of Paul Bierley, a scholar who has made a life's work of examining the March King, his music, and his ensemble. Paul repeatedly opened his home and his mind for my benefit. The Historian of the United States Marine Band, Master Gunnery Sergeant D. Michael Ressler, seems to have the entire two-hundred-year history of this exalted institution at his fingertips. His kindness and generosity sped the completion of this work and opened new doors to inquiry. Finally, I still have a photograph from the commencement exercises at which I received my PhD. Literally towering behind me at a height of six feet and two inches is my graduate advisor, J. Peter Burkholder. Whatever modest success I have had as a scholar or teacher I owe to Peter. With every word I write, I feel him there, still kindly and critically looking over my shoulder.

An academic study relies not only on the help of other scholars but also on loved ones. I thank four furry friends: Master Raro, KC, Rae, and Sonneck. But most of all, I thank my wife. Kirsten, you have been patient, kind, supportive, and enabling. Thank you, my love.

Prelude

A Triumph on the Waves

AUSTIN CORBIN OPENED HIS Manhattan Beach Hotel on the Fourth of July 1877. From the resort's seemingly endless veranda near the eastern edge of Coney Island, overnight guests could enjoy carefully manicured lawns and cool ocean breezes before retiring to lavishly decorated rooms. All of this pleasure was reaped while safely isolated from the island's seedier western edge, an area dotted with the beer gardens, brothels, and sideshows that later earned the island its nickname: Sodom-by-the-Sea. Corbin promoted an unsullied air of refinement removed from such ordinary entertainments. His gleaming expanse of white beach marked the geographic division, but the hotel also provided a security fence and Pinkerton detectives to reinforce its position as a world of class and social distinction.

Despite such trappings, Corbin's scheme relied more on scale than on exclusivity. Brown-bagging day visitors were as free to enjoy the hotel's bathhouses, restaurants, and promenades as were their wealthier compatriots. The Manhattan Beach may have been advertised as a getaway for the highest social orders, but in reality the crowds that mingled there were remarkably democratic. Those looking to enjoy what Theodore Dreiser called a "cool, summery, airy-fairy realm" needed to travel but an hour from New York. On a pleasant summer day about thirty thousand visitors from all walks of life—many brought to the island by Corbin's own railcars—could be found swimming in the ocean or strolling the boardwalk. Here was a place, created by design, for several diverse social classes to revel in sophistication, to be both refined and democratic.[1]

William Engeman opened his competing Brighton Beach within a year of Corbin's triumph, and Corbin responded with the Oriental in 1880. These three resorts strove on every front to delight their visitors' senses. In addition to offering meticulously planted gardens, lighted bathhouses, and a wealth of recreation, each hotel worked to secure the services of America's most accomplished musicians. Whether it was to hear the Seventh Regiment Band led by Claudio Grafulla or the Metropolitan Opera Orchestra conducted by Anton Seidl, visitors lounging near the various band shells could enjoy music from mid-afternoon well into the summer evenings. And what music it was: the preludes of Richard Wagner, the symphonies of Ludwig van Beethoven, the latest social dances, and the newest popular melodies. Visitors flocked to the island's eastern edge for all of these sensory delights and basked in the familiarity of old favorites and the novelty of recent hits.

Amid this diversity of entertainments, none could touch the king of Coney Island: America's most celebrated bandmaster, an immigrant turned superstar, Patrick S. Gilmore. Beginning in the summer of 1879, he and his Twenty-Second Regiment Band—featuring the famed cornetist Jules Levy—delighted audiences by the thousands at Manhattan Beach. For the next decade it was Gilmore who owned the lyre of Orpheus and created waves in the air to accompany those rising from the sea.

Like many celebrities, Gilmore coped with the stresses of fame by neglecting his health, and his reign came to a sudden end in September 1892. Gilmore's death was a blow to Manhattan Beach, but with the summer crowds still months away, the hotel was in an enviable position. With its loyal patrons and easy access to the New York press, Corbin's resort was an ideal place from which to launch a musical career, and candidates to replace the departed bandmaster would not be in short supply. One contender, from the District of Columbia, was a mere thirty-seven years of age and had only recently entered the national spotlight; he was also quietly working to establish himself as Gilmore's rightful heir. Within months of the older bandmaster's death, he had acquired several of the Irish Orpheus's star players and sought to lay claim to his most visible engagements. By the end of January this usurper had been promised the crown jewel: the band shell at Corbin's Manhattan Beach Hotel.

The guests who stepped off the train platform in July 1893 came to that summer's first concert "determined not to like the new band or its leader," but they should be forgiven their lack of faith. After all, by daring to perform on the hallowed ground of Coney Island, the young conductor was challenging not only America's living musicians but also the ghost of Patrick Gilmore himself. The audience that gathered that afternoon, unsympathetic, greeted the new band with "only a slight burst of applause." This hesitant reception left the conductor wary as he stepped onto the platform and "raised his baton in the historic place that seemed still to echo the notes of the old band, and to make his bow to an audience in whose hearts and minds the memories of the seasons past were still fresh."[2]

This summer concert by the sea was hardly John Philip Sousa's first test, and just a year earlier he had left a comfortable position in Washington as the leader of the United States Marine Band. His resignation had not come in haste; rather, it had been part of a carefully orchestrated endeavor to transform a local military musician into a nationally recognized celebrity. Together

Sousa and his manager had striven to find a place within the bustling market of American touring entertainment. At the Columbian Exposition in Chicago, Sousa and his new band had gone toe to toe with the renowned conductor Theodore Thomas. Thanks to the bandmaster's skillful programming, his manager's careful attention to the press, and the conveniently timed death of Gilmore, Sousa had emerged unscathed. By the summer of 1893 he was ready to lay claim to Gilmore's crown at Manhattan Beach.

Sousa's story has been told elsewhere, but it has always been the story of Sousa after Coney Island, the story of a celebrity already made. When his earlier career has been documented, Sousa has seemed somehow predestined for fame as a bandleader, a figure worthy of his nickname: the March King. The story told in this book is different; it is a tale of perseverance rather than predetermination. The musician who stepped onto the podium at Manhattan Beach was not born a band conductor; rather, he grew up in the theater as a violinist. As he built his reputation, first as a composer and later as an entertainer, Sousa drew time and again on his theatrical education. In short, the man who pleased audiences on Coney Island—and across America for the next four decades—was much more than a band conductor; he was a theatrical character, one full of drama, spectacle, and excitement. Put another way, it was not only Sousa's music that inspired Americans to purchase concert tickets, it was the character of the March King himself. As one reviewer later explained: "The non-musical public allows itself to be lured into hearing music which it would vote a bore, if anybody else played it." It was "the exuberant vitality of Sousa, the dash and vivacity of the man," that conquered his audience.[3]

While theatricality plays an important role in this story, so, too, do Sousa's roots as a working-class musician. As a young man he carefully observed his older colleagues and from them learned to court, win, and keep an audience. Fate played no role in creating America's March King; rather, Sousa's success was the result of lessons learned during his earliest years as a professional musician. Sousa came to articulate these lessons, and through them he reached an audience that saw the March King not as some distant musical genius, but as a self-made business success, an entertainer who embodied their own anxieties about modernism, nationalism, and masculinity.

Sousa's story is told here in three parts, each containing three chapters. Part I, "The Apprentice," covers the years 1854 to 1875 and begins with Sousa's early education in Washington and his training as a member of the United States Marine Band. Chapter Two details his career as a violinist, his earliest efforts as a composer, and his first tours away from Washington as a professional theater musician. Chapter Three is a more careful look at two

Washington-based figures who provided Sousa with examples of just how expansive a nineteenth-century musical career could become.

Part II, "The Professional," examines the decade from 1876 to 1886. In it, Sousa moves from Washington to Philadelphia to prove himself as a violinist, arranger, and composer. It was in the Centennial City that Sousa earned his stripes writing songs and stage works, and it was also in Philadelphia that he began to plot a return to the capital. Chapter Five examines the first part of Sousa's tenure as leader of the United States Marine Band and shows how he worked to stabilize that ensemble's membership and modernize its repertoire. Sousa's career was never limited to the military, however, and Chapter Six looks at his involvement in Washington's civilian musical life during the 1880s.

Part III, "The March King," details the emergence of Sousa's new public persona between 1886 and 1893. Chapter Seven shows how, while he was still serving as leader of the Marine Band, Sousa's reputation began to spread beyond Washington. The biographical portion of this book comes to an end with the introduction of David Blakely in Chapter Eight. It was Blakely who organized the first Marine Band tours, thus arranging for Sousa's debut on the national stage. Sousa's theatrical works, dances, and songs are discussed more or less chronologically throughout this study, but since his fame rested on his reputation as the March King, Sousa's works in this genre are treated separately in the final chapter.[4]

Sousa's biography is bound together with that of the town in which he was born and trained. Although this is primarily Sousa's story, it is also the story of a city full of institutions, ensembles, and personalities that would prove useful to the young musician's career. It was Washington—the marble city on the Potomac—that prepared Sousa to face the crowds on Coney Island. Because of his Washington training, when Sousa first lifted his baton in front of the Manhattan Beach Hotel on July 1, 1893, "those who came to scoff remained to pray, for Mr. Sousa and his splendid band made an instantaneous and unqualified success."[5]

The Sousa Band would spend sixty-six days at Manhattan Beach that summer, and the bandmaster made every effort to woo both the island's audiences and the nearby city's press. In mid-July Corbin invited critics and professional musicians from New York to attend—and judge—Sousa's concerts. Their verdict made clear that Gilmore's "mantle had fallen upon a greater leader—if not prophet" and that in this new musician, audiences would find a "new era for band music." By summer's end, Sousa's visage had quite literally taken a place alongside that of his predecessor. In Gilmore's honor the great pyrotechnician Henry J. Pain used his fireworks to represent both the Irish

Fig. 1. The cover of the piano edition of "Manhattan Beach," showing both a dedication to Austin Corbin and the hotel where Sousa secured his reputation. Library of Congress, Washington, D.C.

Orpheus and the March King in the night sky: "The old and the new—the present and the past." Sousa's ensemble now stood "as the best organization of its kind on this continent," and it was clear that "no other leader could so well fill the place of Gilmore as does Mr. Sousa."[6]

Both Sousa and Corbin recognized the importance of these concerts. Just days after leaving to take Gilmore's place at the St. Louis Exposition, Sousa published his latest march, "Manhattan Beach" (fig. 1). When the ensemble returned in 1894, Corbin and his shareholders presented their new bandmaster—and major draw—with a commemorative medal. The Sousa Band and its conductor would take up residence at Coney Island almost every summer through 1901, and it was a fitting home. Corbin's patrons cut across America's economic and social divides in much the same way as did Sousa's March King. While many in the audience may have lacked musical sophistication, they all sought an entertainment that was both enjoyable and in step with the image of elegance that had drawn them to Corbin's hotel in the first place. Sousa courted these listeners by providing them with music that was both refined and accessible, simultaneously catering to sophistication and cultural democracy. Of course, such audiences existed well beyond Manhattan Beach, and Sousa found them at the roughly fifteen thousand concerts he gave across North America. These tours (as well as four trips through Europe and one around the world) made Sousa rich, but that is another story. Ours begins forty years earlier, in a city two hundred miles down the Atlantic Seaboard, where a young John Philip Sousa was training to please audiences very much like those at Austin Corbin's remarkable hotel.

PART I *The Apprentice*

CHAPTER ONE

A Capital Boyhood

THERE IS NO TRUTH TO THE RUMOR that John Philip Sousa was born in England as Sam Ogden and immigrated to the United States with luggage bearing his initials and destination: "S. O., U.S.A." This popular story, which continues to be heard even today, was the work of Sousa's most ambitious press agent, Colonel George Frederick Hinton. Never one to let a good gimmick go to waste, Hinton varied his tale as the Sousa Band made its way across America and around the globe. During the ensemble's travels he created musicians with names such as S. Oulette, Sigismund Ochs, and John Philipso. The goal, of course, was twofold. For some in the audience these names would evoke the musical pedigree of Europe, and for others they could serve as reminders that despite his royal designation, the March King remained one of them: the hard-working child of even harder-working immigrants. Along the way Sousa simultaneously became both musical genius and local son, and in his 1928 autobiography the conductor admitted: "This more or less polite fiction, common to society, has been one of the best bits of advertising I have had in my long career."[1]

At the height of his fame—from the late 1890s to the early 1920s—Sousa was as much a theatrical entertainer as he was a musician, and in the former role he worked ceaselessly to manipulate both his audience and the press. As the band reached town, so, too, did the character of the March King, who happily continued Hinton's efforts to endear himself to local audiences by leading community ensembles, programming the works of resident composers, and complimenting the cultural sophistication of his hosts. Along the way, polite fictions could prove magnificently useful. In Sousa's many interviews the same half-truths, embellished stories, and moral parables appear time and again. This plethora of tall tales should not be terribly surprising: the March King was, after all, a character, and John Philip Sousa wrote the drama in which he played. From the beginning of his professional life to the height of his international fame, Sousa was a storyteller whose tales unfolded during the drama of a march, in the spectacle of a concert, and between the pages of his many books, essays, and libretti. Sousa the storyteller did not spring onto the podium at Manhattan Beach fully formed, however. Rather, his origins can be found in the musical life of the city in which his parents settled and where he was born.

BEYOND THE MARBLE

In 1790 a site just below the fall line of the Potomac River was finally selected for the establishment of a new American capital. The city would encompass two existing ports: on the northeastern side of the river was Maryland's Georgetown, and southwest, across the Potomac, was Virginia's Alexandria. These two small cities were ceded by their respective states, along with valuable farmland and some less desirable swamp, to form the ten-mile-sided diamond called for by the founders. By late 1800, John Adams was able to take up residence in the Executive Mansion and Congress could convene in the unfinished Capitol.

It was widely assumed that the site of the federal government would quickly develop into a center for American commerce, but difficulties were apparent almost from the start. In an effort to prevent the appearance of financial impropriety on the part of the Virginia property owner George Washington, Congress passed a law in 1791 that limited construction of federal buildings to the Maryland side of the river, effectively excluding Alexandria from participation in the federal government. The Organic Act of 1801 established a system of county and city authorities that further divided the district. Worse still, many of Washington's most prominent inhabitants were temporary residents with little attachment to the city and thus were slow to encourage its improvement. As the nineteenth century began, sewage from federal office buildings emptied toward the national mall to create a fetid marsh that threatened epidemics of dysentery, typhoid, and cholera. In 1815 the newly arrived Representative Elijah Mills would tell his family, "It is impossible for me to describe to you my feelings on entering this miserable desert, this scene of desolation and horror. . . . I can truly say that the first appearance of this seat of the national government has produced in me nothing but absolute loathing and disgust."[2]

The decades before the Civil War placed further strain on the national capital. The economy of Alexandria, where residents were already feeling both geographically and politically isolated, was further threatened by calls for abolition in the Virginia State Assembly. The port was a major player in the American slave trade, and in an effort to neutralize more progressive voices, some residents lobbied for a return to state control. They were successful in 1847, just in time to avoid the Compromise of 1850, which outlawed the slave trade (although not slavery itself) within the now geographically reduced District of Columbia.[3]

The census of 1850 revealed fewer than fifty-two thousand residents in the capital, and this number was further reduced during summer months when malaria-carrying mosquitoes encouraged many to flee for cooler climes in the Appalachian Mountains. Mid-century Washington was, in many ways, a city still unfinished. A stroll from the White House to the Capitol took one along muck-filled streets that turned into dusty paths in the summer's heat; livestock grazed in an open pasture where politics and economics seemed to have permanently stalled construction of the Washington Monument; and the grandeur of carefully planned avenues and federal buildings stood in stark contrast to the squalid row houses and scattered hotels they dwarfed.

Despite this fit of half-finished endeavors, however, Washington was the eighteenth-largest urban area in the United States. It was also growing fast: over the course of the 1850s, the population swelled by more than 40 percent to seventy-five thousand. The stability of the federal government helped the city weather the financial panic of 1857, and with the threat of war Congress sought to endow the capital with signs of impregnable strength and unshakable unity. Major improvements were made to City Hall and the Patent Office, and work began to enlarge the Capitol Building and construct its towering dome. Such gestures of grandeur were matched by more humanitarian efforts. The Soldiers' Home opened to needy veterans in 1851, and Dorothea Dix managed to establish the humane Government Hospital for the Insane in 1855. A new system began to provide running water to public fountains at the end of the decade, and soon thereafter it would start delivery to individual residences. Smaller but equally valuable improvements could be found in the installation of gaslights and street signs. All told, as the Civil War approached, Washington was a burgeoning city, growing in population, transforming farmland into urban spaces, and strengthening community ties.

THE SOUSA FAMILY

The city into which the Sousa family moved in 1854 was vitally optimistic, and their eldest son would find it a remarkable playground to be explored from his home in the southeast corner. But while Sousa may have been well acquainted with his geographic surroundings, he seems to have known very little about his own family prior to their arrival in the capital. The adult Sousa readily admitted that his father "never let us know—and if he told Mother, she kept her own counsel—just what his standing was in the Old World." In any case, he may have been correct in imagining himself part of an "illustrious line of ancestral Sousas," since the name dates back to the earliest years of the Portuguese Empire. Sousa was always happy to draw an abundance of familial connections before an eager press, making links to the sixteenth-century governor of Goa, Martim Afonso de Sousa, to a governor-general of Brazil, Thomé de Sousa, and to the seventeenth-century historian Manuel de Faria e Sousa. John Philip even suggested that his own given name derived from Portuguese history because prior to that country's renewed independence in 1640, a Sousa serving as chief justice delivered opinions in the name of King Philip of Spain. The same jurist abandoned Philip after independence in favor of the new king, John. America's future March King thus claimed to have taken his name from the two early seventeenth-century monarchs of his ancestral homeland.[4]

It seems clear that Sousa's paternal grandparents left Portugal for Spain sometime during the Liberal Revolution of 1820. His father, John Antonio, was born soon thereafter, probably in Seville in late September 1824. Antonio's path to the New World was a meandering one, and family stories suggest that he spent time in Italy before crossing the Atlantic as a translator for the British Navy. He may have seen military service in Brazil, and perhaps during the Mexican-American War, before finally settling in New York in the 1840s.[5]

Sousa's mother, Marie Elisabeth Trinkaus, was born on May 20, 1826, in the village of Fränkisch-Crumbach, then part of the grand duchy of Hesse. She immigrated to the United States in August 1849 and shortly thereafter met Antonio, probably in Brooklyn. The two were married soon thereafter, and their first child, Catherine Margaret, arrived on December 6, 1850. A second daughter, Josephine, was likely born in late 1852.[6]

As Sousa would later recall, "my mother was not the least musical," and "the sounds my father extracted from his trombone and cornet were awful!" Nonetheless, Antonio managed to build a career as a musician, something he took to only "by chance, not for love of it, but as a means to make a necessary living." Antonio's reputation as a trombonist must have been reasonably good, for in March 1854 the commandant of the United States Marine Corps ordered Major John Reynolds to "enlist a Musician by the name of Antonio Sousa and send him to Head Quarters." The young couple and their two daughters arrived in Washington later that month.[7]

Fig. 2. Sousa's parents, Antonio and Elisabeth, ca. 1865. Library of Congress, Washington, D.C.

Horse-drawn carriages would not provide regular service until 1862, and so Washington, like other cities its size, developed a geography based on neighborhood employment and housing. Shortly after arriving in Washington, the Sousa family found a home not far from the marine barracks where Antonio would work, and their address at 636 G Street SE placed them squarely within the Navy Yard neighborhood. Situated on the western bank of the Anacostia River (then known simply as the Eastern Branch), the area was well hidden from ships approaching from the Potomac two miles to the south. When the city was first laid out, this unseen corner proved an ideal defense for the new capital, and it soon became a center for American shipbuilding. The yard was burned in 1814 to prevent its capture by British forces, and as the river proved too shallow for modern shipbuilding, the facility was reconstructed to manufacture ordnance and anchors.

The city's mid-century civic improvements brought a heightened demand for skilled labor, and the Navy Yard soon became one of the district's best employers, a haven for black and immigrant workers. But in addition to these carpenters, bricklayers, and blacksmiths, the Navy Yard was also home to an unusually large number of musicians. The presence of these players can be accounted for by the nearby marine barracks, home of the United States Marine Band. When Antonio Sousa moved into the neighborhood to join that ensemble he was hardly alone, and one writer later suggested that the Navy Yard "was a sociable neighborhood, and a man was a man even though he played a saxophone. Of course, that's going pretty far."[8]

In his new neighborhood the elder Sousa strove for assimilation. According to his son, Antonio "came from Seville, and was born in America some twenty-five years later." While the Catholic Antonio found a spiritual home at St. Peter's Church on nearby Capitol Hill, his Protestant wife sought to retain her Germanic heritage. In 1860, 20 percent of the district's free residents identified themselves as foreign-born. Numbering about seven thousand, Irish immigrants constituted the city's largest European ethnic group, with the German-speaking states contributing about half that number. Many of these immigrants—Irish and German—settled near the confluence of the Potomac River and Rock Creek in a neighborhood known as Funkstown (now Foggy Bottom). The area took its name from Jacob Funk, who in 1765 tried to establish a port capable of competing with Georgetown and Alexandria. Although his commercial endeavors failed, Funk's neighborhood, which he called Hamburgh, survived as one of the city's oldest settlements. Among Funk's first acts was the establishment of a church at the corner of what would later become 20th and G Streets. A

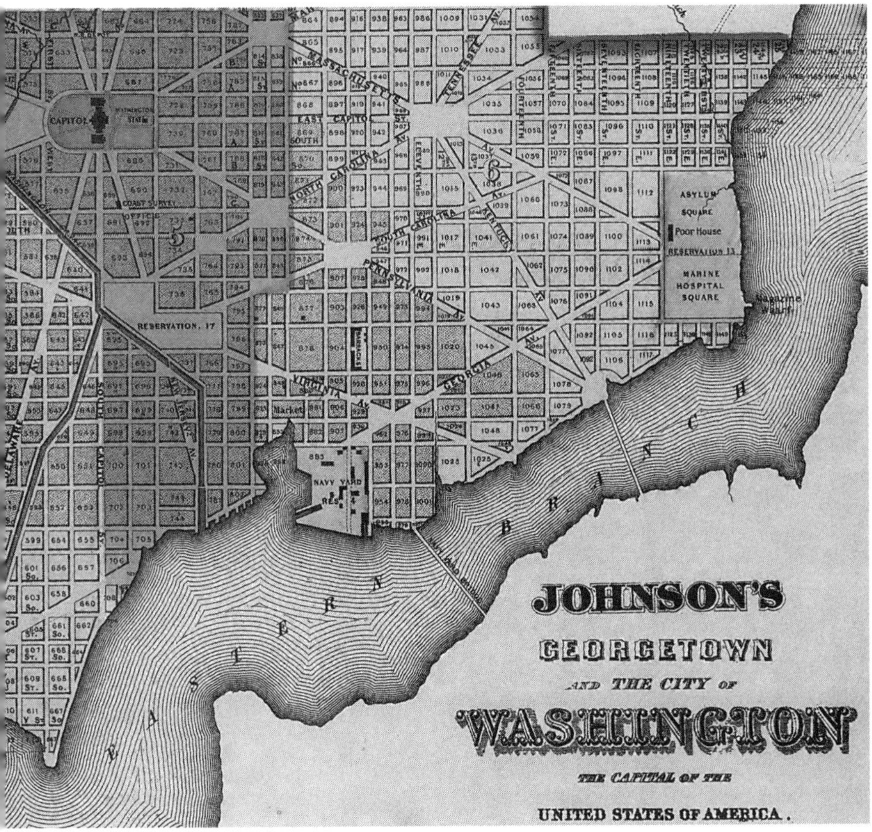

Fig. 3. Detail of an 1862 map showing southeast Washington. Sousa's birthplace was near square 877, and the house where he grew up was near square 903. The marine barracks is shown just north of square 928. Library of Congress, Washington, D.C.

new building was constructed in 1833, and it was here that Elisabeth Sousa found a German-speaking congregation.[9]

In their house on G Street the Sousas suffered their first tragedy, the death of their younger daughter, Josephine, in November 1854. But it was also here that their first son, John Philip, was born on November 6, 1854. He was baptized by the Reverend Samuel D. Finckel at his mother's church on November 26, and soon thereafter the entire family began attending services at Christ Episcopal Church on G Street, just a few steps from their home.

Over the course of the next few years the Sousa family would occupy several properties, all within a few blocks of each other. Early in 1855 they moved west on G Street to a modest brick house between Fifth and Sixth Streets, and it was probably here that Ferdinand M. Sousa was born and died in 1857. In 1856 they had purchased but had not built upon a lot just to the east of the marine barracks. On April 30, 1858, Antonio purchased an L-shaped lot at the corner of Seventh and E Streets, where he built the home he and his wife would share until their deaths. It was also here that several additional children joined the Sousa family: Rosina (1858–60), George Williams (1859–1913), Annie Francis (1863–65), Mary Elisabeth (1865–1940), Antonio Augustus (1868–1918), and Louis Marion (1870–1929). Sousa was correct when he stated, "My parents were absolutely opposed to race suicide and were the authors of a family of ten children," six of whom survived to adulthood. John Philip does not seem to have been close to any of his siblings, and in his autobiography he mentions only his oldest sister, Catherine, who helped raise him.[10]

A WASHINGTON EDUCATION

In 1983 the historian Neil Harris suggested that Sousa's biography seemed to have "no buried secrets" and "no squalid episodes to shock admirers or provoke defenders." This morally upright March King was also plainly evident to his contemporaries. Sousa's one-time road manager William Schneider remembered the bandmaster as "one trying diligently to be the most honorable man who ever walked on the face of the earth." This image of a scandal-free entertainer may well reflect reality, but truthful or not, such a wholesome reputation was clearly a carefully planned part of the March King's public persona. In Sousa's autobiographical statements, the roots of this idealized identity could be traced to his boyhood in the Navy Yard. Time and again, Sousa used his childhood to present a mythology of a youth well spent, one in which boys "toted a gun as soon as they were old enough to shoot" and the ability to "sit out all day in the sun fishing" was a requirement for obtaining social status.[11]

In Sousa's stories he is often accompanied by his father, who along the way imparted bits of wisdom to his eager son. The resulting tales of sport, adventure, and parental bonding would later prove useful to creating a masculine, accessible, and upstanding March King. Indeed, Sousa's recollections of a happy and strenuous boyhood must have been well known to his fans, because they are repeated in his autobiography, in many articles, and in endless interviews. Along the way, nearly every adventure leads to some sort of moral epiphany, and the lessons learned were always the same: hard work would result in just success, while laziness was sure to be punished by failure. As a result, the youthful biography so well known to Sousa's audience was one in which the District of Columbia provided a vast laboratory of physical and moral development and in which a boy's father acted as his most important tutor. Sousa's Washington thus seems hardly a real place but rather a nostalgic world where a father could teach his son the value of physical strength, the worth of moral diligence, and the importance of striving ambition. Sousa had no trouble crediting his success to these very traits, and in 1921 he explained to his faithful readers, "One of the most necessary concomitants of adaptability, talent or genius is capacity for work, hard grinding and never-ending work."[12]

Ambition could—when left unchecked—manifest itself in conceit and stubbornness. But these were, of course, the very faults forgivable in a successful American entrepreneur. Sousa happily hinted at the first: "I was the third child and the first boy. The joy in our household was without bounds, upon my advent, and I became a despot absolute and merciless." According to Sousa, it was the fault of stubbornness that set the course for his early education, when, at the age of five, he committed his most egregious crime. Sousa explained that in an effort to protest a parental limit on doughnuts, "I moved out a plank in our front yard, placed it on two trestles, and then proceeded to make it my bed. In fifteen minutes I was soaked to the skin, and in half an hour my mother discovered me shivering and chattering with cold." The resulting pneumonia confined the boy to bed for two years, during which time his father and older sister taught him to read and write. Antonio was likely an impressive tutor, for Sousa described his father as "one of the best-informed men I have ever met," someone "keenly interested in literature, language and current events."[13]

There is little question that in recounting such stories, Sousa sought to emphasize the parts of his biography that reinforced his image as a self-made, family-oriented, and morally upstanding celebrity. But it is also clear that Sousa's education was not as casual as his tales might suggest. His later admirers often noted the March King's formidable knowledge: "Such a fame, prestige and popularity as John Philip Sousa has achieved . . . is founded upon the broadest lines of intellect, originality and unconquerable force," one critic announced, while another found him to be a "man with ideas and brains"; and another stated that "there are very few musicians, if any, whose thinking covers a wider range." Indeed, the bandleader's extensive library suggests an entertainer of some learning, and at least a portion of his education occurred through channels more formal than those provided by his father and sister.[14]

On recovering from his bout with pneumonia, Sousa entered the Washington school system, later recalling that he attended a "little private school opposite my father's house on 7th Street" and from there went to a "larger one half way down the block." Washington was full of small, privately run schools during the 1850s, and given the family's address in the Navy Yard, it is likely that Sousa first attended the institution run by Jane Spooner and later one organized by the prominent Washington educator Joshua L. Henshaw. Following this neighborhood instruction, Sousa "applied for admission to the primary department of the public school in our district." His family tutors had prepared him well, and he remained only a few hours before being "transferred to the secondary school; it seemed that the teacher thought I knew too much for a primary pupil!" The bandmaster then recalled spending a year at the intermediate level and beginning grammar school at the age of eight or ten.[15]

Public education within the District of Columbia began in a series of fits and starts. Prior to the 1860s most schoolhouses were simply rooms rented from private owners who could find no other tenants. As a result, many schools were isolated, lacked proper facilities, and were often unlighted, unheated, and unventilated. New buildings were authorized for the four school districts in 1862, and each would house four levels of two-year study (primary, secondary, intermediate, and grammar). It was during this reorganization that Sousa was a student in the public system, and since his home was in the third district, he likely attended the first of the new buildings to be dedicated: the Wallach School at the corner of Pennsylvania and South Carolina Avenues. All told, he probably attended a mixture of private and public schools from about 1861 to 1868, between the ages of seven and fourteen. Despite his reputed intellect, Sousa did not distinguish himself scholastically, and he is listed as an award winner only once, in 1865, for "Exemplary Conduct and Punctuality" at Secondary School Number 7.[16]

Music's role in the school system was limited to vocal instruction, which the school board hoped would soften students' manners, "impart to them a taste for amusements within the bosom of their families," and "become the means of saving them from many of the evil consequences of idling away their vacant hours in the streets." In order to achieve such lofty goals, a music teacher was engaged in 1845. From 1856 through Sousa's school years, that instructor was Joseph Humphrey Daniel. The system may have viewed music as an important tool in social reform, but American musical instructors were few and far between, and Daniel was a tailor without any formal education in music.[17]

What Daniel lacked in training he made up for with ambition, and Washington's newspapers frequently announced concerts presented by his students. The admission charged for these performances paid for school pianos, reference books, and various less profitable artistic demonstrations. While the board rejoiced in Daniel's success, it did worry that he might be driving his students to excess, and in 1866 he was advised to confine his efforts to teaching "the science of music" rather than featuring the children in quite so many public performances. Sousa explains that as a boy he sang in the public schools, but his name never appears in the list of prizewinners for vocal performance, an omission suggesting either that Sousa found his musical outlet elsewhere or that he was correct in claiming that "the very worst medium for interpreting my music is, beyond a doubt, my own voice."[18]

There was, however, one event under the direction of Daniel that made a lasting impact on the young man. The defining event of Sousa's childhood was the American Civil War. This monumental struggle transformed his hometown from a small city into the center of American power. Raw volunteers and professional soldiers began to trickle into Washington by early April 1861. At mid-summer the city was host to thousands of soldiers, and it served as the staging ground for the conflict's first major battle at nearby Manassas, Virginia. Following this shocking Union defeat, it was clear to everyone that what had begun as a minor rebellion would in fact become a prolonged conflict. Washington served as host to the Department of the Potomac during the summer of 1861, and the city soon saw a massive expansion of the federal government to support the new war effort. This growth would, of course, become permanent, as the agencies designed to execute battle later shifted to aid veterans and administer Reconstruction.

The city was changing physically and demographically, as well. In late 1861, General George McClellan began to ring Washington with enclosed forts, artillery batteries, and rifle pits. By Sousa's eighth birthday his hometown had become an armed camp, and before the end of the war it would also be a massive field hospital. But wounded soldiers were not the only new arrivals. Slavery was abolished in the district on April 16, 1862, and the city became a convenient stop for African Americans fleeing the South. Once they arrived, many found employment constructing the city's defenses or manufacturing arms in the Navy Yard. In 1860 the city had a population of just over 75,000 residents. By 1870 that number had jumped to nearly 132,000, one-third of whom were African American.

The district saw direct combat only once, when General Jubal Early threatened Washington in July 1864. Sousa would, nevertheless, come to know the heavy price of liberty in the makeshift medical facilities that transformed his neighborhood into a military hospital and prison ward. Given the stresses of war, it is no surprise that a grand festival was held to mark its end, and over the course of two days in late May 1865, more than eighty thousand soldiers took part in celebratory parades. For his part, Daniel massed twenty-five hundred schoolchildren on the north side of the Capitol to serenade troops with "The Star-Spangled Banner," "The Battle Cry of Freedom," "When Johnny Comes Marching Home," and "Victory at Last." It is impossible to know whether Sousa sang with this assembly of youthful voices, but he clearly remembered the arrival of a certain famous general. The event was reported in the *Washington Star*:

> Suddenly a thrill ran through the vast assemblage as a magnificent stallion dashed madly down past the President and his associates, the rider, General Custer, with a large wreath hanging upon his arm, his scabbard empty, and his long hair waving in the wind, vainly striving to check him. On swept the horse, the throng rising from their seats in breathless suspense that changed to a murmur of applause at the horsemanship of the rider, and finally giving place to a long loud cheer as the General checked his frightened steed, and gracefully rode back to the head of his column, the third cavalry division.[19]

Fig. 4. Mathew Brady photograph of the U.S. Capitol during the Grand Review of the Army, May 1865. Library of Congress, Washington, D.C.

A passage from Sousa's 1905 novel, *Pipetown Sandy*, suggests just how much this thrilling event affected the future March King. It is written in the Washington dialect Sousa uses throughout the book:

> We stan's there a little while an' hears 'em sing *Rally Round the Flag*, an' *When Johnny Comes Marchin' Home*, then the old man sez, a-startin' off: "Let's mosey along to where Andy Johnson an' Grant's goin' to review the boys." . . . I wuz jest wishin' it would get a little excitin', when, lickety-split, the devil's own horse comes tearin' up the street fer all he wuz worth. He cert'nly did look bad. The crowd stops cacklin' an' rose up like bees a-swarmin', an' strains their necks peekin'. There wuz 'n officer on the horse, with no hat on. His long lightish hair wuz jest blowin' ev'ryway; ther' wuz a great wreath swung on his left arm, an' that 'ere horse wuz runnin' as if Satan hisself wuz chasin' it. . . . "It's Custer!" bellers er officer, jumpin' on a chair, mos' dead from excitement.[20]

Sousa's school days may not have provided him with much of a musical education, but both *Marching Along* and *Pipetown Sandy* make clear that the young man had an active childhood in the Navy Yard. At least some of this time involved music, and Sousa later recalled: "Washington was, in those Civil War days, an armed camp, and there were bands galore. Strange is the boy who doesn't love a band!" Hearing such music led Sousa to dream of "a day when maybe I would be at the head of a band, a day when I would compose." While these reminiscences are likely colored by the March King's later fame, it is true that the next step in his education involved the most distinguished of the bands Sousa might have heard during his youth in the Navy Yard.[21]

A MARINE CORPS APPRENTICE

In perhaps the most frequently repeated story regarding Sousa's youth, a traveling circus conductor overheard the thirteen-year-old boy practicing his violin. Always on the lookout for new and unusual talent, the bandleader suggested that Sousa secretly join his ensemble as it headed out of town the following morning. Sousa, flattered by the offer and eager for adventure, of course agreed. Like any youngster, he quickly shared his good fortune with a loose-lipped playmate, and it did not take long for the news to return home to his parents. The next morning Sousa was escorted by his father to the nearby marine barracks and enlisted in the United States Marine Corps.[22]

The veracity of Sousa's story is impossible to judge. No circuses were advertised in Washington on the day in question, and it is difficult to imagine that

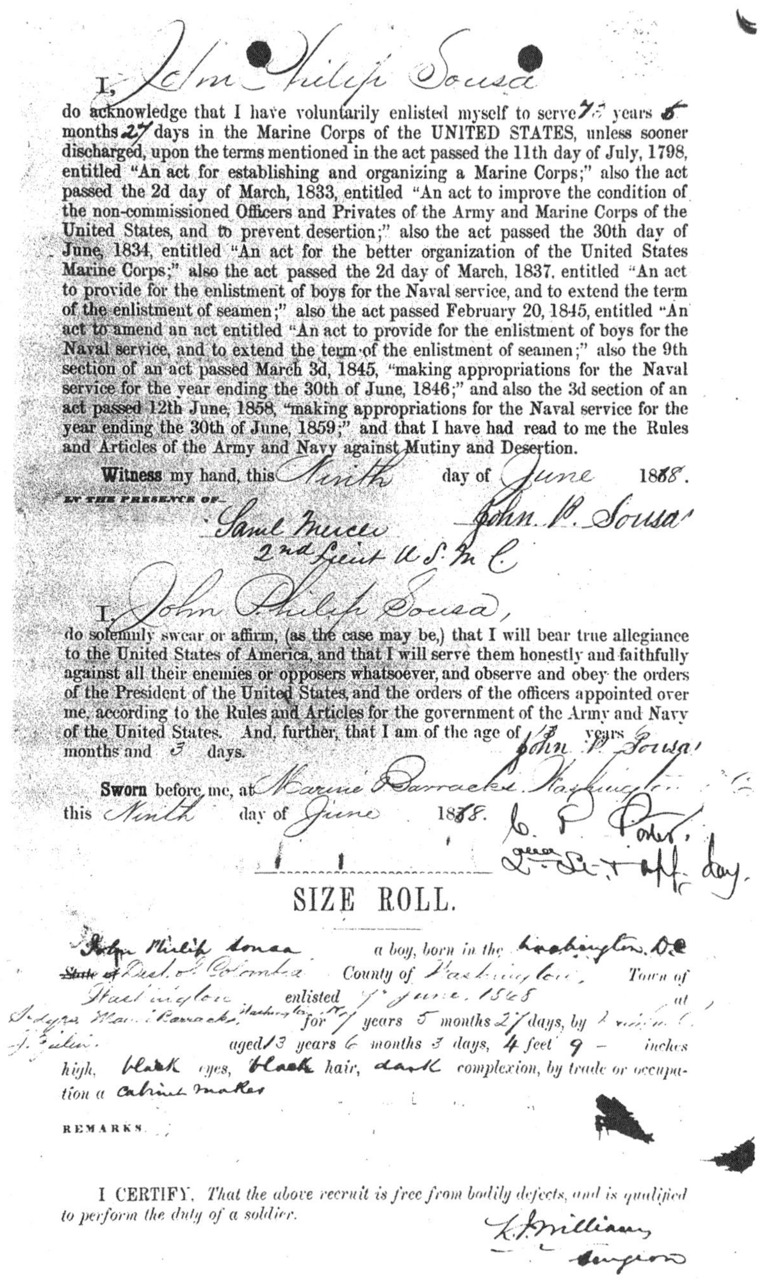

I, John Philip Sousa
do acknowledge that I have voluntarily enlisted myself to serve 7 years 5 months 27 days in the Marine Corps of the UNITED STATES, unless sooner discharged, upon the terms mentioned in the act passed the 11th day of July, 1798, entitled "An act for establishing and organizing a Marine Corps;" also the act passed the 2d day of March, 1833, entitled "An act to improve the condition of the non-commissioned Officers and Privates of the Army and Marine Corps of the United States, and to prevent desertion;" also the act passed the 30th day of June, 1834, entitled "An act for the better organization of the United States Marine Corps;" also the act passed the 2d day of March, 1837, entitled "An act to provide for the enlistment of boys for the Naval service, and to extend the term of the enlistment of seamen;" also the act passed February 20, 1845, entitled "An act to amend an act entitled "An act to provide for the enlistment of boys for the Naval service, and to extend the term of the enlistment of seamen;" also the 9th section of an act passed March 3d, 1845, "making appropriations for the Naval service for the year ending the 30th of June, 1846;" and also the 3d section of an act passed 12th June, 1858, "making appropriations for the Naval service for the year ending the 30th of June, 1859;" and that I have had read to me the Rules and Articles of the Army and Navy against Mutiny and Desertion.

Witness my hand, this Ninth day of June 1868.

IN THE PRESENCE OF—

Saml Mercer
2nd Lieut U.S.M.C.

John P. Sousa

I, John Philip Sousa,
do solemnly swear or affirm, (as the case may be,) that I will bear true allegiance to the United States of America, and that I will serve them honestly and faithfully against all their enemies or opposers whatsoever, and observe and obey the orders of the President of the United States, and the orders of the officers appointed over me, according to the Rules and Articles for the government of the Army and Navy of the United States. And, further, that I am of the age of 13 years 6 months and 3 days.

John P. Sousa

Sworn before me, at Marine Barracks Washington
this Ninth day of June 1868.

C. P. Porter
2nd Lt. & Adj.

SIZE ROLL.

John Philip Sousa a boy, born in the Washington D.C. ~~State~~ of Dist. of Columbia County of Washington, Town of Washington enlisted 9th June, 1868 at [illegible] Marine Barracks, Washington, for 7 years 5 months 27 days, by [illegible] aged 13 years 6 months 3 days, 4 feet 9 – inches high, black eyes, black hair, dark complexion, by trade or occupation a Cabinet maker

REMARKS.

I CERTIFY, *That the above recruit is free from bodily defects, and is qualified to perform the duty of a soldier.*

L. J. Williams
Surgeon

Fig. 5. The document with which Sousa first enlisted in the Marine Corps, June 1868. National Archives and Records Administration, Washington, D.C.

such a *Toby Tyler* opportunity could have presented itself so fortuitously. The story, however, would have been useful to the mature Sousa. It has the spark of adventure, the wisdom of a more responsible choice, and an explanation for Sousa's enlistment in the ensemble that would nurture his career. But it is also misleading. The tale is meant to explain how the March King was born, fully formed, in the nation's capital. There he was weaned on band music and connected from his earliest days to that most American of all ensembles: "The President's Own." To show that his path to fame was inevitable, Sousa's experience that Tuesday morning in 1868 also needs to be unique, and indeed the boy in *Marching Along* seems surprised by his father's sudden order to dress in Sunday clothes and travel with him to work. But given the profession that dominated the Navy Yard, his father's vocation, and the convenient location of a distinguished ensemble, it is hard to imagine that Sousa could in any way have been astonished by his sudden military enlistment.[23]

Like most boys of the nineteenth century, Sousa's most important education was earned through an apprenticeship, in this case one that would teach him the trade of his father. Since the Marine Band served as Washington's principal employer of musicians, that ensemble provided the city's largest musical apprentice program. Simply put, Sousa must have expected—from quite a young age—to be marched to the barracks and bound to learn "the trade or mystery of a musician."[24]

The United States Marine Band was effectively formed by the same Act of Congress that established the Marine Corps on July 11, 1798: "There shall be raised and organized a corps of marines, which shall consist of one major, four captains, sixteen first lieutenants, twelve second lieutenants, forty-eight sergeants, forty-eight corporals, thirty-two drums and fifes, and seven hundred and twenty privates." The drums and fifes called for by Congress were destined for the field music: they were the players who provided the calls and ceremonial signals necessary to regulate life at shore stations and on naval vessels. A few musicians, however, were retained at the capital in Philadelphia to provide music for the newly formed federal government.[25]

Although this early Marine Band was useful for ceremonial work and recruitment drives, the music-loving Thomas Jefferson envisioned a more robust ensemble. He suggested to Commandant William Ward Burrows that he recruit professional musicians from abroad, and a group of about fifteen Sicilian players under the informal leadership of Gaetano Carusi arrived in Washington on September 19, 1805. But Burrows, who had died shortly before their arrival, failed to pass along the presidential suggestion to his successor Franklin Wharton, who was outraged to hear of the enlistments. Equally disappointed were the new musicians. As Carusi explained, Washington was "a desert, in fact, a place containing some two or three taverns, with a few scattered cottages or log huts." After some months of confusion, the Sicilians were finally allowed to take up residence at the marine barracks, but they continued to be administered as a separate ensemble. This situation effectively created two Marine Bands: one that consisted of the original American musicians, and the other consisting of the players from Sicily. The latter were discharged after only two years of service, allowing many to quickly enlist in the original band and thus influence its repertoire for several decades.[26]

The band's modern history began about the time Antonio Sousa joined the ensemble in 1854. Still operating under its original congressional mandate, the organization continued to enlist musicians as either drummers or fifers, regardless of their actual instruments. Instead of a dedicated conductor, the band's de facto leader was its drum major. The Neapolitan clarinetist Francis Maria Scala joined the band in 1842, was soon promoted to fife major, and took over the ensemble in September 1855. Scala later explained just how modest his band remained: "We had one flute, one clarinet, one French horn, two trombones, one bugle, one bass drum, and one pair of cymbals. Not more than five men could read music. I had to direct the bass drummer with my feet." But Scala was an accomplished player and prolific composer who brought with him a large personal library that helped diversify the ensemble's repertoire of marches and popular songs. He was also ambitious. The Civil War provided the Marine Corps with an opportunity to request additional resources from Congress, and in July 1861 that body authorized a principal musician, a drum major, and thirty players for the ensemble. Under Scala's leadership, a band that had begun as an afterthought to the Corps's field-music needs finally had official recognition.[27]

It would be several years before the ensemble could fully demonstrate its new abilities, however. In February 1862 the federal city entered a period of mourning for the final illness and death of the president's third son, Willie Lincoln. With the First Family in little mood for music, the band's activities were drastically curtailed, but by the end of the Civil War Washington could boast of a popular, professional, and adaptable musical ensemble. Like all military bands, that of the Marine Corps was never limited to just one kind of music, nor was it composed exclusively of wind and percussion players. Rather, one might hear at their concerts popular tunes and the latest dances coupled with operatic selections and excerpts from the orchestral repertoire.

The apprentice program into which John Philip Sousa enlisted on June 9, 1868, was not, however, designed to train musicians for this ensemble. Rather, its primary function was to instruct the vast numbers of field musicians required by the military, as indicated by Commandant Archibald Henderson in 1839: "The only way in which Drummers and Fifers can be made is to have boys bound and instructed to play on these instruments. So many of them are required both in the Army and Navy that it is not practicable to enlist them already instructed." In 1885 Commandant Charles McCawley further explained, "All vacancies in the Field Music' of the Marine Corps are filled by the promotion of 'boys' enlisted as 'apprentices to learn music.'"[28]

Boys in the program came from a variety of backgrounds. Some were sent to Washington in the hope that the Corps would provide discipline and structure to otherwise chaotic lives. This practice became so prevalent that in 1881 McCawley wrote to the father of a prospective apprentice thanking him for frankly stating his "son's faults" but also explaining that the Corps required "a certificate of good character with each applicant. It is useless for boys with any vicious tendencies to enlist, because if they develop them, they are shortly discharged as 'unfit for the service.'" One officer went further in 1890, reminding a father that the Corps was not "a reformatory institution." Nonetheless, problematic children did sometimes slip through. One was apparently "so incorrigibly bad that he is an injury to the Service. He has been enlisted about six months, and during that time has deserted twice; scales the wall repeatedly, night or day, and his example is so injurious to the other boys, that I recommend he be discharged as worthless."[29]

Nevertheless, many of the boys were sons of the Navy Yard, and muster rolls indicate that a single family could provide generations of marine musicians. In addition to Antonio Sousa and his son, the Marine Band of the 1860s and 1870s included several Arths, Esputas, Pistoris, and Prosperis. In short, the yard constituted a community of musicians with the band at its center. Many of the neighborhood's musical families, like the Sousas, passed the trade of music from one generation to the next, and in some cases they intermarried, as when two daughters of the Esputa family wed sons from the Prosperi family.[30]

Once boys were bound to the band's drum major they were paid a monthly salary. In addition, and perhaps of greater value, they received both musical training and a formal education, as well as food, clothing, and lodging. This exchange was quite useful to both the Marine Corps, which was able to train musicians to its own specifications, and to the immigrant families of the Navy Yard. With hard work an apprentice might learn his trade well enough to serve an entire career in the Corps. John Roach, for example, enlisted as an apprentice in 1827 at the age of fourteen. After being released on his twenty-first birthday, he reenlisted as a fifer and served on several naval vessels. By the 1850s Roach held the position of drum major, and he would remain in that capacity through the 1870s. Because it was to the drum major that apprentices were formally bound, Roach now found himself instructing apprentices in the very program that had started his military and musical career a quarter of a century earlier.[31]

The apprentice program normally led to relatively anonymous military careers in the field music, so the high command saw little point in carefully documenting its details. One surviving teacher's report suggests that the boys likely received an education more thorough than that provided in the public schools. In 1865, twenty-seven apprentices were rated in conduct, spelling, reading, penmanship, arithmetic, tables, definitions, geography, history, grammar, and attendance. One of the very few descriptions of the boys on drill was provided by Commandant George F. Elliott, who remembered them marching at the barracks:

> In the old barracks here in Washington I've seen from sixty to eighty apprentices out at the crack of dawn for reveille; about half of them were fifers and the rest were drummers. There was also a big bass drum that was beaten on both ends and made a terrific noise. For fifteen minutes they marched

Fig. 6. The Marine Band in formation at the marine barracks, ca. 1864. The drum major is believed to be John Roach. Antonio Sousa is likely the last trombonist to his left. "The President's Own" United States Marine Band, Washington, D.C.

around the old quadrangle playing "The Breaking of the Day," "Hearts of Oak," "Blue Bonnets Over the Border," "Garry Owen," and other airs that had come down from the British regiments of the Colonial days. . . . You had to be an early riser to live in the neighborhood of the barracks; there was no sleep after our fife and drum corps got warmed to their work.[32]

While the apprentices were formally part of the field-music program, after 1859 they earned the same pay and rations as regular musicians, and the most successful of them were allowed to play with the band itself. Indeed, as a son of the Navy Yard, Sousa was likely appearing with the band even before his official enlistment: "Being a boy in the band was not a novel situation for me, for from my tenth year I had played triangle, cymbals and E♭ alto horn (God forgive me!) at various times with the band, and was a great friend of all the musicians in it." Such experiences were almost certainly common among musical sons of the Navy Yard.[33]

For most of his apprenticeship Sousa served under the leadership of Francis Scala, who was much admired by the Marine Corps officers. Scala had encountered one bit of difficulty in 1862, however, when amidst the patriotic fervor of war a Washington newspaper begged him not to perform so much European classical music: "Although Snobs cry 'brayvo!' after a long imported rigmarole, the People prefer the good old-fashioned airs, marches, and dancing tunes." Other journalists piled on, often complaining that Scala had neglected some favorite patriotic melody. Once the conductor modified his programming the complaints dissipated, but despite this reprieve the bandleader soon faced a much more serious allegation. Official charges were filed in 1871 after several band members informed the secretary of the navy that "it is a custom with the present Leader to receive bribes from persons desiring to enlist in the Marine Band." Instead of accepting a reduction in rank, Scala left the Corps later that year, and on December 14, 1871, the German-born Henry Fries was appointed in his place.[34]

On December 31, 1871, just two weeks after Scala's departure, Sousa and several other boys were released from their contracts. Sousa was only seventeen, and it is unclear why he left the program prior to his twenty-first birthday, but perhaps he had already mastered his musical studies. In any case, several of the boys immediately reenlisted as regular members of the band; Sousa, however, waited until July 8, 1872, before rejoining as a third-class musician. Shortly after this enlistment the band's baton changed hands again, and Louis Schneider took over as leader in September 1873. It was under Schneider that Sousa would serve until his discharge on May 18, 1875.

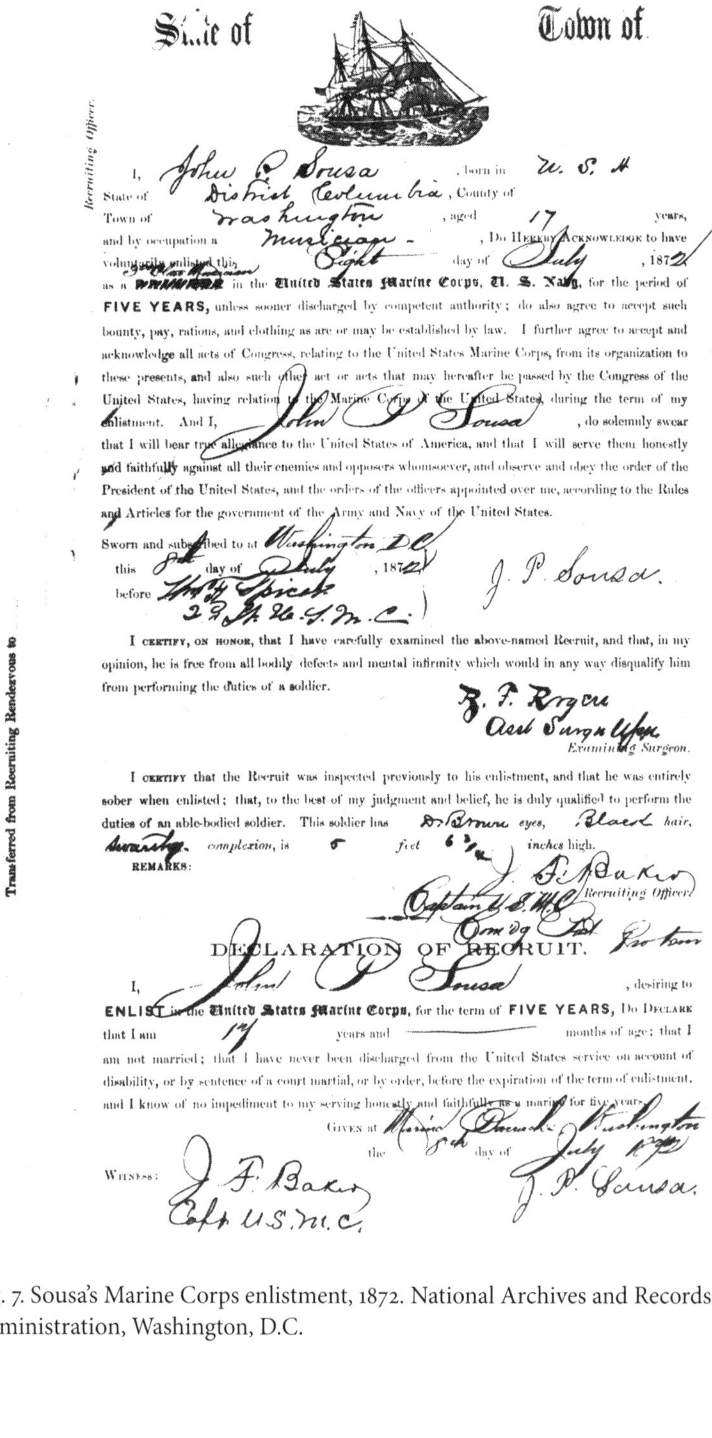

State of Town of

I, John P. Sousa, born in U. S. A State of District Columbia, County of Town of Washington, aged 17 years, and by occupation a Musician, Do Hereby Acknowledge to have voluntarily enlisted this Eight day of July, 1872 as a [illegible] in the United States Marine Corps, U. S. Navy, for the period of FIVE YEARS, unless sooner discharged by competent authority; do also agree to accept such bounty, pay, rations, and clothing as are or may be established by law. I further agree to accept and acknowledge all acts of Congress, relating to the United States Marine Corps, from its organization to these presents, and also such other act or acts that may hereafter be passed by the Congress of the United States, having relation to the Marine Corps of the United States, during the term of my enlistment. And I, John P. Sousa, do solemnly swear that I will bear true allegiance to the United States of America, and that I will serve them honestly and faithfully against all their enemies and opposers whomsoever, and observe and obey the order of the President of the United States, and the orders of the officers appointed over me, according to the Rules and Articles for the government of the Army and Navy of the United States.

Sworn and subscribed to at Washington D.C. this 8th day of July, 1872 before Wm H. Spicer 2d Lt. U.S.M.C. J. P. Sousa.

I certify, on honor, that I have carefully examined the above-named Recruit, and that, in my opinion, he is free from all bodily defects and mental infirmity which would in any way disqualify him from performing the duties of a soldier.

J. F. Rogers Asst Surgn USN Examining Surgeon.

I certify that the Recruit was inspected previously to his enlistment, and that he was entirely sober when enlisted; that, to the best of my judgment and belief, he is duly qualified to perform the duties of an able-bodied soldier. This soldier has Dk Brown eyes, Black hair, Swarthy complexion, is 5 feet 6 1/4 inches high.

REMARKS:

J. F. Baker Captain U.S.M.C. Recruiting Officer. Comdg Post Pro tem

Transferred from Recruiting Rendezvous to

Recruiting Officer.

DECLARATION OF RECRUIT.

I, John P. Sousa, desiring to ENLIST in the United States Marine Corps, for the term of FIVE YEARS, Do Declare that I am 17 years and —— months of age; that I am not married; that I have never been discharged from the United States service on account of disability, or by sentence of a court martial, or by order, before the expiration of the term of enlistment, and I know of no impediment to my serving honestly and faithfully as a marine for five years.

Given at Marine Barracks Washington the 8th day of July 1872

Witness: J. F. Baker Capt U.S.M.C. J. P. Sousa.

Fig. 7. Sousa's Marine Corps enlistment, 1872. National Archives and Records Administration, Washington, D.C.

Although it seems likely that this apprenticeship formed a major part of Sousa's musical education, he wrote very little about his youthful military career (in one article he even condensed his six years of service to a mere eighteen months). Surviving documents are so incomplete that very little detail can be added to Sousa's spotty recollection. Between June 1 and June 18, 1873, he was listed as confined, perhaps indicating some disciplinary or health problem. The entire band took ten days of leave in July 1874, and it was again on furlough from September 7 to September 11, presumably for a performance outside Washington. Both Sousa and his father took sick leave at the end of December 1874.[35]

Sousa does not give much space to his early service in the United States Marine Band, but nonetheless the ensemble did serve three important functions for the young musician. First, he received an education that involved experience in both the field music and in a concert band. Second, it was this ensemble that played some of Sousa's earliest compositions. He explains that "the first march I wrote was played by the Marine Band" and that his first published work, *Moonlight on the Potomac Waltzes*, was also performed by the ensemble. Sousa further reports that he wrote a new piece for the ceremony that welcomed Louis Schneider as bandleader in 1873, a now-lost march called "Salutation." When Schneider discovered that the piece was by such a young composer, he ordered it off the stands. This insult may have prompted Sousa's decision to leave the ensemble a year and a half later. Most important, the band served as a place of professional and social contact where Sousa could work closely with many of Washington's musical families. The value of these contacts cannot be overestimated, and as Sousa began to make a name for himself in and around the capital, he would frequently rely on the good will of his Marine Band colleagues.[36]

THE BOY SOUSA

The Washington, D.C., of Sousa's youth was a rapidly changing city, and the stresses of the Civil War must have been felt by all of its inhabitants. But looking back over his childhood, the March King remembered the 1860s as a period of adventure and the Navy Yard as a neighborhood that allowed youthful play to coexist with military pageantry. The soundtrack of this childhood was provided by military bands, some of which were accompanying Northern regiments to battle, while others were permanent residents of the city. Sousa "loved all of them, good and bad alike." The most important band was, of course, the ensemble that provided Antonio Sousa with employment and his son with a musical education. Sousa later remembered that the Marine Band of his childhood "held forth every Wednesday afternoon in the park at the foot of the Capitol. . . . We children gathered there listening to the red-coated band under the leadership of Francesco Scala and had the opportunity of hearing the choicest bits from the best Italian operas . . . coupled with the popular pieces of the time." While the band played "The Star-Spangled Banner" or "Yankee Doodle," "thousands of children roamed the grounds dancing to the time of the music, playing 'Ring Around Rosy' or stepping in martial array."[37]

Sousa was perhaps one of these stepping children, and music clearly played an important role in his youth. While receiving a public school education, he likely helped welcome Civil War soldiers home with song. By the age of thirteen he had largely committed himself to a career in music. He was helped along the way by a community of musicians that provided him with much more than playmates and an apprenticeship. While the later March King rarely attributed his success to the neighborhood, he certainly recognized the importance of its lessons, lessons that stressed the value of striving, masculine ambition: "From the earliest period of my professional life I had confidence in my ability to win out. A momentary reverse increased my persistency; a lack of appreciation increased my combativeness." For Sousa this striving was only natural, and his active life on the Navy Yard was so full of pleasant memories that he could exclaim: "Golly, but I'd like to go back and do it all over again."[38]

CHAPTER TWO

Into the Pit

DESCRIBING THE SALARIES OF MARINE BAND musicians in 1885, Secretary of the Navy William Whitney explained that "the compensation provided by the Government is based somewhat upon the supposition that enlisted musicians will supplement their Government pay from private employment." That government income has always been dependent on rank, and, of course, it fluctuates with congressional appropriations. In the late nineteenth century most band members could expect a salary of between about $25 and $40 per month, a humble stipend to be modestly augmented whenever a private organization paid the band to appear at a dinner, dance, reception, or excursion. As Whitney noted, however, almost all musicians would have needed to further supplement their wages with some sort of civilian work, and for many that meant turning to another trade altogether. Antonio Sousa, for example, found work building furniture in the Navy Yard.[1]

Antonio was a member of the local musician's union, but he seems never to have considered himself primarily an instrumentalist. Other band members, however, were more devoted to their craft, and some wished to stretch their musical wings. For these players the most attractive and lucrative engagements were to be found in Washington's many theaters. Operas, burlesques, and minstrel shows all clearly called for music, but even seemingly nonmusical productions routinely made use of interpolated songs and dances. Many theaters also entertained their guests with short concerts or other musical diversions in their outdoor gardens, especially during the hot summer months. In short, theater included music at almost every turn, and it was in the city's playhouses that the most skilled members of the Marine Band found nearly nightly work to supplement their military pay.

THE CAPITAL'S THEATERS

Although theaters burned with unfortunate ease, changed names as frequently as they were rebuilt, and often went unlisted in city directories, it seems clear that late nineteenth-century Washington usually had seven or eight playhouses operating at any one time. Each of these theaters offered a remarkable cornucopia of staged entertainments, almost all of which included music in some form. The most coveted musical position in a theater was that of orchestra leader, a job that required talents well beyond mere conducting. Working from the first violin stand, this leader was often responsible for the recruiting, hiring, and firing of musicians and served as the principal provider of music, selecting, arranging, and composing material as needed. Of course, any house required only one leader, and so the majority of musicians found themselves in a middle station: working as regular performers entitled to a consistent paycheck. At the bottom of the ladder were substitute players, hired to temporarily replace absent members or engaged to augment ensembles for more lavish productions.[2]

Given that theater orchestras were usually invisible to their audiences and served little value in advertising, it comes as no surprise that programs detailing their membership are rare. Nonetheless, press reports sometimes name specific conductors and players, and in almost every case these men were connected to the Marine Band as current players, alumni, or family members. The city's military band and its playhouses were so closely intertwined that Acting Secretary of the Navy A. L. Case felt it important to make certain that government duty would not interfere with this lucrative civilian work: "You will be pleased to grant those members of the Marine Band who belong to the orchestra at the National Theatre, the necessary permission to enable them to attend the rehearsals and performances at the Theatre, except when their services are strictly required with the Band." Washington's playhouses, especially those along Pennsylvania Avenue between the White House and City Hall, thus became a second employer for many band musicians, and the band itself acted as a clearinghouse from which theater managers could staff their ensembles. Thanks to this clearinghouse, between about 1874 and 1876 John Philip Sousa came to work as a violinist and conductor in two of Washington's theaters.[3]

The Baltimore-based manager John T. Ford began his Washington career in 1855 by leasing the small Varieties Theater. After a brief and unsuccessful stint managing the National Theater in the mid-1850s, he opened Ford's Athenaeum on March 19, 1862, at 511 Tenth Street NW. This house burned at the end of the year but was rebuilt and reopened as Ford's Theatre in August

1863. It was here that President Abraham Lincoln was assassinated on April 14, 1865, while the orchestra was under the direction of William Withers Jr., who along with his father and three brothers had served in the Marine Band.

Ford had strong ties to Lincoln's assassin, John Wilkes Booth, and he was immediately suspected of complacency in the crime. He and his two brothers would be incarcerated for well over a month, and the government quickly seized his profitable playhouse. The tragedy would not, however, put John Ford out of business. The property at 900 C Street between Louisiana Avenue and Ninth Street NW was variously known as the Varieties Concert Saloon, the Oxford Hall of Music, and Wall's Opera House before it burned on December 6, 1871. The rebuilt structure was leased to Ford in early 1873, opened on February 22 of that year, and remained under his management through 1885. It was here at Ford's Opera House that the young John Philip Sousa likely found his first theatrical employment.[4]

The theatrical scene in Washington was supplemented by houses in the nearby cities of Baltimore and Richmond, and this plethora of venues attracted many touring organizations to the region. Between February 9 and February 21, 1874, Ford hosted the famous Alice Oates Opera Company, which specialized in English translations of French *opéra bouffe*. During her nearly two-week stay in Washington, Oates followed the tradition of American touring companies by treating audiences to a different example of light operetta nearly every evening: *Grand Duchess* (February 9), *Flower Girl of Paris* (February 10), *Les Bavards* (February 11), *King's Secret* (February 12), *Prima Donna of a Night* (February 13), *Fortunio and His Gifted Servants* (February 14 and 21), *Mme. Angot's Child* (February 16–18), *Child of the Regiment* (February 19), and *Bohemian Girl* (February 20). Sousa states that he served as a violinist for Jacques Offenbach's *Les Bavards*, although he may have played for the company's entire Washington run. It is unclear whether he was regularly employed at Ford's, but because Oates required "a complete and very costly combination of principals, chorusters, instrumentalists, etc." and was "much increased in numbers," it is possible that Sousa was simply one of several musicians temporarily hired to supplement the theater's regular ensemble. Whatever his role, by 1874 Sousa had gained at least some experience as a violinist for light opera, the tradition in which he would soon make his mark as an arranger and composer.[5]

During the mid-1870s Sousa also worked at the Washington Theatre Comique, a house run by James Lawrence Kernan. In 1866, after serving the Confederacy, Kernan began managing theaters in Baltimore, and within a few years he had opened a number of vaudeville and burlesque houses along the East Coast. Sometime around 1872 he took over the management of a theater on Eleventh Street between Pennsylvania Avenue and C Street NW that had first opened in 1822 under the management of the Carusi family as the Washington Assembly Rooms.[6]

Very little is known about the productions that occurred at this house, but a description of Kernan's Monumental in Baltimore gives some flavor of his preferred mode of entertainment: "Drinks were served . . . throughout the performance by darky waiters, who called 'Beer, cigars and soda.' The seats were covered with cream-tinted oilcloth, doubtless to protect them from spilled liquors. The gallery gods, two-thirds of them newsboys and bootblacks, sang and whistled the chorus to every song." Clearly Kernan's theater was a somewhat less formal affair than the house run by John Ford.[7]

Washington's seasonal heat encouraged many citizens to leave the city during the summer months, and the various resorts of Virginia and Maryland provided another important source of income for area musicians. During at least one summer in the early 1870s, Kernan's regular orchestra leader left for "a watering-place in Virginia," and his departure afforded Sousa a rare opportunity to serve as a substitute conductor. Kernan had planned for the young musician to make his debut in the theater's outdoor garden, but one of the city's frequent summer rains necessitated a hasty move inside, resulting in what Sousa called "the worst orchestral performance that was ever given in this imperfect world." The manager, however, appreciated the young musician's determination, and Sousa remained at the theater until the start of the winter season. If he found opera, operetta, and dramatic works at Ford's house, Sousa likely conducted a somewhat more varied fare of burlesques, minstrel shows, and athletic demonstrations while employed by Kernan.[8]

It is impossible to date Sousa's first appearance at Kernan's Theatre Comique, but he would have been nineteen when the Oates Company performed at Ford's in early 1874. In a later article, Sousa claims to have been playing first violin for Ford considerably earlier, at the tender age of thirteen. Such a youthful start seems unlikely, but the Marine Band's connection to Washington's playhouses does suggest that he could have made other theatrical appearances during his teenage years. At the least, as a young man John Philip Sousa served two interrelated apprenticeships. From the age of thirteen he worked in the Marine Band. Starting in his late teens he also learned his trade in at least two playhouses. The influence of the band is obvious, but Sousa's theatrical endeavors will prove to have been equally important in creating the dramatic persona known as the March King. These two apprenticeships were not, however, the sum of Sousa's youthful activities, since he was also beginning to test his skills as a composer.[9]

Fig. 8. An early portrait of Sousa, ca. 1871. "The President's Own" United States Marine Band, Washington, D.C.

FIRST COMPOSITIONS

John Philip Sousa was first and foremost a practical composer, capable of turning out new works quickly and adapting older pieces to fresh situations. In 1896 John Lathrop Mathews explained how even the youthful Sousa recognized the importance of having musical material at the ready: "In his younger days, while still a violinist, say from the age of eleven to eighteen, Mr. Sousa kept a 'scrap-book' in which he wrote down suggestions for melodies as they occurred to him. . . . In the course of time this scrap-book reached a considerable size, and it has become invaluable to him. From it he draws for operas, marches and songs." Sousa did, indeed, keep a scrapbook, and in it can be found many of his earliest unpublished efforts at composition.[10]

In 1901 Sousa claimed, "I began to write music when I was eleven years of age, but I have kept nothing of that period." In his autobiography he explains that his first effort at composition resulted in a short piece for violin and piano inspired by Robert Schumann's *Träumerei* and titled *An Album Leaf.* Since this work is now lost, Sousa's first surviving composition is likely "Fall Tenderly, Roses," a song lamenting the end of summer that exists only in an undated manuscript. Given the simple style and youthful hand, it was likely written sometime during Sousa's Marine Corps apprenticeship.[11]

Like many composers, Sousa based his first works on musical models. The anonymous text of "Fall Tenderly, Roses" relies on the pervasive nineteenth-century trope of a dying flower, the most famous example of which is Thomas Moore's "The Last Rose of Summer." For his graceful melody and unpretentious harmonies, Sousa needed to look no further than the repertoires of the Marine Band or the theater pit. But there was an additional world from which the young musician could draw inspiration. Sousa indicates that as he began to perform outside the Navy Yard, he became acquainted with families in the northwest section of Washington. Some of the young friends he made there formed a club called Vis-à-Vis, which celebrated literature, art, and music. It was for this audience of close friends, with their accessible but cultured tastes, that Sousa intended his earliest compositions.[12]

In each of these situations—band concerts, theater performances, and social gatherings—music, while vital, served as an accompaniment to some more important activity. As such, the class of composition into which Sousa took his first steps has variously been called salon music, music of the democratic sociability, and parlor music. Given its accompanying role, such sound was always more functional than reflective, arranged for the ensemble and situation at hand, and altered as needed. Though not completely sympathetic to the tradition, W. S. B. Mathews provided a fair description: "This music usually consists of a very simple and natural melody, set to the most elementary harmony, and brightened up with a few stock passages, arpeggios and the like, simple and easily to be executed by players of small attainment, but modeled upon passages in pieces by first-class writers."[13]

Mathews's words may be dismissive, but he correctly underscores the important relation between a composition and its performers: one in which music was not meant for an attentive audience but, rather, designed for the enjoyment of a cultured, if not particularly sophisticated, class of performer. Such amateurs were no doubt ready to be delighted by well-mannered pieces and were particularly receptive to works that lay well under the hand and in the throat. Their musical tastes were formed by popular but unpretentious composers ranging from Rossini to Offenbach and from Foster to Balfe, composers whose music could move effortlessly between the middle-class parlor, the theater pit, the parade ground, and the dance floor.

"Fall Tenderly, Roses," fits well into this class of composition: it can be learned quickly, and although a seated audience might be bored by its material, the song stands ready to delight the aural and tactile senses of its amateur performers. Such accessibility does not, however, suggest a lack of sophistication. In setting his text, Sousa wrote four equal phrases (ex. 1). The first rises and falls through mostly conjunct motion, with just a single leap. Accented notes are treated with special care, and the song's sense of balance is reaffirmed by its downbeats, which form an ascending and descending palindrome between the pitches a' and d". The second phrase mirrors the first but shifts the listener's attention forward with its heightened ambitus and expanded leap. In the third phrase, Sousa condenses his symmetry and the melodic line becomes nearly reversible. In the final phrase, he begins by writing a descending leap into the second bar. This tumble, along with a slowing of rhythmic momentum, brings the song to a well-earned conclusion. The result is a work quite gratifying to sing and a delightful if straightforward attempt by a young composer to please his friends. The seriousness with which Sousa approached his task is made clear by the song's separate title page, which indicates that it was written "par J. Philip Sousa."

It did not take long for this budding composer to further stretch his musical wings. In 1872 he was approached by a friend named Albert Taylor and asked to compose a piece that might "smooth the road to matrimony." The result was Sousa's first published composition, a dance set titled *Moonlight on the Potomac Waltzes*. The work was brought out in a piano arrangement by the Washington firm of John F. Ellis and designated as Sousa's opus 3. He dedicated the piece to one Miss Carrie E. Foote.[14]

While songs formed an important part of the salon repertoire, piano music was equally popular. In the three decades following 1850 the number of pianos produced and sold in the United States increased enormously, and by

Ex. 1. "Fall Tenderly, Roses" (from the manuscript)

Ex. 1 (*continued*)

1860 almost one in every fifteen hundred Americans was purchasing a new keyboard. Most of these instruments were destined for the parlor, where they would delight the fingertips of marriageable young ladies eager to demonstrate both familial sophistication and personal worth. Given the important social value placed on these instruments, it is no surprise that the appetite for new sheet music was both omnivorous and insatiable, and the number of light piano works published in the last third of the nineteenth century is truly staggering. One writer explained that "the thousand and one waltzes, polkas, marches, and negro melodies, which are weekly thrown out from the presses of this country" came to "cover the land like the frogs in Egypt."[15]

Among the most common types of piano music were dance collections, and while few would sell in any quantity, their collective popularity made them an obvious avenue for a young composer. The waltz was by far the most widespread of such dances, and Sousa's *Moonlight on the Potomac Waltzes* is but one of thousands of such collections. Like many other sets from the 1870s, his begins with a slow, recitative-like introduction. This passage, marked *con espressione*, is followed by five waltzes that pass through several keys with the help of short interludes. Sousa's dances are all unified by a common character, similar melodic and rhythmic gestures, and a consistent structure of two contrasting sixteen-bar periods. In many cases the second of these sections features heightened rhythmic activity or a denser texture than the material preceding it, thus giving the set a strong sense of forward momentum. While it is unclear whether the piece was successful in wooing Miss Foote, with *Moonlight on the Potomac Waltzes* the eighteen-year-old composer had managed to create a work on a par with his models and interesting enough to attract a local publisher.

Sousa wrote several other works in the mid-1870s, including two unpublished songs both labeled "From 'Fountains Abbey.'" It is unclear whether the brief pieces—"Weary and Footsore" (for voice and piano) and "Awake, Awake" (for four-part chorus)—are arrangements or original compositions, but the descriptive headings on each suggest that they are incidental music. "Weary and Footsore" is dated April 1873, and it is possible that these pieces were written or arranged for a Washington theater.[16]

Sousa's next two works were the first to be printed outside Washington: the march "Review" and the galop "Cuckoo," both published in piano editions by the Philadelphia firm of Lee and Walker, reportedly in exchange for a hundred printed copies of each. The march was announced as Sousa's opus 5, and it bears a dedication to Colonel William Moore of the Washington Light Infantry. Sousa reports that the pieces were not particularly successful

Ex. 2. *Moonlight on the Potomac Waltzes*, first waltz

Ex. 3. "Cuckoo," introduction and first strain

but that they "were played by a few bands here and there." Nonetheless, the publisher must have found them promising, and within a year "Cuckoo" had appeared in an arrangement for violin and piano by the celebrated Philadelphia composer Septimus Winner.[17]

Like most mid-century marches, "Review" is in two large sections: a march proper in the tonic and a trio in the subdominant. Each of these units consists of two repeated strains, and the work concludes with a repeat of the opening march. "Cuckoo" follows a similar format. In both pieces, Sousa's writing once again fits skillfully onto the keyboard, offers a light sprinkling of ornamentation, and features some mild chromatic inflections. Although the right hand almost always carries the tune while the left presents a rhythmic accompaniment, there is considerable room for textural variety, and an amateur player's interest is easily kept as the works pass through unharmonized octaves, chordal writing, and contrary motion. A great deal of nineteenth-century sheet music contains references to nature, and Sousa had already alluded to Washington's defining river in his collection of waltzes. In "Cuckoo" he mimics the bird of the title with descending minor thirds, and the piano edition even includes the title word printed at appropriate points in the music (ex. 3). Sousa likely wrote other pieces that could have been arranged for piano, band, or theater orchestra during this period, including the lost march "Salutation."[18]

Sometime around 1873 Sousa became romantically involved with Emma May Swallow, whom he had probably met through the Vis-à-Vis club. In an act common "among all young lovers," Sousa set several of her texts to music. These songs are generally less well polished than "Fall Tenderly, Roses," and in them Sousa experiments with wider-ranging melodies that reveal his roots as a violinist. The first setting of a Swallow text is the thirty-measure unpublished song "Day and Night" from October 1873. After a brief introduction, Sousa asks his singer to make two ascending leaps, followed by a skipping descent. The song later requires negotiation of several other rather large intervals, including an ascending seventh and a downward tritone (ex. 4). Sousa dedicated his

Ex. 4. "Day and Night" (melody only, from the manuscript)

opus 9, the unpublished piano work *La Reine d'Amour Valses*, to Cawthorne Swallow, Emma May's sister. This work follows a pattern similar to that found in *Moonlight on the Potomac Waltzes* but with a much more elaborate introduction and coda.[19]

The only early work by Sousa to set a text by a professional poet is the unpublished song “Wilt Thou Be True?” from November 1873. The poem is by the English author Eliza Cook, famous for writing the text set by Henry Russell in “The Old Arm Chair.” Sousa's tune is once again more instrumental than vocal (ex. 5). He begins with four repeated pitches and an ascending leap of a sixth. Rather than turning around with stepwise motion, he continues upward before skipping down by thirds. The phrase construction is also unusual. The final cadence, which contains the title text, appears an afterthought, lying outside the song's principal sixteen bars. In spite of such oddities, the increased surface rhythm, which rushes the listener toward the song's repeated climaxes, creates an attractive, if instrumental, melody.[20]

In January 1874 Sousa registered for copyright a now-lost song titled “O My Country.” The copyright card was cosigned by Emma's stepfather Benjamin Swallow, and it seems likely that the lyrics were written by this English-born clergyman who worked in the U.S. State Department. Finally, in November 1874 Sousa wrote an untitled song with a text by Emma Swallow simply labeled “Valse.”[21]

In sum, Sousa published three works during the early 1870s, all piano pieces based on dance forms: *Moonlight on the Potomac Waltzes*, “Review,” and “Cuckoo.” He also wrote an unpublished set of waltzes. But most of Sousa's time was spent setting texts, almost exclusively poems by friends and acquaintances, a pattern that would remain true throughout much of his

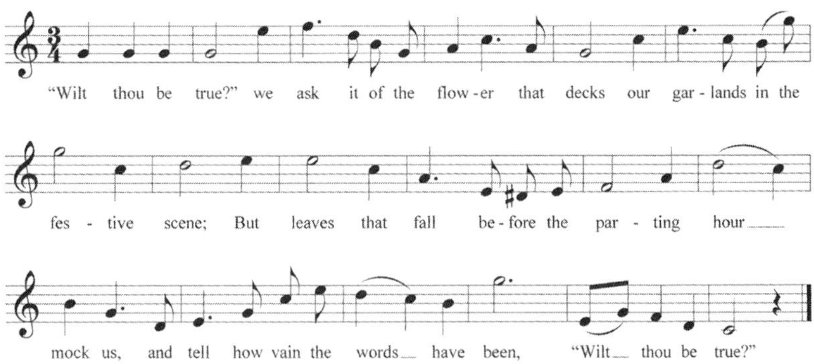

Ex. 5. “Wilt Thou Be True?” (melody only, from the manuscript)

career. An examination of the original songs from before 1875 reveals little that is shocking: all begin and end in the same key with only brief excursions to closely related keys; all have regular phrases, usually of four or eight bars; all are primarily diatonic with only modest chromaticism; all feature regular and unchanging surface rhythms; all are for solo singer and piano; and all are brief settings of simple, elegant, but sometimes awkward verse. Put simply, these songs are not unlike many of those Sousa could have heard in Washington during the 1870s.

In spite of, or rather because of, their directness, all of Sousa's youthful songs are remarkably attractive. Once again, this attractiveness was aimed not at a detached listener but, rather, at a group of amateur performers, likely his teenage friends. With the exception of a few awkward leaps, each of these songs is easy to play and easy to sing. In most cases the piano gently guides the vocalist through doublings and guarantees ensemble cohesion with regularly repeating chords. In every case the text is sentimental, never humorous or vulgar. In these regards, Sousa's early works are like the many parlor songs of the era shortly after the Civil War that focus on nature, warn of the dangers of passing time, and praise the purity of love. While they may not stand out from the thousands of others written during the decade, these pieces do indicate a young composer well in tune with his musical surroundings and cognizant of his performers' abilities and interests.[22]

THE FIRST TOURS

Having played in the city's most visible local ensemble, performed in several important theaters, and composed for area amateurs, Sousa must have been quite well known among Washington's musicians by the mid-1870s. Two events, however, spurred him to temporarily leave the capital. The first was Louis Schneider's reaction to the march "Salutation," in September 1873. Frustrated by the unkind reception, Sousa sought to leave the ensemble, and he found his opportunity when Benjamin Swallow introduced him to William Hunter. Following the 1865 attempt on the life of Secretary of State William Henry Seward (an event that accompanied the assassination of Abraham Lincoln), Hunter had been made second assistant secretary of state, a position he would hold until his death two decades later. Hunter was a deeply dedicated amateur musician, and between about 1873 and 1875, Sousa took part in a series of Tuesday evening string quartet readings at the Hunter residence. The older official was duly impressed with the violinist and arranged for Sousa's military discharge in May 1875.[23]

Not about to allow his newly liberated beneficiary to wander aimlessly, Hunter sought to send Sousa abroad for a European training. In order to fund such a trip, Sousa was introduced to William Wilson Corcoran, a Washington-based banker turned philanthropist who had earned a fortune on government securities floated to finance the Mexican War. Corcoran's name still looms large in Washington's cultural life, both for his building of the Renwick Gallery and for his 1874 founding of the Corcoran Gallery of Art. Sousa would write that after an interview with the older patron, he was instructed to call again and learn of the results. He would, in the end, not return.

Corcoran kept meticulous logs of his correspondence, and there is no evidence to suggest that he ever met with Sousa. On the other hand, Hunter and Corcoran met frequently in the mid-1870s as part of their effort to complete the stalled Washington Monument, and it is possible that the two men discussed Sousa without the formality of correspondence. The veracity of Sousa's story is thus impossible to judge, and it may well be another example of a polite fiction. Regardless of its truth, Sousa's recollection of Corcoran would have been useful to the mature March King since it reinforced two important characteristics of the bandmaster. First, in an era when most art composers active in the United States enjoyed a European training, Sousa could package himself as a native musician through and through: "Though Mr. Corcoran might have sent me to Europe, I feel that I am better off as it is—even without the benefits of a European education—for I may therefore consider myself a truly American musician." Americanism was, of course, a quality of the March King that the press loved to highlight. In introducing Sousa to Chicago in 1892, one reporter explained that the bandmaster "is an American, born in Washington under the shadow of the capitol dome" who "breathed the inspiration of his work from the center of the nation's history." In the end, it hardly mattered if Sousa's exclusively domestic education was a noble choice or simply the result of his parents' social status and income.[24]

The Corcoran story was useful to Sousa in another way as well. The March King was not merely a successful composer and conductor; he was also an entrepreneur, the leader of an immensely lucrative American enterprise. America's business prowess was on full display at the turn of the century, especially in the many fairs and expositions that celebrated the nation's achievements in science, technology, and agriculture. As a result, masters of industry could take their place alongside professional athletes and celebrity entertainers as cultural heroes, and Sousa was again and again depicted as the Henry Ford or Thomas Edison of music: someone whose genius lay not only in invention but also in implementation. In 1899 a Detroit journalist noted how expertly

Sousa created order from chaos. While the language may be military, the image is clearly industrial: "To be able to command men is a gift possessed by comparatively few, and the great general is no more difficult to discover than the great conductor. The strict discipline that promotes a wholesome respect for the commander is as necessary in maintaining the standard of a musical organization as it is in promoting the efficiency of a fighting body. Not the least enjoyable thing about a Sousa band concert is the masterly control of the leader over the human instrumentality before him." Sousa was only too happy to fuel this reputation as a leader expertly controlling a mechanized body of musicians: "That is what I am constantly trying to do all the time—to make my musicians and myself a one-man band! Only, instead of having actual metallic wires to work the instruments I strike after magnetic ones. I have to work so that I feel every one of my eighty-four musicians is linked up with me by a cable of magnetism. Every man must be as intent upon and as sensitive to every movement of my baton as I am myself."[25]

Indeed, Sousa frequently drew from the language of business: "The organizing and maintaining of a superior band I regard in the light of a calm, calculative, business proposition, as much a matter of practical consideration as the selection and training of men for banking or other commercial duties. . . . As the head of a counting-house exercises powers of selection in gathering about him a staff as nearly perfect as possible, so is the bandmaster untiring in his search for the best available talent. . . . The principle of the survival of the fittest is strong." It was important for Sousa that this survival be self-earned, and he never relied on government or philanthropic handouts. Rather, he saw himself as competing in the American marketplace: "If a musician, a writer, or a painter, has anything in him, he will dig it out of himself, if the State will only let him starve long enough. . . . But if he has the Government behind him, it is merely in human nature that he will quote the famous saying: 'The public be damned!'"[26]

In writing his autobiography, Sousa used the Corcoran story to demonstrate that his belief in the self-made businessman dated back to his earliest years in Washington. In finishing the account of his interview, Sousa explains why he never returned to discover Corcoran's decision: "I never got out of a house quicker than I did out of that one, and I *didn't* call in five or six days; in fact, I haven't called up to date! The idea of being under obligations to anybody was very distasteful to me." Whatever the truth of the story, John Philip Sousa never received a subsidized or European education and was thus free to establish his reputation as a distinctly American artist and independent entrepreneur.[27]

Whatever occurred between Sousa, Hunter, and Corcoran, by the summer of 1875 Sousa was a free agent, no longer bound by the rules of an apprenticeship or by the military. All he needed was a reason to venture beyond Washington's borders. At some point in the mid-1870s, Sousa became engaged to Emma May Swallow. Her stepfather liked the young man well enough to collaborate on a song but did not approve of him as a potential son-in-law. Swallow's objection was that "musicians invariably live in poverty," and Sousa thus had his second spur to travel beyond the city. He decided to leave Washington, prove himself as a musician and businessman, and return to marry Emma May.[28]

An opportunity presented itself while Sousa was conducting incidental music for Milton Nobles's play *Jim Bludso, or, Bohemians and Detectives* (later called *The Phoenix*), which was presented at Kernan's Theatre Comique between June 21 and June 26, 1875. Nobles was impressed by the young conductor, and a few days later he sent Sousa a telegram asking that he join the troupe on tour. Sousa's disagreement with Swallow provided all the impetus he needed, and he probably met the company in Illinois early in September 1875. Sousa would tour the Midwest and the southern United States for the next two months as *Jim Bludso* played in Bloomington (September 15–16), Peoria (September 17–18), Omaha (September 30 to October 2), Council Bluffs (October 4), Lincoln (October 5–6), Atchison (October 7), Topeka (October 8–9), Leavenworth (October 11–14), Mobile (November 1–6), and New Orleans (November 7–13).

Along the way, Sousa learned the remarkable variety of duties required of a touring theater conductor. The company traveled without an orchestra, and it fell to Sousa to engage musicians at each stop. He also needed to schedule and oversee rehearsals and conduct nearly nightly performances from the first violin stand. Finally, it was Sousa who supplied both original music and arrangements of well-known songs for the play. In this task, he needed to adjust his music to meet the abilities of each town's musicians, and as he later explained: "I very soon got used to the depth of musical degradation a country orchestra could reach. Their so-called musicians were men employed in other walks of life; and, without an opportunity to practice their instruments daily, they made a sorry mess of the melodramatic music which was used in the performance."[29]

In late 1875 Sousa returned to Washington and rejoined the orchestra at Ford's Opera House, where he played in several productions prior to the April 3, 1876, arrival of Matt Morgan's Grand Art Exhibition of Living Statues, a presentation of twenty young women posed in historical and mythological tableaux that would provide Sousa with his second opportunity to tour the

United States. Sousa described the production as "the first time that America had seen the undraped female on the stage, in any numbers, and America gasped at the spectacle. . . . The audiences were almost entirely men and the performance, though a harmless one, was generally considered as risqué."[30]

Matthew Somerville Morgan began his career in London as a political illustrator, becoming famous for his parodies of the royal family. He came to the United States to draw cartoons for the 1872 presidential race and remained to work with several New York theaters. Living statues such as Morgan's began their modern history in the United States in the 1830s and used classical and biblical subjects—ranging from the temptation of St. Anthony to the destruction of Pompeii—as an excuse for the gauze scarves and flesh-toned tights that led so many men to enjoy the sensual statuary. Companies got away with such productions by relying on the Victorian convention that seminudity was acceptable when placed in the service of high art. Thus, despite Sousa's claim, by the time Morgan opened his production at New York's Theatre Comique in November 1875, American audiences had been enjoying the artistic spectacle of the female body in theaters, ballrooms, and upper-class parlors for four decades.

Critical reaction to Morgan's show varied considerably. Some, such as the theater chronicler George Odell, took issue with Morgan's artistic choices, describing him as "that devastating mongrel that in so many theatres had killed drama." But far more serious were the charges of pornography directed at the show, primarily by the self-appointed antiobscenity crusader Anthony Comstock. As a special agent for the Post Office, Comstock usually focused his attention on articles that could be transmitted through the mail. But as founder of the New York Society for the Suppression of Vice, he also pursued Morgan with unusual zeal. In December 1875, while his show was in New York, Morgan was arrested and forced into "draping the tableaux more than usual." The illustrator, however, found powerful allies in the New York press, and the *Dramatic News* declared that his "tableaux are still, and always the main attraction of the Comique, and their value becomes apparent more and more. The carping opposition which they at first received has given way to a proper idea of their artistic worth." Comstock, on the other hand, was labeled "a narrow brained half imbecile."[31]

While the company was playing at Ford's Opera House between April 3 and April 8, 1876, its conductor was suddenly fired, and Sousa was offered his position. So once again the young musician set off on a tour of the eastern United States, this time with a company under the management of James Kernan's older brother Eugene. Unknown to him, Sousa was entering a fray already in progress. Morgan had faced little criticism in the capital, but things took a turn for the worse when the company arrived in Pittsburgh on April 10 for a week-long run at the Fifth Avenue Comedy Theater. The production was advertised as the latest and best New York sensation, but the first review set the tone for the coming controversy:

> An audience which occupied every seat, filled all the aisles, squeezed into every available corner, and dangled over the balcony rail, witnessed the performance and tableaux at this theater last evening. Most of the persons present, all of whom were men, had evidently expected to gratify their lewd instincts, but such were somewhat disappointed. Only those whose taste stimulated them to search for the bad, and whose imagination supplied what their senses failed to realize found the exhibition dirty. To people of pure taste there was nothing disgusting in the living pictures, though as a matter of modesty, perhaps, they might be questionable.[32]

Not all viewers were so sympathetic, and charges were filed shortly after the first performance. The prosecution had two complaints: first, the company had failed to obtain the necessary license, and second, the show itself was obscene in its use of nearly naked women. The second charge was further expanded to suggest that the nudity on stage provoked unseemly behavior from the audience.

Legal proceedings, which attracted just as much attention as did the show, began on April 12, and Sousa's failure to appear in court resulted in what may have been the first printing of his name in a newspaper outside Washington: "Mr. Souse [*sic*], who is the leader of the orchestra, was not on hand, and a long delay ensued." The court first took up the issue of licensing, to which the company pled not guilty. To the company's misfortune, the prosecutor also happened to be both the judge and the city official responsible for the granting of theater licenses. The troupe's manager, stage manager, and treasurer were each fined fifty dollars for each of the first three performances.[33]

With the matter of licenses resolved, attention turned to obscenity. As in New York, Morgan found a powerful ally in the press. The prosecutor—one Mr. McCarthy—had a single goal: to inconvenience the company. As the first step he delayed the hearing for several days, forcing the performers to remain in Pittsburgh. The newspapers noted the astounding amount of free advertising this tactic unintentionally provided: "He advertises this show which he claims to be indecent—holds a hearing, enters judgment, half opens the case again, and puts it off until Saturday, giving the defendants an opportunity to continue their representations each night and once on Saturday afternoon.

His Honor's advertisement has been so well executed that it might be worth anywhere from $1,000 to $2,000 to the managers of the classically developed company. It will bring to the house thousands of curious persons who otherwise might not have thought of going there." The paper continued its dismissive tone a few days later, writing that McCarthy's "desire for notoriety impelled him to the first act, his mulishness made him adhere to it, and his ignorance now leaves him in an awkward position."[34]

On April 18 the court finally heard complaints regarding the immoral performances themselves. According to members of the police department, the show's near nudity had a demoralizing effect on the audience and caused some in the gallery to make "obscene allusions." Efforts to temper boisterous indications of approval or disapproval from the gallery gods were well under way by the 1870s, and Morgan's company decided that a guilty plea might be the best way to avoid further prolonging its ordeal. In the end it agreed to pay $25 per charged man plus court costs and then left for Baltimore, where the show played between April 19 and April 29. The tour continued to St. Louis (May 9–13), Indianapolis (May 15–20), and Louisville (May 22–27). At some point the company received an offer for an extended stay in California, and so Sousa left the production to return to Washington.[35]

WRITING FOR THE THEATER

Sousa's surviving music for both of these touring shows is unpublished and incomplete. Portions of what he wrote for *The Phoenix* remain in the possession of descendants of Milton Nobles, and these materials include selections from the play's second act and part of an *entr'acte* march labeled "Bludso," opus 19. It is likely that in composing for *The Phoenix*, Sousa reworked music written by the conductors who preceded him, and it is equally likely that his music was later revised by his successors.[36]

The surviving musical materials for Morgan's production consist of parts for a small theater orchestra (two violins, viola, bass, flute, clarinet, cornet, horns, trombone, and percussion). As one might expect, these parts are all quite direct and easy to perform. The first violin, played by Sousa, almost always carries the melody (sometimes doubled by the flute). The other parts all play mainly supporting roles by arpeggiating chords or articulating downbeats. Because each piece is quite short—always less than thirty-two bars—it was likely repeated for as long as the corresponding tableaux were in view. In almost every case the music is slow and expressive, consonant and unassuming, likely meant to go largely unnoticed.[37]

While on tour in 1875 and 1876, Sousa did not write the boisterous marches for which he would later become famous, nor did he compose the self-expressive songs of his youth. This incidental music was purely functional, meant to set a mood rather than focus attention. The music needed to be easily played by musicians of meager attainment and with little opportunity for rehearsal. Nevertheless, its impact should not be underestimated. Because his professional band toured almost constantly, with regular rehearsal a luxury, Sousa often needed to write, and his bandsmen master, new music rather quickly. Like Duke Ellington at the Cotton Club, Sousa knew his players' talents well and was able to complete pieces that would have required virtually no rehearsal. The requisite skills—an ability to write for the talent at hand and a willingness to temper his own artistic desires to the needs of the moment—were always Sousa's greatest strengths. As a touring theater conductor he would have learned and practiced these skills by creating music that could both feature the talents and hide the faults of any musician who happened to be available for hire.

Nobles and Morgan provided yet another lesson for the young conductor. As a mature musician the March King often worked to manipulate both his public and the press, and a large part of his appeal lay in the ability to endear himself to the audience at hand. He succeeded in the same way he composed his earliest parlor songs: by presenting entertainment that was simultaneously accessible and sophisticated. Sousa would have seen further models of this approach to popular culture on tour with Nobles and Morgan. In his autobiography Milton Nobles explains that education is only a secondary goal of the theater and that the playwright would do well not to confuse sermonizing with entertaining. Nonetheless, he hints that sophistication and pleasure can go hand in hand: "The idea that any sane person goes, or ever will go, to the theatre to listen to a moral lecture or theological essay is simple rot. . . . If it is the legitimate object of art to strengthen or to teach, that object must be attained indirectly. Its first and nearest object is to charm and to delight. That dramatist or 'reformer' will live unrecognized and die unsung who writes and argues from the mistaken thesis that a play should be a sermon in disguise."[38]

This conception of art—that it can marry charm and education, with a decided preference for the former—would be echoed throughout Sousa's career. In 1893 he explained that the music that audiences found enticing was more useful than the music designed to educate, and he connected this argument to the theater of his youth: "It is a well-known fact among theatrical people, that fifty comedy companies will prosper where one presenting tragedy will earn a precarious livelihood, showing that many people prefer entertainment to instruction. Therefore, the musician's duty, in catering to the public, is rather to present music clean, brilliant, and entertaining in large quantities, and that of a decided scientific tendency in homeopathic doses." Like Nobles, Sousa admitted education as a worthy goal but one that must be subservient to entertainment. In 1910 he tied this idea back to a distinctly American notion of entrepreneurial democracy:

> My theory was, by insensible degrees, first to reach every heart by simple, stirring music. Secondly, to lift the unmusical mind to a still higher form of musical art. This was my mission. Just as armies were moved and thrilled by simple music to perform great deeds, so I had dreamed that all people by the same means could be led to conquer the more difficult and classical forms of musical expression. It was a perfectly definite project. The point was to move all America, while busied in its various pursuits, by the power of direct and simple music. I wanted to make a music for the people, a music to be grasped at once.[39]

As the March King's words suggest, Sousa recognized that even as they were entertained, his audiences needed to at least believe that their amusements had a nobler value. Here Matt Morgan's efforts would have been instructive. The friendly disposition of the press that benefited Morgan in Pittsburgh was not accidental; it had been cultivated every time he advertised his tableaux as high art rather than burlesque. This wrapping of pleasure within culture was picked up time and again by reporters, as when the *Washington Star* explained that Morgan's living statues had appeared in New York and were there "viewed by all the best citizens" and "praised without stint by all the papers." As a result, the same audiences that had been titillated by the sensual tableaux could congratulate themselves on having enjoyed a sophisticated program.[40]

This playing of the press also aided Sousa's mystique, and he frequently made efforts to flatter local taste as he traveled across America and around the globe. When his band visited Australia in 1911, Sousa told reporters that he was honored to play in the nation that had given the world Nellie Melba, Ada Crossley, and Amy Castles and that he knew Australian audiences "could not fail to appreciate that which was best in music." The press naturally embraced Sousa's flattery, declaring that Australians are "from a musical point of view, and in the gross, a more highly educated body than may be found anywhere outside the great art centres of the Old World." By filling Sousa's concerts they proved "this fact to the full satisfaction of our famous visitor." Sousa concerts, whether perceived as trite or artistic, were a success even before the first note had sounded.[41]

Just as Morgan learned to package sensuality as art, Sousa could adapt the tunes his audiences loved and present them as items worthy of their good taste. In 1893 he explained to a New York reporter that the song "Annie Rooney" was the type of piece "over which the musically ignorant go wild," since it was just a "pretty little air" found as a "frowsy-headed and unkempt child." For Sousa, however, the song—though born on the street—was easily elevated:

> In her original guise Annie is the product of the slums. Now we will suppose that we take Annie in hand. The first thing that we do is to wash her face, next we comb her hair, then we remove her tattered frock and replace it with a nice, clean garment edged with cheap lace. Now Annie has not by any means lost her identity. She is the same Annie Rooney she was before. But how differently she appeared! Even the most captious of critics can take no exception to her, and those who have loved her in her crude condition now admire her the more sincerely in her added grace.[42]

By the time Sousa returned to Washington in the spring of 1876, he was a well-educated journeyman musician. He had apprenticed in the Marine Band, played and conducted in Washington's theaters, and toured the eastern half of the United States. He must have been a fine violinist and a more than competent conductor, not yet twenty-two years old. He was also a blossoming composer, equally at home in the parlor and the theater. He had learned about drama and he had learned to please an audience. In short, John Philip Sousa was well prepared to leave his apprenticeship, begin life as a professional musician, and prove himself to a potential father-in-law. But the 1860s and 1870s had provided Sousa with yet another opportunity to learn his craft, and once again it was centered in the Navy Yard.

CHAPTER THREE

A Nineteenth-Century Musical Career

IN MANY WAYS THE HISTORICAL John Philip Sousa has been the victim of the March King's incredible success. He is today fully his stage name: a musician known only for a handful of three-minute works written for ensembles of winds alone. It is true that Sousa's greatest artistic achievements came in the form of marches and that his public fame was secured from the bandstand. But the Sousa of the late nineteenth and early twentieth centuries was much more than a march king, and to think of his creative career as limited to "The Washington Post" or "The Stars and Stripes Forever" is to misunderstand both Sousa and his musical world.

A concert by Sousa's ensemble usually fell into two halves, and a 1926 performance in Salt Lake City is typical (fig. 9). Sousa began most appearances with an overture, in this case the prelude to Richard Wagner's *Tannhäuser*. Next came a virtuoso brass solo; here William Tong performed Herman Bellstedt's cornet feature "Centennial Polka." The light work was usually followed by a Sousa suite or other medium-length piece, in this case *El Capitan and His Friends*, a collection of materials from several Sousa operettas. The pairing of soloist with longer work was then repeated, here by the soprano Marjorie Moody singing a selection from Meyerbeer's *Dinorah* and a band performance of the slow movement from Dvořák's Symphony no. 9. After the intermission the entire process started again. The first half's soloists were often replaced with a female violinist or, as in this case, with saxophone and percussion features. Along the way almost every work received an unprinted encore, usually consisting of light favorites, most notably Sousa's own marches.[1]

A Sousa concert was thus quite different from most twenty-first-century orchestral performances. Rather than the homogeneity of a Beethoven, Schubert, or Brahms cycle, Sousa aimed for variety: ensemble works and soloists, highbrow selections and those meant to entertain, instrumental numbers and vocal gems. For some devotees of high culture such a range

SOUSA AND HIS BAND

TABERNACLE—SALT LAKE CITY
WEDNESDAY AFTERNOON, FEBRUARY 3, 1926

LIEUT.-COMMANDER JOHN PHILIP SOUSA, CONDUCTOR

HARRY ASKIN, *Manager* GEO. D. PYPER, *Local Manager*

MISS MARJORIE MOODY, *Soprano*
MR. WILLIAM TONG, *Cornet*
MR. GEORGE CAREY, *Xylophone*
MR. HOWARD GOULDEN, *Xylophone*

PROGRAM

1 Overture, "Tannhauser" - - - - - - - - - *Wagner*

The impulse to write "Tannhauser" came to Wagner upon his visiting the Castle of Wartburg in 1842, while en route from Paris to Germany. Three years later (on October 19, 1845), the work was brought out at Dresden.

The sumptuous overture is too well known to call for any extended resume, but a brief recital of its salient features may be of service. All the themes are taken from the opera, the movement opening with the sedate "Pilgrim's Chorus," which is made to do service as an introduction. This is first given out in a subdued, chant-like manner, to expand presently into a majestic anthem, with the broad melody in the brasses against a singularly weird, shimmering counter figure. Finally subdsiding to pianissimo, this stately introduction leads over into the body proper of the overture, whose first theme is a swirling figure (the Tannhauser motive proper). Sundry subsidiary materials drawn from the opening of the opera follow, leading, at length, to the entrance of the second principal theme—the sweeping song of love which Tannhauser sings at the contest in the Wartburg castle, the accompaniment scored for the full orchestra, the trombones excepted.

After a furious development, which halts for a moment to make way for Venus' seductive song, (the Venus motive proper, in the clarinet) the Pilgrim's Chorus is resumed—at first softly and solemnly, and then swelling into the mighty paeon which brings the overture to a gorgeous conclusion.

2 Cornet Solo, "Centennial" - - - - - - - *Bellstedt*

MR. WILLIAM TONG

3 Suite, "El Capitan and His Friends" - - - - - - *Sousa*
a "El Capitan"
b "The Charlatan"
c "The Bride-Elect"

4 Soprano Solo, "Shadow Dance" from "Dinorah" - *Meyerbeer*

MISS MARJORIE MOODY
(Flute obligato by MR. R. E. WILLIAMS)

5 Largo, "The New World" - - - - - - - - - *Dvorak*

INTERVAL

6 Village Scene, "Sunday Evening in Alsace" - - - *Massenet*

7 *a* Saxophone Octette, "On the Mississippi" - - - - *Klein*

MESSRS. STEPHENS, HENEY, GOODRICH, JOHNSON,
WEIR, MADDEN, CONKLIN AND MUNROE

b March, "The National Game" (new) - - - - - - *Sousa*

8 Xylophone Duet, "March Wind" - - - - - - - *Carey*

MESSRS. CAREY AND GOULDEN

9 "Pomp and Circumstance" - - - - - - - - - *Elgar*

Fig. 9. Sousa Band program, 1926. Author's collection.

of material might appear a form of bribery: audiences could be lured to the theater with promises of musical delights and then, once captured, forced to absorb the classical masterworks. But trickery was not part of Sousa's plan. Like Milton Nobles and Matthew Morgan before him, Sousa sought to give audiences what they wanted: a whole world of entertainment—both pleasing and sophisticated—in one evening. In the March King's words: "I believe a programme composed entirely of so-called popular music would now be as dismal a failure as one wholly made up of classical pieces. The people seem to want a combination of the heavy and the light."[2]

Throughout the course of Sousa's career, variety remained always the watchword, and it is as apparent in his output as it is in his programming. Sousa wrote about 130 marches, but he also composed art, parlor, minstrel, and political songs, galops, gavottes, schottisches, and waltzes, descriptive works and suites, and operettas and humoresques. Sousa may today be best known as a composer and bandleader, but to his own audiences he was also an essayist, copyright expert, athlete, and humorist.

From our perspective the variety evident in a Sousa program and the breadth of Sousa's career have taken on contradictory interpretations: he is either a noble genius who denies categorization or a charlatan willing to pander to his audience. But the breadth of his work—from theater violinist to band conductor, from songwriter to march composer, from government musician to capitalist entrepreneur—was really quite typical of his generation. In the midst of an 1889 labor battle Sousa explained that any musician could "cast, daily, into the sea of engagements, at least four lines. Sometimes, it's true, he'll only get a nibble or two, but oftener he'll hook a fish on each line, and I can assure you he only throws away what he can't carry." The boy Sousa had many models for this sort of musical gamut, models to be found in the working-class players of the Navy Yard, men who might "teach music in the morning, write music in the afternoon, and play music in the evening, receiving for each a separate stipend."[3]

GEORGE FELIX BENKERT

Sousa learned something about the financial value of his talents in the late 1860s or early 1870s when he organized a small quadrille band that provided music for the rehearsals and recitals of a dancing academy run by George Thompson Sheldon. In his autobiography Sousa explains that the musicians, who were all much older than their novice leader, convinced him to approach Sheldon and demand more money. When the master refused, Sousa quit in protest. This story—real or imagined—is once again a parable, this time teaching that the value of music is dependent on the marketplace. Sousa returned to Sheldon's academy the following week, only to discover that while someone else was in his place, "the same seven anarchists were meekly playing there at their old wages! It was a lesson I have never forgotten and never shall forget!"[4]

Before his mistake Sousa had earned at least a little money from Sheldon's Fashionable Dancing Academy, and he used it to pay George Felix Benkert for harmony and violin lessons. Sousa may have denied himself a European education, but through Benkert he could be attached to the classical tradition. Born in Philadelphia in 1831, Benkert quickly built an impressive musical résumé. According to press reports, he had composed an overture and an oratorio by the time he was nine, spent five years studying in Germany under Peter Josef von Lindpaintner, and had written a Mass that received performances in Stuttgart and Vienna. Benkert returned to Philadelphia by 1856 and presented a concert of his instrumental works at Musical Fund Hall. While little of his music survives, he seems to have been a reasonably prolific composer. There are reports of several operas, including *Cordelia* and *Viola*, which were based on Shakespeare's *King Lear* and *Twelfth Night*, respectively. He also wrote two Indianist operas: *Logan* and *The Indian Girl: A Scene in the Early History of Pennsylvania*, as well as two comic operas, *Une visite à Pierre le grand* and *The Dragon of Wantley*.[5]

Although Benkert may be largely forgotten today, by the late 1850s he had built quite a reputation as a serious pianist and composer. Correspondents for *Dwight's Journal of Music* often sang Benkert's praises, as when one reported: "As Germany hath given the world a Thalberg and a Mendelssohn, so America, the Young Giant of the West, hath produced a Gottschalk and a Benkert." During an excursion to San Francisco in the mid-1860s he attracted the attention of Mark Twain, and Benkert's reputation even allowed him to find a place in William Upton's 1930 *Art Song in America*, where he is treated alongside William Henry Fry and George Bristow.[6]

Unlikely to earn a living simply through composition, Benkert also served as a piano teacher in Philadelphia and as a conductor at Barnum's Museum. He seems to have settled in Washington sometime around 1868 and there founded the Amateur Orchestral Union, a forty-piece orchestra that likely provided several local premieres of works by Beethoven. As a young man Sousa served as a violinist in this ensemble, and he seems to have begun lessons with Benkert sometime around 1873. From this well-trained musician Sousa received a thorough grounding in counterpoint, based at least in part on the work of Simon Sechter. The Library of Congress's Sousa Collection includes two counterpoint notebooks that appear to have belonged to Benkert and may have made up a portion of Sousa's studies. Some of Sousa's own counterpoint exercises can be found in another notebook, in which he explores two-, three- and four-part writing and practices modulation.[7]

All of this, from Benkert's European training to the surviving counterpoint studies, suggests that Sousa received at least some formal education in composition. It has been tempting for many to sec in Benkert the March King's connection to European art music, the connection he refused to forge with the aid of W. W. Corcoran. In one excellent modern edition of "The Stars and Stripes Forever," for example, the editors write, "As a teenager in Washington, Sousa received sophisticated training in composition, counterpoint and orchestration from an Austrian immigrant, Felix Benkert. Benkert had studied in Vienna with the famed Austrian theorist Simon Sechter, who himself had been taught by Brahms. Sechter's most famous student was Anton Bruckner." Though such descriptions may be a fair way of linking the March King to Europe, it seems clear—given the surviving exercises—that while Sousa's studies may have been thorough in terms of their basics, they were also quite brief. Nonetheless, Benkert proved to be an encouraging instructor and even suggested to Sousa that he might one day make a fine composer of opera.[8]

Benkert died in early 1876 at the age of forty-four. His music may not be well remembered, but during his time in Washington he did provide a young John Philip Sousa with a technical education in composition. More important, however, he proved a model of the kind of musician who was willing to "cast, daily, into the sea of engagements." Benkert was, after all, a composer, conductor, and teacher. He was also an entrepreneur, fully capable of establishing and leading a small orchestra. But these achievements barely scratch the surface of his career, and he never limited himself to European art music. Rather, like almost all nineteenth-century American composers, Benkert found musical employment wherever he could, with very little concern for its high- or lowbrow status. Alongside his operas and chamber music stand a number of more functional pieces, including the parlor songs "Saucy Kate" (1849) and "The Prayer My Mother Taught" (1861), the patriotic songs "God Save Our President" (1858) and "Save the Union" (1861), and a "Funeral March" for one Colonel Baker (1861). Benkert even wrote a piece using a title Sousa would make famous, "The Stars and Stripes" (1861). These works were certainly more widely known than any of Benkert's operas or chamber music, and the Marine Band performed "God Save Our President" at both of Abraham Lincoln's inaugurations, as well as at the first inauguration of Ulysses S. Grant.[9]

JOHN ESPUTA

No programs from Benkert's Amateur Orchestral Union are known to have survived, but a newspaper advertisement for his chamber series suggests that his programs mirrored the repertoire of similar ensembles by presenting a mixture of vocal, orchestral, and chamber selections from such European composers as Handel, Hummel, Beethoven, and Brahms. Between Benkert's orchestra and his chamber activities with William Hunter, the young John Philip Sousa would have come to know at least some of the standard European repertoire. But George Felix Benkert was hardly Sousa's only professional model, and in the Navy Yard the young man worked with another musician whose extraordinary breadth Sousa would strive to emulate throughout his long career.[10]

Sometime in or around the autumn of 1861, prior to his boyhood enlistment in the Marine Corps, Sousa's musical education began in the form of *solfège* lessons with someone he termed "an old Spanish gentleman, a friend of my father's." This friend was Francis Esputa, who had emigrated from Spain in the 1830s. After serving aboard several American vessels, he settled in Washington, where, by the late 1840s, he was teaching music at what was then Georgetown College. There Esputa gave lessons in violin, piano, guitar, flute, bugle, clarinet, cornopean, and voice to more than three dozen students, one of whom was a young James Ryder Randall, who would later write the Civil War poem "Maryland, My Maryland." In March 1853, Esputa followed in the steps of other immigrant musicians and enlisted in the Marine Band, where he would remain until 1857. Naturally, he and his wife Susan settled in the Navy Yard.[11]

Sousa's studies with Francis Esputa did not last long; by the late 1860s he was attending a private conservatory at the home of Francis's son John Esputa. There he studied violin, music theory, and a variety of wind instruments for the better part of the next decade. The relationship between teacher and pupil was strained, and Esputa rejected Sousa's first composition, the now-lost violin solo "An Album Leaf," as "nothing but cheese and bread, and bread and cheese." Nonetheless, Sousa credits the older musician with finding him his first opportunity for public performance (at the age of eleven, in St. Elizabeth's Hospital) and prompting him to hear his first concert of "really fine music" (the Franko family, in November 1869). Sousa apparently did well in his studies, since he is listed as a medal finalist at the Esputa Musical Academy in 1869, just a year after the beginning of his Marine Band apprenticeship. John Esputa may today be remembered only for his most famous pupil, but

ig. 10. Esputa's music class, ca. 1865. Esputa is seated in the front center; Sousa is standing ı the back row to Esputa's right. This is likely the earliest photograph of Sousa. Library of ;ongress, Washington, D.C.

a brief examination of his remarkable career demonstrates just how far a nineteenth-century musical life could reach. While Esputa would prove to be quite successful in his craft, there is no reason to think that he was particularly unusual in the breadth of his activities.[12]

Esputa at St. Augustine's

Like other boys growing up in the Navy Yard, John Esputa served an apprenticeship in the United States Marine Corps. He enlisted as a fifer on February 9, 1844, when he was just twelve years old, and like many boys he followed this apprenticeship with a regular enlistment in the band. Esputa was honorably discharged in the summer of 1860 but returned to the military during the Civil War to serve as drum major for the Fifteenth Engineers Regiment of New York. Esputa was commissioned as a lieutenant, second class in March 1863 and received a disability discharge in September of that year.[13]

Returning to civilian life, the thirty-year-old musician needed a new source of income, which he found in the capital's churches. He likely began by leading the choirs at St. Dominic's and St. Peter's Catholic churches, both near his home in the Navy Yard. At St. Peter's he met the Italian missionary Felix Barotti and followed him to a new congregation in northwest Washington that was creating a remarkable history.

The city's 3,100 slaves were emancipated in April 1862, and many of the codes used to restrict opportunities for black Washingtonians were lifted shortly thereafter. But the Civil War also resulted in massive economic challenges, and the tens of thousands of freed slaves who poured into Washington found a city ill equipped to house or feed them. St. Matthew's Church at 15th and H Streets NW was home to a number of African American congregants who were becoming increasingly frustrated with segregated worship and instruction. In a series of remarkable efforts they were able to establish the city's first African American Catholic congregation, St. Martin's, in 1866, dedicated to the Blessed Martin de Porres. Their first permanent priest would be none other than Felix Barotti, who brought with him from St. Peter's the talented John Esputa.

A large and progressive white establishment in Washington was understandably sympathetic to the postwar trials of their African American neighbors, and as word spread of a talented black choir at a local church, fascination within the white community grew rapidly. It did not take long for St. Martin's to become a Sunday-morning destination for white audiences intrigued by the spectacle of black musicians performing European sacred music. The newspapers were also impressed and often praised Esputa's work. In October 1873 the choir, "which has been carefully trained by Professor John Esputa," sang a Mozart Mass. Through this and other performances the ensemble shortly came to be "justly considered one of the best in the city."[14]

Forming a skillful choir was hardly the extent of Esputa's ambitions, however. In October 1871 Fisk University in Nashville sent its Jubilee Singers on a fund-raising tour of the northeastern United States. Perhaps inspired by this group of African American artists, Esputa selected members of his church choir and formed the Colored American Opera Company, the first all-black organization for the production of opera in the United States. The ensemble's only documented production was of Julius Eichberg's *The Doctor of Alcantara*, first performed in a public dress rehearsal at St. Martin's Hall on January 24, 1873. The press, fascinated with the whole endeavor, had high hopes for its success and announced that Esputa's company, "composed exclusively of colored people . . . bids fair to successfully rival some of the now famous English, French, and Italian Opera Combinations that occasionally throw the fashionable world into ecstasies of delight."[15]

After this modest premiere the company decided to appear in a more public setting, and it issued a circular asking for the aid of Washington's white elite:

> We hope to be able to demonstrate that our race will in time be capable of taking rank musically with our white brothers and sisters, and intend,

should we meet with success here, to make a professional tour of the Northern cities. We appeal to you, who have always expressed so much friendship for our race in our struggles for political and mental elevation, to aid us in our endeavors now. Stimulate us by your presence. Witness our performance of the opera, and see if we are not worthy of encouragement.

This appeal was successful, and the audience that attended the two performances held in Lincoln Hall on February 3 and 4, 1873, included "nearly all the leading colored people of the District and many of our prominent white citizens." At least some of the white Washingtonians in attendance were attracted by the unusual ensemble: "Among them were many representatives of the musical circles of the city, somewhat curious to hear and compare the performance with those they have been accustomed to hear."[16]

Reviews of the Colored American Opera Company's first public performance were favorable, and complaints were notably muted, since critics felt that it would be unfair to hold these amateur singers to too high a standard: "It would be hardly fair to criticise their performance of *The Doctor of Alcantara* by the standard required in the case of experienced artists, but it was certainly creditable for beginners in a profession which requires much experience to attain even mediocrity." Other commentators remembered the limited opportunities afforded to black musicians: None "of the company . . . have had the advantage of musical training in European or American conservatories. They have to depend alone upon their natural gifts and personal acquirements. This fact is one which makes vastly in their favor and protects them from the rules and standards by which Adaline Patti or Louise Kellogg would be judged as artists. Under all the circumstances they sing and perform extraordinarily well, and as for the chorus, it is superior to that of any Italian or German opera heard in this city for years." Emboldened by such reviews, Esputa decided to book the company for three performances in Philadelphia's Horticultural Hall on February 21 and 22, 1873. Here the ensemble's novelty was felt even more deeply. The *Evening Bulletin* attributed the small size of the audience to the assumption that the performance "would be a burlesque," but the paper went on to note that a "greater mistake could not have been made. . . . The effort of these persons to win a place for themselves in the world of art would deserve warm commendation under any circumstances; but such a brave and successful attempt as this should bring a generous pecuniary reward."[17]

There is no evidence that the Colored American Opera Company ever made it beyond Philadelphia, but three months later, on May 12 and 13, "by request of a number of prominent citizens," the company appeared again in Washington, this time at the larger and better-equipped Wall's Opera House. Reviews continued to be favorable, although credit was still given to the white organizers—especially Esputa and the local manager T. Harry Donohue—who had cultivated these black artists and presented them before a paying public: "Prof. Esputa and Mr. T. Harry Donohue, to whom belong the credit of this unique organization, are thorough and energetic gentlemen, as shown by the perfection of this troupe; and the colored people owe them a debt of gratitude for so successfully demonstrating the musical abilities of the race."[18]

While Esputa's opera company may have been short-lived, it was seen as a major achievement for Washington's black musicians. The *National Republican* was proud to note that such an organization could exist in the capital just a decade after emancipation:

> One could not help recalling the dark and bloody pictures of "chains and slavery," of ignorance and degradation that once surrounded these colored people, and how those pictures were irradiated with the colors of hope, ambition and gratitude by Mr. Lincoln's god-like action in his proclamations of freedom and emancipation. Emancipation not only gave liberty to the African race, but it gave the world colored poets and painters, orators and senators, judicial magistrates, and men of science, sculptors and musicians, and as one of the first fruits of liberty a regularly organized opera company at the national capital. This is a long, long step in advance of the condition of the race a few short years ago, and it reveals possibilities for them that are indeed gratifying to all their well wishers.[19]

Washington's principal black newspaper, the *New National Era*, had a different perspective. Rather than noting how quickly such an opera company had been formed, the *Era* wondered whether white audiences recognized that the achievement was long overdue and that slavery had deprived the country of earlier black talents: "If they reflected at all upon the recent condition of the colored race in this country and the certain and rapid progress it has made as evinced by the ability presented to them on Monday night, they could not but realize the check to civilization that the forced ignorance of four million people has wrought. The capabilities of the colored race to do and be all that any other civilized and enlightened race can do or be has been fully demonstrated, and such performances as that of Monday make the evidence stronger and stronger." The paper's most lofty sentiments were reserved for the final Washington performances. The writer notes that the Colored American Opera Company proved that the days of slave song were over, remembers that black Americans had long been viewed as distinctly musical, and gives thanks for John Esputa's charitable work:

> Truly the negro has left his plantation melodies and essayed with no feeble wing the higher flights of music. And why not? It has always been conceded, even by our enemies, that we were gifted in this direction. The performances we have listened to encouraged and cheered us both by what they furnished in the way of entertainment and the promise which they gave of future excellence. All credit must be given to the thorough training given to these vocalists by the able master, Signor Esputa. He has labored with them out of pure sympathy and interest, and he has his reward in the credit they have reflected upon him and the race.[20]

John Esputa must have been quite pleased with his efforts, and likely was proud when James Trotter included the Colored American Opera Company in his 1878 book *Music and Some Highly Musical People*. There can be little doubt that the attention being paid to St. Martin's choir helped the church raise the necessary funds to construct a new building at the corner of 15th and M Streets NW. When the structure was dedicated to St. Augustine in June 1876, Esputa turned to his former employer and expanded the sixty-voice parish choir with eighteen brass and string players from the Marine Band. He also enlisted the talents of his prize pupil and presented Alois Francis LeJeal's *Solemn Vespers* "with arrangements for the orchestra by Mr. Sioussa [*sic*], a pupil of Prof. Esputa." As a result, the music performed that day was "perhaps the grandest ever heard in Washington."[21]

Sousa seems to have prepared additional music for his teacher's work at St. Augustine's. In 1877 Esputa conducted a Mass by Paolo Giorza, and when the same piece was performed on Easter Sunday 1888, the press announced that it was in an orchestration by "Prof. Sousa, of the Marine Band, made for St. Augustine's choir." The choir also performed the Mass at the opening of the first Colored Catholic Congress in January 1889. Sousa certainly knew the work, and a single page of his unpublished orchestration, portions of which were later used in his 1893 fantasy *Songs of Grace and Songs of Glory*, survives at the Library of Congress. Even more intriguing is a work Sousa called his opus 12, an unpublished Te Deum for mixed quartet and organ. Sousa recalled writing this work in the late 1870s, but given its opus number and religious content, it seems more likely that it was meant for Esputa's choir. As a complete English setting of the Te Deum text, this is Sousa's longest early composition. The work passes through homophonic writing, imitative counterpoint, and solos, suggesting the effort of a student experimenting with musical style.

Sousa also takes advantage of the text's sectional layout to explore a much wider variety of keys and a greater degree of chromaticism than he had in any earlier work.[22]

The popularity of Esputa's choir can hardly be overestimated. An Ohio reporter visited the church one Sunday in February 1878 and heard the black musicians sing Haydn, Millard, and Mozart. After noting the importance of the works and the skills of the soloists, he described the scene:

> under the leadership of Professor John Esputa, whose name and fame as a musician is of the first order, and stands No. 1 in Washington city; add to this a chorus of forty-two well trained voices; imagine a grand organ of 34 stops under the master hand of Professor Zierback [Thierbach], who in his beautiful combinations of flute and violincello [*sic*], blended with the bourdon, followed by the reed stop, sixteenth, and this with the swell organ coupled with the choir organ, all concluding with the metallic clash of the double gamba, overpowered by the immense choral wave, and you will have some idea of St. Augustine's choir. The attraction to this church is increasing, Foreign ministers, members of Congress and the aristocracy generally, are frequently seen in this church; the elite and upper tens generally consider it their special privilege to be present.

Of course, a white listener would have been stunned to find all of this in a black church, and so the reporter added, "I mention these facts to impress you with the idea these are *negroes!*"[23]

Esputa and the Public Schools

The brief tour of the Colored American Opera Company was, no doubt, the highlight of John Esputa's musical career. But for Washington audiences, his work was not limited to a single production or to a single church. The city of Washington, D.C., has long had a tense relationship with the federal government that oversees it, and the 1870s marked a period of particular struggle. In 1871 the independent cities of Washington and Georgetown, along with the county of Washington, were combined under a single territorial government. This system lasted only until 1874, when Congress replaced it with a board of commissioners appointed by the president. Under the old system public schools had been run by four independent boards, one for each of the three municipalities and another overseeing African American students. With the new board of commissioners this motley system was replaced by a single board of trustees and two superintendents, one for the black schools and another for the white schools. On September 1, 1874, John Esputa was appointed director of music for the black public schools.

Esputa took to his new job with characteristic vigor, later explaining, "I examined about five thousand pupils, and I am sorry to be compelled to say that, with a few exceptions, they did not know the notes of the gamut." In order to solve the problem, he devised a teacher-training program in which he worked with classroom instructors weekly, "as without this no considerable progress could be made." The superintendent, George F. T. Cook, was quite pleased with the results: "In no year since the introduction of this study into the schools have results in it been so highly satisfactory and capacity for rapid acquisition so fully shown. Excellent progress was made in schools of all grades, and in those of the lowest Primary it was clearly demonstrated that the principles of this study are as readily acquired as those of any other generally given to children of such tender age."[24]

Esputa wisely used his students—just as he had his church choir—to raise money. Four pianos were purchased "through a series of musical and literary entertainments given weekly by pupils. In this commendable effort the schools not only gained valuable accessions to school property, but appreciable contributions to the promotion and maintenance of good discipline." In an effort to learn of other cities' pedagogy systems, Esputa arranged to visit schools in Baltimore, Philadelphia, New York, and Boston. By the late 1870s he was so well known for his work with Washington's African American musicians that the *Church News* called him "an educator to the extent of benefactor among the colored people of this city."[25]

Esputa's efforts in the capital came to an abrupt end in 1878, when illness forced him to spend a portion of the year in Florida. Sometime in or around 1880 he divorced his wife, but he returned to Washington early in 1882 and remarried her in February. John Esputa died a month later, on March 7. The family name remained important in Washington, primarily through the efforts of his daughter Josephine Esputa-Daly, who—beginning in 1899—led St. Augustine's choir.[26]

Esputa and Composition

John Esputa would have been sufficiently busy with his duties as a conductor and educator, but like most nineteenth-century musicians he did not limit himself to just a handful of activities. Since he frequently worked with institutions that did not have established music programs, it comes as no surprise that when materials were needed, he simply created them himself. In 1875, while leading his church choir, he published his Mass in C, a brief setting of the Ordinary for divided chorus. In 1881 he reportedly wrote a now-lost requiem for St. Augustine's founding pastor, Felix Barotti.[27]

Like Benkert, Esputa did not limit himself to large-scale composition but also wrote several lighter works. His first piano piece was the now-lost "Jakey Polka." His earliest surviving work, the "Tuners Polka" (1855), was written while Esputa was still a member of the Marine Band and dedicated to Jacob Hilbus, a Washington piano tuner and organ builder. A few years later he published the "Paradise Waltz" (1858), the sheet music for which indicates that it was performed by Esputa's Cornet Band (yet another activity undertaken by this enterprising musician). Esputa was also an arranger, and in 1874 he prepared a piano edition of pieces by J. Harry Rathbone under the title *Happy Hours*.[28]

There is also an intriguing short fragment of music by Esputa preserved by the Library of Congress. A *Washington Star* column from 1925 asserts that "the first piece of music copyrighted in the United States was composed and copyrighted by Prof. John Esputa. It was a little song dedicated to his daughter, Josephine, and I am told that it hangs, framed and glazed, in the Library of Congress." Indeed, a piece of music at the library, neither framed nor glazed, bears the inscription "Prof. John Esputa to Josie Esputa" and the notation "first proof of music taken at Washington, D.C., June 1874." This is not the first piece to have been protected by U.S. copyright, but it may well have been one of the first musical works submitted to the Library of Congress when that institution took over the copyright office in 1870.[29]

Given that Esputa composed for his choir at St. Augustine's, it comes as no surprise that he also wrote a textbook for his students. *Esputa's Music Instructor*, published in 1870, was probably intended for his private conservatory in the Navy Yard (although the textbook was later put to use in the Washington Colored Schools). The work is fairly typical of mid-nineteenth-century American music tutors. Its seventy-nine pages include about ninety solfège exercises in which Esputa introduces new material at an astonishing rate, thus ensuring the need to hire—and pay—a music teacher. All of Esputa's works naturally needed a publisher and a shop in which to be sold, and he was happy to fit the bill. His Mass setting and textbook were self-published, and by 1877 he was listed in Washington directories as a music printer and shopkeeper. In order to protect his interests, Esputa also served on the executive committee of the local musicians' union.[30]

LESSONS OF THE NAVY YARD

By 1876 John Philip Sousa had begun to build a remarkable musical career. He had studied with two of Washington's best-known musicians, and from them had learned the basics of music theory and advanced on his principal instrument, the violin. He had also played in at least one small orchestra, Benkert's Amateur Orchestral Union. Sousa had, of course, served more formal apprenticeships, first in the United States Marine Band and then in the pits of Ford's Opera House and Kernan's Theatre Comique. By the mid-1870s he had also composed several pieces of parlor music, a small body of incidental material for the theater, and perhaps one sacred work. He had also begun to spread his wings beyond Washington, publishing a march and a galop in Philadelphia and touring with Milton Nobles and Matt Morgan.

Each of these activities would prove important to Sousa's later success. As a member of the Marine Band he became well acquainted with the ensemble he would later lead and with the musicians he would eventually conduct. His time as a violinist and traveling music director allowed him to learn the mechanics of the theater and to see how established artists worked to please their public. Both of these skills would be vital as the apprentice John Philip Sousa transformed himself into the celebrity March King.

But the most important lessons of Sousa's youth did not come from formal apprenticeships or professional employment; they were found in the careers of musicians who lived in the Navy Yard. The most remarkable of these models was, no doubt, John Esputa, a working-class musician who found employment where he could, wrote what must have seemed financially prudent at the time, and had a wide range of musical talents. Esputa's musical career seems quite remarkable in its specifics, but its outlines were perfectly typical of American musical life in the nineteenth century.

Esputa obviously found it quite easy to move between the spheres of America's shared musical culture. His textbook places ditties of his own invention alongside selections from Meyerbeer and Verdi. In nineteenth-century Washington the music of both composers could have been heard in operas but also recast as the waltzes, quadrilles, polkas, and marches that dominated dance cards, resonated in parlors, and entertained at the White House. Like Verdi, Esputa was capable of serving more than one purpose: he could compose a polka and a Mass, lead a cornet band and an opera company, play in the all-white Marine Band and conduct an all-black church choir. In short, Esputa—like most working-class musicians of his generation—moved easily between indistinct and overlapping artistic traditions.

When the future March King combined the high and the low on his concert programs or when he moved from the band podium to the opera pit, he was doing exactly what his teachers and neighbors in the Navy Yard had done and exactly what was expected by his audiences. In 1915 Sousa explained why it was so easy to shift between different kinds of music. His example is ragtime, but the same point could have been made of any repertoire: "The 'low-brows' like to talk about ragtime to deride the 'high-brows' and the 'high-brows' use it to make fun of the 'low-brows.' The fact remains that when it's clever we like to hear it regardless of the kind of 'brows' responsible." In reflecting on John Philip Sousa's career prior to his twenty-second birthday, it is useful to remember that his wide range of musical endeavors was not particularly unusual. As Sousa left the Navy Yard in 1876, such breadth would serve him well. He was now trained as a violinist, practiced as a conductor, and competent as a composer. Just as important, he carried with him models of musical success such as John Esputa and George Felix Benkert as well as his father and neighbors in the Navy Yard.[31]

PART II *The Professional*

CHAPTER FOUR

The Centennial City

SOUSA HAD PROMISED BENJAMIN SWALLOW that he would leave Washington for two years, prove himself financially, and return to marry Emma May. Choosing a career in music may never have been the safest way to achieve this goal, but by 1876 Sousa was a well-trained journeyman capable of finding work in a theater orchestra, traveling show, or publishing firm. By the end of the decade he would succeed in all three types of jobs, and this success would come in a city that offered unique opportunities for a young musician.

The International Exhibition of Arts, Manufactures, and Products of the Soil and Mine was organized to celebrate the centennial of American independence. While the national birthday may have provided an excuse for the fair, it was hardly its underlying purpose. The preceding decades had revealed massive fissures in the democratic experiment, and despite having extracted its price in blood, the Civil War had failed to cauterize the nation's wounds: the panic of 1873 continued to slow the economy, violent clashes with labor were becoming more frequent, Reconstruction's collapse was both obvious and imminent, the struggle for women's suffrage threatened to undermine gender roles, and the question of just what to do with the continent's original inhabitants was swiftly coming to a head.

These stresses, of course, would not be on view at the centennial celebrations. No fair could thrive by dwelling on national challenges, and it was easy enough to relegate African, Native, and female Americans to their prescribed roles in minstrel shows, savage displays, and needlework demonstrations. The exhibition would instead showcase national order and unity, its very organization demonstrating the ability to raise funds, manage labor, and counter resistance. The materials of mechanical, industrial, and agricultural innovation would expose a people at work, not a nation at war. In short, the centennial exhibition that took place along the Schuylkill River in Philadelphia in the summer of 1876 was an opportunity for a socially, economically, and politically reeling country to demonstrate to both itself and the world that the great democracy's national industry was organized for future gain and not distracted by ongoing challenges or past tragedies.

The elderly Sousa would explain that following his tours with Nobles and Morgan, he "decided to go to Philadelphia and see the Centennial. It was a big event in the life of any young American and I believe the first event of its kind that the country had ever had." The centennial exhibition was, indeed, the first of America's world fairs, and funds were quickly raised through private donations, stock sales, local appropriations, and federal loans. About 450 acres were set aside in West Fairmount Park, and a design competition was established. In the end, more than two hundred structures—most of them temporary—were erected. Both weather and advertising caused shifts in attendance over the exhibition's six-month run, but in the end well over eight million visitors—fully one-fifth of the country's population—reaffirmed Sousa's claim that this was an important event for many Americans.[1]

Once at the centennial, visitors were treated to evidence of America's scientific progress ranging from the Bell telephone to the Otis elevator. All eyes were especially drawn to the Corliss engine in the aptly named Machinery Hall. This behemoth of steel and iron caused the visiting Walt Whitman to gaze for fully half an hour and marvel at man's greatest technological achievement. Within the Main Exhibition Hall this focus on craftsmanship and innovation extended even to music. Visitors were asked to appreciate the mechanical improvements made by Steinway, Chickering, and Knabe, companies routinely praised for their "fidelity and taste in workmanship," "excellence in materials employed," and other "practical improvements" to the keyboard. Because so much of the exhibition was designed to showcase American unity through displays of industrial success, it is no surprise that the physical materials of music were prominently featured in sound (the thirteen Centennial Chimes in Machinery Hall), wood (an ornately carved keyboard case in the Women's Pavilion), metal (the multiple displays of hardware used in piano construction), and mechanics (the Schmoele electromagnetic orchestrion in Agriculture Hall).[2]

Such displays of mechanical innovation in music were well matched to the fair's goals, but there was also a need to prove the country's progress in the art's other sciences: composition and performance. This task fell to the Women's Centennial Executive Committee, and in this, too, industry would be the model. In order to compete with the splendor of the 2,704 pipes found on the Centennial Organ, the Women's Committee required a music director capable of harnessing a similarly impressive force. Only a general of the art could prove that performance required the same organizational acumen, industrial discipline, and financial savvy as that needed to build music's mechanical equipment. It would be this leader's task to prove that Americans could both make instruments and appreciate their sounds.

There was in America only one musician who fit the bill. The Irish-born Patrick S. Gilmore had settled in Boston by 1849 and was soon leading several local bands. In 1859 he formed Gilmore's Band with the intent of creating a commercial touring organization. With the onset of the Civil War, Gilmore and his ensemble joined the Massachusetts Volunteers, and he was soon tasked with reorganizing the state's military music. At the conflict's end, Gilmore produced a celebration for the inauguration of Louisiana's first Reconstruction governor, Michael Hahn. The bandmaster, recognizing the financial possibilities of such events, in 1869 organized the five-day National Peace Jubilee in Boston. Although his publicity machine no doubt inflated the event's numbers, press reports indicate that about one thousand instrumentalists and perhaps ten thousand singers took part in Gilmore's celebration. The end of the Franco-Prussian War gave the bandmaster another chance to showcase his organizational skills, and in 1872 he staged the eighteen-day World's Peace Jubilee and International Musical Festival in Boston, which featured a massive pipe organ; military bands from London, Paris, Berlin, and Dublin; the composers Johann Strauss and Franz Abt; and the Fisk Jubilee Singers.

The press naturally urged that Gilmore be anointed music's representative in Philadelphia. One plea drew directly on the military language of industry and organization:

> We must continue to affirm the unequalled merits of Mr. Gilmore as an Organizer and Great Magnetic power. . . . He alone has the Napoleonic genius to gather around him a host of lieutenants, whose genius and power in their respective fields are equal to his own, and whose standing as musicians and conductors make them the natural and legitimate marshals to wield the batons in this grand and unequalled struggle of the countless battalions arrayed in the name of Harmony, Melody, Music, and Musical Art on this Great Centennial battle field of the nations.[3]

Gilmore was happy to perform at the fair, but he had no interest in again organizing such a gargantuan event. Instead he suggested a musician six years his junior: "Who," he responded, "in the profession is best fitted for so important a position? Who will reflect the highest credit upon the country in that position? And who would the cultivated musicians and the true lovers of the divine art elect to that office, could they have a voice in making a selection? I answer these questions, when I say the unanimous choice should and doubtless would be THEODORE THOMAS."[4]

After emigrating from Germany in 1845, Theodore Thomas quickly began a career in the United States as a touring violin protégé and later traveled in the orchestras that accompanied such artists as Jenny Lind, Henrietta Sontag, and Giuseppe Mario. Thomas formed his own ensemble in 1862 and soon began a series of summer concerts in New York. The orchestra conductor had always held more appeal for the Women's Committee than had the bandmaster: Gilmore may have enjoyed greater fame, but Thomas was more distinguished, steeped in the Germanic tradition, and fully ready to demonstrate both the skills of America's performing musicians and the maturing taste of the nation's audiences. If the Music Pavilion was to prove that the country could build instruments, Thomas would show that it could also write for, play upon, and appreciate them. The conductor's efforts began with the commissioning of two new works by American composers: a festive cantata from Dudley Buck and an inaugural hymn by John Knowles Paine. The skills of American artists thus proven, Thomas sought a commission that would demonstrate his adoptive country's cosmopolitan taste. This desire resulted in the payment of an astonishing $5,000 to his professional idol, Richard Wagner.

About two hundred thousand visitors came to witness the centennial's opening ceremonies on the morning of May 10, 1876. The conductor began by leading an arrangement of national anthems, followed by Wagner's brief "Grand March," Paine's "Centennial Hymn," and Buck's *Centennial Meditation of Columbia*. At noon a choir of eight hundred joined Thomas's 150-piece orchestra for a rousing performance of the Hallelujah Chorus. Despite Thomas's grand efforts, things did not go as planned. While he may have gathered a gargantuan orchestra, the open-air space was even bigger, and only those packed close to the ensemble could hear with any clarity. Sightlines, along with Thomas's own "exceedingly tranquil" conducting style, further eroded public interest. The press was largely unconcerned with the newly commissioned works, and even the attention paid to Wagner's music might be deemed a slighting. When one reporter wrote that the potboiler depicted a "world of souls communing together in universal concord and exulting together over the marvelous achievements of the just closing century," Thomas must have wondered just how far American taste had really progressed, especially since the composer himself reportedly claimed that the piece had little to recommend it aside from the commissioning fee. Sad to say, the disappointments of these opening ceremonies would foreshadow Thomas's other musical experiences during the centennial summer.[5]

Music as a science and music as an art were not the only choices open to fairgoers: melodies, after all, could also be entertainment. Once under way, the exhibition offered an endless stream of theater orchestras, German bands, and solo singers who stood ready to delight with familiar tunes in exchange for nominal payment. It was in one of these lighter ensembles that the transplanted Sousa found himself playing during the summer of 1876. The opening ceremonies may have dealt high art a nasty blow, but from his chair in the violin section of an entertainment orchestra, Sousa witnessed its virtual demise.

Plagued by rapidly deteriorating personal finances, the Parisian composer Jacques Offenbach accepted an offer to travel to the United States under the management of Maurice Grau. He was paid the astonishing sum of $30,000 in advance and arrived in New York on May 5, 1876. Although he appeared to great fanfare, New York audiences were unimpressed with his performances. It seems that the composer had misunderstood his appeal: he programmed his own music but appeared without a vocalist, conducted only four numbers per concert, and set ticket prices far too high. Audiences, of course, wanted to see much more of the famous musician, preferably conducting his most popular novelties while dancing the can-can. Embarrassed by the poor ticket sales, Offenbach offered to release Grau from his contract, but instead the manager—who was well versed in American taste—engaged vocal soloists, restructured the program to complement Offenbach's music with familiar works by Weber, Strauss, Gounod, and Berlioz, and cut ticket prices in half. The French composer was soon turning a profit, and in celebration Grau booked the Booth Theater to present performances of Offenbachian *opéra bouffe*. Audiences were delighted.

His schedule just happened to place Offenbach in direct competition with Thomas's orchestra, which was also appearing in the city. Seeing the visiting musician's financial and popular success must have frustrated Thomas, who had worked tirelessly on behalf of serious art in America. The ensuing battle was largely manufactured by the press, but the sentiments attributed to the two men were likely valid. When asked to program more of Offenbach's music, Thomas reportedly refused: "Never will I do anything so degrading." Offenbach's reply was characteristic in its scathing wit: "Please tell Mr. Thomas that I will not be so particular. I shall be most happy to conduct any composition of Theodore Thomas when he reaches the dignity of becoming a composer."[6]

The discord between the two musicians continued as both arrived in Philadelphia. After the opening ceremonies, Thomas began what was to have been a six-month series at the estate of the late actor Edwin Forrest. Travis Quigg, who had purchased the grounds, replanted their lush gardens, opened an art gallery, hired a French chef, and constructed the Women's Centennial Music Hall. In exchange for the kind naming, the Women's Committee, which hoped that the concerts would illustrate "the musical progress of America," promised to sell $100,000 worth of tickets. The length and seriousness of the first concert must have given Thomas's backers pause. Before about three thousand guests he repeated the inaugural music but also added Beethoven's *Consecration of the House* overture, Weber's *Invitation to the Dance*, and works by Mozart, Schubert, and Auber. All in all it must have been a taxing evening for both orchestra and audience. From here Thomas's fortunes deteriorated rapidly. The Forrest Estate was located several miles from the exhibition itself, but Quigg and the Women's Committee had assumed that with the fairgrounds closed in the evening, visitors would be eager to spend their empty hours with Thomas. In practice, however, most fairgoers proved too exhausted to travel and instead retired to their hotel rooms. Those who did make the excursion found the seating arrangement so cramped that there was little access to waiters or the bar. This situation irritated not only patrons but also the management, whose financial plans rested largely on food and beverage sales. Purchases dropped so precipitously that even Thomas was worried. At the start of the third week he stormed off the podium and left a dumbfounded audience to watch his lawyer do battle with Quigg's representative on the stage.[7]

Thomas's difficulties only increased on June 19 when Offenbach arrived in town. His venue was the Alhambra, located downtown at the corner of Broad and Cherry Streets and temporarily renamed in Offenbach's honor. The location, audience size, and feature attraction must have made Thomas nervous. According to one local paper,

> Neither expense nor good judgment has been spared. Indeed, it may be said with perfect justice, that no place more convenient in every way for a summer evening resort is to be found within the city limits. The new hall is one of considerable size, and affords, they say, seating accommodations for so many thousands that we prefer not mentioning the reported number lest our veracity should be called in question. . . . Owing to previous engagements M. Offenbach will not be able to remain long (a week is talked of), so that procrastination should be eschewed.

This report was correct, and Offenbach's engagement at the exhibition lasted just one week. During that time he followed Grau's successful New York strategy by conducting his own works, judiciously mixed with well-known favorites led by the Moravian-born Max Maretzek. Offenbach then spent an additional week in Philadelphia at the Arch Street Theatre, leading productions of his own *opéra bouffe*.[8]

Offenbach had conducted an orchestra of 110 musicians in New York, and about sixty of these men traveled with him to Philadelphia. Once there, this core was joined by local players to form the seventy-five member Centennial Orchestra, and among the violins was John Philip Sousa. Many studies of Offenbach's American tour casually assert that Sousa was part of the New York ensemble, but it is much more likely that he joined the orchestra in Philadelphia through his contact with Simon Hassler, who, along with his brother Mark, contracted players for a number of Philadelphia ensembles.[9]

Thomas's supporters hoped that Offenbach's departure would finally allow for the success of their music director. On July 31, however, the public was informed that the Forrest concerts would come to an end. Thomas had foolishly taken financial responsibility for the venture just as Offenbach was beginning his own performances, and the results were devastating: Thomas's backers found themselves out about $78,000. The conductor too was deep in debt, and to satisfy his creditors, the local sheriff auctioned off his valuable music library, from Wagner's manuscript all the way down to Thomas's own baton.

The lessons of this debacle should have been obvious to everyone involved. Repertoire certainly played a role, but the real culprit was to be found in Thomas's unreasonable demands. Patrons of the Forrest Estate were expected to travel for their art, and once there they were asked to sit through remarkably long concerts while enduring Philadelphia's summer heat and humidity without the relief of refreshment. Such an experience ran counter to the exhibition's atmosphere, where visitors expected to move freely from one display to another.

The sense of casual variety missing from Thomas's concerts pervaded the Offenbach Gardens. The program for the first performance was divided into three sections, the first of which included the overture to Ferdinand Hérold's *Zampa*, Johann Strauss's *Morgenblätter Waltzes*, a paraphrase on "How Fair Art Thou," and a promenade from Offenbach titled *Au tour l'Orphée*. The second set featured the overture to Auber's *Masaniello*, a fantasia on Offenbach's *Geneviève de Brabant*, a selection from Richard Wagner's *Lohengrin*, and Offenbach's own "Polka burlesque." The final set consisted of the overture to Rossini's *William Tell*, a collection titled *Offenbachiana*, a mazurka, and the grand march from Gounod's *Queen of Sheba*. As at Thomas's concerts, Richard Wagner's music was present, but Offenbach couched it in a performance where variety and pleasure were the rule of the day.[10]

In his autobiography Theodore Thomas came close to expressing an understanding of what had happened in Philadelphia. He wrote: "People go to a World's Fair to see and not to hear, to be amused, not to be educated." In this, however, he was still in part mistaken. Music to be both seen and heard was everywhere at the Centennial Exhibition, and Offenbach's success suggests that fairgoers wanted both aural and visual pleasure. Sousa later summed up the lesson more accurately when he explained that Thomas "gave Wagner, Liszt, and Tchaikowsky, in the belief that he was educating his public; I gave Wagner, Liszt and Tchaikowsky with the hope that I was entertaining my public."[11]

FREELANCING IN PHILADELPHIA

After completing his engagements in the Centennial City, Offenbach traveled to Niagara Falls and Chicago before returning to France on July 8. Sousa later wrote, "I also traveled with Offenbach during the time he was in America," but no further evidence suggests that he actually left Philadelphia. In any case, Offenbach's departure did not mean the end of the Centennial Orchestra, and the ensemble continued to perform on the fairgrounds under the direction of Max Maretzek and Simon Hassler. Without Offenbach, however, the orchestra's popularity quickly waned, and by early July the managers found themselves unable to pay their players. On Independence Day the orchestra was finally replaced by a German military band.[12]

Considerable sums had been spent in preparing for the nation's birthday, and not wanting to see the fairgrounds go to waste, a group of Philadelphia businessmen purchased the Main Exhibition Hall and opened the Permanent International Exhibition in May 1877. This private enterprise hoped to recapture the excitement—and dividends—of the previous year's fair, and so it recycled not only the most impressive structures but also the most successful entertainments. Sousa thus found himself playing under the Hasslers in the Permanent Exhibition Orchestra during the summers of 1877 and 1878.

Simon Hassler arranged for Sousa to join the orchestra at the Chestnut Street Theatre sometime near the end of the centennial summer. Sousa later remembered performing with three productions at the Chestnut: Henry James Byron's *Our Boys* (June 26–November 18, 1876); Charles Reade and Tom Taylor's *Masks and Faces* (January 1–13, 1877), and Casimir Delavigne's *Louis XI* (April 22–May 11, 1878). Although these are the only performances Sousa mentioned, he likely used his connection to the Hasslers to find additional work in other area playhouses.[13]

Sousa had at least one additional source of income while in Philadelphia, which he probably acquired with the aid of Thomas à Becket Jr. This composer, arranger, and keyboardist had been working at the house of Lee and Walker when it published Sousa's "Review" and "Cuckoo" in 1873. By the mid-1870s, à Becket was employed at W. F. Shaw, and it was this publisher that hired Sousa, probably in 1877, to correct music proofs. He was also working at the publishing firm of J. M. Stoddart by the fall of 1878.

Each of these employment opportunities—on the fairgrounds, in the theaters, and with publishing firms—gave Sousa a chance to stretch his wings as a composer. The works he wrote during the late 1870s thus encompass a wide variety of genres, styles, and purposes, suggesting a composer quite eager to earn an income from music. In some cases Sousa sold songs, piano pieces, or arrangements outright to a publisher, and such works can be traced through copyright records and sheet music publications. But he was also writing for immediate consumption on the fairground and in the theaters. Pieces for these venues might be performed from manuscript parts and then adapted and recycled for new venues as needed. For many such works only a manuscript source or program reference survives.

Given that Sousa had moved to Philadelphia in order to prove himself worthy of Emma May Swallow, it comes as no surprise that some of the first works he published there were settings of Swallow's texts. It is equally unsurprising that both the composer and his poet were attracted to verses that lamented the separation of sweethearts. Sousa published songs on two such texts in 1877: "The Song of the Sea" and "Ah Me!" The latter, written following a quarrel between the couple, describes a woman wooed and won and the despondency she feels during her lover's absence. The three-strophe setting, with its doubling of the voice by the piano and its largely triadic melody, is very much in the vein of Sousa's youthful songs. A sketch of the piece is dated May 31, 1876, suggesting that Swallow's text may have been inspired by Sousa's absence during the Matt Morgan tour.

"The Song of the Sea," however, is quite different from anything Sousa had written before, and it is indicative of a new maturity entering into his vocal writing. Swallow's text is divided between two speakers: a woman who has lost her beloved sailor and the sea that has stolen him. The human character begins with chromatic and declamatory material as she awaits her partner's return, and Sousa depicts the "cruel, crawling sea" with a chromatic descent through a perfect fourth and twisting diminished chords (ex. 6a). In a nod to Schubert's "Erlkönig," the sea replies with a more metrical and tuneful melody as it explains what has become of the absent lover. After a brief piano interlude that recalls the rocking of waves, the woman's voice reenters, now much more agitated (ex. 6b). She retains her chromatic material, but her fear is further depicted by a less stepwise tune. A reprise of the sea's siren song brings the piece to an end. While "The Song of the Sea" is still straightforward and fairly easy to sing, doublings between voice and piano are more selective, and the work as a whole is as dramatic as it is accessible.

Sousa published two additional works in 1877, both of which were likely begun in Washington. The "Myrrha Gavotte" is his only surviving independent work in that genre. A formal and stately piece, it is an excellent

Ex. 6a. "The Song of the Sea," first verse and chorus

Ex. 6a (*continued*)

Ex. 6b. "The Song of the Sea," second verse

example of Sousa's economy of writing, and a phrase's opening gesture often leads to several measures of musical material. Sousa manages to achieve a remarkable degree of textural variety despite such repetition, and the piece ends with long, sustained notes suggesting the pastoral drones of the dance's ancestors.[14]

As a boy in Washington, Sousa had attended Christ Episcopal Church, whose pastor was Charles D. Andrews. The young musician soon began to serve as violin teacher to Andrews's sister Mary Denison. She was no anonymous Washingtonian; rather, both Mary and her husband Charles Wheeler Denison were writers of substantial local popularity: Mary for her novels, which extolled the virtues of married life, and Charles for his work with abolitionist newspapers. Sousa would collaborate with Mary Denison on several works, the first of which was "Only a Dream," a song very much in the style of his youthful parlor music. The manuscript materials are dated in March 1875, suggesting that the song was drafted in Washington and reworked for publication in Philadelphia.

Holograph materials for "Only a Dream" and "Ah Me!" contain character indications suggesting that the songs may have been meant for theatrical use. There were, however, several works from the late 1870s that Sousa clearly meant for the serious stage. Until this point most of his songs had been written to texts by his Washington friends, but it is not known whether Sousa ever met the lyricist Jefferson Henri Nones, on whose work he drew for two songs. With its female narrator lamenting her separation from a beloved sailor, Sousa's "Hoping" is not unlike "The Song of the Sea." He sets Nones's text with frequent changes of tempo, key, and mood, and the addition of a long piano interlude and complex rhythms suggests that he was reaching for something beyond the parlor tradition. The piece's theatricality is reinforced by the published sheet music, which contains such indications as *andante vezzosamente* and *piangevole ed gentelezza*. That the song was meant for the theater is made clear by its dedication to Emelie Melville, prima donna of the Hess English Opera Company, which performed at Philadelphia's Arch Street Theatre in November 1877. It is likely that "Hoping" was interpolated into one of their productions. Sousa also borrowed from Nones for his earlier and much simpler 1877 song "Lonely."[15]

Sousa almost certainly did not know the much older English writer Charles Swain, who provided the text for two songs: "Only Thee" and "The Magic Glass." The first uses Swain's poem "A Word of Thine," and Sousa's largely diatonic, triadic, and strophic setting is very much in the vein of his earliest songs. "The Magic Glass," however, is an unusual piece relative to Sousa's early work. In it, a group of maidens is invited to view the future through a looking glass. While the three-strophe format is familiar from earlier songs, Sousa creates a rapid, syllabic setting, resulting in the first humorous, patter effect of his output and a significant shift from his earlier, often melancholy love songs. Finally, in 1878 he used an old English ballad for "Love Me Little, Love Me Long," returning to his earlier, straightforward vocal writing.

In 1877 and 1878 Sousa wrote a series of songs that were almost certainly meant for minstrel performance. Entertainments featuring racial comedy were enormously popular during this period, and their most common manifestation was on the blackface minstrel stage, where white actors would capitalize on widely held stereotypes of African American culture. The first of Sousa's racialized songs, " 'Deed I Has to Laugh," is from 1877. The sheet music advertises the piece as a plantation scene, "composed expressly for Griffin and Rice, of Carncross & Dixey's Minstrels," a troupe that enjoyed considerable popularity at Philadelphia's Eleventh Street Opera House. This unremarkable song, which draws on the dialect of the minstrel stage, could have formed a complete scene with its internal dialogue and concluding dance.

"The Free Lunch Cadets" is another 1877 song advertised under the names of Griffin and Rice, and it is the first song to explicitly name Sousa as the lyricist. Racial stage humor in nineteenth-century America was hardly limited to mocking black culture, and other ethnic groups often served as the butt of jokes. In this song Sousa turns his attention to German immigrants with a relatively harmless chorus:

> Oh, sauerkraut and barley soup, and corn-beef by the slice
> Red herrings sprinkled o'er with salt, we tell you they are nice.
> Limburger cheese and mushroom pie, and hot corn by the ear—
> You wouldn't have, you couldn't get, a better bill of fare.

"The Free Lunch Cadets" must have seen some success, since it was also published in a march arrangement for piano by Septimus Winner.

Two songs from 1878 are less obviously about ethnicity but still contain hints of the minstrel stage. "Smick, Smack, Smuck" is about a girl who loves to kiss. The lyric, again by Sousa, contains no ethnic dialect but the conceit of a girl with wide, raw lips suggests the fetishization of the African American mouth that appeared so often on the minstrel stage. "Mavourneen Asthore" sets a text by the otherwise unknown Albert S. Nones, and some editions of the sheet music indicate that it was written for Carncross and Dixey's Minstrels. The title suggests an Irish parody, but the verse has none of the expected dialect, nor does the melody suggest an Irish tune. The four-part chorus with which it concludes is typical of nineteenth-century minstrel works but is unusual in Sousa's output.

It seems clear that Sousa considered himself primarily a song composer in the late 1870s, but he did publish several works in popular dance genres. While these pieces appeared in piano editions, many of them were probably arranged for band or orchestra and intended for performance in Philadelphia theaters or on the centennial grounds. "On Wings of Lightning," published in 1876, joins "Cuckoo" to complete Sousa's production of galops. The piano edition indicates that it was performed by Hassler's Orchestra at the Chestnut Street Theatre but also contains a dedication to one Mrs. M. Louise Redington of St. Louis, suggesting that the work might have been conceived while Sousa was on tour with the Morgan company. Like "Cuckoo," "On Wings of Lightning" contains an introduction and two repeated strains followed by a lyric trio. Two additional strains lead to a lengthy finale, which returns to the home key and reprises the opening material. The different genres of nineteenth-century dance music could be quite similar, and Sousa's galops are very much like his marches except for their varied form, faster tempo, and higher degree of virtuosic writing.

In addition to marches, galops, gavottes, and waltzes, Sousa also wrote one schottische, "Silver Spray" (1878), and dedicated it to one C. F. Eaton of Washington. Like other schottisches, his is little more than a slow polka that makes use of four-bar phrases and an off-beat accompaniment pattern. The origin of the title is unknown, but it may have been a reference to the elaborate fountain Frederic Auguste Bartholdi designed for the centennial's main entrance. If that is the case, the piece was likely performed in ensemble arrangements on the fairground.

At the time of his arrival in Philadelphia, Sousa had published just one march, "Review." In the mid-1870s he would add two more. His march titles often celebrate contemporaneous events, and the first to do so was "Across the Danube," written to commemorate a military battle in the Russo-Turkish War. As the resulting political and military intrigue dominated newspapers during the summer of 1877, a march referencing the event could have been a hit with audiences at the Permanent Exhibition.

The genesis of "Revival March" is more involved. Several of Sousa's newest pieces were published in Philadelphia, but much of his fairground and theater output never made it into print. These works were often fantasies that collected together well-known tunes, and they could thus easily be adapted or arranged as needed. In the late 1890s, after Sousa had become quite famous, Milton Nobles took credit for discovering the young musician and introducing him to Simon

Hassler. According to Nobles, Hassler asked Sousa to compose a piece based on Joseph Webster's hymn "The Sweet By-and-By" for his Exhibition Orchestra. The result may have been the unpublished fantasy *Sounds from the Revivals*. Sousa completed the manuscript on July 20, 1876, and this stringing together of Protestant hymns continued to be used on the fairgrounds until at least the following May. The work includes "Jesus, Lover of My Soul," "Nearer, My God to Thee," "Come Holy Spirit," "Hold the Fort," and "The Sweet By-and-By."[16]

Sousa was not done with Webster's hymn, however, and he returned to it again for the trio of "Revival March," the sheet music for which indicates a performance by Hassler's orchestra at the Chestnut Street Theatre. That Hassler and Sousa would be drawn to the tune is hardly surprising, since it was quite popular in the 1870s, and borrowing from it likely had considerable commercial appeal. The march's reputation quickly spread beyond Philadelphia, and in September 1876 John Esputa reportedly praised it as "deserving of credit."[17]

Taking a cue from Theodore Thomas's opening ceremonies, Sousa also wrote a potpourri of patriotic melodies called "The International Congress." This piece, which was written for the Offenbach orchestra, no longer exists in its original form, but Sousa adapted the work for band and published it in 1887. It is mostly a stringing together of national airs, but Sousa did treat "Yankee Doodle" and "The Star-Spangled Banner" with special care: the first received a short fugue, and the second a scoring marked "à la Wagner." Newspaper reports indicate that in May and June 1877, audiences at the fair could also have heard Sousa's unpublished march "Recognition," which now exists only in a later manuscript, as well as his arrangement of selections from Arthur Sullivan's *Trial by Jury*.[18]

Aside from individual songs, Sousa wrote two other kinds of music for Philadelphia's theaters. As he had with Nobles and Morgan, Sousa sometimes composed incidental music for plays. But nineteenth-century theaters also featured brief concerts before the dramatic entertainment, and on occasion playbills and newspaper announcements list Sousa works as parts of these performances. Given the state of surviving materials, it is not always possible to tell for which of these two traditions an individual piece was intended.

According to the manuscript of *In Parlor and Street*, this unpublished fantasy on tunes ranging from Verdi's "Anvil Chorus" to Sousa's "Only a Dream" and "Smick, Smack, Smuck" was first performed at the Chestnut Street Theatre on February 27, 1877. The unpublished *Phoenix Medley* similarly contains selections from popular songs and operettas, and it is possible that Sousa created the work from his earlier incidental music for Nobles's play. *The*

Phoenix appeared at the Arch Street Theatre in late November 1878, and the medley may have been used for that production.[19]

A number of other works are mentioned on various theater programs from the 1870s. In August 1876 the orchestra at the Chestnut Street Theatre played the otherwise unknown *World of Fancies*. That November it performed something identified as Sousa's "Grand International Pot-Pourri: Airs of All Nations," likely a version of "The International Congress." His only quadrille, "Queen of the Harvest" (a work not published until 1889), appeared at the Chestnut Street Theatre in February 1877. Sousa also provided a lost overture for Richard Brinsley Sheridan's play *The Rivals*, probably for a late November 1877 production at the Chestnut. Finally, an Arch Street Theatre program from September 1878 lists Sousa's lost fantasia *Belle Mahone*.[20]

Other theatrical connections are even more speculative. There is a sketch in the Library of Congress's scrapbook that is labeled as belonging to Shakespeare's *Twelfth Night* and dated November 1876. That play appeared at the Chestnut in November and early December, and it is possible that Sousa provided some of the incidental music. In early 1877 he wrote the unpublished *Sandalphon Waltzes* and called them opus 34. These were likely used in connection to a reading of Longfellow's poem, perhaps one that took place at the Academy of Music in November 1877 with musical accompaniment by Thomas à Becket Jr. One manuscript source is labeled *Sardanapolis*, and perhaps the waltzes did double duty for a production of Lord Byron's drama, which played at the Academy of Music in late January and early February. Whatever the case, the piece was reworked and dedicated to Rose Cleveland, who would serve as White House hostess for her unmarried brother in 1885 and early 1886.[21]

All in all Sousa composed a great deal between his summer 1876 arrival in Philadelphia and mid-1878. Much of this music was performed from manuscript sources, and some of it was later reworked for publication, usually in the 1880s. In total, seventeen new works appeared in print during this period. The majority of these pieces were songs, although they included a galop, a gavotte, a schottische, and two marches. Sousa had not yet settled on a single publisher, and several different houses were issuing his works. Following Sousa's opus numbers (whenever possible), these were the Charles Swain song "Only Thee," opus 24 (published by North); the Mary Denison song "Only a Dream," opus 25 (North); the galop "On Wings of Lightning," opus 26 (Andre); "Revival March" (Ditson); the Swallow songs "The Song of the Sea," opus 27 (North) and "Ah Me!," opus 29 (Meyer); "Myrrha Gavotte," opus 30 (Lee and Walker); the Swain song "The Magic Glass," opus 31 (North); the Jefferson Henri Nones song "Lonely," opus 32 (Stoddart); the march "Across the Danube," opus 36 (Stoddart); the ballad "Love Me Little, Love Me Long," opus 37 (Shaw); the Nones song "Hoping," opus 39 (Stoddart); the minstrel songs "'Deed I Has to Laugh" (Stoddart), "Mavoureen Asthore" (Stoddart), "Smick, Smack, Smuck" (Shaw), and "The Free Lunch Cadets" (Stoddart); and the "Silver Spray Schottische" (Shaw).

Sousa's works were sometimes advertised by association with more famous composers or performers. "Only Thee" lists pieces for sale by the far better known Michael Balfe, James Molloy, Ciro Pinsuti, and Arthur Sullivan. The songs published by F. A. North include an engraving of the famous soprano Adelina Patti, although given this publisher's minor status and Patti's hiatus from the American stage, it is unlikely that she actually sang any of them. By the time of "'Deed I Has to Laugh" (1877), Sousa's name seems to have carried some commercial value, as the piece was advertised as being by the same composer as "The Song of the Sea," "Only a Dream," "Ah Me!," "Magic Glass," and "Revival March."

Sousa was clearly putting into practice the lessons of the Navy Yard, and while in Philadelphia he worked quickly to write music for whatever type of entertainment might provide a paycheck. From the centennial fairgrounds and Philadelphia's theaters to the city's many publishing houses, Sousa was working in all sorts of music from serious song to the minstrel stage. His career was not limited to Philadelphia, either, and for a portion of the summer of 1877 he led an orchestra at Cape May Point, at the southern tip of New Jersey. On the fairgrounds Sousa also had a front row seat to a remarkable spectacle. Here, in Theodore Thomas's failure and Jacques Offenbach's triumph, Sousa saw once again the importance of pleasing his public. By the late 1870s, now with professional experience in several different types of musical work, John Philip Sousa was well on his way to mastering the fast-paced variety that nineteenth-century American audiences demanded.[22]

THE PROMISE OF GILBERT AND SULLIVAN

In mid-September 1877 Sousa happened upon Benjamin and Emma May Swallow, who were visiting Philadelphia. By this point he must have been quite proud of his musical exploits, and he followed his fiancée back to Washington. Now modestly—but gainfully—employed as a theater violinist, arranger, and composer, he had fulfilled his pledge to the Reverend Swallow, and it looked certain that he would soon be married. Emma's mother, however, informed the young musician that there was another suitor, and Sousa returned to Philadelphia doubtful of his fiancée's fidelity. In his jealousy he failed to answer Emma's letters, and she in turn married the military officer J. P. Bartlett on October 3, 1877. This romantic setback once again placed Sousa in the Centennial City, but now he was no longer an apprenticing musician; he was a professional composer, conductor, and violinist, ready to tackle much bigger projects.[23]

The young musician had dreamt of writing an operetta since his boyhood studies with George Felix Benkert, and Sousa expressed his desire to Simon Hassler, who suggested that he seek a libretto from the Philadelphia reporter, humorist, and critic Charles Heber Clark. The effort came to nothing when Clark demanded a fee far beyond the young composer's reach. Sousa did make some headway on an operetta titled *Florine* with his Washington friend Mary Denison, but the librettist soon withdrew because of her husband's ill health.

Sousa next paired with Wilson J. Vance, a writer with broad interests. Vance had been with the Twenty-First Regiment of Ohio at Stones River during the Civil War, for which service he was later awarded the Medal of Honor. After attending Harvard Law School, Vance held staff positions in the U.S. Senate and the Treasury Department. He also made several unsuccessful attempts to run for Congress and for the Ohio governor's office. Vance's collaboration with Sousa, titled *Katherine*, progressed far enough to receive some notice in the press, and according to reports the opera was to be set in the White Mountains and partake of "the beauty of the opera of *Martha*, interspersed with frothy effervescence of the *Pinafore* order." Although parts of this piece were completed in 1878 and 1879, the work was never produced. Sousa would need to wait to see an operetta of his own on the American stage, but he was quickly presented with a chance to further his skills and earn a living by arranging the work of more seasoned composers. As it happened, this opportunity was something that American copyright law unintentionally encouraged.[24]

Nineteenth-century operettas were often published in piano reduction. Such simplified editions allowed potential audiences to familiarize themselves with a work's best numbers at home, thus encouraging the purchase of theater tickets. This arrangement proved to be a double-edged sword: a published reduction might act as a powerful form of advertisement, but it could also be used to create unauthorized orchestrations and lead to productions from which the original composer saw no financial reward. American copyright law was of little assistance in such cases because the publication of a piano edition effectively voided a composer's exclusive right to public performance; once a piece was published, anyone was free to adapt, arrange, and produce it.

In order to address this legal loophole, composers and librettists often declined to publish certain essential elements of their work, including dialogue, orchestrations, and stage directions. There was, of course, nothing to keep a determined impresario from creating a new orchestration from the published reduction and memorizing everything else from an authorized production. The 1860 case *Keene v. Kimball* affirmed that any person who had attended a performance and "committed to memory any part or the whole of the play" could "repeat what they heard to others" and that there was "no right of property in gestures, tones, or scenery, which would forbid such reproduction of them by the spectators as their powers of imitation might enable them to accomplish." Thus, once an operetta's songs were published, they could be reorchestrated at will, and anyone clever enough to remember an authorized performance could reproduce it freely for his or her own profit.[25]

Between February 24 and March 1, 1879, the Arch Street Theatre mounted Gilbert and Sullivan's *The Sorcerer*, and Sousa helped prepare an orchestration from the published piano-vocal score. Sousa's work does not survive, and reviews fail to mention his music, although they were remarkably unflattering to the production as a whole: "To maltreat a decent opera in such a shameful fashion as Sullivan's *Sorcerer* was maltreated at the Arch Street Theatre last night ought to be made an indictable offense . . . the performance was simply the worst we have ever heard."[26]

Never one to be discouraged, Sousa soon tried again, and this time he turned to an even more popular operetta, *H.M.S. Pinafore*. It had opened in London in May 1878, and Gilbert and Sullivan naturally published their songs in piano reduction. As a result, an unauthorized *Pinafore* was playing in Boston by November. Within weeks hundreds of productions were crisscrossing the country, and the show was profitably performed by juvenile organizations, blackface minstrel troupes, and church choirs both amateur and professional. As the theater chronicler George Odell would later note, "Never was there anything before or since like the craze, the madness, the lunacy for this opera." From all of these productions, the original composer and librettist received not a penny, a fact that understandably frustrated Arthur Sullivan: "It seemed to be their opinion that a free and independent American citizen ought not to be robbed of his right of robbing somebody else."[27]

In February 1879, on the recommendation of Thomas à Becket Jr., Sousa was hired as the musical director for a production of *H.M.S. Pinafore* being planned by an organization informally known as the Amateur Opera Company. Just as he had for Nobles and Morgan, Sousa would prepare orchestrations, drill singers, and conduct performances. The young musician likely expected a brief employment, but the amateurs proved surprisingly successful, and Sousa—like much of America—was to be consumed by *Pinafore* for the remainder of 1879.[28]

Despite the organization's name, the principals of the Amateur Opera Company were not, strictly speaking, amateurs, and many of them had been paid soloists in Philadelphia churches. As the company began to inspire reviews, this fact had two beneficial effects. First, since many rival productions did not feature skillful singers, this group of exceptional musicians was able to draw attention away from their rather poor dramatic skills. Second, the wholesome reputation of a group of church singers made it difficult for critics to be overtly cruel.[29]

The amateurs opened under Sousa's direction at the Newsboys' Home in Philadelphia on February 20, 1879, and performed at St. George's Hall on February 24. They then began a brief tour of nearby cities, including Pottsville, Pennsylvania (February 27) and Wilmington, Delaware (February 28). This short excursion was all that the amateurs had planned, but their novel production, which had begun under the management of James F. Gorman, soon attracted the attention of the professional New York manager James H. Meade. Now renamed to capitalize on their wholesome membership (and avoid connection to an established New York business interest), Gorman's Philadelphia Church Choir Company opened at the Broadway Theatre in New York on March 10, 1879.[30]

Sousa's organization was hardly alone in presenting Gilbert and Sullivan to New York audiences, and soon nearly every theater in the city had mounted some sort of production of *H.M.S. Pinafore*. But the church singers proved a hit, probably on account of their better-than-average voices. As George Odell noted, they "unquestionably sang the music better than any other company, thus far, had been able to do. Of course the acting was another matter. But this particular group became a sort of craze, in and for itself, much, probably, to the surprise of regular actors."[31]

Critics accepted the poor acting as a humorous side effect of the company's purely choral training, and in order to maintain their religious identification, the organization periodically returned to perform in Philadelphia churches (and refused to appear in the theaters on Good Friday). All told, Sousa's company presented *Pinafore* to New York audiences for well over a month, from March 10 to April 26, 1879. The *Times* was correct when it reported that the production was "astonishingly successful and profitable," and to distinguish itself from a host of imitators, the Gorman Company soon added the word *Original* to its name.[32]

After leaving New York, Sousa and his singers traveled to Philadelphia for performances until May 3, after which they appeared in New Haven (May 6–7), Trenton (May 8), and Wilmington (May 9). After this excursion, they were back at the Broadway on May 12 to treat New York to another two weeks of Gilbert and Sullivan before closing on May 24. This visit was billed as the company's second voyage, and it included new scenery, an augmented chorus, and a Marine drill provided by the Pennsylvania State Fencibles.[33]

It did not take long for the press to discover Meade's involvement, and once it became clear that Gorman's amateurs were not free of professional management, the critical gloves were removed:

> There can be no doubt, either, but that the connection of J. H. Meade with the Church Choir party has begun to hurt it. As long as his connection was not proclaimed it did no special harm, but when it came to be generally known (through his published notices) that he was the manager of this untarnished troupe of West Philadelphia unexceptionables, the illusion of the Church Choir began to vanish and there remained only the fact—a company of untried, untrained and ungainly bad amateurs, whose vocal powers made insufficient amends for their dramatic capacity.[34]

The organization may have been driven from New York, but Sousa and his singers continued touring until midsummer. They visited New Haven (May 28–29); Hartford (May 30–31); Holyoke and Springfield, Massachusetts (June 2 and June 3); and Providence (June 9–13) before settling in Boston for three weeks (June 15–July 5). They then retraced their steps back through Springfield (July 7–8), Hartford (July 9), and New Haven (July 10–12). To celebrate their phenomenal and unexpected success, the company's principals used their earnings to travel to Europe for a brief respite. Sousa stayed behind to see to some important business in the capital.

Almost unbelievably, the Church Choir Company's success continued unabated. After the European hiatus, *H.M.S. Pinafore* reopened in Trenton on September 30 and played Paterson (October 3–4), New Haven (October 8), Hartford (October 10 and 22), Holyoke (October 11), and Springfield (October 20–21). Next came a swing through Pennsylvania with stops in Maston (November 3), Wilkes-Barre (November 5), Reading (November 6), Pottsville (November 7), and Lancaster (November 8). New York, too, had not seen the end of the Church Choir Company, which opened at the Broadway Opera House on November 10. Reviews continued to be favorable, if somewhat less enthusiastic.

The company remained at the Broadway until November 29, and its timing could not have been better. Most American producers created their Gilbert and Sullivan materials from the published piano-vocal score and failed to provide any financial remuneration to the comic duo. The only exception to this American model of robber-impresario was John Ford, the Baltimore-based manager who had earlier employed Sousa as a violinist and conductor. Ford, along with his son Charles, opened *H.M.S. Pinafore* at the Baltimore Grand Opera House in December 1878 and moved their production to Philadelphia's Broad Street Theatre for the New Year. This run was so rewarding that Ford sent Sullivan $500, becoming, as Sullivan wrote, "the sole manager at present who has offered us any acknowledgement of the success of our piece in America."[35]

Ford's payment was not philanthropic but rather was meant to grease the wheels of his scheme to bring Gilbert and Sullivan to America. After considerable negotiation, the pair arrived in New York in November 1879 and along with the soprano Blanche Roosevelt went to examine the competition. They attended a performance by the Church Choir Company on November 11, and a naturally curious Sousa dispatched a staff member to capture the visiting celebrities' opinion: "Sullivan thought the orchestration excellent. (This of course, delighted me, since it was mine!)"[36]

Gilbert and Sullivan had not crossed the Atlantic just to hear pirated performances of their work, and on December 1, 1879, *H.M.S. Pinafore*, now featuring the original, unpublished stage directions and orchestration conducted by Sullivan himself, opened at New York's Fifth Avenue Theatre, where Ford was a lessee. Given the new competition, Sousa's company simply traded one operetta for another, and in mid-December it opened *The Smugglers*, a reworking of F. C. Burnand and Arthur Sullivan's *The Contrabandista*. Sousa again conducted his own orchestration, likely prepared from a published reduction. The company played in New Haven (December 19–20), Hartford (December 22–23), Springfield (December 24), and Holyoke (December 25). It may have had a few performances in New Jersey, but by the beginning of the New Year the appeal had dissipated, and tickets sales had dramatically declined: "It has been whispered—and not very softly either—that the Philadelphia Church Choir is on its last legs. Salaries are behind, and somewhere in New Jersey the marines executed a new movement—a sort of flank movement. They tried to capture the baggage of the troupe. Tho' silent in their drill, they are hungry on the march—and Jersey is a poor state to forage in."[37]

The year that Sousa spent with Gorman's Original Philadelphia Church Choir Company was important for several reasons. First, though he may have remained in Philadelphia because of a failed romance, he would not leave the city empty-handed. On February 22, 1879, the twenty-four-year-old musician met a carpenter's daughter named Jane van Middlesworth Bellis. At sixteen Bellis was serving as the understudy for the part of Hebe in *H.M.S. Pinafore*, and less than a year later, on December 30, she became Mrs. John Philip Sousa. It is unclear just how large a role Sousa's wife played in his career, and the former Miss Bellis seems to have muted her own ambitions in favor of her husband's: "Mrs. Sousa realized that my life work was to be music, that music was an exacting mistress and that domestic affairs would have to be subordinated to the musical demands of the moment."[38]

Second, at the moment when Sousa was achieving his fame as the March King, there was in America a growing anxiety about the relation between leisure and masculine strength. Urbanization may have promised much to the new

Fig. 11. A portrait of Sousa, ca. 1876. Library of Congress, Washington, D.C.

Fig. 12. Mrs. John Philip Sousa, ca. 1880. Library of Congress, Washington, D.C.

middle class, but between 1870 and 1910 the opportunities once provided by small-scale, competitive capitalism were visibly on the decline. As Jackson Lears has suggested, such economic uncertainty spawned a strong antimodernist backlash, and in the process two modes of masculinity were thrown into conflict. Many men of Sousa's generation had assumed that hard work and moral restraint would lead to financial success, and, indeed, the mature March King seemed to embody this Victorian model of manliness; he was, in the words of one reporter, "the very personification of masculine grace."[39]

With the start of a new century, however, the financial rewards of such self-restraint appeared in doubt, and many Americans began to wonder whether modern civilization was leading them astray from romanticized notions of nature and the primitive. From *The Virginian* (1902) to *Tarzan of the Apes* (1914), popular culture came to celebrate a less restrained sense of manhood that worked to restabilize the heteronormative ideals of untamed masculinity that seemed vulnerable in the face of both financial uncertainty and a physically softening reliance on technology. It was here, in the masculine primitive as much as in the restrained gentlemen, that audiences found the March King.

The European music that made up so much of a Sousa concert—with its foreign roots and growing status as a cultivated art—might undermine the sense of American masculinity on which the March King came to rely. Sousa naturally worked to defuse the conflict by stating unequivocally that his concerts reinforced gender security and that his programming resisted the weakening effects of modern culture. As always, Sousa built a bridge to his audience and gave listeners the credit for his achievement: "The people who frequent my concerts are the strong and healthy. I mean the healthy both of mind and body. These people like virile music. Longhaired men and shorthaired women you never see in my audience. And I don't want them."[40]

In a world that valued musical diversity, a concert's virility could not be built on a repertoire of exclusion. Rather, all music—from a Sousa march to a Wagner prelude—was used to reinforce the sense of manhood that many Americans worried might be stolen by modernity. The key was to present this music with a sense of masculine honesty and avoid the image of artifice. Like his audiences, the March King had no use for "hypocrisy in music" or for performers who wore "long hair, goggles, an air of mystery" and smelled "of Dutch cheese." Rather than being an overly sensitive artist, Sousa was a simple bandmaster who failed to "affect any of the airs of a genius." In the eyes of reporters, the March King was "a tall, burly fellow in the prime of life, and, unlike most of his fellows in the wide domain of art, he combs his hair carefully."[41]

Like the popular fiction of his day, Sousa's writings create a robust sense of masculinity through a celebration of sport and physical culture. Despite his early illness, Sousa regularly depicts an idealized childhood of bodily adventure, and athletics would continue to play an important role in creating the March King persona throughout his career. In 1916 he was documented as traveling nearly a thousand miles on horseback, a trip that allowed Sousa to participate in a number of shooting competitions. The same year, he was elected president of the American Amateur Trapshooters' Association, and in 1917 chairman of the National Association of Shotgun Owners. These sports were so important to Sousa that in 1916 he penned an article for the *American Shooter* titled "A Horse, a Dog, a Gun, and a Girl." Boxing, too, was a favorite pastime, and in 1899 the *Morning World* was invited to observe Sousa at practice. The paper introduced the resulting photographs by connecting strength, conducting, and composition: "You see bared before the camera

Fig. 13. Sousa seated on his horse Aladdin, ca. 1923. "The President's Own" United States Marine Band, Washington, D.C.

Fig. 14. Sousa checking a rifle, ca. 1918. "The President's Own" United States Marine Band, Washington, D.C.

the muscular right arm that has wielded the baton to the delight of millions, the sturdy fist that wrote *El Capitan*."[42]

No physical activity, however, was as important to Sousa as baseball, perhaps because it so perfectly married gentlemanly manhood with masculine power. For years the Sousa Band fielded its own team, and the conductor often acted as pitcher. In 1909 he published an article on the sport ("The Greatest

Fig. 15. Sousa striking a masculine pose, ca. 1899. "The President's Own" United States Marine Band, Washington, D.C.

Fig. 16. The Sousa Band baseball team, 1904. Sousa is seated in the middle. The young man in the Nassau uniform is John Philip Sousa Jr., a first baseman with Princeton University. "The President's Own" United States Marine Band, Washington, D.C.

Game in the World" in *Baseball Magazine*), and in 1925 he wrote a march in honor of the National League's fiftieth anniversary ("The National Game").

Sousa claimed to have begun playing baseball at the age of six, but the first documented notices of Sousa the athlete appeared while he was leading his church choir singers. While on tour the opera company fielded a team, pulled primarily from the Pennsylvania Fencibles, the chorus, and the orchestra; Sousa himself regularly played center field or shortstop. The *Pinafore* company seems not to have been particularly skilled, as one newspaper noticed: "The Pinafore men do not play as well on the ball field as on the stage . . . and the result was their defeat by a score of 16 to 2." What is noteworthy, however, is just how often the local press took an interest in the company's athletic efforts. By appearing on the ball field, Sousa and his musicians once again made clear that they were not professional artists but simply talented Americans. It was this humanizing value of sport that the March King would use throughout his career to reinforce his masculine, American, and accessible image.[43]

Sousa recognized how important a role the Amateur Opera Company played in launching his musical career. On the road he was expected to orchestrate, to rehearse, to conduct, and to manage. It was he whose name was listed on the program, and it was his success or failure that reviews noted. In short, Sousa was the professional among these amateurs, and it was his reputation that stood to rise or fall with their success. In 1928 the mature March King celebrated fifty years on the podium by writing the "Golden Jubilee" march. He clearly saw the *Pinafore* tour, with its successful run in New York and endless press notices, as the start of his professional career.

OUR FLIRTATIONS

The beginning of 1879 may have marked the end of Sousa's amateur opera organization, but it was not yet the end of his time in Philadelphia. In 1878 and 1879 he prepared arrangements for several of the city's publishing houses. The W. F. Shaw Company published his *Evening Pastime* (1879), a collection of eighty-seven simple arrangements—largely from popular operettas—for violin or flute with piano accompaniment. For some pieces in this collection, Sousa is given credit as composer: *Adamsonia*, a collection of songs by Stephen Adams; the "Carmen March," a potpourri based on Georges Bizet's opera; a set of variations on "Home, Sweet Home"; a "Medley Quadrille" on popular songs; "Melange," consisting of well-known melodies; and a new march called "Resumption." Also included was James Molloy's march "The Triton," which Sousa would rework in 1892. Shaw also published a second collection the same year, this one for cornet and piano and titled *Evening Hours*. Of the twenty-eight pieces, only one is a fully original Sousa work: the polka "La Reine d'Amour," a piece distinct from the 1874 set of waltzes by the same name.[44]

Sousa also completed a number of piano arrangements for the Stoddart company between 1878 and 1880. Once again, they are mostly selections from light operetta, including Bizet's *Carmen* (1879); Richard Genée's *The Sea Cadet* (1880); Charles Lecocq's *The Little Duke* (1879) and *La Camargo* (1880); Victor Massé's *Paul and Virginia* (1880); Johann Strauss's *Indigo and the Forty Robbers* (1878); Arthur Sullivan's *Trial by Jury* (1879), *The Sorcerer* (1879), and *H.M.S. Pinafore* (1879 and 1880); Franz von Suppé's *Boccaccio* (1880); and Giuseppe Verdi's *La Traviata* (1880).

There is also a single song that was likely conceived during this period. "A Rare Old Fellow" was not published until 1881, but Sousa dedicated the piece to G. T. R. Knorr, a church choir director who joined the *Pinafore* amateurs as Dick Deadeye. Sousa's song is a sinister piece about King Death, and he uses the same text by Barry Cornwall (a pseudonym for Bryan Waller Procter) that was set by several other composers, including George W. Chadwick.

Knorr would go on to pursue a professional career in comic opera but is not known to have had any further contact with Sousa, making it likely that the song was composed in the late 1870s.

By 1880 John Philip Sousa had established a successful career in Philadelphia as a composer, arranger, and conductor. He would make one final foray into the world of theatrical touring before leaving the city for good. In the summer of 1880 he was asked to provide music for a play by James Bird Wilson that starred the comic duo Frank F. Mackay and Louise Sylvester, whom Sousa had likely met at the Chestnut Street Theatre. Wilson's play centered on several sets of couples involved in a series of flirtatious activities. Sousa quickly retired to Cape May, where he wrote about twenty-one numbers for a show to be called *Our Flirtations*. While a complete score was never published, several individual songs did appear in print in 1880. Two songs use texts by Sousa's earlier collaborators: "The Lily Bells" sets a lyric by the former Emma Swallow and is part of the parlor tradition with which Sousa was now so familiar, and "Love's Beguiling" is a charming patter song with a waltz chorus to a text by Wilson J. Vance. Two songs use lyrics by Sousa himself: "Oh My! De Sight" is a minstrel piece, and "Flirtation!" is a coy song with a patter verse. Sousa also published *Our Flirtation Waltzes*. Finally, for the first entr'acte, he wrote the "Our Flirtation" march. This piece was not published until 1890, when it was dedicated to Henry L. West, a reporter for the *Washington Post*.

Our Flirtations began rehearsals in late July 1880, and Mackay's production appeared at Philadelphia's Park Theatre from August 30 to September 4 before setting out on tour to Reading (September 7), St. Louis (September 12–19), and probably Kansas City. While the plot was "only just strong enough to hold" the production together, audiences enjoyed the singing, dancing, and comic antics of the company. Sousa was also well praised: "The music, with the exception of two numbers, is not of a character likely to become popular—not because it is not good, but because it is too good. It is of too high a class, and is far above the character of the play." The two excepted numbers were "The Lily Bells," described as "just the thing to please all neat song and dance artists and their audiences," and the minstrel tune "Oh My! De Sight," which the same critic expected to become a "bonanza to performers who want a new jubilee end-song."[45]

The surviving manuscript materials for *Our Flirtations* suggest that Sousa was thinking beyond the mere arrangements he had completed thus far, and the settings of texts by his former collaborators indicates that Sousa may have borrowed from original songs and operettas he had earlier failed to complete.

The show may not have been a suitable vehicle for Sousa's ambitions, but it provided him with a bit more experience on the road and another set of publications. He also now had considerably more contact with professional actors and musicians. For example, one of the members of the play's orchestra, the flutist John S. Cox, was quite fond of difficult passages, and Sousa wrote an appropriately challenging part for the overture. He might have met Cox when he soloed with the Exhibition Orchestra or while he was musical director of the Carncross and Dixey's Minstrels. When Sousa formed his own band in 1892, he would again draw on his Philadelphia connections and make Cox a part of the ensemble.[46]

Sousa's entire Philadelphia career, from the performances with Offenbach in the summer of 1876 to *Our Flirtations* at the end of 1880, suggests a composer headed for the musical theater. Sousa had written a few marches and a handful of dance pieces and fantasies, but the vast majority of his output (and almost all of his published music) was made up of original songs and arrangements for the theater. In both of these areas he was maturing rapidly. His songwriting, which had begun as romantic parlor settings for friends, now encompassed minstrel tunes, patter numbers, and several fairly complex and dramatic works. His writing for the theater had also undergone a metamorphosis. For Matt Morgan he had composed brief, repetitive background music that helped set the mood for a series of tableaux. By the time he left Philadelphia in 1880, Sousa had orchestrated several complete operettas. When called on to write incidental music for a play, he seems to have already had a body of material for use, some of which pushed the boundaries of the task at hand. Sousa's personal life had also changed. No longer was he an apprentice musician; by the end of 1879 he was a husband, and he would soon become a father. In short, John Philip Sousa was now an adult and a professional. But the biggest change in his career was still to take place, and it would occur while he was on the road with *Our Flirtations*.

CHAPTER FIVE

A Presidential Musician

EVEN BEFORE BECOMING THE LEADER of the United States Marine Band in 1873, Louis Schneider had been a proud musician: he often boasted of his days with Napoleon III's Royal Band, Theodore Thomas's orchestra, Patrick Gilmore's ensemble, and Adelina Patti's tour, and by all accounts he prominently wore the medals awarded to him by such admirers as the king of Italy, the emperor of France, and the pope. Despite his exalted résumé, Schneider's first years in Washington had not gone particularly smoothly. One summer evening in 1878 he was even more drunk than usual. Making his way home to the Navy Yard after a Saturday ceremony, Schneider stumbled off a streetcar and fell into the road. There to help him was Frank Boidi, a Marine Band member whom Schneider had dismissed just three weeks earlier. The bandleader mistakenly felt himself under attack, and since he was still dressed in his ceremonial uniform, Schneider drew his saber and charged. Boidi responded with his cane just as two off-duty police officers arrived on the scene.

While this fracas may have been brief, it brought Schneider unneeded attention. His public lack of restraint had become all too notorious, and a drunken stumble only added to the Corps's disappointment. It was, however, Schneider's abuse of his public office that finally ruined him. He had of late been accused of various financial improprieties, and for some time had taken advantage of his government office to avoid paying tariffs on imported instruments. Once they were procured, he would sell the untaxed goods in exchange for a handsome commission. "For this and his *other* misconduct," Louis Schneider was dismissed from the Marine Corps on October 1, 1880.[1]

John Philip Sousa, meanwhile, was doing quite well in Philadelphia, but with a new wife, he was no doubt eager to find a more stable source of income than that offered by a traveling theater troupe. Sousa had likely heard of Schneider's difficulties from his father, who had retired from the Marine Band in March 1879 and continued to build furniture on the Navy Yard. A return to his hometown—and to the ensemble that had nurtured his career—must have seemed quite attractive, but Sousa was hardly an obvious candidate to take over as bandleader. If he desired Schneider's position, he would need to find some way of attracting the attention of the Marine Corps.

By late 1878 some of Sousa's Philadelphia music had become known in the capital. The *Washington Post* mentioned "Silver Spray Schottische" and "Smick, Smack, Smuck" in November, calling the latter "one of the most catchy, ridiculous, rib-tickling absurdities ever thought of in the way of a musical composition." In August Sousa completed a march, his opus 45, and dedicated it to the librettist Wilson Vance. Most Americans who purchased W. F. Shaw's piano edition likely did not recognize the dedicatee, but they might well have noticed the title, a phrase often used by the Marines: "Esprit de Corps."[2]

The new year provided Sousa with an opportunity to go a step further. On January 1, 1879, the federal government returned to the practice of settling its public debts with gold. In honor of the occasion Sousa included an original march (called "Resumption") in his collection *Evening Pastime*. When Shaw extracted the piece and published it for piano, Sousa dedicated the new version to Norval L. Nokes. Once again, audiences might not have recognized the name, but the dedicatee—a captain in Washington's Marine Guard—was no doubt flattered. Perhaps because of (or in exchange for) the dedication, Sousa's work was played by the Marine Band, a fact advertised on the sheet music. The band had performed some of Sousa's music when he had been a young member of the ensemble; now, after several years' absence, it had returned to the stands. In retrospect, it seems certain that John Philip Sousa was plotting his own return to Washington.

In the summer of 1879, while the singers in his production of *Pinafore* were celebrating their success with a trip to Europe, Sousa visited his hometown. He was in the city to meet with Wilson Vance, who was now working at the Bureau of Indian Affairs. On September 3 the two men entered into a contract and agreed to complete an opera titled "*Love's Lilting* or such other name as may by the said parties be agreed upon." No opera with this title appears in Sousa's output, but the parties were likely formalizing their unfinished work on *Katherine*, which was submitted for copyright just a few days later. Sousa took another opportunity to flatter the Marine Corps while in Washington: on July 20 he named a new march after their emblem, the "Globe and Eagle." After completing his business in the capital, Sousa returned to Philadelphia and resumed work with the Church Choir Company. He did not, however, give up on the Marine Corps. Almost a year after his trip home, on May 5, 1880, he finished the *Paroles d'Amour Valses* and dedicated them to Marine commandant Charles McCawley. This publication must have gotten the Corps's attention, because the Marine Band performed the new work in June.[3]

For his part, McCawley was intrigued by the young musician's progress. In the summer of 1880 he attended a production of *Our Flirtations* and was duly impressed. Perhaps inspired by Sousa's skills at arranging music from operettas, McCawley wrote and asked him to prepare music for the Marine Band: "I would like you to arrange for the Band selections from *Paul and Virginia, Trial by Jury, Sorcerer, Little Duke, Royal Middy, Aida, Boccaccio, Camargo, Princess Toto*, and *Carmen*. I enclose the number of instruments, and will thank you to select the best airs from each opera named." Since Sousa had already written potpourris based on several of these operettas, the task could not have been very difficult.[4]

RETURNING TO WASHINGTON

Prior to McCawley's request, Sousa, of course, could not afford to wait idly for a job offer, and he continued to compose in Philadelphia. In 1879 he published a march titled "On the Tramp" based on Septimus Winner's song "Out of Work." He would use the same melody again as the basis for a fantasy published for flute as well as violin. He also wrote a companion set of variations titled *Under the Eaves*. In May 1880 Sousa published his second collaboration with Mary Denison, the parlor song "When He Is Near."

Perhaps the most interesting of his pieces from 1880 is the reverie "Nymphalin," published in April. On later editions Sousa included a passage from Edward Bulwer-Lytton's novel *Pilgrims of the Rhine*: "But presently soft music was heard floating along, something like the sound we hear on a still night, then forth issued the fairies—Ghost-like and shadowy floated on that Shape through the abyss of time, governing the world with an unquestioned and noiseless sway." It seems clear that Sousa's intent was to capture Bulwer-Lytton's fairy queen in this flowing work. The piece is dominated by an eight-bar ritornello that stretches out the first half of each measure before fluttering in sixteenth notes (ex. 7). This material is repeatedly interrupted with changes in key, tempo, and mood that allow the listener to peer in on the fairies' dance. Sousa's career had thus far been dominated by the theater, and even as the March King he would remain driven to create musical drama. "Nymphalin" seems to have been his first effort at writing a descriptive, if textless, piece of music.[5]

Ex. 7. "Nymphalin," ritornello and first episode

As word of Schneider's troubles spread, applications for his place began to arrive at the commandant's office. They would prove too late, however. While on tour with *Our Flirtations*, Sousa was informed by telegram that the leadership of the United States Marine Band was his for the taking. Perhaps his portfolio of dedications had paid off, or maybe it was simply Sousa's connections with the Navy Yard that secured his new position. Whatever the case,

Figs. 17 and 18. Two early portraits of Sousa in his Marine Band uniform. "The President's Own" United States Marine Band, Washington, D.C.

on September 30, 1880, John Philip Sousa and his wife arrived in Washington. The following day he enlisted in the Marine Corps for the third time, now as the band's seventeenth director, its youngest leader, and its first American-born conductor. The *Washington Star* announced the city's new bandmaster: "Mr. John Philip Soussa [*sic*] was informed by telegraph at Kansas City, Mo., (where he was engaged with Mackey's Flirtation Combination) on Saturday last that the leadership was at his disposal. Yesterday Mr. Soussa reported to Colonel McCawley, was formally mustered into service and granted ten days leave of absence to settle his business in Philadelphia, which place he has made his home for several years past."[6]

Given the nature of Sousa's later fame, his appointment to the Marine Band seems only natural. But at this stage of his career he had never led a band or military ensemble. He was a published composer, but very little of his music was for ensembles of winds alone, and marches were not yet an important part of his output. As he later admitted: "I began my apprenticeship as an orchestral player—a violinist, and I paid little attention to wind organizations until I led the Marine Band. Like most people who are, so to speak, brought up on the fiddle, I didn't have a proper respect for wind combinations." Despite this lack of experience, Sousa's new appointment was little more than a fine-tuning of his career. The Marine Band's repertoire included many of the same dances and operetta selections that he had performed and arranged in Philadelphia. Its outdoor public concerts were not dissimilar to those he had played on the centennial fairgrounds. Most important, the audiences he found in Washington in 1880 had tastes just as varied as those he had encountered in Philadelphia. In short, as Sousa began his first long-term musical employment, his experiences as an apprentice and young professional would not go to waste.[7]

Over the course of the next twelve years, Sousa's career would flourish, and the decade from 1880 to 1890 was in many ways his workshop period. Like other composer-conductors from Franz Joseph Haydn to Duke Ellington, Sousa had an impressive ensemble at his daily disposal. He would develop a symbiotic relationship with this musical organization, likely cultivated by his long affiliation with many of the musicians he now conducted. The Marine Band stood ready to rehearse Sousa's newest works, help fine-tune them, and present them before an inquisitive audience. At the same time, Sousa was knowingly sympathetic toward his players' financial situation, and he worked tirelessly to improve it. Finally, over the course of the decade Sousa's reputation would become intertwined with that of his band, and he had a vested interest in seeing it prosper. A great deal would change in John Philip

Sousa's life by the start of the 1890s, and it is therefore useful to examine this period in several stages, beginning with the early 1880s, when the future March King found his bearings as a military musician.

THE NATIONAL BAND

Sousa's tenure as leader of the Marine Band spanned the administrations of five U.S. presidents: Rutherford B. Hayes, James A. Garfield, Chester A. Arthur, Grover Cleveland, and Benjamin Harrison. As "The President's Own," the United States Marine Band was the primary source of musical diversion for these executives, but Sousa's duties extended well beyond the White House. The band frequently provided music in and around the capital for government functions, military and civilian, and these ranged from state receptions to military funerals, from troop reviews to civic dedications.

The Marine Band of the 1880s, however, belonged as much to Washington the city as to Washington the capital, and it thus often provided public concerts. On summer afternoons these occurred on Wednesdays at the Capitol, on Thursdays at the marine barracks, and on Saturdays at the White House; during the winter there were Sunday appearances at the National Theatre. Given their bright uniforms, spirited repertoire, and military precision, it is not surprising that the band was often asked to accompany special events, both military and civilian. For all of this activity, Sousa was constantly at work preparing new music and crafting arrangements of favorite tunes. Tracing just a handful of these appearances demonstrates how closely intertwined Sousa's role as the band's conductor became with his unofficial position as America's court composer.[8]

Referring to the White House party that welcomed 1881, Sousa later explained that the "first appearance of the band under my direction was at a New Year's reception," although there is a possibility that he led the band at Baltimore's sesquicentennial two months earlier. Now that he was again a military musician, Sousa's music took on a somewhat more patriotic flair. In early 1881 he wrote two marches dedicated to Captain Richard Strader Collum, a former commanding officer of the marine barracks. He called these pieces "Right Forward," opus 128, and "Guide Right," opus 129; their titles come from the military signals used to regulate troop movement that Sousa likely learned as an apprentice. The command for "forward" consists of two pitches of equal length, a rest, and a sustained note, while that for "guide right" is simply an ascending fourth. That the field music is invoked by the marches' titles is obvious, but given the relatively nondescript nature of these musical calls, it is impossible to determine whether Sousa really incorporated them into either march. Both do, however, contain melodies that resemble bugle calls, and "Guide Right" even begins with a three-chord military salute (this march also features the call's defining interval throughout its trio). The pieces were published as a pair by William A. Pond, and the piano sheet music prominently advertises Sousa as the leader of Washington's Marine Band. Clearly, at least this publisher saw a marketing advantage in Sousa's new position.[9]

The first major public event for which Sousa provided music was the March 4, 1881, inauguration of James Garfield. As today, nineteenth-century inaugurations involved not only the ceremony itself but also countless balls and receptions. On March 2 the band provided music for the Michigan State Association, and in honor of the occasion Sousa composed "The Wolverine March." For the inaugural ceremonies, he wrote his opus 131, the slow and majestic "President Garfield's Inauguration March." William A. Pond published piano editions of both pieces and advertised their use at government ceremonies, further connecting Sousa to the country's official musical life.

James Garfield's presidency would be short-lived; on the morning of July 2 he was shot in the back while walking through Washington's Sixth Street Rail Station. The injured executive lingered for eighty days before finally succumbing to his wounds on September 19. Sousa wrote a funeral march on learning of the president's death, and "In Memoriam" was used to escort the slain executive's body at ceremonies in Washington. Because Garfield had been born in Ohio and had represented the state's Nineteenth Congressional District, he was interred in Cleveland. This funeral presented an unusual opportunity for the Marine Band. Through the early 1880s this was still primarily a local ensemble, and it only rarely left the area immediately surrounding the capital. The burial of a slain president, however, warranted the Marine Band's presence, and so Sousa and his ensemble traveled to Cleveland. Citizens there were understandably excited to hear their national band, and their first opportunity came at the funeral on September 25: "The playing of the Marine Band of Washington yesterday afternoon at the catafalque was magnificent. Every one was waiting impatiently to hear them play 'Nearer, My God, to Thee,' which it is claimed they render better than any other similar body of musicians in the world. A murmur of delight ran through the crowd as the band finally commenced playing the grand sacred air, but the rain compelled them to stop just as they had fairly started." Sousa would make up for the delay the following day: "All at once the famous marine band began playing 'Nearer My God, to Thee,' soft and sweet as a lullaby hymn. Then the tears gushed from Grandma Garfield's eyes, and her lips quivered while Mrs. Garfield, sitting opposite her, sank back into the corner of the carriage and covered her face with her veil." Similar press reports from across the country perhaps constitute the Marine Band's first national exposure, although Sousa is rarely mentioned.[10]

A period of mourning settled over the city with Garfield's death, but there were a few additional concerts involving Sousa in 1881. In June he conducted a military demonstration for which he wrote the now-lost "Memories of the War," a piece that depicted "camp life from Reveille to Tattoo" with the accompaniment of cannons and fireworks. On October 17 the band joined many of Washington's most prominent citizens aboard a flotilla in commemoration of the Siege of Yorktown. For this occasion Sousa completed the march "Yorktown Centennial," his opus 135 and his last piece to carry an opus number. Also in that year came the birth of Sousa's only son, John Philip Jr., on April 1.[11]

Garfield's successor was Chester A. Arthur, the only president for whom Sousa had unkind words: "The austerity of President Arthur was reminiscent of the effete aristocracy of the Old World." Sousa's distaste may have been prompted by an unfortunate miscommunication. In February 1882 he was asked informally by the new president's private secretary to make his first appearance at the White House following the period of mourning for President Garfield. No official notice was sent through the commandant's office, however, and so the band failed to report. After being berated, Sousa told Secretary of the Navy William H. Hunt, "I get my orders from the Commandant, who gets them from you—not from a private secretary, and I did not receive any orders from you to appear at the White House." After some concern regarding Sousa's future as a Marine, the matter was dropped with the help of Senator John F. Miller. Sousa later dedicated the *Intaglio Waltzes* to the senator's daughter Dora, and this piece was given its premiere at the White House on September 27, 1884.[12]

During the Arthur administration there were several major events for the Marine Band. In late August 1882 it traveled to Cape May for a series of concerts at the Congress Hall Hotel, likely arranged by Sousa's Philadelphia friend Simon Hassler. Sousa wrote the march "Congress Hall" for these performances and dedicated the piece to the inn's owners, H. J. and G. R. Crump. On April 19, 1883, the band played for the dedication of a statue of the Smithsonian Institution's first secretary, Joseph Henry. As president of the National Academy of Sciences, Henry had helped improve observations of Venus's movement across the sun, and Sousa wrote the march "Transit of

Venus" in his honor. Such events formed a major part of the band's work, and the ensemble was present at the unveiling of the statue of Admiral Samuel Francis DuPont (December 20, 1884) and the dedication of a statue of James Garfield (May 12, 1887).[13]

Sousa wrote three new marches in the summer of 1883. At a May 26 concert on the White House grounds the band played "Pet of the Petticoats." Sousa never explained the title, but it likely refers to the operetta by John Baldwin Buckstone. At a public White House concert on June 2, the band played "Triumph of Time," another march whose title remains a mystery. The march "Bonnie Annie Laurie" was based on the Scottish ballad of the same name and perhaps intended for the American Pharmaceutical Association, which met in Washington in September. The band provided music for the event and performed several other pieces inspired by Scotland. Also from 1883 was "Right-Left," another march that takes its name from the military parade ground. Like "Guide Right" and "Right Forward," "Right-Left" does not contain obvious references to any particular bugle call, but in both the published piano edition and the band arrangement, Sousa includes indications for shouts of the march's title. Finally, it was during the Arthur administration that Sousa's second child, Jane Priscilla, was born on August 7, 1882.[14]

On March 4, 1885, Grover Cleveland was sworn in as president, and as Sousa later noted, "If I had seemed to lose the beat at the beginning of the Arthur administration, I was in perfect tempo with the Cleveland régime." At modern inaugurations each of the premier service bands plays an important

Fig. 19. The Marine Band at Cape May, 1882. "The President's Own" United States Marine Band, Washington, D.C.

role, but in the nineteenth century the lowest-bidding musical ensembles were hired to play at the balls and the ceremony. In 1885 Sousa was in competition with the Germania Orchestra Society of Philadelphia and Dodworth's Band of New York. Sousa proposed to make a grand ensemble by adding 150 civilian musicians to the Marine Band, but despite his ambitious efforts the Germania Orchestra was awarded the ceremonies. The Marines did, however, perform at what must have been a grueling "continuous concert" the following day. The Washingtonians not well enough connected to attend the inaugural ball were invited to view the decorations and hear the band as it played almost nonstop from 11 A.M. to 10 P.M.[15]

The next few years proved quite busy for Sousa and his band. Former president Ulysses S. Grant died in July 1885; the event likely prompted Sousa to compose his second funeral march: "The Honored Dead." Although the band did travel to New York for the interment, this piece is not mentioned in press reports, and Sousa's manuscript is dated 1886, suggesting that he may have written the work only for publication. The Garfield and Grant funerals were the most visible such events, but the Marine Band was regularly asked to play at memorial services such as those for Rear Admiral Robert H. Wyman (1882), former surgeon general of the army Joseph Barnes (1883), and General Philip Sheridan (1888).[16]

The major social event of 1886 was President Cleveland's wedding to Frances Folsom on June 2. Although the ceremony was a private affair, one newspaper noted that the Marine Band provided a conduit for evading White House security:

> The first visible evidence of the approaching ceremony was the arrival of some of the musicians of the Marine Band, gorgeous in their red uniforms. The members of the band came straggling along in such a manner that their number appeared much greater than it actually was. Some of the spectators declared that at least 150 men in red coats, with horns and trombones, went into the mansion, and this gave rise to a report that the newspaper reporters had gone in disguise, like Nanki-Poo, as second trombones.

Another major ceremony requiring the band's appearance was the October 1886 unveiling of the Statue of Liberty in New York. While the ensemble is known to have been present, Sousa does not seen to have written anything for the occasion.[17]

There are a number of pieces from the early and mid-1880s without any obvious connection to specific events. In 1885 Sousa wrote an additional parade march titled "Sound Off" and dedicated it to Major George Porter Houston, commanding officer of the marine barracks. In February 1886 he dedicated his *La Reine de la Mer Valses* to the wife of Secretary of the Navy W. C. Whitney. It is likely that an unpublished set of variations on the French song "Tyrolienne" was also composed for the Marine Band during this period.[18]

During his apprenticeship years Sousa had focused primarily on writing songs, but on taking charge of the Marine Band, his output swung dramatically toward the composition of marches. Although many of these were played by his new ensemble, most were first published only in piano editions, likely prepared in-house from Sousa's piano draft. During the early 1880s Sousa continued to use several publishers, including New York's William A. Pond, Washington's John F. Ellis, and Philadelphia's Harry Coleman, J. W. Pepper, and J. M. Stoddart. In several cases the sheet music advertised the fact that Sousa was leader of America's most famous military ensemble, but none of Sousa's 1881 or 1882 marches were actually printed in editions for band. In fact, prior to 1883 the only Sousa march to have appeared in a publication for band was "Globe and Eagle," printed by W. F. Shaw in 1879, perhaps for a Marine Band performance.

This state of affairs changed in the summer of 1883 when J. W. Pepper brought out "Bonnie Annie Laurie," "Pet of the Petticoats," "Right-Left," and "Transit of Venus" for band. The floodgates opened in late 1885 when Harry Coleman, who would come to serve as Sousa's principal march publisher, released several of his new marches in editions for band. Coleman seemed to recognize the value of such works, and he began to mine Sousa's catalog for pieces that until then had appeared only for piano. As a result, in the mid-1880s several older works—"Congress Hall," "Guide Right," "Right Forward," "Sound Off," "Triumph of Time," "The Wolverine March," and "Yorktown Centennial"—were finally printed for band. This new set of publications suggests that Sousa's appeal was shifting from the parlor to the bandstand. With this shift came a substantial increase in fame and a greater, although not an exclusive, public identification as a march composer. Before exploring Sousa's new national reputation—which seems to have begun to form in the mid-1880s—it is worth considering the other side of his symbiotic relationship with the United States Marine Band.

IMPROVING THE MARINE BAND

After the band appeared at President Garfield's funeral in 1881, the Washington press expressed pride in the hometown ensemble and its new conductor: "This band, which under the leadership of Mr. John P. Sousa has shown such rapid improvement, was the recipient of great praise during its visit to Cleveland, whither it went to participate in the funeral ceremonies of President Garfield. The papers of that city were emphatic in their commendation of the playing of the band, and the beautiful *In Memoriam* march, which was composed by Mr. Sousa and played during the procession, was warmly lauded, its tender strains and perfect harmony being especially mentioned."[19]

Despite such local pride, the ensemble that Sousa inherited in October 1880 was not particularly impressive. While there must have been some satisfied and satisfactory players, most reports suggest that the majority of the musicians were barely capable of playing their instruments, that few spoke English well enough to rehearse effectively, and that there was considerable frustration regarding the financial rewards offered by military employment. All of these problems fomented such strife that Commandant McCawley impressed on Sousa the need for a "complete reorganization of the band. The men were dissatisfied with the present state of affairs, and to use the Commandant's words, 'The band gives me more trouble than all the rest of the corps put together.'"[20]

On joining the ensemble, band members were enlisted into the Marine Corps, meaning that Sousa could not simply fire weak players; rather, dismissing them required authorization from the commandant's office. Given the time and effort needed to recruit and train replacement musicians, such permission was rarely forthcoming. The band thus had within it many members interested in leaving and several more that any leader would have been happy to see go. During his first year as director, Sousa made clear to his superiors the need to remove unhappy and musically inept men, and a number of documents demonstrate just how aggressively he worked with the commandant to eliminate them. For example, in July 1881 Sousa requested that one musician be discharged "for the following reasons: 1st a total disregard of the directions for the proper performance of the part assigned him. 2nd a want of proper respect for me as leader of the Band, by which action he continually causes quarrels and bickerings among the musicians of the band, greatly detrimental to a proper observance of the rules and regulations governing the Band." Another musician was released because he was "of no use to the Band."[21]

Given the increased musical demands Sousa placed on the ensemble, few of these players objected to their dismissal, but on some occasions a musician did fight back. In his autobiography Sousa mentions a "perpetual grouch" who caused him considerable difficulty during his first year as leader. This musician, who remained unnamed by Sousa, was probably Filippo Manco. In September 1881 Sousa recommended that Manco be discharged, reporting that the musician showed "continuous insubordination and insolence; together with a very inferior performance of his part, and a totally [*sic*] disregard for the instructions given, for a proper rendering of the part assigned him." Normally such a report would have been enough to see a player removed, but Manco was equally unhappy with Sousa, writing: "Ever since the arrival of the present Leader of the Band, J. P. Sousa, he began a continuous unjust treatment of myself and several other members of the Band." Manco continued by accusing Sousa of conduct "unbecoming any Leader of a Band" and claimed, probably correctly, that Sousa had "spoken to members of the Band reprimanding them publicly saying they did not know how to play."[22]

Given Manco's accusations, the commandant had little choice but to form a board of inquiry, which met in September 1881, quickly dismissed the charges against Sousa, and found Manco to be "insubordinate and rebellious of authority." Manco, still unwilling to let the matter rest, sent a letter to the *Evening Critic* in which he claimed that the board was unfairly "composed of Sousa's friends" and that the witnesses against him spouted "unsworn nonsense." Whatever the merits of Manco's argument, this airing of military matters in public ended his marine career. For his "false and lying report against his Commanding Officer and the members of a board," Manco was discharged as unfit for the service.[23]

Sousa did manage to quietly remove a fair number of unsatisfactory players despite such objections, an act that led to a substantial decline in the band's overall size: "By the end of the first year the band was reduced to thirty-three men and even the Commandant was a little alarmed." The bandleader therefore began an effort to recruit more accomplished musicians. In 1882 he described the talents he desired, and his words suggest that he was looking for players who were both accomplished and motivated: "Musicians required for the band, must be good sight (*prima vista*) readers, first-class executants, and ambitious to excel. The class of music performed by the band embraces everything from the ancient classics to the modern dramatic compositions of Verdi, Meyerbeer, etc. Musicians for the band must also possess good quality of tone and correctness of style."[24]

Even the commandant became involved in Sousa's quest to find better players, and like his predecessors, McCawley looked overseas for new recruits: "There are several vacancies in the Band of the U.S. Marine Corps which we find it very difficult to fill in this country. I am credibly informed that there would be no difficulty in enlisting suitable men in Italy or France and in sending them here." Despite such efforts, the commandant's foreign enterprise does not seem to have been successful, and Sousa instead turned to his contacts in Philadelphia and New York to find replacement players.[25]

By 1883 the ensemble's membership seems to have stabilized, but even at its full strength, Sousa's Marine Band was quite small compared to the military ensembles of Europe. The 1880 naval appropriations bill calls for one leader, one drum major, and thirty musicians. These numbers could be modestly augmented by assigning regular soldiers to the band, and photographs of the ensemble suggest that Sousa had about forty players at his disposal. The local press agreed that such numbers were far too small and that the United States deserved a band that could compete with those of Europe: "In the musical carnival at Paris in 1868 the Prussian band had 87 pieces, the Russian 71, the Austrian 70, the Spanish 64, the French 62, the Belgian 59 and others about the same number. . . . Our country, about as large as all Europe, has a band less pretentious in numbers than those of some petty kingdoms across the way."[26]

Both the quantity and the quality of the ensemble's players were limited by the meager funds Congress was willing to appropriate to the band. In 1882 Sousa explained that improved pay would be vital to attracting the best musicians:

> When the law of Congress was enacted creating the Band and classifying its members, music was scarcely recognized as a profession in this country, and a musician's means of livelihood were precarious and uncertain, but with the progress of the country the art of Music has been elevated to a higher standard and as a natural result a greater demand for musical talent has been developed. . . . While the pride of organization keeps the Band up to a high standard of musical excellence and soldierly discipline, I can not but feel that its *esprit-du-corps* will vanish, and that this Band, with all its popularity and old associations, will sink into oblivion, unless the fostering hand of the 'powers that be' come to its rescue.[27]

This was hardly the first time that pay had been an issue for the ensemble. A number of musicians requested discharges in 1877 and 1878 on the grounds that they could make much more money in the theaters. Indeed, the pay for band members was remarkably low, and in 1880 Congress authorized payment for the leader and the drum major of only $1,080 per year. The thirty bandsmen were divided into three categories: seven first-class musicians earning $40 per month, eight second-class musicians earning $26 per month, and fifteen third-class musicians earning $23 per month. These annual salaries of between $276 and $480 were, as Sousa pointed out, "pitifully small."[28]

It was not until Sousa's last years as leader that the issue of band size and pay gained any real traction. In May 1890 he suggested that the rating structure be altered to provide the men with higher salaries: "I respectfully recommend that all second and third class members of the Band of the U.S. Marine Corps, who have served fifteen years or more be promoted and added to the first class as a reward for faithful service." This change was made, but in August 1891 the acting secretary of the navy ordered that the increased ratings be revoked since the Treasury Department would not pay the higher salaries.[29]

If an internal change was impossible, Sousa's next option was to appeal directly to Congress. In January 1891 he convinced Representative William C. Wallace to introduce a bill that would increase both the size and pay of the ensemble. Under the terms of Sousa's proposal, the total number of musicians would be seventy-two: thirty first-class musicians at $60 per month, thirty second-class musicians at $50 per month, and ten apprentices at $13 per month. The leader would earn an annual salary equal to that of a second lieutenant: $1,400. In addition, there was to be an assistant musical director with the rank of sergeant major. To bolster the bill, Sousa argued that the weekly salaries of $14 to $42 offered by theater managers were more or less equal to the monthly salaries of the government's musicians. He went on to explain that a comic opera conductor could earn up to $450 per month, while as Marine Band leader he made only $94. Sousa even suggested that an increase in pay might actually help the government earn money:

> I beg to present the commercial side of the question: The present duty on musical merchandise and books, based on the value of imports of former years, amounts to between $800,000 and $900,000 a year. . . . There can be little doubt but that the professional musician creates the demand for musical literature and musical merchandise. Were it not for him the national revenue would lose to that amount. As a plain business proposition it is but reasonable to assume that the Government should use a portion of this large sum in further developing the musical culture and musical resources of our land. No better way can be devised than by proper equipment of the musical bodies in its employ and especially the organization that represents it musically on official occasions.[30]

Wallace's bill was introduced shortly before the World's Columbian Exposition was to be held in Chicago, where the country's premier military band would be on display with those of Europe. The Washington press took Sousa's cue and argued that without better compensation, America's band would compare unfavorably with those of the Old World:

> While the skill and ability of Prof. Sousa have brought this National band up to a degree of excellence that it has never before attained, it can not be

> disputed that it is very far inferior to the National bands of other countries. The pay is so much less than good musicians can command in private employment, that the band can not be kept full. There are vacancies now that the utmost efforts of Prof. Sousa have failed to supply on this account. . . . National pride alone should prompt every Member and Senator to vote for this bill. The matter of additional cost is too small to be taken into consideration at all. This great country can well afford and should by all means have here at the National Capital a band that will compare favorably with the best in the world, one in which every citizen of the greatest Republic on earth can feel a National pride.[31]

Despite such support, Sousa was never able to officially increase the size of the Marine Band or significantly improve its members' pay. In February 1893, just after leaving the ensemble, he revisited the issue of congressional action: "I interested many members of both branches of Congress in its favor, the press were unanimous in support of the measure, the Naval Committee of the House reported it favorably, it was introduced to the Senate, and there it sleeps. . . . My hopes were crushed." By this point Sousa was the leader of a commercial band, and he added, "Private enterprise has made it possible to accomplish elsewhere what I hoped to do here. Pluck, energy, and liberality are potent factors of success, and have a fashion of winning with unvarying regularity."[32]

There was another avenue for Sousa to pursue in bettering his musician's lives. Each player had before him three potential sources of income from music. The first and most important was his modest military compensation, in exchange for which the band provided music at various government functions and presented the free concerts at the White House, the Capitol, and the marine barracks. Individual players also used their contacts within the band to find civilian work, as Sousa did in the early 1870s when he played alongside other band members in Washington's theaters. But sometimes a civilian organization would want to capitalize on the band's local fame by hiring the ensemble, or some portion of it, to appear in uniform, not as civilian musicians who happened to be Marine Band players, but as a privately engaged version of that band itself.

Sousa later explained that it was the equitable distribution of supplemental engagements that caused the greatest difficulties for the ensemble: the "main cause of trouble was 'outside business'—the engagements the men made apart from their Governmental duties." Though unable to enlarge the Marine Band or increase its players' salaries, he could at least hope to better regulate how the band as an ensemble was paid by civilian organizations and thus augment his players' total income. He hoped that by building up "the private practice of the band something would be gained."[33]

In the normal order of business a civic organization would request the band's presence from the commandant or the secretary of the navy. These officials would then determine whether the request fell within the band's salaried duties or whether the players could charge for their services. In the former case an official order would be sent to the bandleader, while in the latter the request was forwarded to Sousa, who would privately contract his players. It is likely that several of the events discussed above, including the band's appearances before the Michigan State Association and at Cape May, were treated as such outside business.

The difficulty with this work stemmed from two sources: its frequency and its equitable distribution. The issue of frequency was a result of the overlapping authority of the secretary of the navy and the commandant of the marine corps, and these two officials did not always agree on an event's disposition. Because the secretary had little financial interest in the ensemble, he would often authorize the uncompensated use of the band at events that Sousa, his men, and the commandant felt deserved extra payment. Each year, for example, the Grand Army of the Republic would request that the Marine Band accompany its honor guard to Arlington National Cemetery for services on Decoration Day. This was, on one hand, a request from a fraternal organization and, on the other, a military ceremony. The secretary usually ordered the band to appear, and the commandant would routinely object on the ground that there were no marines interred in the cemetery. In a typical, though not altogether satisfactory compromise, the band would appear at Arlington without additional compensation, but the Grand Army of the Republic would be held financially responsible for the ensemble's transportation and meals.[34]

Sousa considered such engagements a misuse of his players' time, and requests had become so frequent that the bandleader complained that good men were leaving the ensemble due to overwork. McCawley forwarded Sousa's concerns to his superior: "A mistaken idea seems to prevail in the mind of the public as to the right it has to the services of this Band. No such agreement is made by the men on enlistment as the public seems to claim and it is to be observed that the number of applications for the services of the Band (without pay) increases yearly. If it is desired to retain the efficiency of the Band, it will be necessary to limit such occasions to purely official ceremonies to which there can be no objection."[35]

The secretary's office clearly felt some political pressure to provide the band for unofficial functions. In 1883 it requested the ensemble's indulgence in playing music for a charitable event: "This is not a public occasion, although it is somewhat of that character, as the President and some of the Cabinet and Diplomatic Corps are expected to be present, and I cannot, therefore, order the attendance of any portion of the Band. It is for a charitable object—one that commends itself to all—and I would be glad if the Band, or part of it, could furnish music for the occasion."[36]

Sousa, himself once a member of the ensemble, wanted to limit these unpaid appearances. He seems to have had some success, and letters from the commandant's office suggest that McCawley was eager to classify many requests as civilian engagements. In 1884, for example, the principal of the Miner Normal School asked that the band provide music for its commencement exercises. She was informed that "the Band having enlisted for Military duty cannot legally be ordered to do what you request. The men are allowed to make engagements for such purposes and do make many." They made so many, in fact, that the ensemble was already privately engaged for the day in question. Other examples abound. In September 1887 the band traveled to Philadelphia to take part in the constitutional centennial celebration, and while there it was asked to play at a private reception for the president. McCawley explained that he would not order the band to appear but that the sponsoring organization was welcome to privately engage the ensemble. On another occasion Vice President Levi Morton asked the band to play for a children's hospital charity. Given the noble cause, it was agreed that the men would attend, but only if they had not already made other engagements.[37]

The other concern within the ensemble centered on the equitable distribution of this outside work. In 1872, prior to Sousa's tenure as leader, a governance document was drafted for the band, and the fair allotment of private engagements was clearly the principal concern:

1. No member of the Band shall hereafter make an engagement to perform with any Band, or with any person, not a member of the Band of the Corps, except at the Theatre or in Churches.
2. When one-half, or more of the Band are wanted on a private engagement, the Leader of the Band will be with them, and will have direction, he receiving double compensation with the others.
3. Each member of the Band will be permitted to make private engagements with citizens to perform at any time, when not required for public duty, the person making the engagement to have the right to select from the Band such members as he may desire to

Fig. 20. The Marine Band in a casual pose, probably at the constitutional centennial celebration in Philadelphia, 1887. "The President's Own" United States Marine Band, Washington, D.C.

accompany him, and no member so selected, shall refuse to perform unless previously engaged or sick; but, if it is for street music, each member must play on the instrument he is accustomed to play in the Band.

4. When the entire Band shall be wanted, the Leader of the Band alone shall be authorized to make the engagements, in which case he will have charge and direction of the Band. He will be allowed to receive for his services double more than any one member, the additional amount, however, not to be deducted from the pay of the members but to be stipulated for with the person making the engagement.
5. When any member makes a private engagement, he will furnish the Leader of the Band with a written list of the members engaged, and the purpose of the engagement, which list shall be copied by the Leader in a book kept for the purpose to be subject to the inspection

of the Adjutant and Inspector, or the officer in charge of the Band, when required.

6. The Leader of the Band should at all times be able to account for the absence of its members should the Band be called upon for public duty; it is, therefore, expressly ordered, that no member will absent himself without first notifying the Leader, as above directed. When the Leader is absent notice in writing must be left at his place of residence.
7. In all private engagements, whether by day or night, it is expected by the Commandant that good order, sobriety and neatness in personal appearance will be observed, as much so, as if the members were in performance of public duty.
8. As good feeling and harmony should exist among the members of the Band, it is expressly directed that no combinations shall be made to favor certain members or to exclude certain others from performing, it being the desire of the Commandant that in as much as all are required to perform the same public duty, that all shall share alike in the benefits accruing from private engagements, a due regard being had to the wishes of the public.
9. The regular practice for the Band will be two hours twice a week, but the Leader can require more frequent practice should he deem it necessary.
10. During practice [members] are required to give strict attention; loud talking, whistling and any noise calculated to interfere with the practice is prohibited.
11. The Leader of the Band is required to report any inattention on the part of members of the Band.

Such regulations failed to completely eliminate strife within the ensemble, and several Marine Band leaders were accused of unfairly distributing funds from outside sources. Even Sousa faced this problem, as when Filippo Manco accused him in 1881 of "having appropriated certain sums of money belonging to members of the Marine Band to his own use."[38]

All in all, however, Sousa seems to have been quite successful in engaging the band and seeing its members paid for their services. After Manco made his charges, several musicians responded by testifying that "they had received more money and better engagements under the present leader, than ever before and were perfectly satisfied with Mr. Sousa." Indeed, surviving programs reveal just how busy the ensemble was. In addition to its official duties, the band provided music for commencement ceremonies at Washington's various universities and made appearances at charity concerts, picnics, excursions, and dances for organizations as diverse as the Baltimore Letter Carriers' Association, the Clothing Cutters and Trimmers of Baltimore, the Iron and Steel Institutes, and the Loyal Temperance Legion. For many of these events Sousa composed (or perhaps recycled) music, often titled or dedicated in honor of the occasion. A survey of programs from events in and around Washington, D.C., reveals a number of now-lost (or perhaps retitled) pieces. A program from 1883, for example, indicates that Sousa wrote an otherwise unknown march, "The Wheelmen," for the Capital Bicycle Club's October races. The band appeared at Georgetown College's commencement in 1885, and the program suggests that Sousa wrote a now unknown march for the school.[39]

Throughout the 1880s, Sousa made an effort to increase his own standing through the publication of sheet music that announced his connection to the President's Own. Sympathetic to his players' working conditions, he had also tried to improve both their government and their outside compensation. But as Sousa's own reputation became intertwined with that of his ensemble, he also found that he had an interest in improving the musical product of the Marine Band, and he began this process by addressing the ensemble's repertoire. On becoming director, he had discovered that its library was limited to "some selections of old Italian operas, a few of the standard overtures, and a great number of ordinary marches, polkas, etc." but that "there was not a sheet of Wagner, Berlioz, Grieg, Tschaikowsky, or any other of the modern composers who were attracting attention throughout the musical world."[40]

The Marine Band of the early nineteenth century had performed works from the private library of its director; it was Sousa who finally organized the band's first permanent music collection. In 1885 the Government Printing Office published a catalog of this library, which suggests that the ensemble remained very much at home with the operatic selections and light dance pieces that made up the bulk of late nineteenth-century band repertoire. Composers represented frequently in the catalog include Giuseppe Verdi, Johann Strauss, Emile Waldteufel, Arthur Sullivan, Fred Godfrey, Jacques Offenbach, Franz von Suppé, Gioachino Rossini, Gaetano Donizetti, Charles Gounod, Felix Mendelssohn, Adolphe Adam, Giacomo Meyerbeer, Richard Wagner, and Carl Maria von Weber. Naturally, most of the works by these composers were played in transcription, and the catalog includes sections devoted to overtures, dances, songs, and chamber arrangements. Sousa's name appears just five times, as the composer of "In Parlor and Street," "The

International Congress," the *Paroles d'Amour Valses*, the *Intaglio Waltzes*, and the "Myrrha Gavotte."[41]

This catalog suggests a fairly conservative repertoire, but surviving programs indicate that Sousa did sometimes present more ambitious material. In 1886 band member Walter Smith told a reporter that "there is probably no band in the country that plays as heavy music as does the marine band. . . . New music of the most difficult character is constantly being imported." Indeed, Sousa seems to have added a fair amount of more modern repertoire, including overtures and selections from Wagner's *Tannhäuser*, *Rienzi*, *Lohengrin*, and *Der fliegende Holländer*. President Benjamin Harrison may well have been among the first Americans to hear portions of Pietro Mascagni's *Cavalleria rusticana* when the Marine Band performed selections from the work at an 1891 New Year's reception (even before the opera had been given its American premiere).[42]

When Louis Schneider became leader of the Marine Band in 1873, the Washington press had great expectations for the city's troubled ensemble: "It is to be hoped that the band, under the immediate charge of the able adjutant and inspector of the corps, will be increased and take a front rank in the leading bands of the country. It should, at least, number fifty of the best musicians whose services could be secured, and the men should receive a better compensation than that now paid." Up to that point the ensemble had faced "an up-hill road, probably from the fact that the band needed a leader of great force of character in addition to eminent musical ability. . . . The new director has plenty of work on his hands before he can make an entirely happy family of it."[43]

Schneider would prove unable to modernize the Marine Band, but to a remarkable degree his successor did achieve these goals, and Sousa turned the ensemble into a satisfied musical family. He might not have been able to increase the band's size or its players' military pay, but Sousa did increase their overall compensation by insisting that members receive extra money from civilian engagements. Furthermore, he not only formed a permanent library for the ensemble, he also modernized and diversified its repertoire. Most important, the symbiotic relationship between John Philip Sousa and the United States Marine Band would help increase the fame of both bandleader and ensemble. Sousa's musical interests, however, were never limited to the band, and before he became America's March King, Sousa was Washington's most prominent musician, a composer and conductor often called on to work with civilian organizations. By the mid-1880s, Sousa found himself in demand not only on the bandstand but also in Washington's concert halls, theater pits, and opera houses.

CHAPTER SIX

Civilian Music in Washington

IN DECEMBER 1880 THE GERMAN VIOLINIST August Wilhelmj presented a concert in Washington's Lincoln Hall. The press fawned: "The exquisite production of beautiful echoes and rapid variations of sound which he gives is simply a wonder of delight to lovers of music. He holds the audience in a trance." Entranced along with the rest of the audience was the eight-year-old Martha Leavitt Beckwith Saxton, who, in annotating her program, was far more direct: "My first concert—I was delighted with it." Mattie attended a second concert in March 1881, this one by the young Brazilian violinist Mauricio Dengremont. The third followed that winter, this time featuring some of Washington's own musicians. Mattie Saxton's childhood scrapbooks are full of programs from such performances, sometimes given by visiting celebrities but just as often by local music teachers or dedicated amateurs. In each case, she found the evening a delight.[1]

The National Symphony Orchestra was founded in 1931, the Washington National Opera in 1956. Such dates seem to place the capital somewhat behind other major metropolitan centers in the creation of a vibrant musical culture. To focus exclusively on such permanent, professional ensembles, however, is to miss many of the most important features of a city's musical life. When John Philip Sousa returned to Washington in October 1880, he may have found the District of Columbia without a full-time orchestra or opera company, but it was, nonetheless, a growing city that brimmed with amateur ensembles, semiprofessional organizations, and visiting artists. The resulting concerts delighted listeners such as Mattie Saxton and also provided musical opportunities for the district's newest bandleader.

As the conductor of Washington's most stable ensemble, Sousa suddenly became one of the city's most prominent musicians. Although he may not have known Mattie Saxton personally, she must have been aware of him through the Marine Band's many public concerts on and around the National

Mall. Such performances would not, however, have been young Mattie's only opportunities to hear and see John Philip Sousa. In the same way musical marines found theater work through their band, Sousa's new position provided him with the opportunity to serve as a guest conductor and featured composer for Washington's many other ensembles. Just as his relationship with the band was symbiotic, Sousa and Washington's amateur organizations found their shared work mutually beneficial. A local orchestra or opera company could clearly profit from the young musician's expertise, while Sousa was able to cultivate the theatrical interests that had so successfully sustained him in Philadelphia.

WASHINGTON'S AMATEURS

In June 1883 Mattie Saxton made her debut as a violinist in a recital offered by the pupils of Josef Kaspar, a Bohemian who had settled in Washington to open a teaching studio. Saxton must have done quite well, because the next year she appeared in Baltimore with the Haydn Musical Association, advertised as "the Child Violiniste, aged ten years." Mattie likely had a leg up in attracting public attention since she came from a prominent Washington family. Her father was Major S. Willard Saxton, who after the Civil War became one of the city's most distinguished citizens, first by working with his brother General Rufus Saxton at the Freedmen's Bureau and later as a member of the city's Association of Oldest Inhabitants.[2]

Many of Josef Kaspar's students were similarly well connected in the city's political and social life: Mabel Clare Money was the youngest daughter of a Mississippi senator, and Nona Stosch was the child of a Silesian count. Some went on to garner a degree of musical fame. In 1891 Mattie Saxton moved to New York to become a student of Richard Arnold, and she later returned to Washington to open her own violin studio before her untimely death in 1896. Nona Stosch would study music in Brussels, play under the baton of Anton Seidl, and win a Pulitzer Prize in poetry in 1927 as Lady Leonora Speyer.[3]

There were a few such star pupils, but most of Kaspar's students remained amateurs. Like many other nineteenth-century American cities, Washington was full of dilettante musicians, and on some occasions these players banded together to form rather impressive ensembles. The Georgetown Amateur Orchestra, for example, was founded in the parlor of the unified district's first governor, Henry David Cook, in 1877. As inaugurated it was a mere trio consisting of Cook's financier son (also named David), the artist Charles S. Hein, and the dentist Francis Sinclair Barbarin. These men did not fancy themselves professional musicians; rather, their meetings were a way of pursuing music "as a recreation and pleasure in the evening, after their regular avocations of the day were over."[4]

It is impossible to know just how technically competent this amateur trio was, but by the early 1880s their musical fellowship had begun to attract notice: "The enjoyment experienced by these gentlemen, and the improvement they derived from their practice[,] attracted the attention of other performers, and so gradually their number increased until they found they had a very fair orchestra." This larger ensemble presented its first concert on January 19, 1882, at Curtis Hall, where it played a Haydn symphony "with a degree of expression and precision that would have been creditable to a much older organization."[5]

Like many of the city's amateur ensembles, the Georgetown Amateur Orchestra included prominent members of Washington's social and political elite, including the chief of the engraving division at the Bureau of Engraving and Printing, the chief of the loan division of the United States Treasury, the superintendent of the National Bank Redemption Agency, the chief clerk in the Quartermaster-General's Office, two chemists from the Department of Agriculture, a notable local architect, and the curator of the Corcoran Gallery. As the *Washington Post* explained: "On its bead-roll of honor are men prominent in our official, social, and business life, who, for now some ten years past, have devoted themselves, heart and soul, to the cult and gospel of the best music rendered by the best methods." Some of these amateurs were remarkably devoted to music. Beginning in 1881 Ernest Szemelényi served as a translator in the Patent Office. The son of a prolific parlor composer, he likely studied with John Knowles Paine while a student at Harvard University. Reflecting on Szemelényi's decade-long career in Washington, one reporter noted that there were "few musical undertakings in which he has not taken an active part." In addition to serving as conductor of the Georgetown Amateur Orchestra, Szemelényi was a periodic concertmaster, violinist, violist, and pianist with a variety of other amateur groups, including the Choral Society, the Richard Wagner Society, the Travel Club, and the German Club.[6]

In 1885 the Georgetown Amateur Orchestra assisted in a production of Gilbert and Sullivan's *Patience*, "rendered entirely by ladies and gentlemen prominent in society." This high-profile event brought them a measure of fame, and the orchestra was soon able to establish a subscription series. On the heels of this success, the amateurs decided to engage a professional conductor, and Josef Kaspar brought with him many of the young women from his violin studio. Such additions delighted the press, which could not resist commenting on the orchestra's new visual appeal: "It is wholly without the bounds of competent criticism to speak rationally of a performance which deliberately intrenches [*sic*] itself behind a double-banked row of blushing young womanhood, mostly still in the 'teens, a charm of 'waving arms and woven faces,' wielding the bow like so many virgin Dianas."[7]

Among these musical Dianas was Mattie Saxton, whose first orchestral appearance likely occurred in December 1886. The concert featured Schubert's "Unfinished Symphony," along with the overtures to Weber's *Der Freischütz* and Rossini's *William Tell*. In order to support such lofty works, Kaspar announced, "Professional players will be engaged to supply deficiencies." Fulfilling this promise naturally meant turning to the ensemble that had long supplied players for all types of musical events within the District of Columbia: the United States Marine Band.[8]

The Georgetown amateurs may not have been able to financially compensate these professional players, but the orchestra could provide something almost as satisfying as a paycheck. Then, as now, employment in a military band allows for limited artistic expression, and many players found themselves eager to broaden their musical experiences by performing works from the orchestral repertoire. Furthermore, an engagement with the Georgetown amateurs allowed marine musicians to rub shoulders with Washington's social aristocracy. By 1886 six band members were assisting the Georgetown orchestra, and in 1891 the ensemble had to arrange its concert schedule to finish the season "before the 1st of April, when the Marine Band, from which the brass and wood wind of the orchestra are obtained, will leave on a six week's tour."[9]

Sousa is not known to have led the Georgetown Amateur Orchestra, but the ensemble did play several of his pieces. An April 1890 concert, for example, included "Nymphalin" and a new caprice—which Sousa called a characteristic dance—derived from Longfellow's translation of the German ballad *Beware* and titled "The Coquette." That Sousa had some local fame is made clear by one critic who noticed that both works were now "familiar to Washington audiences."[10]

More important to the Marine Band's leader were two other local organizations. The Washington Philharmonic Society was a choral group designed to render "oratorio and music of a kindred devotional character in an artistic manner." In 1881 they engaged Sousa to organize a two-day May Festival at the National Theatre featuring the professional soloists Imogen Brown, Italo Campanini, and John Winch. Sousa programmed Rossini's *Stabat Mater*, Haydn's *Creation*, and several lighter works, including "Nymphalin." The press was appreciative of the ensemble's efforts and noted that "one could easily have thought himself in the presence of one of the best drilled and most competent choruses in the country." Later in the decade Sousa also conducted the Washington Symphony Orchestra, an amateur ensemble formed by Robert Camp Bernays to compete with the Georgetown players. Like Kaspar, Bernays supplemented his amateurs with professional players, many of whom came from the Marine Band. In 1887 Sousa led the group in his dance "The Coquette," and the following season he acted as the ensemble's regular conductor. In addition to arias and instrumental solos, the programs featured overtures such as those from Karl Goldmark's *Sakuntala*, Rossini's *William Tell*, and Beethoven's *Leonore*. On March 10, 1888, Sousa combined the orchestra with the amateur Washington Choral Society (supplemented by professional soloists from New York, Cleveland, and Baltimore) to present John Francis Barnett's cantata *The Ancient Mariner*, in what was advertised as the work's first American performance with orchestral accompaniment.[11]

Despite the best efforts of Sousa and Bernays, this combination of professional and amateur musicians proved difficult to maintain. Like many other conductors who had hoped to establish professional orchestras in Washington, Sousa discovered that attracting audiences meant playing "music of the lightest, frothiest character." This repertoire failed to excite the professional players, who were being asked to donate their time: "The men who really desire to add to their musical education by reading meritorious works, even at some sacrifice, are not willing to lose time and money without adding to their intelligence."[12]

A RETURN TO GILBERT AND SULLIVAN

Performances with such amateur ensembles would have helped Sousa re-engage with Washington's civilian musical life. While in Philadelphia, however, he had developed a reputation as a conductor and arranger of operetta, endeavors that Sousa continued on his return to Washington. In May 1882 a touring ensemble featuring the actress Emily Rigl opened Anson Pond's *Her Atonement* at the National Theatre. Since this entertainment required a military display, Sousa and his band were engaged for the week. On June 9, Sousa conducted amateur productions of Offenbach's *The Rose of Auvergne* and the farce *Penelope* at Ford's Opera House as part of a fundraising benefit for the Society for the Prevention of Cruelty to Animals.

Most of Sousa's operatic experiences of the 1870s revolved around the work of W. S. Gilbert and Arthur Sullivan, and he continued to find value in this comic duo during the 1880s. When Gilbert and Sullivan came to the United States in 1879, they recognized the importance of securing the financial benefits of their work. Since international copyright remained largely unsettled, they had hoped that an American premiere of *The Pirates of Penzance* might give the new work some measure of legal protection. In an effort to claim both British and American rights for their operetta, it was produced in a secret matinee at the Bijou Theatre in Paignton, England, on December 30, 1879, and received its official premiere in the United States the following evening at New York's Fifth Avenue Theatre.

Such dual international premieres may have bolstered Gilbert and Sullivan's claims to exclusive performance rights to their work, but there remained the more practical issue of pirates unconcerned with such clever legal wrangling. To thwart this competition, the pair concocted a multipronged defense. Just as they had with *H.M.S. Pinafore*, Gilbert and Sullivan opted to keep their orchestrations and stage directions unpublished. This time, however, they also declined to prepare a piano reduction; anyone wishing to pirate *The Pirates of Penzance* would need to do so solely through memorization. To guard against such borrowings, lawyers vigilantly searched for unauthorized performances (and frequently filed local injunctions), while a host of official touring companies were dispatched to flood the performance market.

Despite these precautions, it did not take long for Sullivan's tunes to appear in unauthorized piano reductions, and one arrangement printed in Boston by Louis P. Goullaud ended up in the Massachusetts Circuit Court. There, to everyone's surprise, an American judge granted an injunction in favor of the British duo and stopped the sale of *Favorite Melodies from the Pirates of Penzance*. As other cases began to appear on the horizon, however, it became clear that this antipiracy ruling would not settle the matter.[13]

In 1881 Richard D'Oyly Carte and Edward Rice opened the operetta *Billie Taylor* by Harry P. Stephens and Edward Solomon at the Standard Theatre in New York. Charles Ford had asked permission to produce the operetta in Baltimore, but Carte had refused. Ford, therefore, followed standard practice and commissioned a new version of *Billie Taylor*, created from the published libretto and his uncle's memory of Carte's production. Carte quickly filed suit, charging that "a more reliable agent" than memory had been used, likely "a little money judiciously administered to some of our under people." The Maryland Circuit Court sided with Ford, ruling that his production could continue so long as the advertising material did not too closely resemble Carte's. The legal issues were now more unsettled than ever. Emboldened, Charles Ford opened Gilbert and Sullivan's *Iolanthe* in February 1883. In order to create the missing orchestration, he turned to a musician with considerable experience adapting Sullivan's music: John Philip Sousa, who took to the task and prepared "an orchestral accompaniment for the published vocal score . . . relying solely upon his own skill as an arranger of orchestral music."[14]

Carte promptly filed suit alleging two injuries. First, Ford's traveling company was beating his own troupe to many cities, and demand for the authentic *Iolanthe* was thereby diminished. This argument was quickly rejected when the court noted that the publication in print of a work "is a complete dedication of it for all purposes to the public." Since the orchestration was legally deemed to be of only secondary value, a violinist might be added to aid the pianist with no loss to the original work. Such a process could continue instrument by instrument until an entire orchestra had been assembled. Because Sousa's arrangement had been created "by his independent skill and labor" and not obtained "in any surreptitious or unauthorized manner" it was not only perfectly legal, but it was also such "an original work that it could itself be protected."[15]

Hedging his bets, Carte further contended that the "inferior and incomplete" performance mounted by Ford was damaging the reputation and success of his more genuine production. Sousa's arrangement, which might be "blundering or mechanical," could potentially harm the reputation of Sullivan himself. Here the court substantially agreed, but noted that Carte's argument was not enough to restrict Ford's production, which could continue so long as notices were "coupled with a reasonably-conspicuous announcement" that the audience would not be hearing Sullivan's original orchestrations. Ford was only too happy to comply and use his advertising to highlight the now locally famous John Philip Sousa.[16]

This squabble over *Iolanthe* was Sousa's first legal battle involving copyright; it would not be his last. It did, however, mark a change in his approach to operetta. In 1885 Sousa published his "Mikado March," a piece that again plundered from Gilbert and Sullivan. Despite this borrowing and a few later examples, by the mid-1880s Sousa was more or less finished riding the coattails of Gilbert, Sullivan, and Offenbach; he had already moved on to writing original operettas.

CREATING AN AMERICAN OPERETTA

In January 1882, Sousa led yet another amateur organization—the Washington Operatic Association—in a production of Robert Planquette's *The Chimes of Normandy* at Lincoln Hall. The press showed considerable fondness for the city's new conductor, who had brought with him eighteen members of the Marine Band:

> The care that Mr. Sousa has given in his instruction was apparent in the precision, the time, and the phrasing of every choral number, and he may well be proud of the results of his labors. It is by far the best drilled chorus that has ever been heard here. The well-balanced orchestra should come in for its share of just praise, the members obeying the baton of Mr. Sousa perfectly. When it is stated that the orchestra was composed of the best members of the Marine Band, the excellence of their playing is a decided compliment to Mr. Sousa's leadership.

Such reviews reveal at least a little local pride, and in response to this warm reception, the Operatic Association revived *The Chimes of Normandy* in May 1882. In the meantime, however, they had moved on to a new and rather unusual work.[17]

The Smugglers was Sousa's second attempt at revitalizing Burnand and Sullivan's *The Contrabandista*, but this time the composer discarded much of his 1879 arrangement and joined with Wilson Vance to fashion a fresh libretto. This new version of *The Smugglers*—Sousa's first original operetta to be completed and staged—opened at Lincoln Hall on February 17, 1882. The three performances came under the auspices of Washington's National Rifles, and just as the militia announced its involvement, Sousa was elected an honorary member. Having this popular and local organization directly involved with his operetta had obvious benefits; the Rifles quickly announced prizes for the "two ladies selling the greatest number of tickets," and there can be little doubt that a significant portion of Sousa's audience consisted of militia members, their families, and friends. Local critics were not entirely convinced by the work, noting that the plot was "somewhat defective in continuity," but thanks to the Rifles, the opening night saw "scarcely a vacant seat." The city's pride extended beyond the press, and on March 4 Sousa received a letter signed by fifty prominent Washingtonians, including General William Tecumseh Sherman, Senator John F. Miller, and Representative John Floyd King, who were "desirous of hearing the opera again before its introduction elsewhere." On March 25, the fourth performance was duly offered at Lincoln Hall.[18]

Riding on this local success, Vance and Sousa formed a touring company and headed to Philadelphia, where they opened at the Chestnut Street Opera House on March 27, 1882. After a single performance in Lancaster the following evening, the company returned to Philadelphia and gave performances until April 1. Sousa's success at home had relied in large part on an understanding audience and a sympathetic press, an environment that could not be re-created on the road. In Pennsylvania, Vance's dialogue was roundly criticized for being "either vapid or ludicrously stilted," while Sousa's music showed a composer "more prone to nice detail and finish than to the dash of genius." The company was called "the worst we have ever seen," and one reporter wondered how Washington could have so enjoyed a score with such a "painful paucity of merit." The press could only conclude that the city's "abundance of untamed congressmen from the boundless prairies of the West" accounted for "the otherwise singular circumstance" of the operetta's local success. The disgraced company had to borrow money simply to return home, and Sousa was devastated by the catastrophe: "I examined myself and could only see that I was a colossal failure as a composer, as a dramatist, and as a man."[19]

Sousa was not quite finished with *The Smugglers* despite this setback. In March 1883 he traveled to New York to secure a new cast, which included Richard Mansfield's brother Henry. The Operatic Association—now with some professional soloists—produced *The Smugglers* again on April 2, 3, and 4, 1883. These performances appear to have been the last staged versions of Sousa's operetta, but selections from the piece continued to appear sporadically on Washington programs. It was not until 1885 that a critic could write of *The Smugglers*, "I think Mr. Sousa will now agree with the general opinion that it is not a success." Sousa did, indeed, agree, and the operetta was "buried in the vast dramatic cemetery of musical failures."[20]

The Smugglers was not, in fact, a complete loss. Sousa's music was attractive enough to warrant a piano-vocal score, becoming his first stage work to reach publication when it was printed by W. F. Shaw in 1881. The overture and a number of vocal selections were later used by the Sousa Band on tour, and Sousa cannibalized the operetta for several later stage works. Most important, however, *The Smugglers* introduced the dramatic side of the composer to Washington, D.C., and likely impressed many of the city's musical amateurs. Sousa continued periodically to lead the Washington Operatic Association. Gilbert and Sullivan's *Patience* was performed by the organization in January 1883 and *H.M.S. Pinafore* in May of that year. The following year Sousa paired the latter work with *The Pirates of Penzance*. Finally, in January 1885 he conducted the organization in *Paul and Virginia* at Albaugh's Opera House.[21]

In his autobiography, Sousa frequently explains that the March King achieved his fame through hard work, perseverance, and attention to his audiences' taste. For Sousa, a public failure such as that surrounding *The*

Smugglers was simply a chance to learn and adjust. Back on his horse, he soon paired with Edward M. Taber to create an operetta based on John Maddison Morton's 1856 play *Our Wife, or, The Rose of Amiens*. Like many of Sousa's collaborators, Taber was hardly a professional librettist. Nonetheless, this Pension Office clerk fashioned a text that was "unusually smooth" and gave the songs "poetic qualities more noticeable than comic operas usually" command. The result was *Désirée*, in which a musketeer colonel works to alter the social status of his lieutenant's beloved and thus make her a suitable bride.[22]

Désirée was first produced by the John McCaull Opera Comique Company, a professional organization that drew many of its members from the Washington-Baltimore region. The work played at the National Theatre between May 1 and 3, 1884, and McCaull then took the company to Philadelphia for a three-week engagement at Haverly's Theatre between November 10 and November 29. Finally, it was produced at Boston's Bijou between December 15 and December 27. With this modest run, *Désirée* proved to be Sousa's first operatic success, albeit a limited one. The locally grown cast, of course, aided the production in Washington, but on the road attention turned to the work itself. The Philadelphia press admitted that Taber's libretto was well written and that Sousa's music was generally "very sweet and pleasing." Sousa was nonetheless criticized for being overly reliant on the language of Offenbach and Sullivan, and the *Boston Globe* called the entire work "undeniably dull."[23]

In spite of such weaknesses, a single member of the cast and McCaull's own clever promotion seem to have saved the tour. The manager had considerable misgivings about engaging an untested performer for the role of Désirée's father, but one critic noted that DeWolf Hopper "may, in fact, be said to 'carry the piece.'" The sensation Hopper created as Pomaret secured his fame, and he later explained that he was never "able to live down that success. At the outset I was hugely gratified with it, as one is likely to be with first victories, and when I had tired of it, it was too late. I was catalogued in the card index of the theater and of theatergoers as a singing comedian and a singing comedian I have remained. There are worse destinies."[24]

Just as important to the operetta's success were McCaull's efforts to surround the work with an aura of Americanism. Early advertisements called *Désirée* an "American Comic Opera," and debates about its national style began almost at once. Just a few days after the work's premiere, a writer identified only as "Musician" complained: "Can *Désirée* be rightly called 'a new American comic opera,' when its plot is laid in Amiens, its characters are French, its music a combination of Audran, Planquette and Sullivan, and when there is nothing in the entire work distinctively American? One of its librettists, too, is an Englishman. It may be a meritorious work, but it is not an American opera." A reply from "A Spectator"—almost certainly McCaull, Taber, or Sousa himself—appeared just a few days later:

> In your issue of this morning, "Musician" presents some peculiar notions as to what constitutes an American opera[;] according to his mode of reasoning, *Hamlet* is a Danish play and *Richelieu* French, because the action takes place in Denmark and France, although these tragedies are productions of two of the greatest men England ever produced. Surely Mr. Taber's lyrics in *Désirée* are "distinctly American" enough even for the prejudiced notions of your correspondent. I should be pleased to have "Musician" prove his statement that Mr. Sousa's music is a combination of the works of Sullivan, Audran and Planquette by pointing out the parallel passages in the score of *Désirée* and those of any opera by the above named composers. It is easy enough to make a general statement of this kind, but "Musician" must produce "proof positive" to convince.[25]

On the road McCaull made even more serious efforts to highlight the work's American qualities. In Philadelphia "the lobby and theatre were profusely decorated with the American and tri-color flags," and after the first act McCaull gave "a patriotic speech, expressing his justifiable pride in having produced a successful American opera, the joint work of an American author and an American composer, sung by an American company to an American audience in an American city." Sousa was, of course, quite pleased by all the attention and noted that ticket receipts topped expectations.[26]

While Sousa may have been happy to ride the waves of musical nationalism, turning *Désirée* into a distinctly American work was almost certainly a gimmick created by John McCaull. As the March King, Sousa came to rely on his audiences' patriotism, but in aesthetic terms he had little use for nationalism. As the 1884 reply by "A Spectator" in the *Post* suggests, Sousa saw nationality as a personal trait, not an artistic asset. For him, success in music was necessarily the result of personal effort: "It is the individuality and the genius of the composer that matters," he later wrote, "not the individuality of his race." But in the early 1880s Sousa was not yet the March King, and as he worked to find success beyond Washington, it was sometimes helpful to step into whatever voids might be perceived in the musical marketplace. Filling a void was, no doubt, McCaull's goal in tagging *Désirée* as an American work. Reviews indicate that his efforts were successful on the local level, but national critics were not yet ready to declare *Désirée* an opera written in a distinctly American style. According to the *Dramatic Mirror*: "That is yet to come."[27]

Like *The Smugglers* before it, *Désirée* appeared in a piano-vocal reduction, this one printed by J. W. Pepper. Thus, by the end of 1884 Sousa had published two operettas, each of which enjoyed considerable success in Washington but only lukewarm reviews on the road. For his next venture Sousa again teamed with Taber, but this time they decided to stay with the audience most sympathetic to their talents. In March 1885 a correspondent for the *Washington Post* explained that "Mr. Sousa has two of the brightest little girls that a father could be proud of. Their great amusement is to have him repeat to them the rhymes of Mother Goose, which we remember so well as a part of our childhood. The enjoyment which the children find in these rhymes has led Mr. Sousa to compose a little operetta, which, I think, cannot fail to be bright and popular."[28]

The result of Sousa's efforts was *The Queen of Hearts, or, Royalty and Roguery*, a short "Juvenile Jingle" in three tableaux finished in January 1885. The libretto was published by the Washington firm of R. O. Polkinhorn, and the work was produced by the Washington Operatic Association between April 12 and April 14, 1886, at Albaugh's Opera House, where it shared the bill with *Trial by Jury*. *The Queen of Hearts* was not Sousa's first attempt at children's music. In October 1880 he had written a march titled "Mother Goose" that included several children's songs. This work was followed in 1885 by the "Mother Hubbard March." Like the "Mikado March," these works freely change key and meter to accommodate well-known borrowed material, but with *The Queen of Hearts* Sousa seems to have written his first original music for young listeners. The piece received excellent reviews, which probably should be attributed to the press's sympathy for a homegrown cast that included several Washington schoolchildren. Although the work never made it beyond the capital, Sousa did recycle portions of it for his later operettas *El Capitan* (1895) and *The Charlatan* (1898), as well as for the march "The Loyal Legion" (1890).[29]

Taken together, Sousa's activities during the 1880s demonstrate a musician eager to build a name for himself. He may have hoped that this reputation would spread beyond his hometown, but during this period, at least, John Philip Sousa was Washington's prize. His work with amateur orchestras and local opera companies solidified his standing in the capital, and the Marine Corps officers must have known that they had made a wise decision—at least in terms of local public relations—in hiring back one of their own.

Sousa's civilian activities also demonstrate just how vibrant and close-knit a musical community Washington, D.C., enjoyed. Programs from the 1880s reveal, time and again, the same individuals and families enriching the city's artistic life. At one December 1885 Marine Band concert, for example, Sousa conducted vocal selections by Ponchielli and Bizet. The soloist that evening was Josephine Esputa-Daly, the daughter of his boyhood teacher. Other connections abound, the most striking of which was the 1890 wedding of Robert Bernays, Sousa's colleague in the Washington Symphony Orchestra, to the March King's youngest sister, Mary Elisabeth. Even the 1886 production of *The Queen of Hearts* was full of familiar faces. Offstage, acting as prompter, was George Hinton, the very man who would later serve as Sousa's professional manager and invent his alter ego Sam Ogden. In the operetta's title role was Annie Roemer, wife of Mattie Saxton's violin teacher, Josef Kaspar.[30]

Sousa's civilian activities also demonstrate that he remained a man of the theater. Despite earning a comfortable military income, he continued to invest considerable time and effort in creating works for the stage. By 1885 his three complete operettas—*The Smugglers*, *Désirée*, and *The Queen of Hearts*—had been produced and published. Sousa would have to wait until 1896—two and a half years after he left the Marine Band—before he would see another on the stage. He did not, however, abandon his interest in theatrical music. In 1888 he fashioned his own libretto for yet another reworking of *The Smugglers*, a project he called *The Wolf*. Sousa later explained that on offering the piece to a producer, he was told that it "violated every known principle of comic opera construction." Nevertheless he was able to sell performance rights to the work to the actor Francis Wilson and later to DeWolf Hopper, although the piece was never produced. Always the practical composer, Sousa reused much of the failed material in *El Capitan* (1895), *The Bride Elect* (1897), and *The Charlatan* (1898).[31]

Original operettas were not, of course, the only possible outlets for a theatrically inclined composer, and while leader of the Marine Band, Sousa provided music for several staged plays. He came to know the California poet Joaquin Miller sometime in the early 1880s and wrote an overture and a single song, "Tally-Ho!," for Miller's play of the same name. He also provided an overture for Adolphe Eugene Philippe d'Ennery's play *Vautour*. The song was published in 1885 by John F. Ellis, and the two overtures in 1886 by Harry Coleman, but it is unclear whether any of the pieces were used in actual productions.[32]

Sousa likely met the actor Francis Wilson while working at Philadelphia's Chestnut Street Theatre in the late 1870s, and at the end of his Marine Band career he orchestrated music for several Wilson productions. The first of these was likely *The Oolah* (1889), an adaptation of Charles Lecocq's *La Jolie Persane*. This work was followed by *The Merry Monarch*, which played at New York's Broadway Theatre in the fall of 1890. The original music was by Emile Chabrier and Woolson Morse, but Sousa's orchestration was singled out for praise: "Much of the good effect of the music is due to the admirable instrumentation, which is the work of John Sousa, leader of the Marine Band of Washington. He has scored the numbers with great taste and skill." Wilson engaged Sousa again in late 1891 to orchestrate *The Lion Tamer*, an operetta with music by Richard Stahl. For this work Sousa wrote an original march, later published as "On Parade." He may well have completed orchestrations for several other operettas under Wilson's management, and in 1893 he began work on an original operetta for Wilson titled *The Devil's Deputy*.[33]

SOUSA AND SONG: COMEDY AND ART

While working in Philadelphia in the late 1870s, Sousa clearly saw himself primarily as a theater composer and songwriter. As a military musician in the 1880s, he was more fully occupied with band music, but his civilian activities demonstrate just how much his ambitions continued to center on the stage. Nonetheless, in addition to writing stage works and marches, Sousa kept expanding his catalog of songs. He had always been in the habit of setting texts by close friends, and this pattern continued well into the 1880s.

On August 2, 1884, Sousa conducted at a campaign event for the Republican presidential nominee, James G. Blaine. With Edward Taber he used the candidate's nickname—The Plumed Knight—as the title of a campaign song: "We'll Follow Where the White Plume Leads." The five-verse setting is musically brief, tuneful, and full of militaristic rhythms, all of which make it the perfect vehicle for a political rally and ideal for adaptation as a march. Indeed, the "White Plume March" appeared in print alongside the song in 1884.

In 1887 Sousa and Taber wrote a more dramatic song, "The Window Blind." In it a young lover wishes he had some "mystic method" to pierce the opacity of the "tantalizing, latticed green Venetian window blind" that keeps the object of his affection from view. Taber's wistful and witty text would have been well suited to an operetta, as would have Sousa's setting, which alternates between three declamatory verses and a waltz chorus. This is clearly a parlor song, but Taber's lyric makes it much more amusing than the songs of Sousa's youth. Indeed, Sousa and Taber collaborated on several forthrightly comic songs. The first of these pieces was 1889's "O'Reilly's Kettledrum," an ethnic novelty song in which an Irish family attempts to host a cotillion but misunderstands the word and instead fills a kettle with whisky punch and hires an Irish drummer. A fight naturally breaks out, putting an end to "Pat O'Reilly's first and only kettledrum." Sousa's tune is unremarkable, but it provides a snappy, march-like setting for Taber's text, complete with a percussive fanfare for an introduction. In the same year they produced the song "2-15," in which a ribbon clerk who makes $2.15 per week stays up nightly with his love until 2:15 A.M., when he is chased by her father for 2.15 miles. He then learns a new trade to earn $2.15 per hour, and the couple elopes aboard the 2:15 express. Sousa sets Taber's five-verse text to a charming waltz melody that includes just an eight-bar refrain. In 1890 the pair wrote one additional comic song. The four verses of "You'll Miss Lots of Fun When You're Married" praise the joys of wedded bliss, but Sousa's long melodic descent and rocking upper neighboring tones suggest that the narrator is not quite convinced of his own words. A four-bar refrain, introduced by spoken interjections of "still," "nevertheless," "notwithstanding which, however," or "but, all the same," confirms the suspicion aroused by the song's title. Sousa's music is again a swaying waltz that would have been perfectly at home on the comic stage.[34]

In August 1893, Sousa named four songs that he considered to be "of the better class of English ballads . . . in a vein with those of Sullivan." One of these, "I Wonder" (1888) had a text by Edward Taber. This is the only independent Taber song on a melancholy theme, and in it the poet asks if after death there is a world as joyous as life. Unlike most of Sousa's earlier sentimental songs, this one does not focus on love but rather reflects simply on the joys of living. Sousa's music is uncharacteristically chromatic and contains a more active and varied piano part than those found in most of his earlier songs.[35]

Two of the other pieces Sousa named were collaborations with Francis C. Long, a Treasury Department clerk who frequently contributed verse to the *Washington Post*. "My Own, My Geraldine" and "O Ye Lilies White" are both from 1887. The first is a remarkably dramatic and nostalgic song that has new music for each verse. In the first, a pair of lovers prepare for what appears to be a brief separation, guided by a completely diatonic melody (ex. 8a). The second verse is more cheerful as the narrator returns home to his bride (ex. 8b). Only in the final verse is the beloved's death revealed, and here Sousa writes in a style that is largely new for him (ex. 8c). The passage spans just a tritone, but the music is remarkably chromatic and begins fully outside the home key as the narrator finds his wife buried in the churchyard. This declamatory tune, with its sudden changes of dynamic and varied expressive markings, suggests that Sousa was reaching for something well beyond the parlor songs of his youth. The piece's emotional power is further heightened by Long's text, perhaps the most accomplished Sousa had yet set, with its reframing of sleeping, smiling, and gilding moonbeams in the three verses. "O Ye Lilies White" is similarly charged with dramatic changes in meter and mood, and it shifts between declamatory speech and a lilting melody. Before turning to the fourth song Sousa places among

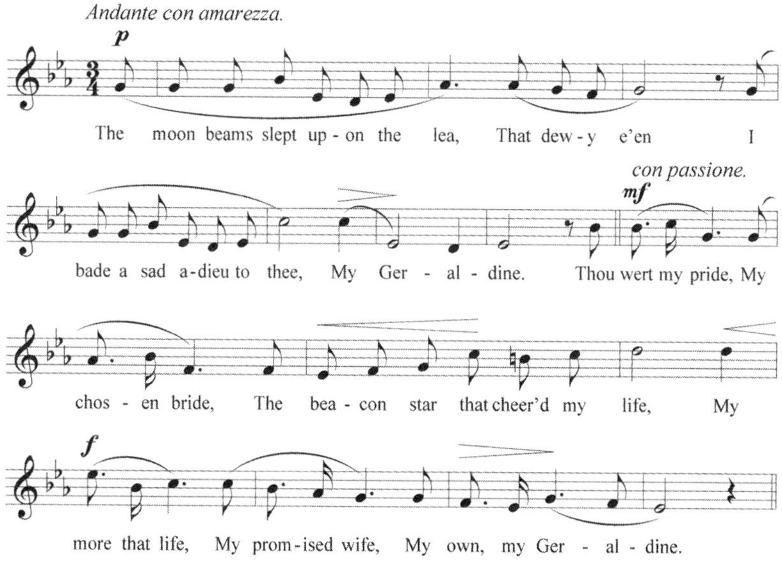

Ex. 8a. "My Own, My Geraldine," first verse and chorus (melody only)

Ex. 8b. "My Own, My Geraldine," second verse and chorus (melody only)

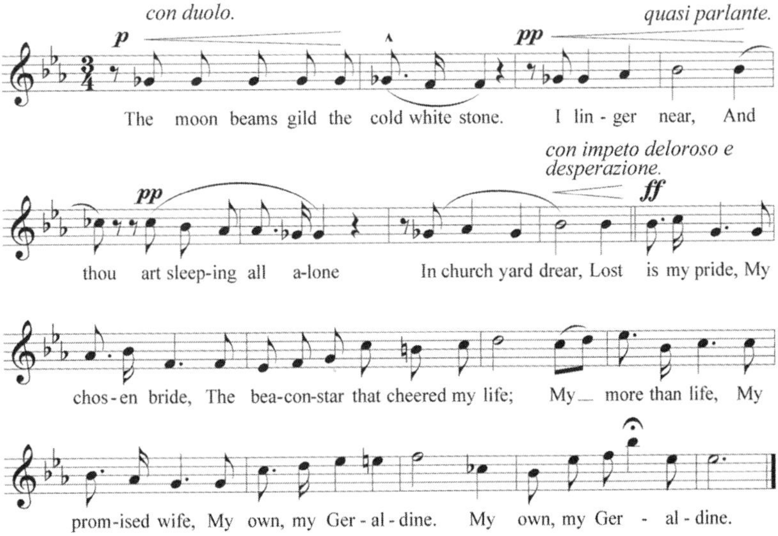

Ex. 8c. "My Own, My Geraldine," third verse and chorus (melody only)

his favorites—"Reveille"—it is worth considering his nonmilitary musical output as a whole.[36]

During the 1880s, Sousa was writing songs in several styles. Some pieces, such as "The Window Blind" and "I Wonder," continued the nostalgic parlor tradition. They were dramatic but remained tuneful and easy to perform. Others, such as "2–15" and "O'Reilly's Kettledrum," were effectively comic, with accessible melodies and repeated verses. But "My Own, My Geraldine" and "O Ye Lilies White" represent a third kind of song. Here Sousa's tunes become deeply chromatic, and his music is in the service of dramatic expression rather than parlor entertainment. To divide these works into popular and art songs would be to make a value distinction often rejected by musicians of Sousa's generation, but it is clear that in some cases the composer was rapidly setting texts for humorous or melodic effect, while at other times he was more concerned with emotional depth. It is telling, too, that the songs Sousa listed as among his favorites were those that told the most compelling stories. Once again, the future March King reveals his concern for, and attachment to, the theatrical.

There are several other minor works from the 1880s. In 1882 Sousa set a text by the local poet Mrs. M. D. Lincoln, who wrote under the pseudonym Bessie Beach. Their joint effort, "Star of Light," is a sentimental song about a guardian angel dedicated to the otherwise unknown "Ellen in Heaven." The strophic melody is plainly accessible and is supported by a straightforward, chordal accompaniment. The unfinished "Love That Comes When May-Roses Blow," sketched in the summer of 1889 to Sousa's own text, would likely have been a similarly sentimental parlor song. "Wissahickon Waltz" first appeared in the April 1885 edition of *Strawbridge and Clothier Quarterly*, a Philadelphia department store magazine. In the summer of 1889 Philadelphia newspapers printed a text by Hunter MacCulloch titled "Something Most Mysterious" and promised that a Sousa setting would be published in the June issue of the *Strawbridge and Clothier Quarterly*. Since MacCulloch served as editor of this publication, it seems clear that Sousa maintained his Philadelphia connections even as the leader of the Marine Band.[37]

Two of the comic songs Sousa wrote during this period were settings of texts by poets he likely did not know personally. In July 1881 he published "Pretty Patty Honeywood," drawn from the 1853 novel *The Adventures of Mr. Verdant Green* by the English writer Cuthbert Bede, a pseudonym for Edward Bradley. Here a narrator proclaims his love for the "fair and plump" Patty Honeywood. Sousa provides a running melody in sixteenth notes, and the piano reinforces his patter effect by hammering out triads. "Sweet Miss Industry," from early 1888, is a similar song on a poem by S. Conant Foster that Sousa found in the December 1884 issue of *St. Nicholas Magazine*. As might be expected, he wrote a patter verse paired with a waltz chorus to tell the story of a young girl deciding between marriage and housework.

Perhaps the most remarkable song from Sousa's Marine Band years was the fourth piece he placed among his favorites. "Reveille" (1890), dedicated to the army, is a setting of a poem from Robert Jones Burdette's war memoir *The Drums of the 47th*. The piece begins by referring to the rituals of field music, and Sousa's piano introduction starts with Assembly of Trumpeters, a fanfare used to bring together the buglers who will awaken the camp (ex. 9a). In the first verse, an uncertain musician sees the morning approach, but he is still half asleep, and Sousa's single carefully placed melisma suggests his drowsy yawn. When it comes time for the bugle to sound, the protagonist can only muster a *pianissimo* Reveille, as if his efforts create a mere echo. The text suggests his disappointment: "I can't get 'em up, I can't get 'em up, I can't get 'em up in the morning" (ex. 9b). The camp begins to come to life in the second verse. As the

Ex. 9a. "Reveille," introduction stating Assembly of Trumpeters

Ex. 9b. "Reveille," first verse and chorus (melody only)

Ex. 9c. "Reveille," third verse and conclusion

Ex. 9c. (*continued*)

Ex. 9c. (*continued*)

bugler prepares to blow his signal again, a triplet fanfare in the accompaniment eggs him on, but still he can only reach a *piano*. Sousa mixes his original melody with the bugle call in the final verse, but each time he tries to sound the tune, the player remains too soft and out of synch with the camp. Only at the end of the song, with the field musician now fully awake, does Reveille sound with its full and glorious power, complete with a drum roll in the piano (ex. 9c on pp. 143–45).

What makes "Reveille" so remarkable is its summary of Sousa's career to 1890. It is a parlor song, published for amateur performance. The melody is largely diatonic, stepwise, or triadic, but it contains enough light chromaticism and changes of mood to retain a performer's interest. The piano part is accessible, requiring some practice but leading to little frustration. The borrowed bugle calls are familiar, easing the performers' task while delighting the listeners' ears. But "Reveille" is simultaneously a dramatic, artistic song, with careful text painting, a clever plot, and a humorous conclusion. Sousa's growing fame in Washington was due in large part to his position as leader of the United States Marine Band, and with its military references this song encapsulated that fame more than any other vocal work up to that time.

Throughout the 1880s John Philip Sousa was Washington's native son and favorite musician: he conducted the city's most famous band, led amateur productions of operettas and orchestral music, and wrote his own stage works. In all of these tasks, he remained primarily a local musician: his operettas saw their greatest success at home, most of his song settings drew on the work of local writers, and the vast majority of these songs were published by the Washington firm of John F. Ellis. But Sousa clearly harbored a desire for a wider reputation, a desire that manifested itself in a series of brief, and only marginally successful, operetta tours. He would soon discover, however, that the financial rewards of national fame were not to be found through operas or songs. He was now, after all, an entertainer of presidents and America's most important public musician. While in Philadelphia, he had seen one celebration of national pride, and as the 1880s came to a close, another was on the horizon. Soon, John Philip Sousa's position as leader of the Marine Band would take on a new value, and he stood ready to seize that opportunity. Along the way, he would become an ever more patriotic musician and would create a new persona that combined national pride with the dramatic theatricality he knew so well. It is hardly surprising, therefore, that when Sousa created a new operetta in 1909—*The American Maid*, written at the height of his fame—he recycled "Reveille." It was, after all, within the world of military, patriotic, and official music that Sousa was soon to achieve his greatest fame.

PART III *The March King*

CHAPTER SEVEN

America's Court Composer

IN 1898 THE *MUSICAL COURIER* DECLARED: "It is Sousa in the band, Sousa in the orchestra, Sousa in the phonograph, Sousa in the hand organ, Sousa in the music box, Sousa everywhere. The American composer is the man, not of the hour or of the day, but of the time!" Such claims for Sousa's reach into American culture were commonplace by the late 1890s, but they demonstrate a level of fame unfathomable to the bandmaster just a decade earlier. Sousa was still a merely local musician: a composer and conductor who may have dreamt of success on the national stage but had thus far found triumph only in his hometown. His transformation from local son to March King would begin in the late 1880s as he focused his ambitions, put his dramatic skills to greater use on the bandstand, and sought out a musical niche by connecting himself ever more intimately with American patriotism.[1]

AMERICA'S COURT COMPOSER

In the process of securing the leadership of the Marine Band, Sousa had written two marches with evocative military titles: "Esprit de Corps" and "Globe and Eagle." Such martial titling would become commonplace after his return to Washington, where he wrote "Guide Right," "Right Forward," and "Right-Left." As Marine Band leader, Sousa was responsible for the parades and public concerts where such pieces might have been put to good use, but in the early 1880s most of his marches continued to be published only for piano. While Sousa's military music may have been written for the parade ground and bandstand, it circulated primarily in local parlors.

There was, however, a kind of military music that had little value to the amateur pianist but through which Sousa could make his mark among bandsmen. During the 1880s, Sousa was—at least nominally—the chief musician for the Marine Corps. In fulfillment of these duties he wrote *Four Marches for*

Regimental Drums and Trumpets. These pieces, published in 1884, were each a mere sixteen bars long and thus brief enough to be printed together on a single page. They consist only of tunes for one or two natural trumpets and rudimentary percussion, and given the technical restrictions of these instruments, the marches could not have been especially difficult to compose. Even so, they mark Sousa's first foray into a musical world that did not focus on the home parlor, concert hall, or theatrical stage. The marches were, of course, meant as field music, and they were Sousa's inaugural efforts at composing for a purely military ensemble.

His next outing as a ceremonial composer would be much less modest. In the summer of 1881 the Marine Corps ended its field use of fifes. It fell to the bandleader to update the field repertoire, and so, in 1886, Sousa published his first book: *The Trumpet and Drum*. This pocket-sized manual contains training instructions for both instruments, as well as a complete set of garrison signals, several original field marches by Sousa, and two more pieces from his collaborator F. W. Lusby, a drum instructor for the Marine Band.

Both of these collections were designed for the relatively insulated market of music for the field, but they reveal Sousa's attitude toward his new responsibilities. Since taking control of the Marine Band, he had instituted a systematic series of improvements to the ensemble by working to advance the musical skills of his players, increase their compensation, and diversify their repertoire. He began a similarly ordered reorganization of the field music itself with *The Trumpet and Drum*, as suggested by his introduction: "The belief that a book of instruction for the field music of the Service is greatly needed, has suggested to the author the publication of this work. At the present time there is a lack of precision in the performance of the trumpet-signals of the Service, both as to intonation and division of time." Sousa did not take his duties lightly, and the layout of the book suggests that he carefully based his work on the musical sections of Emory Upton's infantry tactics manual. In short, Sousa's activities suggest a marine musician considerably more diligent and ambitious than his predecessors, and this ambition would soon attract the attention of the national press. For the moment, however, he was focused on a systematic overhaul of America's official music.[2]

In his autobiography Sousa explains that dignitaries visiting the White House were required to assemble in the East Room, where "they were informed of the approach of the executive by the pompous strains of an old Scotch boating song, 'Hail to the Chief.'" President Arthur asked his bandmaster one evening if the tune was appropriate to the occasion, and Sousa answered in the negative: "No, sir. . . . It was selected long ago on account of its name, and not on account of its character." The president replied just as Sousa had hoped he would: "Then change it!"[3]

Sousa composed two pieces at Arthur's urging, both meant to replace "Hail to the Chief." One was designed for indoor events and the other to render honors on parade. The indoor piece, completed on November 25, 1886, was scored for band and titled "In Echelon Polonaise." Its earliest known performance occurred at a public concert on the White House grounds on July 9, 1887. Sousa rescored the work in January 1889 for orchestra and used it at the inaugural ball of Benjamin Harrison. In publishing the piece that year, Harry Coleman capitalized on its association with the executive and retitled the work "Presidential Polonaise."[4]

For his outdoor piece, Sousa envisioned a march in which the full band would drop away and leave only the "roll of the drums and the sounding of the trumpets" to honor the reviewing official. He wrote a fairly typical march to achieve this effect, but instead of composing a new trio, he inserted his field march "With Steady Step," first printed in *The Trumpet and Drum*. The result was "Semper Fidelis" (1888). "Hail to the Chief" is, of course, still the official tune used in greeting the president of the United States, but "Semper Fidelis" is today known by tradition as the official march of the Marine Corps. It is also the earliest of Sousa's marches to have entered the permanent repertoire.[5]

In these efforts to regularize America's official music, Sousa's achievements would have been noticed only by other military musicians. In 1889, however, he undertook a project that would garner his first exposure in the national press. Because the Marine Band was often required to perform the national anthems of visiting dignitaries, Sousa suggested to the secretary of the navy that the nation's military would be well served by a volume that collected together such anthems. Benjamin F. Tracy agreed, and in a Special Order dated October 18, 1889, the secretary wrote: "John Philip Sousa, Bandmaster of the Band of the United States Marine Corps, is hereby directed to compile for the use of the Department the National and Patriotic airs of all Nations."[6]

Sousa, of course, had collected together several national anthems for his U.S. centennial composition "The International Congress." But now, with the secretary's blessing, he could create a comprehensive reference work of such tunes. After contacting foreign consuls, consulting with music publishers, and visiting dozens of libraries, Sousa published *National, Patriotic, and Typical Airs of All Lands* in 1890. This volume is remarkable on two fronts. First, it is likely the first effort by an American official to create a comprehensive collection of national airs. Sousa includes more than two hundred pieces, ranging from officially recognized national anthems to popular and folk songs typical of various countries, tribes, and ethnic groups. Second, in this project he acted not merely as a compiler but rather saw himself as a scholar: someone learned enough to provide commentary on each work and clever enough to outline a scheme for their organization.

He divided his selections into the three categories reflected in his title. National airs were those that "either by official decree or by the voice of the people, are known as the principal patriotic airs of their respective countries." Patriotic tunes are "those which embody words of a patriotic character, or are used at times for patriotic purposes." Finally, typical airs are "indigenous to the soil, or the people" and represent "national music in the broad sense of the term." Sousa provides written commentary for a number of pieces, sometimes original but often heavily reliant on standard reference sources.[7]

Sousa's second book was well timed. With the upcoming celebration of the four-hundredth anniversary of Columbus's historic voyage, Americans were fascinated by all things national. Sousa's name had appeared in the press whenever he launched a new operetta or when the Marine Band took part in an event of national importance, but most of these notices were confined to cities in and around Washington, Philadelphia, Boston, and New York. With the publication of *National, Patriotic, and Typical Airs of All Lands*, however, newspapers from Savannah to Salt Lake City reported on Sousa's achievement. Most praised his skillful attention to detail, and one writer noted that the secretary's original order imposed a "herculean task" that "would have fairly paralyzed any other than a man possessing the most indomitable energy and extraordinary ability in his profession, coupled with ambition and confidence in his power." According to this critic, Sousa had produced a volume that was not only complete in content but also magnificent in presentation. He had given

> the world the masterpiece before us, a large quarto book of 283 pages, handsomely bound in cloth and embellished with its title and the author's name in gold, and actually containing the National, patriotic and typical airs of every nation and tribe of people on the globe including even the islands of the sea, arranged for the piano, giving generally the words in the language of the country or people, and also the English translations, with copious historical notes, preserving for posterity the history of each of our own National airs, as well as those of France and England and some other countries, with a copious index giving the name of the country, character of the air, whether National, patriotic or typical, its title, name of author and composer, the form of government and location, alphabetically arranged.

This work was so impressive that it placed Sousa—now both bandmaster and scholar—"in the front rank of the composers of our time." It was a volume that "no musician can afford to be without, and that should be found in the music rack of every parlor."[8]

Several papers sought out the compiler, who spoke at some length about America's own patriotic songs. He explained to an astonished press that while many countries had legally prescribed works for ceremonial occasions, there was no such consistency in the United States: "In Europe they have national airs because they have been made so either by the Government or by the people, and on all ceremonial occasions they are played as a matter of course. . . . But with us, when the President takes part in any ceremony, one band may play 'America' and another 'The Star-Spangled Banner.'"[9]

In representing the United States, Sousa included "Hail, Columbia!," "The Star-Spangled Banner," "Yankee Doodle," "Columbia, the Gem of the Ocean," and "My Country, 'Tis of Thee," all songs that he personally found inappropriate because they were either of foreign origin or lacking in musical dignity. Asked if Congress could mandate a new and improved national song, Sousa replied: "Well, hardly. Congress can do a great many things, but it cannot do that. The national air of a people must come from some great event in the life of the Nation, perhaps some crisis. It must be spontaneous; it must appeal to national pride and the national sentiment, and then, when it does that, the country takes it up and clings to it as jealously as it does to its other traditions."[10]

Sousa did not make such statements idly; rather, they came just as he was learning how completely an American community could identify with a familiar tune. In November 1889, the Marine Band was given permission to travel to Fayetteville and take part in the celebration of North Carolina's ratification of the U.S. Constitution. Sousa was worried that a federal band, sent by a Republican president, might be challenged in courting a southern audience. He programmed a familiar and well-loved song to put his public at ease. As the band began, he noticed the crowd's reaction: "It was like an electric shock! A rebel yell, starting on the grandstand, went booming down the street, through the surging crowds. Never was there so tremendous and thrilling a shout! The very air seemed to quiver with excitement. A myriad hats went rocketing upwards. Grim old warriors cried aloud, the women turned and hugged each other, and for fifteen minutes pandemonium reigned." The tune, of course, was "Dixie," and the Marine Band spent the remainder of the concert alternating it with the planned works on the program. Sousa later advised that any musician daring to enter the South without this melody in his repertoire would be "mentally, morally and physically damned by everybody—and doubtless should have been."[11]

"Dixie," though not included in *National, Patriotic, and Typical Airs of All Lands*, was just the sort of song Sousa admired: a piece of popular origin by an American composer, whose text and tune had been adopted as a rallying cry for a patriotic cause. He also praised "The Battle Hymn of the Republic," not for its musical characteristics but for its embrace by audiences. Such works might have begun life as minstrel tunes or sacred songs, he wrote, "but when the populace want a thing they take it wherever they find it." This concern for his audience's desires would help define the future March King. For Sousa, however, both songs shared a fatal flaw: they were drawn from the period of the Civil War, and the bandmaster made it clear that the nation needed a unifying crisis to create a truly national melody.[12]

The press notices about Sousa's collection reflect his growing reputation as an expert on patriotic music, but they also reveal an unpleasant element of his personality. His biography is largely devoid of scandal, but his writings demonstrate that he harbored the racial views so common to his generation. His anecdotes are littered with casual references to comic, insolent, impertinent, or ignorant "darkies," "colored men," and "niggers," and this sort of racism—often couched as jingoism—is apparent both in interviews regarding his patriotic tunebook and in the volume itself.[13]

In the preface, Sousa explains that he corresponded with a large number of foreign and domestic consulates. From them he received various national tunes, many of which came without harmonic treatment. For his part, he "endeavored to supply that deficiency." While he took care not to alter the melodies, he did provide harmonizations without any real concern for national or ethnic traditions. In this sense, Sousa was not unlike many other collectors of the late nineteenth century, and since he was creating a reference volume for military bands, the violence done to his source material was perhaps more due to practical necessity than to insensitivity.[14]

Sousa's casual racism was made more obvious in interviews: "With hardly an exception," he noted, "the national airs of all the savage or semi-civilized nations are written in a minor key, while those of highly civilized nations are invariably written in the major key." He went on to observe that "the national airs of the great countries are short, while those of the little countries are very long," implying that European composers were more economical in their writing. Sousa cites as examples "God Save the Queen," whose melody is a mere fourteen measures long, and the national air of China, which "is so long that when the people want to hear it, they have to take half a day off to be [able] to listen to its dulcet strains." Sousa is clearly speaking off the cuff. The two Chinese songs he prints, "The World's Delight" and "Moo-lee-wha," are a mere sixty and thirty-two bars long, respectively, and in other interviews China is replaced with San Marino, whose tune—which consumes ten pages in Sousa's arrangement—is, indeed, among the longest in the collection.[15]

Regardless of Sousa's credentials in anthropology, he did manage to compile an impressive volume, but perhaps more important, he broadened and deepened his own reputation. A few of his published pieces likely were known to amateur pianists and bandsmen, but with *National, Patriotic, and Typical Airs of All Lands*, he added the label "scholar" to his résumé: "Mr. Sousa, everybody knows, is the leader of the United States Marine Band, and he has long been generally recognized as a skillful and forcible musician; this work shows him also to be a thorough student, with a large acquaintance with history and literature." Such notices were quite common; a Chicago paper, for example, declared that the bandmaster's efforts "must not only enhance Mr. Sousa's name as a musician, but give him also a place in literature." Most impressive is the *Brooklyn Eagle*'s declaration that Sousa was "a capable conductor, a critic, a literary investigator, and a philosopher."[16]

The military, for its part, was ecstatic with the bandmaster's work. Rear Admiral John G. Walker, who was scheduled to sail aboard the *Chicago* on November 1, 1889, delayed his departure until Sousa's volume was available. Like a proud father, he collected fifty copies to present to dignitaries in the Mediterranean. And although Sousa doubted that a national melody could be created by decree, some of his American choices did quickly achieve official recognition. In a General Order dated July 26, 1889, Secretary Tracy followed Sousa's advice and ordered the playing of "The Star-Spangled Banner" at morning colors and "Hail, Columbia!" at evening colors.[17]

The fall of 1930 would see a new push to designate "The Star-Spangled Banner" as the national anthem of the United States. As recently as 1928, Sousa had outlined the characteristics of a good anthem, which included a narrow range, expressions of virility, and a beautiful melody. Any anthem would, of course, need to avoid "modern conceptions of harmony" and stay away from jazz inflections: "Spare us that!" he exclaimed. "The Star-Spangled Banner" may have avoided the worst affronts, but Sousa rejected the tune, along with "Hail, Columbia," "Columbia, the Gem of the Ocean," "America," "Yankee Doodle," and "Dixie," because of its foreign origin and wide range. As the push for "The Star-Spangled Banner" became stronger, however, he agreed to sign a statement endorsing congressional action. But his enthusiasm was muted: "The only possible chance that we might have a new National anthem would be when the eyes of all America are directed toward some particular cause and another genius captures the spirit of the moment in a thrilling song of patriotism. Until that time I do not believe the veneration for Francis Scott Key's anthem will ever be displaced." The efforts were successful, despite Sousa's reservations, and Herbert Hoover signed an act naming "The Star-Spangled Banner" the national anthem on March 3, 1931.[18]

MECHANICAL MUSIC

The flurry of press notices and interviews concerning *National, Patriotic, and Typical Airs of All Lands* helped heighten Sousa's profile. But while many Americans outside Washington may have played from Sousa's sheet music or heard his marches performed by local ensembles, few had actually heard the dulcet strains of their national band. This situation would change in 1889 with the formation of the Columbia Phonograph Company. Organized by a group of Washington businessmen, Columbia acted as a regional distributor for the American Graphophone Company. The organization at first focused on selling equipment to aid in office dictation—a widespread enterprise in the capital—but by November 1889 it was advertising musical recordings for the entertainment market. Given the uncertainty of public interest in the new technology, Columbia turned to inexpensive local artists such as the government clerk and artistic whistler John Y. AtLee, the student pianist Fred Gaisberg, and the baritone errand boy Len Spencer.

Just as the Marine Band had long acted as Washington's principal clearinghouse for live musical performance, it now provided some of Columbia's earliest talent. In February 1890 the company announced that it would begin selling recordings of Henry Jaeger, "the celebrated flute and piccolo soloist of the Marine Band." Jaeger was not the first person to make musical recordings, but he was the first of Columbia's artists to be identified by name and probably the first Marine Band musician to be heard on record.[19]

Columbia was soon looking for a larger group on whose reputation it could build, and, as Sousa wrote, men from the company "came over to the barracks while we were rehearsing and put their machines into operation." Assuming it to be a private experiment, the bandmaster allowed the intrusion, but when he discovered that "the disks were being used and our names advertised, we put a stop to the business." Wanting to protect his men's financial interests, as well as his own, Sousa arranged for a contract. Columbia soon agreed to pay "each man a dollar an hour for playing selections into the phonographs."

Sousa could state: "The phonograph people were great nuisances to me for a long time, but I am not complaining much now."[20]

By the middle of 1890 the Marine Band became the first large musical ensemble to undertake the commercial recording of music. The earliest surviving Columbia catalog to indicate individual selections is a typed sheet dated October 1, 1890, and it lists sixty numbers available from Sousa's ensemble. These works are divided by genre, and of the twenty-three marches, nearly half are by Sousa (there are also five waltzes, nine polkas, a galop, and a yorke). The remainder of the list is headed "Miscellaneous," and it includes several of the national airs Sousa had so recently published. Additional lists would soon appear, and the Marine Band went on to record about two hundred cylinders during Sousa's tenure as leader.[21]

The sound of the band is often hidden behind pops and scratches on the surviving cylinders, but these recordings do capture something of the excitement surrounding this early technology. The cylinders were, after all, not merely documentations of musical performance but also exhibitions of a fledgling industry. A fascinated public naturally inspired the press to publish accounts of the recording process like this one:

> While the Marine Band plays into the five great horns, an expert manipulates the machines. Each phonograph being supplied with a smooth and fresh cylinder of wax, the expert in charge shouts into each horn separately the title of the piece to be played. When he has done this the electric motor is turned on again, the cylinders revolve beneath the recording needles, the band starts up at a signal, and the music pours into the big trumpets until each cylinder is as full of sound impressions as it can hold. Then the expert holds up his finger and the band comes to a full stop at the end of the next musical phrase. . . . Now and then, if there is a little space left at the end of the cylinders, the band indulges in a wild burst of applause, stamping and shouting in approbation of its own performance. This passes for demonstration by a suppositious audience, of course, when one hears the phonograph reproduce it.[22]

Such descriptions reveal several things about these early recordings. First, each cylinder is an original. The band would play the same selection again and again—into several different machines simultaneously—and thus produce about $10 worth of cylinders every ten minutes. Second, the material on the recordings was limited by the two-minute duration of the cylinders; each piece came to an end, not with the end of the printed music, but with the

Fig. 21. The Marine Band in the studio of the Columbia Phonograph Company, ca. 1891. "The President's Own" United States Marine Band, Washington, D.C.

signal of an engineer. This process sometimes necessitated the chopping off of strains, while at other times it allowed for added repeats or the enthusiastic shouts of an imaginary audience. The third issue revealed by this description, and by the only photograph of the Marine Band in a recording session, relates to Sousa's relationship with Columbia, one that necessitates leaping forward a decade to when he was securely established as the March King.

THE MENACE OF MECHANICAL MUSIC

In 1906 *Appleton's Magazine* published a vitriolic and now quite famous article "The Menace of Mechanical Music." In it, America's best-known bandmaster warns his readers of an impending disaster: "Sweeping across the country with the speed of a transient fashion in slang or Panama hats, political war cries or popular novels, comes now the mechanical device to sing for us a song or play for us a piano, in substitute for human skill, intelligence, and soul." The new technologies of player pianos and recordings were so dangerous that Sousa felt compelled to spur his public to action before music was reduced to a mere "mathematical system of megaphones, wheels, cogs, disks, cylinders, and all manner of revolving things." Should he fail in this missionary quest, it would be "simply a question of time when the amateur disappears entirely."[23]

Sousa was no longer a local bandmaster at the time he wrote this article; rather, he was one of America's most celebrated entertainers, one whose livelihood depended on both ticket receipts and sheet music sales. These two forms of income were, of course, interdependent, and in this his career parallels those of W. S. Gilbert and Arthur Sullivan, whose work Sousa knew intimately. The amateur musician who purchased Sousa's latest march—and learned it at the parlor piano—might be inspired to attend one of Sousa's concerts. Conversely, hearing a march in performance might prompt the same amateur to purchase sheet music for use at home. Sousa's career thus rested on a reciprocal pathway in which sheet music advertised performance, and performance promoted sheet music. Any technology that threatened this two-way financial street also threatened the March King's income.

Sousa's article did not appear in isolation, however; rather, it was written in the midst of an ongoing debate regarding American copyright law. In 1906 the legal framework that had allowed Sousa to freely orchestrate the music of Gilbert and Sullivan remained. By publishing their music, composers effectively dedicated it to public performance. With the law still well behind new technologies, recordings constituted simply another kind of performance, and manufacturers of player piano rolls, cylinders, and disks were thus free to record any piece that had appeared in print, with no financial remuneration to its composer.

Several professional organizations had lobbied for a revision to the copyright law in hopes of addressing this issue, and Theodore Roosevelt—himself an aggrieved author—brought presidential authority to bear in his December 1905 State of the Union address: "Our copyright laws urgently need revision. They are imperfect in definition, confused and inconsistent in expression; they omit provision for many articles which, under modern reproductive processes, are entitled to protection." Indeed, the Librarian of Congress had already sponsored a series of conferences that proposed new legal language granting to composers and their publishers "the sole and exclusive right . . . to make, sell, distribute, or let for hire any device, contrivance, or appliance especially adapted in any manner whatsoever to reproduce to the ear the whole or any material part of any work published and copyrighted."[24]

With a proposal pending, Congress held hearings to explore its ramifications, and Victor Herbert organized composers on behalf of the new language. Looking for a celebrity spokesperson, Herbert engaged John Philip Sousa to appear before the joint Congressional Committees on Patents in June 1906.

There Sousa articulated three types of arguments in favor of the bill. With the first he addressed the legal issue of "writing" as understood by the Constitution, which grants to Congress the power to secure "for limited times to authors and inventors the exclusive right to their respective writings and discoveries." If recorded disks, cylinders, and piano rolls were "writings," then they constituted copies that should be controlled by the author. Sousa argued that whatever doubt there was regarding a record's readability, it was "simply that no method has been found to read them up to the present time, but there will be. Just as the man who wanted to scan the heavens discovered a telescope to do it. No doubt there will be found a way to read these records."[25]

His second argument focused on his sense of moral equity. As the law then stood, a record company could legally purchase one set of band parts for a Sousa march and from it make thousands of identical records, thus multiplying their profits exponentially. To Sousa, each record represented a loss in sales for which he wanted compensation: "If they would buy one copy from my publishers . . . and sell that one copy, I would have no objection." Instead, they "take one copy of a copyrighted piece of music and produce by their method a thousand or more disks, cylinders, or perforated rolls."[26]

Sousa, of course, had already seen American copyright fail to protect composers. He had borrowed the work of Gilbert and Sullivan for his own profit, and with Charles Ford's 1883 production of *Iolanthe* he had actually been named in a lawsuit over musical appropriation. In 1906 Sousa was as successful in America as Gilbert and Sullivan had ever been, and he knew that mere legal or ethical arguments focused on preserving his own financial interests would have little sway with an audience eager for easy access to his latest music. In an effort to win public support for a new law, Sousa formulated a third argument, one that rested on an idealized notion of America's past and predicted a cultural loss for the country:

> When I was a boy—I was born in this town—in front of every house in the summer evenings you would find young people together singing the songs of the day or the old songs. To-day you hear these infernal machines going night and day. . . . Last summer and the summer before I was in one of the biggest yacht harbors in the world, and I did not hear a voice the whole summer. Every yacht had a gramophone, a phonograph, an æolian, or something of the kind.[27]

As the June hearings came to a close, Congress's position remained unclear, and there was no indication that Herbert and Sousa enjoyed the support of the public or the press. Many journalists were simply unconvinced that amateur music making was on the decline, and some suggested that talking machines would, if anything, help spread high-quality performances to smaller communities: "The talking machine will do no harm, but it does impart an infinite amount of pleasure to millions of people who are enabled through its instrumentality to get an idea of the powers and beauties of the voices of great singers whom they otherwise never could have hoped to hear." Others suggested that recordings might act as inexpensive teachers and thus increase the quality of home performance: "In reality the graphophone, so far from supplanting the human singing voice, is a most active agent in its cultivation. In thousands of homes the graphophone takes the place of a vocal instructor. The children gather about the instrument and learn to sing the new songs correctly and with expression."[28]

The March King had been in this position before. During a trip to London in January 1903, Sousa discovered that pirated editions of his pieces were being sold on the street. Furious, he wrote a letter to the *Times* of London asking that the British government enforce existing law: "I have been labouring under the delusion that, as I have complied with the requirements of the international copyright laws, your Government would assume the responsibility of finding a way to protect my property. Apparently no such responsibility exists. There surely must be a remedy to protect a composer from such a deplorable injustice?"[29] Sousa was hardly the only musician to suffer under this state of affairs. In turn-of-the-century England musical piracy was merely a civil offense, and British publishers discovered that their only recourse involved lengthy and expensive litigation, which might at best result in a small fine. By the time Sousa returned to London in 1905, several publishers were lobbying to introduce stricter penalties for piracy. Their leading spokesperson was William Boosey, general manager of the Chappell Publishing Company and chairman of the Music Publishers' Association. Parliament had blocked the proposed legislation prompting Boosey to take the matter public. With Sousa in town he did not need to look far for a spokesperson, and he asked the visiting March King to write two public letters, "one dignified and the other satirical." Because Sousa's compositions continued to appear in pirated English editions, he was more than happy to comply.[30]

The dignified piece appeared in the *Times*, and in it he reminded readers that British piracy was depriving at least one composer of a well-earned income:

> I have before me a pirated edition of my latest composition, which was printed and hawked about the streets of London, within a few days of the

authorized publication of this march, at a price at which my publishers could not afford to print it. And this has been the case with all my compositions in Great Britain for several years. It has had the effect of practically stopping the sale of my genuine publications, thus depriving me of the substantial income from that source that the popularity of my music in this country gives me every reason to expect.[31]

The opposition's public argument had rested on the idea that music must be made available to the masses at low prices. Sousa's satirical letter carried this line of reasoning to its extreme: "The music pirate had a philanthropic mission. This mysterious and mercenary Messiah, noticing the dire distress of the tune-starved masses—whoever they may be—said, 'I will save them. . . . I will gorge them with gavottes, build them up with ballads, and make muscle with marches. They shall become comely with comedy conceits, and radiantly rosy with ragtime rondos—and all at 2d. a throw.'"[32]

These efforts led to considerable press commentary, almost entirely in favor of the new law. As a result, in 1906 British publishers persuaded Parliament to pass a copyright revision that provided a prison sentence for the possession of pirated music. Sousa had learned something as well. Now that his music was as susceptible to piracy as Arthur Sullivan's had once been, he knew that convincing the public to alter the law might require a direct, emotional appeal, rather than a more nuanced legal argument.

As he left the 1906 American copyright hearings, Sousa must have remembered Boosey's advice, and he decided to write a series of articles, serious and satirical. "The Menace of Mechanical Music" was Sousa's principal "dignified" article. Recognizing that greed would not be met with public sympathy, he quickly admitted that he was "swayed in part by personal interest." All too aware of the public's growing fondness for recordings, he was also willing to allow that "where families lack time or inclination to acquire musical technic, and to hear public performances, the best of these machines supply a certain amount of satisfaction and pleasure." Sousa's task was to arouse public support, not to debate the law, and so he quickly conceded the point: "Let the ambiguities in the text of law be what they may; let there be of legal quips and quirks as many as you please." He would focus instead on what he felt sure the public would see as a more devastating loss: the decline of amateur culture.[33]

Sousa's greatest fame coincided with an early twentieth-century American optimism, in which urbanization, industrialization, and technological advancement promised to raise all boats. For many, however, this period of change also elicited nostalgia for the certainties of the nineteenth century. While Sousa's primary motivation in writing "The Menace of Mechanical Music" may have been financial, his argument and rhetoric allowed him to tap into the antimodernist sentiment that caused many Americans to seek out more authentic aesthetic experiences, unmediated by technology.

The March King served, for many, as a symbol of masculine success. He was no soft entertainer, and despite a childhood illness, he had spent his boyhood hunting and fishing in the Navy Yard. On the bandstand he was a leader of men, and in the press he was photographed as a boxer, trapshooter, and horseman. In short, the March King's body had not been softened by technology. He had already warned Congress of the bodily dangers threatened by talking machines. Thanks to mechanical music, the transcript of the hearings stated, Americans would soon "not have a vocal chord [*sic*] left. [Laughter.] The vocal chords will be eliminated by a process of evolution, as was the tail of man when he came from the ape. The vocal chords will go because no one will have a chance to sing, the phonograph supplying a mechanical imitation of the voice, accompaniment, and effort."[34]

Appealing to his adoring public, Sousa expanded this warning of a weakened national body. Along the way he connected physical health and the antimodernist movement to amateur culture and promised to stand firm in the face of an emasculating technology. Knowing that musical practice was an important part of "the curriculum of physical culture," Sousa questioned the strength of an unmusical country: "Then what of the national throat? Will it not weaken? What of the national chest? Will it not shrink?" If the record companies had their way, masculinity and its connection to nature would be lost along with amateur culture: "The ingenious purveyor of canned music is urging the sportsman, on his way to the silent places with gun and rod, tent and canoe, to take with him some disks, cranks, and cogs to sing to him as he sits by the firelight, a thought as unhappy and incongruous as canned salmon by a trout brook." Such mechanization even threatened the very fabric of American home life: "It is at the fireside that we look for virtue and patriotism; for songs that stir the blood and fire the zeal; for songs of home, of mother, and of love, that touch the heart and brighten the eye. Music teaches all that is beautiful in this world. Let us not hamper it with a machine that tells the story day by day, without variation, without soul, barren of the joy, the passion, the ardor that is the inheritance of man alone."[35]

Following Boosey's earlier advice, Sousa did not limit himself to one public appeal, and he also wrote a satirical article. In it he imagined himself a newspaper columnist summarizing a year in music after the takeover of recordings.

Following the establishment of "talking-machine conservatories," Sousa discovered that just as recordings had weakened the bodies of amateurs, so, too, had they destroyed the minds of performers. No longer could graduates "tell a barcarole from a boiler explosion, a rallentando from a railroad smash-up." Instruments that required physical prowess to play and disciplined practice to perfect were "fast becoming archaic," and, posing as the champion of mechanization, Sousa praised their demise: "When it is considered that a whole man is necessary to manipulate each separate one of these nearly-obsolete instruments, the waste of space and energy seems appalling."[36]

Whatever the wisdom of this argument, Sousa had shifted the discussion away from the economies of copyright to the perceived cultural cost of mechanical reproduction. Along the way, however, he exposed himself to charges of hypocrisy. By 1906 the Sousa Band had made hundreds of recordings, and it seemed impossible that the bandmaster could really be worried about the moral hazards of the technology. One S. T. Cameron, who represented the American Graphophone Company and thus knew something of Sousa's activities, made this very point before Congress:

> Mr. Sousa himself does not scorn, as he pretended to the other day, these "infernal talking machines." The day has been when Mr. Sousa himself came with advance scores and begged to have them put upon the machines, in order that they might popularize his own music. Nor is that all. He today is under contract, and he plays into these "infernal machines" with his band, and he is contributing, as he told you a few days ago, to stifle these "beautiful young voices that now have disappeared throughout our city and our land." [Laughter.] He does it for the almighty dollar.

In December 1906 Paul Cromelin, vice president of the Columbia Phonograph Company, made a similar argument before Congress, pointing out that Sousa had already gained in both payment and reputation from recordings: "We started in business in the District of Columbia about the time Mr. Sousa, then leader of the United States Marine Band, won his first laurels as a composer. The first band records I have any recollection of were made by Mr. Sousa and his band, and I have very distinct recollection of advance scores of Mr. Sousa's being sent to our laboratory to be played on our records before the sheet music was out."[37]

In his efforts to woo the public, Sousa had staked out a claim that the new technology could do real damage to American culture. As a celebrated representative of that culture, it would not do to have his earlier involvement too directly revealed, and so Sousa twice denied ever having appeared on a recording. In June 1906 he explained that his band had, indeed, made discs and cylinders but that he had never actually been involved: "An organization known as 'Sousa and his band,' employed just as any other body of musicians, in which I have no part myself, plays into the instrument," he stated. "I am the director of that band, but I have no personal part in the performance of those pieces. I have never been in the gramophone company's office in my life." At the December hearings he was even more direct: "I will not deny that my band played for their records, but I never was in the laboratory of the phonograph company in my life."[38]

Over the course of its existence the Sousa Band made about 1,770 recordings, but the March King himself seems to have conducted only three sessions, none of which occurred before 1906. His statements before Congress, along with his absence from the 1891 photograph (fig. 21 on p. 158), have been taken to mean that he also did not personally conduct the Marine Band during any of its recording sessions. While there is no reason to doubt the veracity of Sousa's testimony, it is worth bearing in mind that he gave it as part of a larger effort to reform American copyright to his own benefit. It is thus impossible to know whether his later professed distaste for the phonograph was already in place by the early 1890s or whether it prevented him from leading any Marine Band recording sessions.

Sousa's efforts to bring about a revision of the copyright law were successful, and on March 4, 1909, a new bill was signed into law granting to composers the exclusive right to control their music. As a reward for his service, Sousa was made an officer in the newly formed American Society of Composers, Authors, and Publishers. The efforts at recording the Marine Band two decades earlier had been successful as well, whether or not Sousa was actually present or even approved. Columbia frequently featured the Marine Band in its catalogs and launched what was effectively the first advertising campaign on behalf of a particular recording ensemble. Just as *National, Patriotic, and Typical Airs of All Lands* solidified Sousa's reputation as America's national musician, in October 1891 Columbia focused on the Marine Band's connection to the federal government: "The music of the WORLD-RENOWNED UNITED STATES MARINE BAND, which plays at the WHITE HOUSE for President Harrison, and has played for his predecessors, is not, and will never be, the cheapest band music, although our prices are very reasonable. You do not want the cheapest. You want the very best and most attractive music that money will buy. . . . And for reproduction IN THE HOME, what can be more delightful than to hear the same band that plays for the President?" The company had been even more direct in May of that year: "*YOU AND PRESIDENT HARRISON*

. . . may enjoy together the world renowned U.S. Marine Band if you have a phonograph."[39]

Given the advertisements, it is hardly surprising that newspapers across the country ran stories on the new technology, and while the recordings may not have been easily available, by 1890 the notion that America had a national band—and national bandmaster—was beginning to grow, as made clear by one Omaha reporter:

> [The Marine Band] now discoursed not alone to officials or to the great public in open air concerts, but is also heard in the parlors of many Washington residents through the agency of the latest addition to a modern home and office life, the phonograph. . . . The average citizen of Washington can thus at any moment produce in his own home for the gratification of his family or friends the full Marine band. . . . These reproductions of the renditions of the Marine band are so complete in their detail that it needs but a faint stretch of the imagination of the listener to believe himself in the presence of the great Sousa and his red-coated artists and their costly silver and silver-toned instruments.[40]

MUSIC FOR WASHINGTON

As the article from Omaha suggests, interest in the Marine Band may have been spreading, but in the nation's imagination, it and its leader remained attached to the capital city. Indeed, Sousa continued to act as Washington's most important composer throughout the late 1880s, a composer whose music was becoming more and more closely associated with the city's military and official life. As the decade came to a close, however, a handful of his pieces began to circulate beyond the capital.

Sousa later recalled that while walking through Philadelphia sometime around 1887, he heard a hand organist playing a familiar melody. On further inspection the tune proved to be his own march "The Gladiator," which he had written the year before and dedicated to the editor of the *Boston Traveler*, Charles F. Towle. Sousa's compositions had long been available in printed form, and there are occasional reports of performances in other cities. In 1885, for example, a Philadelphia band played his march "Mother Hubbard." But such appearances outside of Washington were still rare, and Sousa was both surprised and ecstatic to hear "The Gladiator" away from home: "I was exultant. My music had made enough of a hit to be played on a street organ. At last I felt that it had struck a popular chord."[41]

It is not known for what occasion Sousa wrote "The Gladiator," but several of his marches from the mid-1880s seem to have been inspired by his membership in the Society of Freemasons. Many of the Marine Band's musicians—including Sousa's father—were Masons, and the composer joined Hiram Lodge No. 10 in July 1881. In January 1888, shortly after being knighted in the Columbia Commandery No. 2, Knights Templar, Sousa wrote "The Crusader." The sheet music for this march, with its band of knights and white cross, makes its Masonic connections quite clear (fig. 22). In 1889 Sousa borrowed from "Here's Your Health, Sir!," an original march in *The Trumpet and Drum*, to complete "The Thunderer," a march dedicated to the Columbia Commandery and likely performed at a conclave in October of that year. Several other marches, because of their titles, rousing minor-key sections, or decorative sheet music, suggest Masonic connections as well, including "The Occidental" (1887) and "The Picadore" (1889). The Society of Freemasons would remain important to Sousa throughout his career, and a year after joining the Shriners in 1922 he wrote a march for that organization: "Nobles of the Mystic Shrine."[42]

The most famous of Sousa's works to be dedicated to a local institution was written shortly after Benjamin Harrison's inauguration in March 1889. On April 7, one of the city's many newspapers announced the formation of an Amateur Authors' Association for the purpose of "encouraging the pupils of the Washington public schools in the directions of their studies," and students were invited to submit essays for a competition. Frank Hatton, editor of the *Washington Post*, happened to meet Sousa on the street shortly before the awards were to be announced and asked him to compose a new march in honor of the competition. Sousa complied and wrote "The Washington Post," dedicating it to Hatton and his partner Beriah Wilkins.[43]

According to press accounts, the Marine Band performed Sousa's new march at the award ceremony, which was held on the Smithsonian grounds on June 15, 1889. The holograph score, however, is problematically dated July 3, three weeks after the piece's premiere. Sousa—still a relatively little-known figure—was now in the habit of selling his marches outright to the Philadelphia publisher Harry Coleman, often for as little as $35. It is possible that Sousa, not needing a score from which to conduct his own composition, completed one only to aid in the piece's later publication.[44]

There is, however, a more likely scenario. Since marches were generally published without full scores, Sousa was required by Coleman to submit parts. His holograph scores were thus designed for his own use in completing the parts needed for both a premiere and publication. Given that Sousa's increasing local

Fig. 22. The cover of the piano edition of "The Crusader." Library of Congress, Washington, D.C.

fame resulted in a great many requests for new marches, he may have simply substituted an already written work on the Smithsonian grounds and finished the real "Washington Post" several weeks later. Such casual titling can be found throughout Sousa's career. In 1884, for example, he had been asked to provide a march for the unveiling of a bronze statue depicting Chief Justice John Marshall. Press accounts note that the Marine Band rendered a march "composed for the occasion by Prof. Sousa" titled "The Jurist's." No such work survives, and Sousa never mentions the piece, suggesting that he likely recycled music from some other request. His career had already seen such flexible dedications (the marches written for Georgetown College and the Capital Bicycle Club), and there would be others, such as "Foshay Tower Washington Memorial" (1929) and "Kansas Wildcats" (1931).[45]

Whatever its genesis, "The Washington Post" was submitted for copyright in August 1889 and quickly entered the Marine Band's regular repertoire, appearing on a Columbia recording no later than October 1. According to the bandmaster, an association of dancing instructors heard the piece and adopted it "to introduce their new dance, 'the two-step.'" No doubt because it could travel so successfully as dance music, the march quickly became one of Sousa's most popular pieces (indeed, by the early 1890s new works meant to accompany the two-step were published as Washington Posts). Sousa later recalled that on entering an Italian music store and inquiring after the march, the shopkeeper presented an edition by one Giovanni Filipo Sousa. When the composer revealed his identity, "the Venetian was so overcome that he insisted on retailing the pirated copy of the march at cost price, and the respect with which he bowed us out of the shop would have done honor to his emperor." In short, despite being sold to Harry Coleman for just $35, the march provided Sousa "a small fortune in reputation."[46]

By the late 1880s Sousa was so well known as a Washington composer that he was frequently sought out by local organizations. Like later Marine Band leaders, he served as a limited member of the Gridiron Club, an association of Washington-based journalists. For them he composed an ode to wine, women, and music titled "Do We? We Do." Sousa's twelve-bar song, published by the Washington firm of John F. Ellis, is little more than a fraternity chant, but it made quite a hit when performed as part of the club's satirical dinner in 1889. Sousa would return to the organization in 1926 with his march "The Gridiron Club."[47]

Like many American cities, the capital was once home to a large number of military drill teams, the most active of which was the National Rifles. This group had been involved in *The Smugglers*, and in February 1882 it made

Sousa an honorary member. The city's various militia units were reorganized in 1887, and the cadet corps of the National Rifles was disbanded. The National Fencibles was formed in its place, and in 1888 Sousa wrote a piece for the new organization: "The March Past of the National Fencibles," which was published by Harry Coleman in arrangements for piano, orchestra, and band. The piano edition is unusual in that its trio had a text, likely by Sousa himself: "Forward to battle, the trumpet is sounding; 'come if you dare!' we loudly sing / Shoulder to shoulder, with hearts rebounding; onward we march with the Fencibles swing." The march appeared on a Marine Band program on July 21, 1888, in what was likely its premiere.[48]

The popularity of this march prompted the drill team at Washington's Central High School to request a similar piece. As Sousa explained: "While I was conductor of the United States Marine Band I composed and dedicated certain marches to organizations. When my *National Fencibles* became immensely popular, the high school boys of that date came to me and asked if I would write a march for them, adding, 'and be sure to make it as good as the *National Fencibles*.'" The result was "The High School Cadets," which he completed in February 1890. On May 8, he finished another march for a drill team, this one named for his prospective childhood patron: "The March Past of the Corcoran Cadets." Once again he supplied what appears to be an original trio lyric: "Hark, hear the battle cry, onward, soldier daring! Forward to do or die, naught for danger caring / List, tis the bugle's ring, conquest will glory bring; then march with the Corc'ran swing, onward soldier daring!"[49]

The texts to Sousa's militia marches celebrate the glories of battle for men too young to have served in the Civil War. There were, however, three works from this period with more direct military connections. In 1886 Sousa completed "The Rifle Regiment," a march written in honor of the Third Infantry, the oldest in the United States Army. In 1887 he wrote a "medley in marchform" titled "The Blending of the Blue and the Gray." This piece contains Civil War songs from both the North and the South and is dedicated to "the Maryland Line on their return to Virginia twenty-six years after (1861–1887)." The 1890 song "Nail the Flag to the Mast" sets a text by the doctor and pension office clerk William Russell Frisbie, a frequent contributor of poetry to the *Washington Post*. The song seems never to have been successful, but Sousa did recycle a portion of the melody for his 1914 march "Columbia's Pride." It is unclear just why he wrote these pieces, but their borrowed materials, lyric content, and dedications suggest that they may have been meant for commemorative events.[50]

There were, of course, other pieces written during the late 1880s whose histories and connections are less clear. These works include two marches based on borrowed material. "Ben Bolt," published by Harry Coleman in 1888, uses several popular songs, as does the unpublished march "The Quilting Party." It was also during the Harrison administration, on January 21, 1887, that the Sousas' third and last child, Helen, was born.[51]

A GROWING FAME

The election of the New York banker Levi P. Morton to the vice presidency prompted the visionary patron of music Jeannette Thurber to take a new interest in the capital's musical life. In March 1890, she arranged for a Grand American Composers' Concert at Lincoln Hall, an event that featured works by Arthur Foote, Edward MacDowell, John Knowles Paine, Arthur Whiting, George W. Chadwick, and Dudley Buck. Nowhere on the program was the name of Washington's favorite local musician. This slight was not left overlooked by Sousa's friend Major George Porter Houston, who had served as commanding officer at the marine barracks. It was Houston who showed the bandleader a press report that not only ignored Sousa as a composer but also relegated the Marine Band to a back room at the postconcert reception: "In the smoking room, concealed behind tall palms and portieres, Sousa's Marine Band played popular airs in violent contrast to the music that had been heard earlier in the evening." This incident led to one of Sousa's first public letters, and in it he corrected the record:

> It behooves me to gently remind you that in your highly-interesting account of the "Grand American Composers' Concert"—to quote the billboards—a slight error appears. . . . The corrections I desire to make are:
>
> First. The Marine Band was not concealed behind tall palms and portieres in the smoking-room.
>
> Second. The Marine Band did not play popular airs in violent contrast to the music heard earlier in the evening.
>
> Third. The Marine Band was not present.
>
> Outside of these slight inaccuracies, the rest of the paragraph is substantially correct.[52]

It is clear that Sousa was unhappy with his limited reputation, and just a few months later the *Washington Star* ran a profile of the bandleader: "Since taking charge of the band he has developed great talent as a musical composer, among his works being the pretty operas: *The Wolf, Désirée, Queen of Hearts,*

Katherine, The Smugglers, and others equally popular. A wooden-legged man could keep step to the marches he has written that have traversed the globe about as fast as sound can go." Given that the journalist could not possibly have known Sousa's unpublished and unproduced *The Wolf* or *Katherine*, it seems certain that the article was, at least in part, fed to the reporter by the composer. It thus reveals something that should by now be clear about the thirty-six-year-old musician. In listing only his operettas, Sousa reaffirmed his primary interest in theatrical music, but he could not claim that these works had begun to traverse the globe. Rather, he recognized that he was now viewed primarily as a composer of marches: it was they that could circulate most easily as sheet music, could appear most readily on Columbia recordings, and could be most easily reconciled with his position as a government musician and expert on patriotic music.[53]

Sousa's early marches had been published only in piano editions, but in 1885 Harry Coleman began to issue Sousa's back catalog for band. By 1886 new marches were regularly being printed for both piano and band (and often for small orchestra and other ensembles). "The High School Cadets" of 1890 appeared in arrangements for piano solo, piano four hands, mandolin and piano, banjo and piano, mandolin and guitar, guitar solo, zither solo, zither duet, zither trio, banjo solo or duet, and piano six hands. The in-house preparation of such editions suggests something of the new market potential for Sousa's works, and such variety would become standard practice in the printing of his music by the early 1890s. It was probably in advertising such publications that Coleman first issued an announcement remembered by the mature Sousa: "You can hear his music from the Atlantic to the Pacific, from the St. Lawrence to the Gulf Stream. The March King reigns supreme!" It would take some time for this nickname to catch on, but by the late 1880s—whether he liked it or not—Sousa's transformation from theater musician to March King was well under way.[54]

With a growing reputation and improved band, Sousa naturally wanted to venture beyond the capital region. He had already had the opportunity to do so on a handful of occasions: President Garfield's 1881 funeral in Cleveland, the 1882 concerts in Cape May, and the 1886 unveiling of the Statue of Liberty. But the marine commandant and secretary of the navy generally disapproved of such excursions, which continued to be quite rare in the latter part of the decade. Sometimes the leadership was simply concerned about the band's ability to handle its duties both at home and on the road. In 1888, for example, a Philadelphia militia requested the ensemble's presence at a celebratory ball, but the secretary declined the invitation: "I think that the request should not be granted. There is duty enough at Washington, and establishing this precedent would give us great trouble." At other times money was at stake, and the commandant would insist that trips be taken only "*without cost* to the Government." The needed funding was rarely forthcoming.[55]

Such military objections were matched by concerns among civilian ensembles. As marines, Sousa's musicians had guaranteed government salaries and might therefore be able to underbid civilian players. A group of Philadelphia musicians was particularly insistent that a federal band not be allowed to take business away from organizations that were without government support. Sousa, who desperately wanted to travel, dismissed the argument and insisted that the National League of Musicians simply wanted "to place a stigma on the members of the musical profession who are employed by the government. A disinterested person would imagine that it is their wish that the liberties guaranteed us as citizens should be curtailed because we serve Uncle Sam in a musical capacity. It smells suspiciously like an attempt to build a Chinese wall around the nation's music-makers, so that no sound shall escape for the benefit of a music-hungry public."[56]

Despite such challenges, in the late 1880s Sousa was able to manage several short excursions, such as the 1889 trip to Fayetteville. The most important of his engagements away from Washington, however, began in 1888 when the Marine Band was invited to take part in Hannah Harris's Star Course at the Academy of Music in Philadelphia. Reviews of the performances given over the course of the next few years reveal just how rapidly Sousa's reputation was changing.

The Star Course season generally featured a variety of entertainments, and the Marine Band concert of March 24, 1888, was sandwiched between a French satirist and a lecture on Apache culture. The first performance does not seem to have merited a review in the Philadelphia papers, but it must have interested audiences because the band was invited to return on April 13, 1889. The ensemble then gave a series of three concerts for the 1889–90 season. The first, on October 19, received several brief notices in which Sousa was called "a good musician" and his program "generally well selected." The December 17 performance faired little better: the band was criticized for being too loud, and its rendering of Mendelssohn's *Die Hebriden* was said to contain "noisy and impetuous crescendos" that "might not have troubled the stormy dwellers of the Hebrides, but they would have certainly frightened the composer."[57]

Figs. 23–25. Three views of Sousa's Marine Band: standing at the marine barracks (ca. 1887), in an advertising poster (1889), and onstage at Cape May (1891). "The President's Own" United States Marine Band, Washington, D.C.

Prior to their third concert, which took place on April 19, 1890, the band participated in the twenty-fifth anniversary meeting of the Loyal Legion on April 15 and 16. This time, perhaps because of the event's military connection, the press took notice and proved to be especially interested in an otherwise unknown Sousa work called *An Episode in a Soldier's Life*. Given the audience—men who well remembered the Civil War—this descriptive piece was an enormous hit. In it Sousa borrowed from war-era popular songs, including "The Vacant Chair" and "Marching Through Georgia," as well as bugle calls to depict "a surprise, the battle, the return to camp after the engagement, [and] the roll-call," all of which were "faithfully portrayed in music's imaginative tongue." He also recycled material from his 1885 operetta *The Queen of Hearts* to create a march named in honor of his hosts: "The Loyal Legion." The Marine Band combined this trip with its third Star Course concert of the season, and this time the reception was a bit friendlier. The performance "indicated all the excellences and all the demerits of Mr. Sousa's band," and despite repeated complaints about volume, the paper was willing to admit that "few better military band concerts have been heard here."[58]

Figs. 23–25 (*continued*)

Figs. 23–25 (*continued*)

A benefit was held for the West Penn Hospital in Pittsburgh in June 1890. Since one of the sponsors was the widow of the vice presidential candidate John Logan, Sousa was able to secure permission for the band to take part in the celebrations. Here, in a city that had not before heard his ensemble, the press was ecstatic. Reviews indicate, however, that interest lay as much in the idea of a national band as in Sousa's music: "The great United States Marine band, with its blue and red uniforms, its big horns and general air of distinction, arrived in the city" and was "accorded a reception in perfect keeping with their position as military band at the capital of the United States."[59]

Sousa later wrote that he had been warned of the highbrow tastes that permeated Pittsburgh and so had programmed the best works of Brahms, Bach, Wagner, and Strauss. Expecting wild applause after the first number (the overture to Rossini's *William Tell*), Sousa turned to the audience but was greeted with only silence. After several repetitions of this cold reception, the bandmaster ordered his men to pull up "Annie Rooney," and suddenly "strong men wept with delight, husbands threw their arms about their astonished wives, and the rest of the evening was, without question, Annie Rooney's!" This story might be taken for an exaggeration had it not been substantially confirmed by the press, one paper noting that the audience was so delighted to hear "Annie Rooney" just as the First Lady "hears it every time the band plays at the white house . . . that they had to have 'Annie' over again."[60]

Here, then, were Sousa's great selling points: the powerful reputation that the president's band carried even before its arrival in town, and Sousa's willingness to please his audience no matter their musical preferences. When he returned to Philadelphia for three concerts during the 1890–91 season, he added to this mix his remarkable skill for drama. At some point in the late 1880s or in early 1890 he had strung together a series of popular songs—mostly about the pleasures of alcohol—to create an unpublished descriptive humoresque. The first known performance of "The Stag Party" came on October 18, 1890, at a Star Course concert. According to the program, "A Rhinelander hums a tune he loves; an American thinks 'Home Sweet Home' will fit the same harmony; a Scotsman chimes in with 'Comin' Thro' the Rye,' bagpipe and all, while the representatives of the Clover Club insist that there is 'One More Bottle.' The guests join hands and sing 'Auld Lang Syne,' they are interrupted by a still, small voice, a convivial scion of the Bassoon family murmurs something about being his sweetheart."[61]

Reviews made little of Sousa's new piece, but the concert was a hit, and the Marine Band was proclaimed "the sole evidence of any artistic sense that the National Government has ever exhibited." The Star Course's manager, Hannah Harris, must have sensed Sousa's storytelling skills, and she sent him a suggestion: "I know how easily and how charmingly you adapt any fancy to music, and will you think of this suggestion? It is that you prepare a piece of music and call it *The Chariot Race from Ben Hur*. No doubt you are familiar with the spirited description, and if you are not, a single reading will give you the inspiration, I am sure. . . . There is opportunity for a grand climax, and anything with the name of Ben Hur draws." Sousa, of course, had already written several descriptive works for band, but "The Chariot Race" was his first such piece not to be based on borrowed material. It was completed on November 19, 1890, and played for a select group of Washington musicians on December 12. The public premiere came at the Academy of Music the following evening, where Philadelphia concertgoers were given detailed program notes drawn mostly from General Lew Wallace's immensely successful 1880 novel *Ben Hur: A Tale of the Christ*.[62]

The five-minute rendering begins by depicting Wallace's line "the trumpeters blew a call at which the absentees rushed back to their places" with a solo cornet fanfare. The ensemble's lower voices then enter with a *pianissimo* sextuplet figure depicting the horses in their stalls, "for all the time the tramping of eager horses and the voices of the drivers scarcely less eager, were heard behind the stalls, so that one might not look away an instant from the gaping doors." The fanfare then returns to announce the race's start. The remainder of the work is a musical bolt down the track, dominated by rushing sixteenth notes, militaristic fanfares, and percussive effects to imitate the hooves of horses and the whips of their riders.[63]

Sousa's efforts met with incredible success, and one Philadelphia paper noted that he had outdone even the king of programmatic composition: "The late Hector Berlioz, a consummate master of orchestration, . . . laid hold of anything in the shape of a musical instrument, in order to produce piquant, bizarre or impressive effects. But Mr. Sousa has gone ahead of Berlioz in that respect in the *Ben-Hur* piece." Another critic simply wrote that the audience liked the piece immensely and "would not be satisfied until it had been played over again, which shows that Mr. Sousa knows just what his audiences want."[64]

When the band returned to the Academy of Music on March 14, 1891, for its final concert of the season, Sousa was, quite simply, a minor celebrity. If Philadelphia's press had shown him a cold shoulder a few years earlier, it was now eager to sing his praises: "The last of the Marine Band Concerts took place at the Academy of Music last evening under the direction of John Philip Sousa, who has brought the organization up to such a high standard of efficiency. . . . The concert was a delightful one and was received enthusiastically by the audience. This closes the season of Marine Band concerts, which has been successful beyond all anticipations. The Marine Band fills an entirely distinct place in music and it is yearly becoming more appreciated."[65]

During the 1870s and early 1880s, John Philip Sousa blended into a crowd of American song, march, and dance composers. But during his decade-long career as leader of the United States Marine Band, a local reputation slowly transformed into a national fame. Press notices of the band in Philadelphia between 1888 and 1891 make this change apparent. While the band's increasingly positive reviews were, no doubt, due in large part to the men's careful playing and their leader's skillful conducting, the ensemble must have also benefited from its growing reputation as the national band, aided in no small part by *National, Patriotic, and Typical Airs of All Lands* and a growing catalog of recordings. Simply put, the more audiences had heard of the Marine Band, the more eager they became to actually listen to the ensemble.

In many ways the March King was educated in Washington, D.C., but it was Philadelphia that first presented him to audiences. In the capital Sousa was a local son, a talented and hardworking musician, but one not much different in kind from the dozens of other musical men who lived in and around the Navy Yard. For his Academy of Music concerts, however, Sousa began to create a character that could entice and please audiences. Thus, it is in Philadelphia that one can find hints of the March King to come. The later Sousa Band would almost always tour with female violin and soprano soloists. For the Philadelphia concerts, in addition to featuring his own men—including the cornetist Walter F. Smith, the flutist Henry Jaeger, and the clarinetist Felix Jardella—Sousa also toured with singers. In October 1889, Mrs. Theodore Toedt was featured in selections by Ambroise Thomas and Robert Schumann. The next year Sousa brought along Josephine Esputa-Daly, who sang works by Schubert and Luigi Denza. Documents from Philadelphia concerts also reflect Sousa's habits of programming, which allowed him to move happily between Wagner and popular songs and from Rossini to patriotic numbers. Encores were frequent, and newspapers often noted that the printed programs were short enough to allow for the insertion of favorite tunes and the replaying of successful numbers. When coupled with new dramatic and descriptive works, such as "The Chariot Race," these traits of Sousa's programming would become a hallmark of the March King's success. Marketing these skills to a national audience, however, would require Sousa to break free of the capital city, and for that he needed a professional manager.

CHAPTER EIGHT

Making the Sousa Band

EDUARD STRAUSS WAS BUSILY PREPARING for a tour of the New World in the spring of 1890. He had largely taken over the family dynasty and was now looking to capitalize on the popularity of his last name in the United States. A transatlantic excursion was no minor undertaking, but Strauss had been convinced to make the journey by a former Minnesota secretary of state named David Blakely. As one-time proprietor of the St. Paul *Pioneer Press*, the Minneapolis *Tribune*, and the Chicago *Evening Post*, as well as founder of a successful Chicago printing company, Blakely had already proved that he had the promotional skills needed to organize large-scale public events. His interest in music had spurred him to establish the Minneapolis Philharmonic Society, and in 1883 Blakely had served as the local manager for a visit by Theodore Thomas. In the wake of these successes, this politician-printer-impresario established an office in New York from which he could more effectively oversee his growing interests as a concert manager.

The Strauss tour presented Blakely with an unusual problem. Under normal circumstances, touring artists would have been immune from the regulations that limited the activities of foreign contract workers while in the United States. Given the Strauss orchestra's profile—and the potential competition its players might impose on New York musicians—some labor leaders argued against the legality of its visit. This position required some gymnastics, and so the New York unions suggested that Strauss's players were more craftsmen than artists, and thus subject to work restrictions while in the country. Such opposition to the visit led the Port Collector in New York to question his own authority to even allow the orchestra into the country.

Blakely worked quickly to contact potential signatories who would attest to the artistic value of the Strauss ensemble, and on March 2 he was able to publish endorsements from such figures as William Tecumseh Sherman, the writer George William Curtis, and the former interior secretary Carl Schurz.

Fig. 26. Sousa's manager, David Blakely, ca. 1893. Author's collection.

It would, of course, prove helpful to have the nation's highest-profile musicians on board, and so Blakely turned to the piano manufacturer William Steinway; the general manager of the Metropolitan Opera House, Edmund Stanton; and the bandleader Patrick Gilmore. On April 19 Blakely sought to add another name to his list of advocates, and he wrote to the leader of the United States Marine Band in Washington: "I have a number of splendid endorsements from such leaders as Anton Seidl, Dudley Buck, and others well known throughout the country, and I should be glad if you will add your testimony to that of the others."[1]

Blakely's efforts to promote Strauss in the United States were successful, but his reward would be much larger than a single tour by a foreign orchestra. In 1889 and 1890 his most important attraction was none other than America's most celebrated bandmaster, Patrick Gilmore. But at the start of the new decade, Gilmore was considering either a well-earned retirement or a dramatic curtailing of his touring schedule. The departure of his band would leave a significant hole on Blakely's roster, and as rumors of the Irish Orpheus's exit spread, applications to replace him flooded into Blakely's New York office. Inquiries came from such luminaries as the cornetist Alessandro Liberati and the leader of the Elgin Watch Factory Band, Joseph Hecker, but the most passionate plea came from the famed cornetist Jules Levy: "If Gilmore is soon to retire, as I hear he intends doing, why should you not take hold of *me* and *make me*, as you have *him*. I will agree to all reasonable proposals, and you shall be allowed to bind me to an ironclad contract. . . . With your assistance and wonderful management I can become the first Bandmaster in the Universe, but never under any other manager, 'No a thousand times No.'"[2]

Despite such offers, Blakely already had other ideas. Levy, Liberati, and Hecker were well-established musicians who could extract significant sums of money from any manager willing to promote them. Blakely, however, was looking to mold a bandmaster, not merely represent one. Through publications, sheet music, and recordings, he had become aware of a musician residing in the national capital: a conductor, composer, and mere public servant whose salary could be easily matched, and one whose growing fame—with the right guidance—just might prove to be more profitable even than Gilmore's.

MARKETING THE NATIONAL BAND

John Philip Sousa could not simply be snatched away from Washington. His job may have been restrictive, but it was stable and safe, with none of the financial uncertainties that came from civilian touring. He was also a military musician, and though nineteenth-century enlistments were considerably more flexible than their modern counterparts, Sousa was still tied to the federal government. Most important, Blakely's ambitions were not without risk. The manager was looking to build a touring attraction, and Sousa was untested before a national audience. So instead of asking the Marine Band leader to leave his post, the manager suggested a less drastic alternative: "Will you inform me if you have as yet learned whether you could make a tour with your band or not?"[3]

The modern Marine Band makes a tour each fall in which it gives free public concerts in rotating geographic regions across the United States. Blakely, however, was not looking to spread the glory of the Marine Corps; his aim was—quite simply—profit. Given the commandant's previous opposition to excursions by the band, Blakely must have known that a request to borrow the ensemble for a capitalistic enterprise was sure to fail. He thus couched his plans in terms more appealing to the Corps:

> It is impossible for more than a very limited number of the people of the nation to hear the national band in Washington, and since the Marine Band has reached its present high state of excellence, and enjoys a more than national reputation, would it not be possible for me to secure the services of yourself and the band for a tour of from four to six weeks, in order that the principal cities may be visited, and this desire on the part of the public satisfied? It would seem to me that the people might be served in this matter, and the public service thereby actually advanced, and that it would not be at all unwise for the authorities to permit the band to make such a tour in the interests of first-class music in this country.[4]

There was no precedent for what Blakely was asking, and the manager knew that it would take more than a single letter to secure the secretary's blessing. As luck would have it, one of Blakely's former Minneapolis business partners was none other than the sitting assistant secretary of the treasury, Alvred B. Nettleton. Blakely wrote to the official in January 1891 and made his ambitions abundantly clear: "I have made an application to take out the Marine Band for a month's tour. The people outside of Washington have never heard the band, and as they pay the taxes, it seems to me they ought to have the privilege of paying a good price for tickets to listen to the Nation's Orchestra. . . . What I write for is to inquire whether you could do me the good turn to say a word to Secretary Tracy." Nettleton immediately endorsed his friend's proposal.[5]

Eager to undertake his first national tour, Sousa also worked to grease the wheels. After speaking to the First Lady, he discovered that Benjamin Harrison was sympathetic to the enterprise. Sousa later recalled the president's words: "I was thinking myself of going out of town, and . . . it would be tough on Washington if both of us were away at the same time. I have thought it over, and I believe the country would rather hear you, than see me; so you have my permission to go." Authorization for the Marine Band's first national tour had been granted.[6]

When the modern Marine Band makes its annual tours, it travels as a representative of the Marine Corps, but the 1891 outing was to be a commercial enterprise. Every bandsman was granted leave from the military and then personally contracted to Blakely. As a result, from April 1 to May 3, 1891, the band functioned as a civilian ensemble (although its players continued to wear their military uniforms and were advertised as the national band). Performances would not be free, nor would they be spread evenly across the country. Venues were instead selected on the basis of the band's likely draw, and ticket prices were negotiated with local managers. This was to be a commercial enterprise with David Blakely at the helm.

Despite Blakely's skills, the effort was not free of risk. In 1891 the Marine Band leader was familiar to many Americans as a composer of popular marches, the leader of a recording ensemble, and a scholar of national anthems, but he was hardly a celebrity on the order of Levy, Liberati, or Gilmore. Very few Americans had actually heard the band, and they thus had little reason to think that Sousa could provide an evening's entertainment that was worth the price of admission. Even Blakely had not actually heard the ensemble for some time, as he wrote to Charles W. Johnson, the chief clerk of the United States Senate and one of his local managers in Washington: "Do you think the band will make a hit in the country, and can I extoll them as having no superior as a military band? I have not heard the band for 20 years, and of course can form no opinion of them myself. I shall be glad of your estimate, because I have had no qualified opinion expressed of the band's work except that of Mr. Sousa himself."[7]

Worst of all, Sousa was poorly versed in the mechanics of a national tour. He had traveled as a young man with Milton Nobles, Matt Morgan, and the Philadelphia Church Choir Company. He had also managed to take the Marine Band on a handful of excursions, but they had been rare and always brief. On hearing of the light concert schedule and high sums Sousa had promised his players, Blakely's assistant Howard Pew described his new client's naiveté: Sousa, he wrote, "has not much of a practical idea of a tour. He has based his ideas somewhat on the large prices and great successes of a few single concerts he has given in Philadelphia, Pittsburgh, etc., but with ordinary expense we cannot make the tour a success." After demanding that Sousa lower his salaries and accept some of the financial burden, Blakely expressed his own concern about the tour's prospects, telling Sousa: "Enclosed is an estimate made by Pew of the cost of the Marine Band. I confess that it staggers me."[8]

As Washington's favorite musical son, Sousa's appearances in the capital were always guaranteed success. On the road, however, the bandleader would have no good will on which to draw, and Blakely recognized that a financial victory would require a two-part scheme. First, audiences would need to be wooed to concerts, and this would happen not with promises of seeing Sousa but with the enticement of hearing the Marine Band, the entertainer of presidents. Frederick Phinney, the leader of the Iowa State Band, understood this element of Blakely's enterprise: though Sousa "has not the soloists that Gilmore has he is a good drawing card on account of being the government band of the U.S. I am pleased you are going to run them because I know you will make a great amount of money for you both." Every element of the tour—from advertising to program booklets—would focus on the Marine Band's capital connections. Enticing local theater managers to engage the ensemble, Pew promised programs decorated with images of "Washington views, the Band on the street, historical matters, fine picture[s] of Sousa and the singer, and just the kind of matter that will stir up the patriotism of everybody" (fig. 27). Once at the concert, audiences would be reminded that the organization was both "the pet of the Presidential household" and the "pride and charm of official life in Washington."[9]

Lured with promises of a presidential entertainment, the public would expect the appropriate music, and here the second part of Blakely's scheme came into play. At home Sousa was given free rein to entertain his audiences, but his new management made clear just who was now in charge. In preparing for a meeting between the bandmaster and his new manager, Pew reminded Sousa: "Mr. Blakely understands the public thoroughly, so I think it will be well to bring along your items of programme so that he can help you arrange here." The factors for success were plain: familiar numbers, new music, Sousa's own descriptive works, and patriotic tunes. Pew continued, "I think the *Rienzi* Overture will be a good one, and hope you will wind up the programme with your *Ben Hur* number. We must bring in a large amount of patriotic music. This will be what the public will expect. Your band can no doubt open her eyes some in this line."[10]

Sousa and Blakely crafted two principal programs, one each for matinee and evening concerts. A performance typically began with an overture, either Mendelssohn's *Son and Stranger* or Wagner's *Rienzi*, and ended with a patriotic song, either "Hail! Columbia" or "The Star-Spangled Banner." In between were other orchestral transcriptions such as the first movement of Schubert's "Unfinished Symphony," the overture to Rossini's *William Tell*, or excerpts from Berlioz's *Damnation of Faust*, Bizet's *Pearl Fishers*, or Delibes's

Fig. 27. The cover of a program from the Marine Band's 1891 tour, featuring the band on parade as well as views of the Capitol and the White House. "The President's Own" United States Marine Band, Washington, D.C.

Fig. 28. Promotional photograph of the Marine Band, probably for the 1891 tour. "The President's Own" United States Marine Band, Washington, D.C.

Sylvia. One of Sousa's longer works, either "The Chariot Race" or "The Stag Party," was always included, as were featured numbers for members of the band and the guest soprano soloist, Marie Decca. As he had for the Marine Band's Philadelphia concerts, Sousa kept the printed program brief so that pieces could be repeated or followed by encores.

Permission for the tour had not been secured until the end of January 1891, and the band would be at Blakely's disposal only during the month of April. As a result, the manager's team had very little time to plan a route, finalize contracts, and distribute promotional materials. Given the rushed planning and relatively modest reputation of the ensemble, Blakely avoided direct competition with more established organizations and booked the band into relatively modest cities (table 1). The tour began on April 1 in Bridgeport, Connecticut. The band then traveled north through Massachusetts and Rhode Island. On April 6 it headed west to present a concert in Albany, where it also visited the capitol to serenade Governor David Hill. After winding through New York, it traveled to Ohio and Michigan before arriving in Chicago for a series of three concerts. The ensemble then continued its journey west, stopping in Iowa and Nebraska. A performance in Springfield allowed the band to visit the Lincoln homestead before continuing through Indiana,

Table 1. Marine Band tour, 1891

Apr. 1 (Wed.)	Bridgeport, Conn.	Apr. 16 (Thu.)	Grand Rapids, Mich.
	New Haven, Conn.	Apr. 17 (Fri.)	Chicago, Ill.
Apr. 2 (Thu.)	Worcester, Mass. (× 2)	Apr. 18 (Sat.)	Chicago, Ill. (× 2)
Apr. 3 (Fri.)	Boston, Mass.	Apr. 20 (Mon.)	Sioux City, Iowa
Apr. 4 (Sat.)	Providence, R.I.	Apr. 21 (Tue.)	Lincoln, Neb.
Apr. 5 (Sun.)	Boston, Mass.	Apr. 22 (Wed.)	Omaha, Neb. (× 2)
Apr. 6 (Mon.)	Albany, N.Y.	Apr. 23 (Thu.)	Des Moines, Iowa (× 2)
Apr. 7 (Tue.)	Poughkeepsie, N.Y.	Apr. 24 (Fri.)	Quincy, Ill.
Apr. 8 (Wed.)	Rochester, N.Y. (× 2)	Apr. 25 (Sat.)	Springfield, Ill.
Apr. 9 (Thu.)	Buffalo, N.Y.		Decatur, Ill.
Apr. 10 (Fri.)	Akron, Ohio	Apr. 27 (Mon.)	Indianapolis, Ind. (× 2)
Apr. 11 (Sat.)	Cleveland, Ohio (× 2)	Apr. 28 (Tue.)	Louisville, Ky.
Apr. 12 (Sun.)	Detroit, Mich.	Apr. 29 (Wed.)	Cincinnati, Ohio
Apr. 13 (Mon.)	Lansing, Mich.	Apr. 30 (Thu.)	Columbus, Ohio (× 2)
Apr. 14 (Tue.)	Jackson, Mich.	May 1 (Fri.)	Zanesville, Ohio
Apr. 15 (Wed.)	Battle Creek, Mich.	May 2 (Sat.)	Pittsburgh, Pa. (× 2)
	Kalamazoo, Mich.	May 4 (Mon.)	Washington, D.C.

Kentucky, and Ohio. It played twice in Pittsburgh—where it was joined by three hundred schoolchildren in patriotic songs—and on May 4 it returned to Washington and gave a homecoming concert in Lincoln Hall. All told, the Marine Band's first tour consisted of forty-three concerts, played in thirty-two different cities over the course of just thirty-four days.

Along the way, Blakely's team worked overtime to advertise the band and feed stories to the local press. Despite some complaints about the group's volume and intonation—especially during the orchestral transcriptions—reviews were generally quite positive. One Chicago critic noted that "the playing of the band, so far as accuracy of note and purity of tone are concerned, is so nearly faultless, that it is virtually the perfection of band music." Sousa's theatrical skills were also on full display, and an "excruciatingly funny performance" of Charles Godfrey's *The Contest*—which required band members to compete against one another—elicited "peals of laughter" and "volleys of applause" while Sousa was described as a "born humorist."[11]

Sticking to his plan, Blakely placed the spotlight most directly on the band itself. Several newspapers ran profiles of Sousa, but most were steered toward stories of the ensemble's history, uniforms, membership, daily routine, and relationship with the president. One reporter noted that all of the musicians "are subjected to the most rigid physical and musical examination and must be over 5 feet 6 inches in hight [*sic*]. The strictest discipline is maintained, and the members all take pride in the military character of their organization."

An Akron paper compared the Marine Band to other touring ensembles and concluded that "the audience felt a more direct, personal interest in the concert . . . because the Marine Band is essentially the great musical organization of the people of this country." These and other reports indicate that Blakely, like the Columbia Phonograph Company, had successfully sold Washington's Marine Band to the American public as its national ensemble.[12]

With such reviews under his belt, Sousa must have been quite pleased, and midway through the tour he demanded that additional performances be scheduled. The band was set to return to Philadelphia's Academy of Music on May 9, but Sousa also wanted a performance in New York. Pew tried to explain that given the short notice, such a concert could not possibly be successful: "My dear Mr. Sousa, New York is the most uncertain and most critical musical centre, in this country—and whether they will turn out to hear your very delightful music, without knowing more about it, remains to be seen." Sousa stood firm, and Blakely's team agreed to add the concert on the understanding that Sousa "share either profit or loss, whichsoever it may be."[13]

Thus the Marine Band ended its first tour with a New York performance on May 10, 1891. The city's newspapers largely ignored the event, but a review in the *Musical Courier* proved Sousa's manager to be correct in his warning: "Why Mr. John Philip Sousa and his band of [the] United States Marine Corps should have given a concert last Sunday night at the Lenox Lyceum is a difficult problem to solve. The music they made was fit for a picnic excursion or a political torchlight procession. They butchered Wagner, Weber, Berlioz and other composers, until the air was as sanguinary as their uniforms."[14]

The lesson must have been clear: Sousa and his band had considerable promise, but the bandmaster still needed the expertise of a professional manager. This point was driven home by J. H. Laine, one of Blakely's assistants, who explained just whose skill had been on display: "I find the Marine Band did not take with the public so well *on advance work*, as Gilmore or Strauss—and you will pardon me for saying it, but it is damn hard work to boom or work up the Marine Band and to take them out on this first tour and come in *even* (*saying nothing about any profit*) is a miracle—the advance work has been *the star*, not the Band."[15]

Despite the disappointment of the reception in New York, once he received his share of the profits, Sousa must have been ecstatic. After deducting the band's pay and various expenses, the two men split the receipts equally, and each walked away with $2,635; this month-long tour had provided the bandmaster with nearly twice his annual military salary. It was clear that with a bit more planning and more careful bookings, another outing could be even more profitable. In his congratulatory note to Sousa, Blakely outlined the promise of a second tour:

> It seems to me that, as a whole, the tour is one, regarding which, you can congratulate yourself. It has certainly redounded greatly to your musical name and fame, and the financial result, ought, I am sure, to please you. A tour of a month, which gives you more money than your hard work for the entire year in your regular employment, would, I think, be considered by anybody, a happy issue. . . . I should like to have you indicate, by note, in return, whether you wish to have me make the next tour with you. In that event, I will have Mr. Pew keep our literary bureau in motion, from this time on.[16]

While Blakely was eager to plan for 1892, Sousa was exhausted: "The tour," he wrote, "was a very trying one, with two concerts a day, luncheons, banquets, civic demonstrations and incessant travel. The drain on my energy and the lack of sufficient sleep finally caused me to break down on my return." Sousa was exaggerating in his recollection of two concerts per day, but there can be little doubt that he found planning and implementing this first tour stressful. On returning home, the Marine Band repeated its tour program at Lincoln Hall on May 15, but Sousa did not take the podium; according to press reports he instead lay in bed, ill from overwork. The post surgeon suggested a vacation, and with their newfound wealth, Sousa and his wife dropped their children off in Atlantic City, boarded the *City of Richmond*, and sailed for Europe on June 3.[17]

As a boy Sousa had declined a European education, and thus his first Atlantic crossing did not occur until he was thirty-six years old; it was hardly pleasant. After just a few days at sea, cotton in the ship's hold caught fire. Another vessel was enlisted as an escort, but when its captain died suddenly, rumors of yellow fever began to spread. Sousa's ship finally arrived in Liverpool on June 15, and the bandmaster ended his first transatlantic voyage by disembarking from a smoldering vessel.[18]

The Sousas spent some time in London and then traveled to Paris to view the Bastille Day parade. The couple went on to Berlin and Bayreuth, where Sousa was able to watch the first act of *Tannhäuser*. The entire trip was, in theory at least, a vacation, but along the way Sousa took the opportunity to examine the military bands of Europe. Returning home two months later—his health much improved—he continued his fight to increase the band's pay and turn his newfound European expertise to his advantage. He used an interview with the *Washington Post* to compare German and French military bands and argued that where players were treated as artists rather than soldiers, bands thrived. The band of the *Garde républicaine* thus stood above all others, while the military ensembles of Germany proved far too noisy. If the U.S. government would simply provide the proper financial backing, he wrote, America could "have a far superior band to anything I heard in Europe." All in all, it is difficult not to wonder if the vacation was planned less for Sousa's health than for the opportunity to observe other bands in action. He would not, of course, achieve his goal of increasing his players' pay, but Sousa was about to put his new knowledge to use and experience his own financial windfall.[19]

SELLING SOUSA

The band continued to give regular concerts in the Washington area, and on October 24 it returned to Philadelphia for the Star Course. Just a few days earlier, Blakely had written to the commandant stressing the successes of the recent tour and asking once again to borrow the band. He wisely omitted any hope for financial reward and instead focused on the many ways another tour could enhance the reputation of the Marine Corps, educate the American people, and promote patriotism. The manager's timing could not have been better as he hinted that such a tour might be an appropriate way for the Marine Corps to contribute to the upcoming celebrations surrounding the four-hundredth anniversary of Christopher Columbus's historic voyage:

> The exceedingly high musical merit of the Marine Band had never been known by the country at large excepting by reputation. On this tour, however, not only was this merit made manifest to the utmost gratification of all, but Mr. Sousa, the conductor, was found to be a musician of the highest order, most amiable in his personal character, and endowed with the many rare essentials of popularity. The fine appearance and conduct of the men throughout the tour, were everywhere commented upon to the immeasurable credit of the discipline of the Marine Corps. . . . I suggest whether the coming spring, it being the anniversary of the discovery by Columbus, would not be a peculiarly appropriate time for a tour by the National Band in commemoration of this great event.[20]

Blakely did not plan to merely repeat the successes of 1891. Sousa was asked to reserve a full seven weeks for the tour, promised Pullman cars to transport the ensemble, and assured that he "would come home, crowned with glory, and loaded with ducats." Blakely planned for the 1892 tour to be "the grandest ever undertaken by any band in America. It shall be a 'Hail Columbia' and 'Star Spangled Banner' all the way from the Potomac to the Golden Gate."[21]

During the previous tour Blakely had worked to promote the Marine Band and draw in audiences with this ensemble of presidents, but now his goal had changed. The manager could never completely control a government organization, so in an effort to woo Sousa away from the Marine Corps, Blakely set out to promote the bandmaster himself. The 1892 advertisements would feature Sousa just as prominently as they did the ensemble, and the conductor was coached about how to appear in publicity photographs. One of Blakely's assistants, Frank Christianer, explained that Sousa should sport an easy and composed bearing, with his left hand between his coat lapels, and avoid any appearance of having his "pictur tuk." Even Patrick Gilmore was enlisted, and while his endorsement focused on the band, credit for success was clearly given to its conductor:

> With such a leader, whose aim is perfection, and with the beauty, the culture, and the brain of the nation at the Capital for his audiences—enough to inspire both him and his men to bring forth the most charming effects of which the divine art of music is capable—is it not to be expected that the Marine Band of Washington should stand *peerless and unrivaled on the American continent?* Go, then, and hear them play when you have an opportunity, and you will doubtless be convinced that Uncle Sam has a band of which the Government and the people ought to feel, and do feel, justly proud.[22]

In planning for the 1892 outing, Blakely was already looking forward to the national celebrations that would commemorate Columbus's arrival in the New World. In the spring of 1890, Chicago had been selected as the site for the World's Columbian Exposition, which would open to the public in the summer of 1893. After a March 19 concert at the Academy of Music in Philadelphia, Blakely placed the Marine Band in Chicago, thus unambiguously tying his ensemble to the Columbian city. The tour opened on March 21 when Marie Decca rejoined the band to begin a series of four concerts. The group then headed west through Missouri, Nebraska, Colorado, Wyoming, and Utah. It arrived in California on April 4 and spent the next thirteen days touring the state before heading to Oregon, Washington, and Montana. Sousa and the band then headed back to Chicago through Minnesota and Wisconsin. The journey home began on May 2, and the band played in Michigan, Ohio, Pennsylvania, and Maryland before finally arriving in the District of

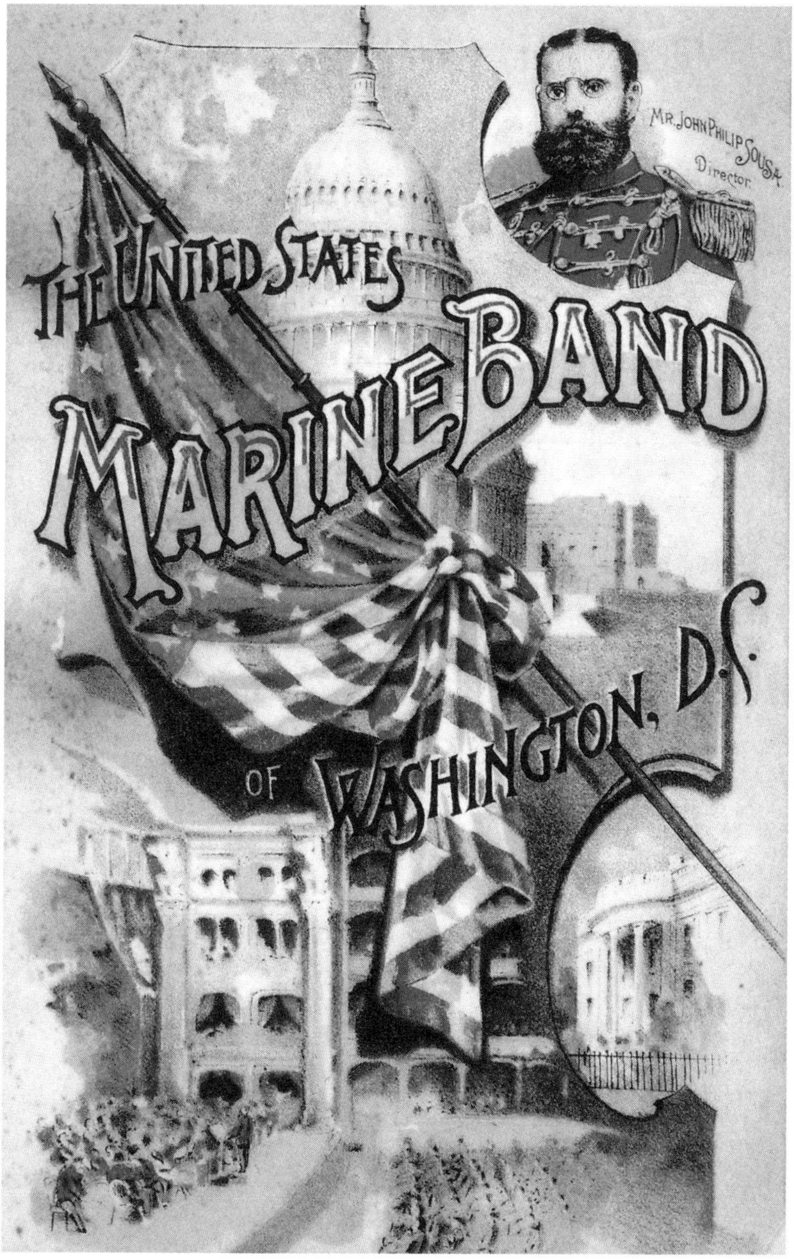

Fig. 29. The cover of a program from the Marine Band's 1892 tour. "The President's Own" United States Marine Band, Washington, D.C.

Fig. 30. The Marine Band at the Palace Hotel, San Francisco, 1892. "The President's Own" United States Marine Band, Washington, D.C.

Columbia on May 9 (table 2). All told, the ensemble played seventy-two concerts in thirty-eight different cities over the course of seven weeks.

Blakely, who had already enjoyed a long career as a newspaper proprietor, knew how to lead the press. Reams of releases were fed to the nation's newspapers, and while they continued to promote the Marine Band as a national ensemble, they always stressed its conductor's lifelong attachment to the capital city, his military bearing, and his accessibility to the common man. One Chicago reporter suggested that Sousa had overcome the immigrant status of his parents and thoroughly integrated himself into American life: "He is an American, born in Washington under the shadow of the capitol dome, and breathed the inspiration of his work from the center of the nation's history. He was brought up there, educated at a public school and is about as near one of us as anybody could be, with his name. John is a fine-looking, military-toned man, with good carriage and unaffected grace." A Los Angeles newspaper went further and published a lengthy profile of the bandleader that stressed Sousa's musical discipline, public integrity, and sexual appeal:

Table 2. Marine Band tour, 1892

Mar. 21 (Mon.)	Chicago, Ill.	Apr. 15 (Fri.)	Stockton, Calif. (× 2)
Mar. 22 (Tue.)	Chicago, Ill.	Apr. 16 (Sat.)	Sacramento, Calif. (× 2)
Mar. 23 (Wed.)	Chicago, Ill. (× 2)	Apr. 18 (Mon.)	Portland, Ore.
Mar. 24 (Thu.)	St. Louis, Mo. (× 2)	Apr. 19 (Tue.)	Portland, Ore. (× 2)
Mar. 25 (Fri.)	Kansas City, Mo. (× 2)	Apr. 20 (Wed.)	Olympia, Wash.
Mar. 26 (Sat.)	Omaha, Neb. (× 2)		Tacoma, Wash.
Mar. 28 (Mon.)	Denver, Colo.	Apr. 21 (Thu.)	Seattle, Wash. (× 2)
Mar. 29 (Tue.)	Denver, Colo. (× 2)	Apr. 22 (Fri.)	Spokane, Wash. (× 2)
Mar. 30 (Wed.)	Colorado Springs, Colo.	Apr. 23 (Sat.)	Helena, Mont. (× 2)
	Pueblo, Colo.	Apr. 25 (Mon.)	Minneapolis, Minn.
Mar. 31 (Thu.)	Cheyenne, Wyo.	Apr. 26 (Tue.)	Minneapolis, Minn.
	Laramie, Wyo.		St. Paul, Minn.
Apr. 1 (Fri.)	Ogden, Utah	Apr. 27 (Wed.)	Duluth, Minn. (× 2)
Apr. 2 (Sat.)	Salt Lake City, Utah (× 2)	Apr. 28 (Thu.)	Oshkosh, Wis.
Apr. 4 (Mon.)	San Jose, Calif.		Fond du Lac, Wis.
Apr. 5 (Tue.)	Oakland, Calif.	Apr. 29 (Fri.)	Chicago, Ill.
Apr. 6 (Wed.)	Oakland, Calif.	Apr. 30 (Sat.)	Chicago, Ill. (× 2)
	San Francisco, Calif.	May 2 (Mon.)	Detroit, Mich.
Apr. 7 (Thu.)	San Francisco, Calif. (× 2)	May 3 (Tue.)	Cleveland, Ohio (× 2)
Apr. 8 (Fri.)	San Francisco, Calif.	May 4 (Wed.)	Warren, Ohio
Apr. 9 (Sat.)	San Francisco, Calif. (× 2)		Youngstown, Ohio
Apr. 11 (Mon.)	San Diego, Calif.	May 5 (Thu.)	Pittsburgh, Pa. (× 2)
Apr. 12 (Tue.)	Los Angeles, Calif.	May 6 (Fri.)	Harrisburg, Pa. (× 2)
Apr. 13 (Wed.)	Los Angeles, Calif. (× 2)	May 7 (Sat.)	Baltimore, Md. (× 2)
Apr. 14 (Thu.)	Fresno, Calif. (× 2)	May 9 (Mon.)	Washington, D.C.

> Mr. Sousa is said to be the most severe and painstaking drillmaster of all the band leaders. He makes the musicians who are enlisted under his care work till they attain a satisfactory rendering of every bar of music they are to play for the public, and the rehearsals at the Marine Corps Music Hall are frequent and thorough. Personally Mr. Sousa is what the ladies call a charming gentleman. He is fine looking, of a dark Southern type. No leader before the public is more conscientious, and he is always rigidly careful not to advertise or promise more to the public than will be carried out to the satisfaction of all.[23]

Since "The Chariot Race" had proved so popular in 1891, Sousa decided to feature another original descriptive work for the 1892 tour. "Sheridan's Ride" was completed on November 14, 1891, and given its premiere by the Marine Band in Philadelphia on December 12. It would serve as the ensemble's featured work during the 1892 tour, and there was little doubt of its success.

"The Chariot Race" may have been based on a well-known novel, but Sheridan's Ride was an event remembered by many in Sousa's audience. After defeating Confederate forces in the Shenandoah Valley, Philip Sheridan left his troops camped at Cedar Creek and traveled to Washington. He was returning when news arrived that Jubal Early had launched a surprise attack. Sheridan raced the remaining twelve miles from Winchester, Virginia, and his sudden appearance on the battlefield rallied the Union troops for a stunning victory on October 19, 1864. Sousa described his motivation for composing the piece: "I thought another descriptive composition, founded on a subject nearer the hearts of the American people, would stand an excellent chance of success."[24]

The piece is in five sections, each based on a Civil War poem. The work begins with a low, rumbling melody interrupted by the sounds of a military encampment. Sousa was inspired by Thomas Wentworth Higginson's "Waiting for the Bugle," and to depict the scene he borrows two camp calls that he had already used in songs and descriptive pieces: Assembly of Trumpeters and Reveille. As the soldiers awaken they hear a muffled tramp, and Sousa introduces a descending figure to represent the Confederate forces. Following the famous story, Sousa called the second section "The Attack" and based it on a portion of Thomas Buchanan Read's "Sheridan's Ride." In it Sousa juxtaposes the Confederate motive with an ascending, chromatic gesture representing the Union Army. The Confederate theme gradually soars above the Union motive during this battle sequence, and triumph for the North appears in doubt.

For the third section Sousa turned to Nancy Priest's "The Soldier's Death" and wrote a funeral march for Colonel Joseph Thoburn, who was killed leading his troops into battle. The highlight of the piece, however, occurs in the fourth section, when Sheridan finally arrives. The band first imitates the distant sound of approaching hooves, but rhythmic and dynamic intensity slowly increase. As Sheridan succeeds in rallying his troops, the opening musical struggle is reversed and the Union motive gains the upper hand. Sousa called the final section "The Apotheosis," and it is dominated by a triumphant Union. The eight-minute work ends by returning the audience to the present: Sheridan had died less than four years before the premiere of the work, and the composer pays tribute to the late general by instructing the band to sound Taps.

As Sousa had predicted, "Sheridan's Ride" met with considerable acclaim. He had successfully depicted "a thrilling war passage more graphically and powerfully than it could have been presented on the stage." At concert after concert, it was this piece that was promoted, this piece that received the greatest press coverage, and this piece that "roused perhaps the loudest demonstrations of applause on account of its realistic simulation of the exciting events depicted in the celebrated story." Programs often included selections from the corresponding poems, and in Los Angeles musical examples of the two opposing forces were even reprinted in newspapers. Despite its popularity, however, the piece was never published for piano, and not until 1908 did a band edition become available.[25]

Also featured on the 1892 tour was a new and never-published humoresque titled "Good-Bye." In this piece members of the band take "umbrage at a sharp criticism of their leader" and leave the stage while playing songs of loss or farewell. The conductor remains unconcerned, since he knows that payday is fast approaching. The piece ends as the instrumentalists "all suddenly and precipitately march back on their duty, playing, as an index of their repentance, the emotional old song of 'Annie Laurie.'" The manuscript is dated February 5, 1892, and the piece was often used on the band's second tour. The work, however, is essentially a potpourri of borrowed songs, and concert reviews suggest that it had been performed in other manifestations somewhat earlier.[26]

Once again, Sousa must have been quite happy with the results of his outing: in less than two months he earned $8,250, more than five times his annual Marine Corps salary. He also now had in place much of what would soon make him famous. Sousa was already well admired as a composer of marches, and these pieces saw success both under his baton and in piano arrangements for the amateur market. With Blakely's aid, he had now skillfully transplanted his theatrical inclinations to the bandstand by writing a series of descriptive instrumental works. Most important, Sousa had created a method of programming that pleased both casual listeners and critics. As a result, his concerts were rendered at once sophisticated (with the frequent presence of orchestral transcriptions and operatic excerpts) and accessible (with humorous works and a nearly endless stream of encores drawn from popular favorites).

The mixed programming was one of the most commented-on aspects of the March King, and late in his marine career the bandmaster noted, "I try to cater to all tastes. Every one of my programmes will have one or two pieces of a high character, then three or four of a lighter character, and the rest is of the intensely popular order." Critics of the 1890s were often surprised by Sousa's willingness to present all kinds of music, but in reality he was simply remembering the lessons of the Navy Yard. It was not his place to judge an audience's taste; rather, he was present simply to please: "All audiences are necessarily of mixed musical taste, and it is necessary to mix the programme."[27]

Despite the objections of some critics, Sousa was proved right time and again in his assessment of audience desire. One reporter complained that Sousa's programs were "marred by the trivial, not to say trashy, airs that he offers with singing, whistling and clog-dancing accompaniments as 'encorés' for classical selections." Nonetheless, this writer was forced to accept that Sousa "is the best judge of what will please an audience, and his success last night is another proof, if any were required, of the correctness of his judgment." In the end, "the house was with him every time." Sousa, of course, would find many ways to introduce variety. In addition to combining symphonies with popular songs, he alternated numbers for the entire ensemble, selections highlighting instrumentalists drawn from the band, and solos for Marie Decca. All of these programming tricks were destined to stay with the March King.[28]

These two years of professional success were tempered, however, by personal loss. While still on tour in 1892, Sousa was informed by telegram of his father's death on April 27. One of his brothers wrote simply: "Father died this morning. Mother insists you continue your concerts and not disappoint the public. Will have funeral postponed until your return." This would be Sousa's second homecoming as Marine Band leader, and along the way he likely wrote the unpublished march "Homeward Bound."[29]

LEAVING THE MARINE BAND

For David Blakely these Marine Band tours were profitable but restrictive. The ensemble was at his disposal for only a few weeks each year, and every season required new permission from the commandant. Blakely had begun the outings as a test of Sousa's financial value, a test the bandleader had clearly passed. By the spring of 1892 the manager's next step was obvious: 1893 would see a massive World's Fair in Chicago, and Blakely needed an ensemble on his roster that could reap the rewards.

As early as February, the manager had hinted at the possibility of forming a commercial band: "One of these days, when the great and good Gilmore has done with terrestrial music, he may want to put Sousa at the head of his Band. I think there would be a better opportunity for you than even the Marine affords." It was during the 1892 tour that Blakely made the offer formal, but before Sousa could thoughtfully respond, the manager leaked his plans to the Chicago press. On April 8, while the Marine Band was playing in San Francisco, the *Tribune* announced a Sousa ensemble that was still unformed: "If the negotiations that are now in progress are successful Chicago will soon have one of the finest military bands in the world. Its leader will be John Phillip [*sic*] Sousa, who is now at the head of the United States Marine Band."[30]

Throughout its history the Marine Band has been allowed to operate with a certain independence from the Corps itself. Sousa's official government obligations were flexible, therefore, and he was more or less free to leave the Corps as he wished. When the Chicago rumors reached Washington, the capital sprung into action. The *Post* urged Congress to increase Sousa's salary and that of his musicians, for unless "it is willing to pay the compensation to Mr. Sousa and his men that is paid to artists of similar rank in civil life," the conductor would likely accept Blakely's offer, and "the Marine Band would speedily return to its old listless state."[31]

While the press worried, the Marine Corps remained steadfastly silent. Rumors of Sousa's departure caused applications to pour into the commandant's office, but there was as yet no official word on Sousa's decision. As Commandant Heywood explained to one curious colleague: "I have to inform you that I have no knowledge relative to Mr. Sousa's place being vacated, except what I have seen in the public prints. He has not made any application for discharge nor do I believe he has any present intention of doing so." Nonetheless, rumors were spreading wildly, and marine musicians felt certain that Sousa's parting was imminent. Worried about his replacement, a number of players petitioned on behalf of Sousa's assistant Salvadore Petrola. By mid-July the commandant had a fistful of applications, some from quite seasoned conductors including David Wallis Reeves (leader of Reeves's American Band), Charles A. Zimmerman (from the Naval Academy Band), and the man who seems to have been Sousa's personal choice, Arthur Clappé (bandleader at West Point).[32]

The exact chronology of Sousa's decision is uncertain, but on June 27 he signed the contract that would bind him to Blakely for five years. The plan provided Sousa with an annual salary of $6,000—four times what he earned as a marine—plus 10 percent of the profits during the band's first year and 20 percent per year after that. In return, Blakely received an interest in Sousa's compositions and ownership of Sousa's music library. This contract, along with Sousa's resignation from the Marine Corps, was quickly reported in the press, and on July 30 the commandant wrote to his bandmaster wishing him well: "It is a matter of extreme regret to me that you desire to sever your connection with the band of the United States Marine Corps, but the reasons stated in your application for discharge, and the knowledge of the advantages offered you to improve your condition leave no other course open to me but to grant your request."[33]

In a scheme to finance this venture, Blakely began to contact investors. His letters make clear just how lucrative he believed a new band led by John Philip Sousa might be. He explained that in less than fifty days the most recent Marine Band tour had earned nearly $20,000. This sum would have paid Sousa's new salary "for an entire year, and left a balance of over $13,000, and given us the entire remainder of the year in which to make additional tours, and to multiply the profits of the engagement." Blakely's goals were clear. Over the course of the next year he would work tirelessly to create the greatest band in America and to enjoy the financial fruits of his efforts: "It is my ambition and purpose and to my interest, to produce a band which will be much more than a representative of the military music of America. It will be a band which will challenge comparison with any organization under the sun. And whatever you do, you can act upon that assurance. I am enlisted in this enterprise for the war."[34]

Notes of congratulation flooded into Blakely's New York office throughout late July, and they reveal just how attached Washington was to its bandleader. Blakely's Treasury Department friend Alvred Nettleton jokingly warned the manager to avoid the capital: "I congratulate you most heartily upon your success in abstracting Director Sousa from the National Capital, but what shall be said concerning the loss to Washington? You could hardly have done a more incendiary thing if you had placed dynamite under the popular branch of Congress, and as your friend of long standing . . . I advise you not to put in an appearance in this burgh until the storm is somewhat allayed!"[35]

Several members of Congress, the secretary of the navy, and the vice president of the United States begged Sousa for one more concert. They, of course, got their wish. Sousa's testimonial, held on July 29 at the National Theater, featured not only the Marine Band but also several of the civilian musicians Sousa had encountered during his twelve years in the capital. Since the new band was to be based in Chicago, he had written a new march, completed on July 23, premiered at this concert, and titled "The Belle of Chicago." As the performance came to an end there were calls for Sousa to address his audience, and stepping to the footlights he spoke: "If I have accomplished anything for the good of music in the past twelve years I will not spoil it now with a speech." With that Sousa turned to his band and struck up "Hail! Columbia," which closed the program. Much of the concert was repeated the following afternoon on the White House lawn, and thus, John Philip Sousa's military career came to an end. The *Post* would lament: "Sousa has gone. Washington's Orpheus is lost to us forever."[36]

Sousa moved his family to New York to be near Blakely's offices and organize his new ensemble. For its part, the Marine Corps was slow to replace its bandleader. It was not until November 1 that the Roman clarinetist Francesco Fanciulli enlisted to fill Sousa's former position. He had been recommended by none other than Patrick Gilmore, for whose band Fanciulli had written several descriptive works, a good reminder that these were hardly the purview of Sousa alone. Unfortunately, Fanciulli's career is also reminiscent of the difficulties faced by so many of the Marine Band's earlier leaders. Because of a perceived unwillingness to play the most popular marches, Fanciulli was arrested at the 1897 Memorial Day parade. It seems that a superior had ordered him to perform more martial music, and Fanciulli had refused. This insubordination soon ended his Marine Corps career.[37]

BUILDING A BAND

Given Sousa's later fame, it is easy to forget just how risky a venture he was undertaking in 1892. For the previous twelve years Sousa's military position had shielded him against the difficulties of a civilian musical life, and he therefore had remarkably little experience as a businessman or public figure. His greatest successes had occurred at home, and whatever praise he received on the road was due in no small part to the status of his ensemble. As Sousa entered this new venture, he would no longer be able to rely on his position as America's national bandleader, nor on the crimson uniforms of his players. He would also have no government paycheck in reserve should the endeavor turn sour. For his part, Blakely also faced considerable risk in taking out such an untested musician. The general manager of the Western Pennsylvania Exposition, J. N. Johnston, advised Blakely that while his new protégé may have been an accomplished composer and conductor, he was not yet a proven entertainer: "A great deal depends upon his manner with the public, upon his *personal* popularity as well as his musical ability, success or failure depends. . . . Every musical Director must be in *sympathy* and *accord* with the people who are his patrons, as you well know. Possibly Sousa has all the qualifications necessary to make him successful, but I simply suggest that *you* see to it that he *unbends* before his audiences like the great *Patrick*, otherwise, he will fail."[38]

Such warnings were not uncommon, and Blakely must have wondered if it was wise to select such an inexperienced conductor instead of the more worldly bandsmen who had begged for him to take up their causes. Hoping to gain a position at the upcoming fair, Blakely had already promised the new band to Chicago, and the press there was uncommonly optimistic about the enterprise. Elsewhere, however, reactions were more cautious. The *Musical Courier*, which had so harshly judged Sousa's 1891 visit to New York, proved to be among the most pessimistic voices. In an article tellingly titled "A Curious Musical Engagement," the magazine declared the Marine Band "a travesty in comparison with great brass bands here or in Europe." Under Sousa "it was a blaring, glaring noise producer, and its success, wherever it had any, was due to the lack of discernment on the part of the public." More important, the *Courier* doubted that Blakely could simply will a profitable ensemble into existence: "A brass band is not created by special design; it is a matter of evolution, even if all the material is acceptable. It takes a long time to make a brass band a musical organization." There was, of course, little reason to think that Washington's favorite son was up to the task: "Mr. Sousa may be a genius, but thus far he has not demonstrated it."[39]

Blakely pressed on despite such misgivings, and his first task was to select a name for the new ensemble. Since Sousa looked forward to the 1893 season, he lobbied for "Sousa's Chicago Band." Blakely, however, wanted to capitalize on the successes of the previous two years, and so he settled on Sousa's New Marine Band. Because the Marine Band was scheduled to appear at the fair's opening ceremonies, the commandant objected to having a civilian competitor borrow his name. Sousa's public reply made his level of frustration with the Corps—and hopes for the future—clear:

> Until two years ago I had no reputation outside of a certain circle, except what I had derived from my compositions. For ten years I had worked incessantly to place the Marine band on a higher plane. . . . During all this time I received no credit for my work whatever. . . . There is no man who has so little vanity and egotism that he has no desire to receive credit for what he has done. I felt that all there was in the marine band was due to my efforts; but I was not even known by name by half the persons who heard the band play. . . . We have none of the members of the old Marine band in our present company. It is composed of the best players we could find, and I think that Colonel Heywood might well be proud to have us use the term 'marine' in any connection with the band we have now.

For a time, at least, Blakely's ensemble would be known as Sousa's New Marine Band.[40]

Next came the matter of players. Publicly, Blakely claimed that Sousa was "restricted in his selection neither in expense nor to locality." As contracts were being negotiated, however, the bandmaster was reminded to stand firm

Fig. 31. The cover of a program from the New Marine Band's 1892 tour. "The President's Own" United States Marine Band, Washington, D.C.

Fig. 32. Promotional photograph of Sousa, ca. 1892. "The President's Own" United States Marine Band, Washington, D.C.

on salaries and remember that profit was the central goal: "We are in this thing for glory and money. . . . Too much of this matter is my own individual burden, and I cannot stand, and won't stand a salary list which is going to eat up all the profits. Moreover, there is no necessity for it. Make your figures what they ought to be, and the men will come to them."[41]

The membership of Sousa's ensemble was never stable, and over the course of its forty-year existence more than one thousand musicians spent time on the road with the March King. Making matters more complicated, midway through the 1892 tour Sousa significantly reshuffled his personnel. It is thus almost impossible to re-create the roster for the band's first tour. Interviews given by Sousa and Blakely are not particularly helpful because both men casually bent the truth to fit their needs. In any case, it is clear that Sousa worked personally to gather musicians and that he was aided in this enterprise by his Philadelphia publisher Harry Coleman. Sousa told the curious Chicago press, "I got the players everywhere—from New York, Boston, Philadelphia, one from Chicago, one from Grand Rapids, Mich.—indeed, nearly all the cities contributed. It didn't matter where a man came from if he could play well." Blakely, hoping to impress, noted the band's foreign pedigree: "The first cornet was brought from London, where he was long the admired soloist of the famous Covent Garden concerts. The entire cornet and trumpet section is worthy of its head. One of the first clarinets was soloist of the band of the *Jardin d'Acclimation*, of Paris, and a graduate of the Paris Conservatory. Two are graduates of the Leipsic Conservatory, and another was for years the first clarinet soloist of Gilmore's Band." One reporter even claimed that during rehearsals Sousa had to shout out instructions "in Italian, German or English, according to the needs of his cosmopolitan orchestra." Such claims were clearly planted, and in one interview Sousa announced that all of his players came from New York.[42]

The players who did sign contracts were generally paid about $35 per week and in exchange agreed to render services for nine weeks' worth of parades and concerts, including matinee, evening, and Sunday performances. Nineteenth-century touring ensembles were often cobbled together, and in order to keep expenses low it was not unusual for professional groups to forgo dedicated rehearsals. Sousa, however, insisted that he have twelve days with the band prior to his first concert. Blakely balked, but in the end agreed to pay the players for an extra two weeks of rehearsal.

A TRAGIC BEGINNING

Even with bandsmen gathered, the success of this venture was hardly assured, and by the middle of August Sousa's fears were palpable. He wrote to the London-based trombonist Arthur Smith: "There are an unusual number of bands leaving New York this fall. . . . Gilmore's goes to St. Louis with 100 men, Cappa with 50, to Tacoma, Innes, with 45, to Minneapolis, Levy with 45 to Pittsburgh, Brooks with 45 to Pittsburgh, and it makes things unusually lively in the military band line." The reason so many bands were hitting the road was the very reason Blakely had paired with Sousa in the first place. The 1892–93 season would mark the four-hundredth anniversary of Columbus's voyage, and the country would be awash in celebrations. By August 6, Blakely had managed to place his new attraction at the most important of them: the World's Columbian Exposition in Chicago, where the band was scheduled to take part in the dedication ceremonies held between October 19 and 22, 1892. In order to prepare for this spectacularly high-profile event, the band would spend two weeks traveling through New Jersey, Pennsylvania, New York, and Michigan (table 3).[43]

In planning routes for the 1891 and 1892 tours, Blakely had carefully avoided putting the Marine Band in direct competition with other touring ensembles, especially that of Patrick Gilmore. Such efforts would no longer be necessary; on September 24, 1892, Gilmore died unexpectedly at the St. Louis Exposition. Sousa's first concert as a civilian was scheduled to occur just two days later, and both the bandmaster and his manager must have breathed a guilty sigh of relief.

Table 3. Sousa's New Marine Band tour, 1892, part 1

Sept. 26 (Mon.)	Plainfield, N.J.	Oct. 14 (Fri.)	Chicago, Ill.
Sept. 27 (Tue.)	Trenton, N.J.	Oct. 15 (Sat.)	Chicago, Ill. (× 2)
Sept. 28 (Wed.)	York, Pa.	Oct. 16 (Sun.)	Racine, Wis.
	Harrisburg, Pa.	Oct. 17 (Mon.)	Chicago, Ill.
Sept. 29 (Thu.)	Danville, Pa.	Oct. 18 (Tue.)	Beloit, Wis.
	Williamsport, Pa.		Rockford, Ill.
Sept. 30 (Fri.)	Corning, N.Y.	Oct. 19 (Wed.)	Chicago, Ill. (dedication/ball)
	Elmira, N.Y.		
Oct. 1 (Sat.)	Towanda, Pa.	Oct. 20 (Thu.)	Chicago, Ill. (parade)
	Ithaca, N.Y.	Oct. 21 (Fri.)	Chicago, Ill. (dedication/concert)
Oct. 2 (Sun.)	Buffalo, N.Y.		
Oct. 3 (Mon.)	Detroit, Mich.	Oct. 22 (Sat.)	Chicago, Ill. (dedication)
Oct. 4 (Tue.)	Ann Arbor, Mich.		
	Jackson, Mich.	Oct. 23 (Sun.)	Lima, Ohio
Oct. 5 (Wed.)	Owasso, Mich.	Oct. 24 (Mon.)	Ada, Ohio
	Saginaw, Mich.		Fort Wayne, Ind.
Oct. 6 (Thu.)	Flint, Mich.	Oct. 25 (Tue.)	Bucyrus, Ohio
	Lansing, Mich.		Mansfield, Ohio
Oct. 7 (Fri.)	Battle Creek, Mich.	Oct. 26 (Wed.)	Johnstown, Pa.
	Kalamazoo, Mich.		Altoona, Pa.
Oct. 8 (Sat.)	Muskegon, Mich. (× 2)	Oct. 27 (Thu.)	Washington, D.C.
Oct. 9 (Sun.)	Grand Rapids, Mich.	Oct. 28 (Fri.)	Washington, D.C. (× 2)
Oct. 10 (Mon.)	Chicago, Ill.	Oct. 29 (Sat.)	Wilmington, Del.
Oct. 11 (Tue.)	Chicago, Ill.		Philadelphia, Pa.
Oct. 12 (Wed.)	Chicago, Ill. (× 2)	Oct. 30 (Sun.)	New York, N.Y.
Oct. 13 (Thu.)	Chicago, Ill.		

Programs from the New Marine Band's first concert, which took place in Plainfield, New Jersey, on September 26, do not survive. Press reports, however, allow for a partial reconstruction of the event, and they indicate that the ensemble performed the overture to Rossini's *Semiramide*, a suite from Grieg's *Peer Gynt*, short selections by D'Arcy Jaxone and Alphons Czibulka, the ballet music from Schubert's *Rosamunde*, and "The Star-Spangled Banner." Three Sousa pieces also appeared: "Sheridan's Ride," "Good-Bye," and the newly written "March of the Royal Trumpets" (an unpublished work featuring a set of five-foot long Egyptian instruments). Gilmore's death put the memory of the Irish Orpheus front and center for many audience members, and in an effort to dissolve any tension between the old and the new, Sousa began the concert with a signal for the band to rise and render honors to Gilmore's memory by playing the fallen bandleader's own "Voice of a Departing Soul."[44]

Despite Sousa's best efforts, his New Marine Band immediately got off to a rocky start. The tour's featured soloists were to be the renowned Italian baritone Antonio Galassi and the almost completely unknown American soprano Marcella Lindh. Galassi would sing "The Evening Star" from Wagner's *Tannhäuser*, and Lindh the mad scene from Donizetti's *Lucia di Lammermoor*. The baritone, however, missed the Plainfield concert when his ship was quarantined, and Lindh was forced to sing with a substitute partner, to the disappointment of the audience.

Looking to build up the band's experience, Blakely had scheduled eleven to twelve concerts per week as the ensemble traveled to Chicago. Along the way, however, he sought to avoid too critical a press, and thus chose mostly smaller cities and towns. By and large this scheme was successful, and at almost every stop critics praised Sousa's judicious mix of elevated selections and popular favorites. In Elmira, New York, the conductor was thanked for "not catering to popular taste" and instead presenting "a better quality of music than brass bands usually play or brass band audiences care to hear." In Grand Rapids the program "covered a wide range and was of a nature to convince the most critical that the organization proposed to win on artistic merit and not by mere musical fireworks." Sousa's decision to rehearse the band also paid off. In Williamsport, Pennsylvania, a reviewer noted that "no such elegant tone shading, tenderness of expression and perfection of execution was ever heard here before." In Muskegon, Michigan, Sousa's ensemble proved itself to be "the greatest military band in the country or the world."[45]

Sousa was naturally compared to Gilmore, and in these small towns he proved equal to the task. A Saginaw critic noticed that Sousa was less flamboyant than his predecessor but that the sound of his band was just as good:

"Unlike the great Gilmore, Sousa does not make himself conspicuous by his vigorous work, but is very quiet and unassuming. Yet the result is the same." Along the way, Sousa maintained his habit of presenting short programs liberally peppered with encores. A Grand Rapids reporter stated: "If there was one thing more than another which endeared Gilmore to the public it was his good nature in responding to encores. His programs contained pieces that appealed to all conditions of men. These were characteristics of the dead bandmaster. They are also those of Sousa." In the end, newspapers agreed that Sousa would "not suffer by comparison with Cappa or Gilmore."[46]

On October 10 the players arrived in Chicago, where they performed at the Chicago Auditorium for a full week, followed by run-out appearances in Racine and Beloit, Wisconsin, and Rockford, Illinois. Sousa added several programs to accommodate the longer engagement, and new pieces included the overtures to Gustave Wettge's *Mysora*, Ambroise Thomas's *Raymond*, and Richard Wagner's *Rienzi*. Both Blakely and Sousa had sold their band as a Chicago ensemble from the start (although its real base of operations had been, and would remain, New York). Given this public tie to the exposition city, it is no surprise that the band received a hero's welcome from the interests hoping to bring Sousa permanently to Chicago.[47]

The real reason for the band's presence became evident on October 19, when the ensemble played for a series of building dedications and provided promenade music for an opening reception at the Auditorium. The next day it took part in a massive parade that included ensembles from all over the country and was reported to be ten miles long. On the morning of October 21, federal troops escorted visiting officials to the Hall of Manufactures and Liberal Arts for the official dedication ceremonies of the World's Columbian Exposition. Covering four city blocks, it was likely the largest building in the world, and its mass gave an indication of what was about to occur.

Theodore Thomas, who shortly beforehand had agreed to direct the newly organized Chicago Symphony Orchestra, was made musical director of the World's Fair in late 1891. This was a fateful decision for Thomas, who had, after all, some experience with such celebrations. Sousa had seen his efforts on behalf of formal music succumb to more popular forces at the nation's centennial, and Thomas must have been wary of repeating that debacle. Nonetheless, he accepted responsibility for music at the exposition, and once again Sousa would be on hand to view the results.

The October ceremonies were Thomas's first test. The maestro's 190-piece orchestra was joined by a choir of nearly six thousand voices and several auxiliary ensembles. Sousa's task was to prepare his own band to assist in the playing of John Knowles Paine's newly commissioned "Columbus March and Hymn." Thomas would conduct the performance, so Sousa was able to listen to the mighty forces during a rehearsal at the Auditorium, and he must have been quite pleased when the older musician stopped to pay his respects and invite the bandmaster to lunch, an experience Sousa later called "one of the happiest afternoons of my life."[48]

The preparation may have gone well, but after a dress rehearsal in the massive performance space, Thomas must have had a hint of the disaster about to unfold. With 150,000 people in attendance (including Vice President Levi P. Morton, members of the Supreme Court, and former president Rutherford B. Hayes), the dedication began. Without amplification the speakers' voices were lost to the crowd, and despite the forces assembled, music faired little better. Thomas was forced to overcome the distance between his various ensembles by signaling with drum rolls and handkerchief waves. Even Sousa's band stood little chance in the massive space: "Poor John Philip! He might have had forty bands just as fine as his own and scattered about those thirty or more acres and he could not have brought even a shadow or flimsy film of Sappho or Euterpe or Melpomene to the arch of the vast canopy above. . . . His greatest artists blew and puffed their cheeks till they looked like victims of the mumps, but it was no use. At the great dais now and then a strain could be recognized if one knew the air, but not else."[49]

For Sousa there was little to be salvaged. His band had been inaudible at the dedication, and despite a warm welcome Chicago was not entirely convinced by his earlier concerts in the city, either. His newest march—"The Belle of Chicago"—was panned. A reviewer for the *Record* wrote: "Sousa has made his Chicago belle a strapping kitchen wench with a disposition to be hilarious. The piece, like others given last night, could stand a little toning down." Certainly his band was good, but to these urban critics the best he could accomplish was to prepare audiences for more serious art. According to one reporter, Sousa could only endear himself to listeners with a tacit promise that "if they will only be patient and listen to the number on the programme, which may occasionally be of a somewhat more serious nature, their patience shall be rewarded with sweetmeats that are presented as encores." With any luck these same audiences would one day be ready to appreciate the real art provided by Thomas: "It is to be hoped that Mr. Sousa will bear in mind the fact that upon him, in a measure, devolves the responsibility of educating the taste of the people so that they may eventually learn to appreciate the higher forms of orchestral music. For band music always appeals to the masses and can thus be made a stepping stone to something better."[50]

It is worth noting that Sousa and Thomas were not the only musicians disappointed by the exposition's opening ceremonies. Given the importance of the event, the commandant had granted permission for the Marine Band to travel to Chicago. The men, who had toured under Blakely's management in 1891 and 1892, were accustomed to jumping off the train, seeing the sights, and enjoying their meals at liberty. This trip, however, was an official engagement and not a private enterprise; the players quickly discovered that they were expected to sleep in local barracks, muster for meals, and live otherwise as a military unit. As one bandsmen complained: we were "treated like a lot of recruits traveling under a sergeant, or a gang of convicts." Washington audiences were not the only capital residents who missed their bandmaster.[51]

After the Chicago debacle, Sousa's New Marine Band spent a week heading back east through Ohio, Indiana, Pennsylvania, and Delaware (table 3 on p. 206). Once again it played two concerts almost every day, primarily in small towns. The tour was brought to a close with a series of concerts in Washington and a final homecoming performance on October 30 in New York. Once again, reviews were less than stellar. A Pennsylvania reporter noted that the ensemble played military music well enough, but "in the works of the standard composers they show a crudeness and a lack of rehearsal that can only be effaced by much hard work." The *Musical Courier* also continued its harsh treatment. In reviewing the closing concert, its critic wrote that a mosaic on Wagner's *Lohengrin* should be dropped because "there is so much better music that is adapted for brass and wood that it seems a pity to sacrifice the tender beauties of Wagner's poetic music drama." The *Record* agreed, declaring that Sousa "should let *Lohengrin* severely alone hereafter." For Blakely these first fifty appearances of 1892 had been a loss: owing to lackluster reviews, tickets sold poorly, and he was forced to contribute $2,900 to cover expenses.[52]

The band rested in New York for two weeks of rehearsal. On November 9, Blakely convinced the usually hostile *Musical Courier* to reprint many of the most positive reviews from the fall of 1892 as part of a trumpeting of Sousa's "new departure" in military music. He also proudly announced that several of Gilmore's former players had decided to join Sousa. According to Blakely these additions included Joseph Raffayolo (euphonium), August Stengler (clarinet), Charles Petit (cornet), John S. Cox (flute), and Thomas Shannon (saxophone). Reorganized and reinvigorated, the band opened a new tour in New York on November 13 and played two concerts nearly every day as it traveled the Northeast through Connecticut, Rhode Island, Massachusetts, New Hampshire, Maine, New York, and Pennsylvania (table 4). Along the way, players from Gilmore's band were often featured as soloists.[53]

Table 4. Sousa's New Marine Band tour, 1892, part 2

Nov. 13 (Sun.)	New York, N.Y.	Nov. 26 (Sat.)	Portland, Me. (× 2)
Nov. 14 (Mon.)	Bridgeport, Conn.	Nov. 27 (Sun.)	Boston, Mass.
	Meriden, Conn.	Nov. 28 (Mon.)	Salem, Mass.
Nov. 15 (Tue.)	New Britain, Conn.	Nov. 29 (Tue.)	Marlboro, Mass.
	New Haven, Conn.		Worcester, Mass.
Nov. 16 (Wed.)	Middletown, Conn.	Nov. 30 (Wed.)	Northampton, Mass.
	Hartford, Conn.		Springfield, Mass.
Nov. 17 (Thu.)	Woonsocket, R.I.	Dec. 1 (Thu.)	Schenectady, N.Y.
	Providence, R.I.		Gloversville, N.Y.
Nov. 18 (Fri.)	Amesbury, Mass.	Dec. 2 (Fri.)	Little Falls, N.Y.
	Haverhill, Mass.		Utica, N.Y.
Nov. 19 (Sat.)	Exeter, N.H.	Dec. 3 (Sat.)	Oneida, N.Y.
	Dover, N.H.		Rome, N.Y.
Nov. 20 (Sun.)	Boston, Mass.	Dec. 4 (Sun.)	Rochester, N.Y. (× 2)
Nov. 21 (Mon.)	Lowell, Mass.	Dec. 5 (Mon.)	Geneva, N.Y.
Nov. 22 (Tue.)	Brunswick, Me.		Auburn, N.Y.
	Lewiston, Me.	Dec. 6 (Tue.)	Syracuse, N.Y. (× 2)
Nov. 23 (Wed.)	Bangor, Me. (× 2)	Dec. 7 (Wed.)	Scranton, Pa.
Nov. 24 (Thu.)	Skowhegan, Me.	Dec. 8 (Thu.)	Wilkes-Barre, Pa. (× 2)
	Augusta, Me.	Dec. 9 (Fri.)	Allentown, Pa. (× 2)
Nov. 25 (Fri.)	Bath, Me.	Dec. 10 (Sat.)	Philadelphia, Pa.
	Rockland, Me.		

Despite Blakely's best advertising efforts and generally positive reviews, Sousa's New Marine Band was still not a powerful draw at the box office. The manager recognized that reports of half-full houses might hurt his negotiations with local managers for the following year, and so while the band was playing in Boston he summoned Sousa and announced, "I'm going to close down this tour to-night." Sousa replied by blaming his manager: "The route laid out for the band has been hopeless, but that is not my fault. You booked me in a territory where Gabriel with a horn of gold wouldn't draw. And now you have the effrontery to propose ruining my career. You would disgrace me as a musician; the authorities at Washington would laugh at my humiliation, after I left them in such a high feather. I won't permit you to close! We have two weeks more, and I insist that you carry out your contract!"[54]

Sousa evidently won this argument, and the band finished its tour, wrapping up the 1892 season with a concert in Philadelphia on December 10. Along the way critics continued to see Sousa as a promising replacement for Gilmore but one not yet ready for the national stage. A Massachusetts reviewer noted: "What it needs to equal the lamented Gilmore's musical aggregation (which must be accepted as the standard in judging of merit) is concerted experience and the personal presence and ability of that matchless bandmaster. This Professor Sousa does not possess at present, although he may acquire it in time." Likely owing to low income at the box office and the high salaries paid to several soloists, Blakely was forced to cover another $500 worth of losses.[55]

STRATEGIC PLANNING

Even before his new band set out in 1892, Blakely had begun to plan for the 1893 season. His strategy rested on a complex calculation of the nation's many fairs and expositions. As work began, Gilmore was still alive and Blakely assumed that America's senior bandmaster would be occupied from July to October with his regular engagements at Manhattan Beach and the St. Louis Exposition. While the fair in Chicago would be the season's crown jewel, it was unlikely that Gilmore would risk losing his yearly residencies for a single summer in the Windy City. Blakely could thus safely hope to win a contract with Chicago, and he was in negotiations with Theodore Thomas by late 1892. Blakely impressed on the conductor the need for a band to demonstrate America's strides in the musical arts: "Pardon me for asking you to consider whether it is not a most desirable thing to have on the ground at all times, the very best American Band, as a standard by which to measure the accomplishments of our country in this direction. Your great orchestra will do this for the orchestral branch of the musical art of the new world. Our band will not fail to do its part, in its sphere, to confer equal honor upon the country."[56]

The Western Pennsylvania Exposition in Pittsburgh also overlapped with Gilmore's St. Louis engagement, and Blakely felt secure in his chances of success there. Throughout August 1892, then, Blakely must have imagined an 1893 season with Sousa's band at the Chicago and Western Pennsylvania expositions. With Gilmore's unexpected death in September, however, that bandleader's more lucrative engagements suddenly became available. Blakely quickly wrote to Frank Gaiennie, manager of the St. Louis Exposition, even while he continued negotiations with Pittsburgh.

On January 5, the manager in Pennsylvania, J. N. Johnston, tried to lower Blakely's asking price by explaining that Sousa was still unknown to most audiences. If the new leader appeared in St. Louis, he would be forced to compete directly with Gilmore's legacy, but if he accepted the more restrictive offer from Pennsylvania, the bandleader would have a chance to make a name for himself away from the memory of Gilmore:

> You know Gilmore owned that town, and it will be very difficult for any one, be he ever so capable, to please its people. It may be if they engage some other Band for a year or two (which will have the effect of taking the curse off) and preparing them to appreciate Sousa, that eventually he may gain a strong foot-hold in that city, but my dear fellow, that will take time, for you well know that it was Gilmore's strong personality that carried the day there *not his Band*. In this city it is different. Pittsburgh has made the reputation of several musical organizations which have played at our Exposition; keep this fact in mind. Of Sousa's *personal characteristics*, I know absolutely nothing. That you have gathered around him a thoroughly competent body of musicians I have not the slightest doubt, but you know as well as I do that everything depends upon the *personal magnetism of the Leader*. He may indeed possess all the qualifications of a popular and successful public favorite, but *he has to prove his worth in this respect*.[57]

As negotiations with the Pittsburgh organizers continued, the managers in St. Louis acted more swiftly, perhaps pushed by the January 6 death of another major bandleader, Carlo Alberto Cappa. On the ninth they extended to Blakely an offer for the full seven weeks of the Exposition. Informing Johnston in Pittsburgh of his decision to accept Gaiennie's offer to appear in St. Louis, Blakely bragged: "They heard the old band under its new leader the last night of the last St. Louis engagement. And they were so pained by the contrast between the old leader and the new, and their recollection was so fresh of two performances by Sousa only a few weeks before, that they came to the instant and unanimous conclusion" that they must engage Sousa.[58]

While still negotiating with Gaiennie in St. Louis, Blakely began to eye Gilmore's other major engagement. On January 4 he wrote to the vice president of Coney Island's Manhattan Beach Hotel. Once again he was happy to find a reluctance to engage Gilmore's revived ensemble, and Blakely's offer to play in July and August was quickly accepted. Thomas, meanwhile, had yet to act on Blakely's proposal for Chicago, and the band's dance card was rapidly filling. A letter was sent to Thomas offering the band for a truncated appearance; it would, of course, be accepted.

By April 1893, Blakely had finalized his plans and arranged an unprecedented season for John Philip Sousa and his band. They would spend May 22 to June 28 in Chicago, playing two concerts per day at the exposition. July 1 to September 4 would find them at Manhattan Beach, again playing two or sometimes three concerts daily. September 6 to October 22 would be spent in St. Louis, often playing four concerts per day. There would also be tour

Table 5. Sousa Band tour, 1893

Date	Place
Apr. 30 (Sun.)	New York, N.Y.
May 1 (Mon.)	Trenton, N.J.
	Philadelphia, Pa.
May 2 (Tue.)	Philadelphia, Pa.
May 3 (Wed.)	Norwalk, Conn.
	Bridgeport, Conn.
May 4 (Thu.)	Boston, Mass.
May 5 (Fri.)	Boston, Mass. (× 2)
May 6 (Sat.)	Boston, Mass. (× 2)
May 7 (Sun.)	Boston, Mass. (× 2)
May 8 (Mon.)	Syracuse, N.Y. (× 2)
May 9 (Tue.)	Buffalo, N.Y. (× 2)
May 10 (Wed.)	Detroit, Mich. (× 2)
May 11 (Thu.)	Louisville, Ky. (× 2)
May 12 (Fri.)	St. Louis, Mo.
May 13 (Sat.)	St. Louis, Mo. (× 2)
May 14 (Sun.)	Kansas City, Mo. (× 2)
May 15 (Mon.)	Omaha, Neb. (× 2)
May 16 (Tue.)	Des Moines, Iowa (× 2)
May 17 (Wed.)	Minneapolis, Minn.
May 18 (Thu.)	Minneapolis, Minn. (× 2)
May 19 (Fri.)	Duluth, Minn. (× 2)
May 20 (Sat.)	St. Paul, Minn. (× 2)
May 21 (Sun.)	Milwaukee, Wis. (× 2)
May 22–June 28	**Chicago, Ill., World's Columbian Exposition**
June 29	**Pittsburgh, Pa. (× 2)**
June 30	**Lancaster, Pa. (× 2)**
July 1–Sept. 4	**Manhattan Beach, N.Y.**
Sept. 6–Oct. 22	**St. Louis Exposition, Mo.**
Oct. 23 (Mon.)	Indianapolis, Ind. (× 2)
Oct. 24 (Tue.)	London, Ohio
	Delaware, Ohio
Oct 25 (Wed.)	Columbia, Ohio (× 2)
Oct. 26 (Thu.)	Cleveland, Ohio
Oct. 27 (Fri.)	Warren, Ohio
	New Castle, Pa.
Oct. 29 (Sun.)	Washington, D.C.
Oct. 30 (Mon.)	Baltimore, Md.
	Wilmington, Del.
Oct. 31 (Tue.)	Philadelphia, Pa.
Nov. 1 (Wed.)	Harrisburg, Pa. (× 2)
Nov. 2 (Thu.)	Batavia, N.Y.
Nov. 3 (Fri.)	Hamilton, Ontario
Nov. 6–19	Chicago, Ill., Trocadero
Nov. 20 (Mon.)	Detroit, Mich.
Nov. 21 (Tue.)	Woodstock, Ontario
	Hamilton, Ontario
Nov. 22 (Wed.)	Syracuse, N.Y.

performances in April and May preceding the Chicago engagement, and after the residencies the band would continue traveling until late November (table 5). This careful planning resulted in what the *Musical Courier* called "the longest continuous tour ever undertaken by a musical organization in this country."[59]

No doubt Sousa and Blakely were both concerned about the financial difficulties that had led to their fight the previous November, and from this point on they would not allow any opportunity to pass them by. Sousa had usually avoided Sunday concerts during the Marine Band tours, but with so much now on the line, not a single day's potential ticket sales could be spared. During the New Marine Band's initial tour, Sunday appearances had been advertised as sacred affairs, but this was done mostly to placate the prevailing religious sentiment and had very little actual effect on the programmed music. In 1892 one critic in Buffalo had noted that with few exceptions, "the instrumental numbers were of the decidedly popular order, the only sacred characteristic being found in the negro melodies played for encores." This critic chastised Sousa that "while 'Annie Rooney' and songs of its kind are all very well in their way, it is not a way leading to a sacred concert and advertisement promises should be fulfilled." In 1893 Sousa hoped to avoid this problem with a new piece: *Songs of Grace and Songs of Glory*. This unpublished "Religious Meditation" was little more than a stringing together of hymn tunes, and it was used throughout the Sousa Band's existence. The particular borrowed songs changed from season to season; in 1893 the work included excerpts from Verdi's *Requiem*, as well as the hymns "Rock of Ages," "Beulah Land," "Steal Away," and a piece that had long been associated with the United States Marine Band: "Nearer, My God, to Thee." No longer could Sousa be accused of misrepresenting his Sunday appearances.[60]

Sousa's real problems, however, lay in continued comparisons to Gilmore, whose band had finished its St. Louis engagements under the baton of assistant conductor Charles Freudenvoll. Feeling his chances of success too low, Freudenvoll quickly resigned, and the band invited David Wallis Reeves to take up the baton. It was this Gilmore Band that provided Sousa with his most threatening competition. The bandmaster and his manager, however, had a plan: rather than engage with Reeves directly, they would simply position Sousa as Gilmore's rightful heir. Blakely had already placed the band at Gilmore's most important engagements, and now he would begin to harvest players directly from the celebrated ensemble.

Before Gilmore's death some members of his band had made overtures to Sousa. Not wanting to appear improper, Blakely had told the men that they must secure Gilmore's permission before entering into negotiations. After Gilmore's death, however, Sousa and Blakely felt free to contract with his players, and by the second half of 1892, Sousa was claiming that he had nine of Gilmore's men, including the famed cornet soloist Alessandro Liberati. Reeves was left with little choice but to attack, and he almost immediately accused Sousa of stealing players who were rightfully his. In March 1893, Reeves wrote to the *Musical Courier* and claimed that the Sousa Band was "selected haphazard from various parts of America" and "hastily formed." It first tried to cash in on Sousa's reputation as the leader of the national band by calling itself the "New Marine Band, trying plainly enough to steal the honors" from the President's Own. Next Blakely "set to work to induce Gilmore's Band to join their party, that they might perhaps share in their great reputation." Blakely was only partly successful in this subterfuge, since the players he enticed were just a "few fossiled and worn out members of Gilmore's Band." Reeves seemed certain that the American public would see through "the unscrupulous methods of speculators, whose only object in connecting themselves with a musical organization is to make money." He signed the letter "Gilmore's Band."[61]

Blakely immediately denied the charges and fired off a letter to Gilmore's widow asking whether Reeves had her support. Ellen Gilmore responded by noting that Reeves's article "amazed and shocked" her. Although she ordered Reeves to expunge his misleading charges, she also accused Blakely of having "done far from generously by the Gilmore Band." In hiring Gilmore's musicians and taking over his engagements, it seemed clear to her, Sousa and Blakely were trying to revive the Gilmore ensemble under their own direction, and as a result "the struggle of the band to retain its place without Mr. Gilmore was made infinitely harder, from the start, by your speedy and conspicuous association of the Gilmore name with the Sousa band." Reeves, meanwhile, accused Blakely of advertising the Sousa Band as Gilmore's rightful heir, "thereby giving the impression that Gilmore's Band was no more."[62]

Reeves had stated that the transferred players were fossilized and worn-out, and the offended men were not about to let the insult pass. Eleven musicians signed a letter to the *Musical Courier* absolving Sousa of any wrongdoing. Because Gilmore's soloists and his engagements were now in Sousa's possession, the musicians wondered whether "Sousa's organization, if he wished it, could not lay greater title to being 'Gilmore's Band' than the organization whose leader, by his wanton and gratuitous attack upon the favorite musicians of Gilmore, has so belied the latter's character as a competent judge of the qualifications of the musicians whom it was his pleasure to employ." Reeves, of course, replied by leaving the matter to public opinion. Audiences would determine the "final judgment of men brought into prominence by association with Gilmore's Band, . . . who at the first opportunity deserted, so to speak, to the enemy."[63]

It is unclear whether Blakely and Sousa attempted to entice players away before Gilmore's death. It is, however, quite obvious that Reeves had cause to worry. The letter in the *Musical Courier* was signed by eleven of Gilmore's greatest players, who were now with the Sousa organization: Frank Wadsworth (flute); Joseph Lacalle, August Stengler, and Fred Urbain (clarinets); Edward Lefebre and Thomas Shannon (saxophones); Albert Bode and Herbert L. Clarke (cornets); Joseph Raffayolo (euphonium); Herman Conrad (tuba); and Ernst Mueller (percussion). In his negotiations with managers, Blakely often stressed his own ensemble's core of former Gilmore soloists, and he even visited Gilmore's widow in an attempt to purchase that band's music library, a move that would have crippled any attempt to revive the ensemble. The 1893 program booklets also stressed the band's connection to Gilmore: "In less than one brief year, this Band has fairly leaped to the front of American military music. . . . It was tendered and accepted the engagement of the St. Louis Exposition of seven weeks, as the successor of the lamented Gilmore's Band. . . . [And] it was tendered and accepted the ten weeks' engagement at Manhattan Beach, which, until his death, had been filled by Gilmore's band." Of the thirty-five men singled out for mention on the 1893 program, fourteen had come from Gilmore. Reeves was right to be frustrated; as Sousa's ensemble set out in 1893, it held a season of lucrative engagements, was well stocked with prominent players, and had left the primary competition largely unarmed. Blakely's efforts would, indeed, cripple Reeves, who left the band later that year.[64]

THE MARCH KING ACHIEVED

On the evening of January 23, 1893, Sousa's ensemble gave a single concert at Carnegie Hall. It appeared there again on April 16, this time in a joint performance with Walter Damrosch and the New York Symphony Orchestra. Although the two ensembles were merged for selections from Meyerbeer, Wagner, and Verdi—which few critics found particularly satisfying—they spent most of the evening alternating appearances on the stage. Performances such as this, held in conjunction with well-loved local ensembles, would form the basis of the 1893 season, which the band opened as Sousa's Festival Tour in New York on April 30 (a concert for which the ensemble donated its time on behalf of the Press Club Fair). Blakely, now more interested in comparing his organization to Gilmore than to the Marine Corps, called the reorganized group Sousa's Military Band, or simply Sousa's Band.

Sousa engaged a host of vocal soloists for this outing. The band traveled with two sopranos: the very famous Emmy Fursch-Madi and the much less well-known Marie van Cauteren. He also included Minnie Behne (alto), Albert Guille (tenor), William Mertens (baritone), and Ludovico Viviani (bass), along with a handful of other singers for briefer engagements. For the first time Sousa also traveled with a female violinist, a player he likely remembered from Washington, Leonora Stosch (who had been a student of Josef Kaspar). Traveling with such a distinguished roster of soloists was not without its difficulties, and Sousa reported complications with both Fursch-Madi and Guille (the latter left the tour by the close of the second week).[65]

Over the course of three weeks the band made its way to Chicago, again playing two concerts almost every day. This time, however, it would not avoid major cities but instead appeared in Philadelphia, Boston, Louisville,

St. Louis, Minneapolis, and Milwaukee. During 1892 it was not uncommon for the band to play matinee and evening performances in two different towns, but the 1893 schedule often allowed for two and sometimes three performances in a single city. Multiple programs were thus required, but a typical concert would alternate selections for the band alone with operatic performances by the vocal soloists. One evening program, for example, opened with the prelude to Wagner's *Der fliegende Holländer* and the ballet music to Rubinstein's *Feramors*, both adapted by Sousa. These selections were followed by the polonaise from Ambroise Thomas's *Mignon*, sung by Marie van Cauteren. The band then rendered Liszt's second Hungarian Rhapsody, and Albert Guille sang Verdi's "Celeste Aida." These pieces were followed by Charles Orth's humoresque *In a Clock Store*, which depicts a cacophony of cuckoos, cathedral bells, and chimes. Additional solos, including Leonora von Stosch's performance of Miska Hauser's *Rhapsodie Hongroise*, led to a new descriptive work by Sousa. The concert ended with the combined soloists performing the prayer and finale from *Lohengrin*. Additional concerts followed the same pattern, often adding Sousa's new *Songs of Grace and Songs of Glory* for Sunday performances.[66]

The conductor had learned the value of a fresh descriptive work for each season, and his feature for 1893 was *The Last Days of Pompeii*, a three-movement suite finished in Washington on January 18, 1893, and based on Edward Bulwer-Lytton's extraordinarily popular novel. The first movement, "In the House of Burbo and Stratonice," is used to set the scene, and in it Sousa depicts a pre-eruption world with the jovial sounds of clinking glasses and rolling dice. The second movement, "Nydia," introduces the principal character, a blind slave, and assigns to her a soaring theme played by the English horn. The real action of the work—and audiences' favorite section—occurred in the two-part third movement, "The Destruction and Nydia's Death." Here Sousa depicts the ominous quaking of Mt. Vesuvius, its eruption, and Nydia's suicide.[67]

The piece was not released for publication until 1912, but Sousa took considerable pride in the work, writing: "I have carried chromaticism about as far as it can be carried. It is a piece which I expect will maintain my reputation after I am dead." The March King was overreaching on both counts. *The Last Days of Pompeii* may well have been Sousa's most chromatic work, but its dissonances are largely confined to the final movement, and even there they are limited to frantic lines of diminished chords and chromatic scales, tempered by a sentimental conclusion that reprises Nydia's wholly diatonic theme. The piece also did not outlast the March King, but it did remain a regular part of his concerts throughout his career.[68]

On the way to Chicago, and in order to warm up for the exposition, Sousa's Band took part in a number of local celebrations. The first was Boston's Columbian Musical Festival, where the band spent four days. There, and at similar events, it performed a new work by Sousa, the unpublished *Salute of the Nations*. This piece—an updated version of "The International Congress"—was rewritten in late March 1893 to include national tunes from many of the countries involved in the Chicago celebrations. The band was routinely joined by hordes of hometown musicians as it performed this work as part of various local festivals. The event in Boston included a chorus, a women's orchestra, a drum corps, a group of Swiss yodelers, a mandolin ensemble, and a bagpipe club. In Syracuse the ensemble was aided by the local oratorio society in vocal selections from Handel, Verdi, and Rossini; in Omaha it took part in a May Festival; in Des Moines it was joined by the local philharmonic society; and in Minneapolis it played for a series of carnival concerts. In Detroit Sousa was honored by the National League of Musicians, and perhaps to mend some old wounds, he dedicated a new march, "The Beau Ideal," to the organization.[69]

Reviews from these concerts are almost unanimously positive in their descriptions of the band's technical skill and Sousa's masterful conducting. When complaints did surface, they usually focused on the programming, some critics wondering whether the bandmaster was a bit too highbrow in his selections. One of the Boston performances, for example, was given over entirely to preludes and vocal selections from Richard Wagner, a choice called "an overestimate of the strength of the Wagner cult hereabout." More often, however, the reverse was true. Sousa's printed program was always liberally sprinkled with encores, almost exclusively popular favorites ranging from songs to his own marches. One St. Paul writer found such encores—at least when contrasted with the more serious pieces—unbearably trite: "Lovers of the best music suffered untold agony when Mr. Sousa selected jingling tunes as encores to great compositions. With such fine material as this band contains it is not necessary to persistently cater to primitive ears."[70]

Whatever the complaints, by placing Sousa onstage with so many local ensembles, Blakely curtailed harsher criticism; local writers instinctively praised homegrown talent, and invariably it was talent that Sousa's Band could hardly help but outshine. The real benefits, however, came from Blakely's crafty borrowing of Gilmore's reputation. The Sousa Band now had, after all, many of the late bandleader's best players and all of his most lucrative engagements. All that remained was to make Sousa's name synonymous with that of Gilmore.

The first signs of Blakely's success came when the band gave three concerts in St. Louis on May 12 and 13. Following these appearances, Frank Gaiennie, the local manager, appeared almost giddy: "I tell you I made no mistake when I recommended Sousa's Band to succeed Gilmore's Band at the Exposition," he told a reporter as he delightedly rubbed his hands together. "Sousa is like Gilmore, bows like him, wears glasses and his power of selecting pleasing programs resembles Gilmore's." The local press agreed: "It can be truly said that it is an excellent musical aggregation and a worthy successor to Gilmore's band. In fact, in scope, character and make up, it is Gilmorean." One Kansas City writer went a step further and proclaimed Sousa to be not only Gilmore's rightful heir, but also the fulfillment of his promise:

> If Gilmore was the pioneer of military music in America, John Philip Sousa is the reaper. The former prepared the way for high class band music and in his later years largely and almost exclusively supplied the demand he had created. He had a magnetic personality and he knew how to feed public taste. . . . If there had never been a Gilmore, certainly we would not have known how to appreciate a Sousa, and this is said with eminent regard for the memory of the former. It is gratifying to know that the deceased leader not only had a successor, but one who does even better than to begin where the former left off.[71]

The Sousa Band arrived in Chicago on May 22, 1893. The bandmaster had already placed his ensemble at the front rank of American touring organizations, and in Chicago he would further solidify his reputation. On the road Sousa was still a bit of a novelty: he breezed through town with an outstanding organization that performed orchestral and operatic standards alongside popular airs. During his month at the exposition, for the first time since leaving Washington, he would, in effect, conduct a resident ensemble. Here he could prove himself again and again as a musician not only able to read his audiences' tastes but also willing to satisfy their every musical desire. As it happens, Sousa would also benefit from the fact that in Chicago there was another artist whose goals were quite different, and in contrast to whom Sousa would emerge a musical hero.

Theodore Thomas had been tasked with organizing music not only for the exposition's dedication but also for the entire duration of the fair. While Thomas tolerated popular music and found a place for it in his plans, his real interest was in bringing "before the people of the United States a full illustration of music in its highest forms as exemplified by the most enlightened nations of the world." In order to achieve this goal, he was determined to complement the fair's free daily popular concerts with ticketed performances by a permanent orchestra as well as solo and chamber artists who would play only the best music by European (and on a few occasions, American) composers.[72]

Thomas's carefully laid plans seem to have been frustrated at virtually every step. After the chaos of the opening ceremonies he was forced to deal with charges from the Federation of Musicians regarding his use of foreign players and from New York labor organizations about his heavy reliance on Chicago musicians. He was then confronted with the acoustical nightmare of Music Hall, made worse by frigid Lake Michigan winds that caused the temperature in the unheated space to plummet. Thomas also found himself at the center of a fierce controversy over the types of pianos to be used at the fair, a fight the press dubbed the "Piano War."

But worst of all, Thomas's efforts to educate his audience in the higher forms of art met with indifference. The free light orchestral and band concerts drew crowds of thousands, but the more elevated, and costly, symphony and chamber performances did very poor business. Four appearances given in May by the Boston and New York symphony orchestras resulted in receipts totaling only $964. The famous Kneisel String Quartet's three concerts saw only $83 in ticket sales. In May, June, and July, Thomas had overseen thirty-two ticketed performances, and sales had come to just a tiny fraction of what the fair's organizers had expected. Thomas had few friends in the press, and many writers took glee in reporting his failures. In late May the *Musical Courier* noted that "Theodore Thomas' Orchestra, the Boston Symphony Orchestra and Walter Damrosch's Orchestra have all played at Music Hall since the opening of the Exposition, and the attendance, at $1 a head has averaged receipts of about $100 per performance, which tells the story of music at the Fair up to date." Such poor numbers forced Thomas to tender his resignation in August. In the letter he admits the failure of artistic music at the World's Fair and grudgingly suggests that band and light orchestra concerts be multiplied: "For the remainder of the Fair, Music shall not figure as an *Art* at all but be treated merely on the basis of an *amusement*."[73]

The roles of high- and lowbrow culture were changing rapidly in late nineteenth-century America, and Thomas's efforts to define a new class of music that could be understood as distinctly serious served as a precursor to the clearly drawn lines so apparent in the twentieth and twenty-first centuries. When Sousa arrived in Chicago, however, the distinction between art and entertainment remained quite murky for most Americans, and it varied widely between different cities and among different audiences.

Before the band arrived at the exposition, most of its performances were given in concert halls and balanced operatic and symphonic selections with lighter airs. Newspapers noticed this mixture, sometimes celebrating it and sometimes accusing Sousa of too obviously pandering. In Chicago, the situation changed. Here the band would play outside on the fairgrounds, just as Sousa had in Philadelphia twenty years earlier. In this space Sousa maintained both types of music but skewed his performances strongly toward popular tunes and his own most accessible arrangements. The vocal soloists he used on the road were largely replaced by instrumentalists. Audiences continued to hear operatic selections, but they were more often in the form of caprices for euphonium than arias for soprano. Likewise, the band was now playing more potpourris of operatic material than complete overtures or unadulterated arias. In short, Sousa's repertoire did not change as he played on the Chicago fairgrounds—Wagner, Meyerbeer, and Mendelssohn were still on the program—but the presentation of this repertoire was altered substantially. Unlike Thomas, Sousa discarded the trappings of the concert hall in favor of a more accessible approach. Along the way, audiences could rest assured that any piece smacking of art would be followed by a popular, familiar, and entertaining encore.

As musical director, Thomas discovered that fair audiences in Chicago were no more ready for extended concerts of classical selections than Philadelphians had been in 1876. While Thomas and his exclusively high-class concerts foundered, Sousa and his mixture of selections—all arranged to be eminently accessible—triumphed. Sousa played much of the material that Thomas presented, but he played it as popular entertainment rather than as edifying art. As a result, Thomas attracted audiences of dozens, but a single Sousa performance, according to the *Chicago Herald*, "comprised by far the larger portion of the 62,000 people who yesterday paid to see the fair." Again and again, visitors were reminded that the band's engagement had been "one long triumph" and that "day and night crowds in uncounted numbers have listened enraptured to their music."[74]

Such reports must be taken with a grain of salt. The *Herald* rarely had kind words for Thomas (and reportedly once fired a critic for writing too kind a review), and Blakely had deep roots in Chicago's journalistic world. Both of these facts unfairly damaged Thomas, but it is nonetheless clear that Sousa's reputation only benefited from side-by-side comparisons with the older musician. Announcing the band's final concerts, one reporter explained that Sousa's crowd-drawing skills should offer a lesson "as ought to convert even Director Thomas to the belief that the public really do like 'Yankee Doodle' when well played better than a Wagnerian symphony in 'E.'" Another reported that "Director Thomas believes the people ought to be pleased with classical music, while the visitors apparently prefer Bandmaster Sousa and the old every day tunes." The *Herald* described Thomas as a "director of music at the fair who entertains opinions directly contrary to those of Mr. Sousa. He is paid a large salary to entertain the people, but he does not choose to entertain them." While Sousa "attracted large crowds of auditors," Thomas gave "performances to rows of empty benches."[75]

It is too easy, however, to draw a line between Thomas the educator and Sousa the entertainer. As early as November 1890, Sousa had explained how music should function at the World's Fair. He indicated the need to please three audiences: the music student, the music lover, and the common auditor. The first—which Sousa rarely addressed—would need "material for enlightenment." The second was his audience while on tour, and it required a program embracing a variety of musical literature. It was for the third group that Sousa would play on the Chicago fairgrounds, and the common auditor "should be amused—educated if possible—but amused by all means." On leaving the city, Sousa was again asked about his programming, and his reply indicates a two-part approach. He would first please: "The whole idea of music is to give its hearers pleasure. It is foolish to try to play above the heads of one's listeners. The audience at big out-door concerts is composed largely of the masses, and they love light and pretty tunes that have a swing and dash to them. They don't care for what some folks are pleased to call classical music." Through such pleasure, Sousa could accomplish the secondary goal of education: "Much of the high class music will be appreciated by the public and become popular in time if it is mixed judiciously with favorite tunes and dealt out in small doses."[76]

Thomas aimed to create a new musical world, one that celebrated high art. Although he may have failed at the Columbian Exposition, in many ways Thomas's vision came to rule the American concert hall during the twentieth century. Sousa, however, had learned the lessons of the Navy Yard well. As a young man he had seen that audiences both yearned for sophistication and desired pleasure; as the March King he would never fail to give them both. Sousa had no interest in banishing any kind of music from his programs, and as he sought to entertain audiences, he remembered what he had learned as a young man on tour with Milton Nobles:

> It is possible that a properly constituted man, while not a musician, can, by familiarizing himself with the brightest thoughts of the masters, derive as much pleasure in hearing a symphony as a simple melody. It does not follow, though, that any conductor who is catering to the million, shall say

> that he will supply only the musical solids, to the exclusion of the lighter viands served as dessert. His duty is to respect the wishes of his audience and his art. In doing so he will devote a portion of his program to that which appeals to their intelligence solely, interspersed by numbers appealing to the ear only.[77]

It was the season of 1893 that finally produced the March King. By performing at local fairs, Sousa had insulated himself from the critics; in programming symphonies, preludes, and arias, he had satisfied his audiences' desires for sophistication; and by presenting encores of familiar songs and marches, he had kept listeners coming back for more. Along the way, his reputation was constantly protected by his manager, who came to Sousa's aid just as the band left Chicago. The *Herald* had become particularly hard on Theodore Thomas, writing: "The one musical success of the World's Fair was made by this (Sousa's) band. That Thomas should have engaged it for the entire period of the fair everyone knows. One blast from Sousa's band would be worth more to the exposition than all the music the Thomas-Liesegang Band [*sic*] trust could furnish in a year." Sousa must have appreciated the compliment, but Blakely saw no upside to criticizing the most celebrated conductor in America. He therefore set the record straight by praising both Thomas the conductor and Thomas the wise judge of musical merit. He underscored his own ensemble's success in the process.

> You do Mr. Thomas a great injustice. Even supposing that the value to the Exposition of Sousa's Band were not so obviously exaggerated, to Mr. Thomas is due the first and continuous public acknowledgement of the merit of Sousa's Band. . . . As soon as the Exposition put it in his power to do so he tendered Mr. Sousa an engagement for the entire World's Fair season of six months. This tender would gladly have been accepted but for the fact that the band had already contracted to play at Manhattan Beach, at the St. Louis Exposition, and upon a concert tour. . . . Mr. Thomas has in many ways shown himself the generous friend of Mr. Sousa, both as a man and as a musician; and Mr. Thomas has no greater friend or more ardent admirer than John Philip Sousa.[78]

In late June 1893, John Philip Sousa and his band left Chicago in triumph. His national reputation was now secure, and his success had been achieved in no small part through his own skills as a composer, arranger, and conductor. But Sousa had also benefited from circumstance. Patrick Gilmore's decision to leave the management of David Blakely, his subsequent death, and the humiliating missteps of Theodore Thomas all played a role in securing the March King's fame. Public reaction to Sousa's final concert in Chicago might have horrified Thomas, but it was a reaction to which Sousa would soon become accustomed. After the last piece, "Auld Lang Syne," the *Herald* reported, the "crowd broke loose. They clapped their hands and shouted; they [threw] their hats into the air and yelled for more, 'Just one more.' The programme had been gone over twice and the musicians were tired. To escape they grasped their caps and fled the stand, while the leader was bowing an acknowledgement. Mr. Sousa was powerless to do more. The people saw it, and realizing the situation, they shouted long and loud: 'Good-by, Sousa.'"[79]

It was this Sousa—a theater violinist turned celebrity conductor, a local bandleader turned public figure—who arrived at the Manhattan Beach Hotel in the summer of 1893. Sousa may have bested Thomas in Chicago, but at Manhattan Beach he was replacing Gilmore himself. Sousa had often been compared to his illustrious predecessor over the course of the previous season, but these audiences could have heard Gilmore only sporadically on tour. Now the Sousa Band was playing on Gilmore's home turf, in a place "that seemed still to echo the notes of the old band," wrote the *Commercial Advertiser*, and to an audience "in whose hearts and minds the memories of the seasons past were still fresh." It was Sousa's success here—where "those who came to scoff remained to pray"—and his following triumph in St. Louis that transformed Sousa from one manager's idea into America's most celebrated musician. By July the *Musical Courier*, which had earlier been so dismissive, would marvel at the March King's rapid rise to fame: "Sousa and his men now stand at the very head of band music in America, having won this place in little over a year." Much of his fame, of course, rested on his marches, and so before leaving John Philip Sousa, it is worth reflecting on how the march as a genre proved so useful to this dramatic entertainer.[80]

CHAPTER NINE

Theater on the Bandstand

JOHN PHILIP SOUSA'S MUSIC IS TODAY almost unavoidable as it travels across the American soundscape, appearing on concert programs, at sporting events, during patriotic celebrations, in films, and in advertisements. For the modern listener this Sousa is all and only the March King, a view that, at least in part, is in keeping with the historical record. After their success at Manhattan Beach in the summer of 1893, Sousa and his ensemble settled into a comfortable routine of tours and residencies. Along the way, the director's own marches always served as an important part of the draw: a new march was featured virtually every season, and well-known favorites peppered concert programs as encores.

This celebrity entertainer may have been best known as a march composer, but the Sousa examined in these pages—the one active in the 1870s and 1880s—saw himself primarily as a theater musician. He was, after all, trained in the pit, his earliest professional experiences were with traveling theater companies, and during his twelve years as leader of the United States Marine Band, Sousa continued to search for success on the operetta stage. Even as his reputation as a bandleader overtook his work in the theater, his musical outlook remained thoroughly dramatic. During the early 1890s his concerts often included new storytelling pieces such as "The Chariot Race," "Sheridan's Ride," and *The Last Days of Pompeii*. Such efforts at program music did not cease as Sousa's fame spread. While traveling the country, and eventually the world, the Sousa Band often presented audiences with descriptive works such as *Dwellers of the Western World* (1910), *Tales of a Traveler* (1911), and *Impressions at the Movies* (1915). Sousa, meanwhile, continued his quest for an operatic success with *El Capitan* (1895), *The Bride Elect* (1897), *The Charlatan* (1898), *Chris and the Wonderful Lamp* (1899), and *The American Maid* (1909).

These two Sousas, the March King and the theatrical musician, are not as different as they might first appear. Critics often noted that there was something overtly dramatic about this musical entertainer. The *Seattle Post Intelligencer* wrote: "A concert by Sousa's band is more than a mere concert—it is a dramatic performance, a stirring lesson in patriotism, and a popular musical event, all on the same program." At least one of Sousa's artistic contemporaries noted that the March King himself was a theatrical creation: in the mid-1890s the American stage actor Otis Skinner told a reporter, "Sousa is away ahead of us all. Watch him in his exquisite art of dress, his make-up, his fascinating stage manner, his abandon to the character of the music his band plays and his magnetic capture of his audience. Of course, his band is the greatest on earth and that has something to do with it, but Sousa is the best actor America ever produced."[1]

Sousa was an actor in the same way many modern pop icons are actors, and it was through the character of the March King that the bandsman and the theatrical musician were reconciled. At the heart of this character stood the Sousa march. These three-minute works became theatrical delights when performed under the composer's baton, and every element of the Sousa march—from its initial announcement to its appearance in concerts and in middle-class parlors—converged to create the dramatic persona recognized not only by Otis Skinner but by audiences across America.

THE MATERIALS OF A MARCH

Sousa followed a multistep process when composing. He would first sketch out melodic ideas, usually in pencil, and these were often signed and dated. His most famous bass drum player, August Helmecke, later explained that because of the band's almost constant touring, such sketching often occurred in haste: "In odd moments on trains, in hotel rooms, or shipboard he'd simply jot down his immortal themes, hand them over to the band copyist, and then snap right into action on them."[2]

This snapping into action meant drafting two piano versions of the march. The first (in pencil) was used to create a full band score. From this score two sets of hand-copied parts were then extracted. One was sent, along with the second copy of the holograph piano version (usually in ink), to the publisher. The other was used by the Sousa Band to premiere the new march and play it on tour until the published edition became available. Sousa was, of course, quite unusual in following these steps. Nineteenth- and early twentieth-century bands were often led by their first cornetist, and given the conventions of early wind band scoring, this player-conductor could simply deduce a piece's likely orchestration from his own part. Publishers therefore found the production of a full score financially wasteful. As a result, almost all printings of band music from this period (including Sousa's) contain only individual parts. Because a full score would not be published, many bandleader-composers dispensed with producing one and simply turned their holograph short scores over to a seasoned copyist who could easily produce appropriate parts. Sousa's fastidious habits in this regard mean that we now have access to an unusually large number of holograph scores, as well as a few sets of copyist parts.

Sousa's publishers found new marches extraordinarily lucrative, and they were often rushed into print. Working from the copyist parts rather than a full score, multiple engravers could ready the printed band edition quite quickly. Sousa's ink piano holograph, meanwhile, led to a version destined for the parlor market. These arrangements would then be pressed into service to prepare an endless list of editions for various combinations of piano, guitar, banjo, mandolin, zither, and theater orchestra, all of which could be printed and reprinted as the piece's popularity demanded (fig. 33).

This process became a matter of habit only as Sousa's fame increased; as a younger man his music was more practical than commercial. A piece from the 1870s might be played in Philadelphia from manuscript sources but not found worthy of publication, or a youthful composition might be printed in an inexpensive piano edition but not arranged for full band. This state of affairs means that some early pieces are known today only from printed piano editions, though they were once played by bands and orchestras from now-lost manuscript parts. As demand for Sousa's marches increased in the mid-1880s, many older works were pressed into service for various combinations of instruments. In some cases such arrangements drew on Sousa's manuscript performance materials, but in others new editions were almost surely created from scratch. It is often impossible, therefore, to determine whether printed arrangements of early works reflect a piece's original layout or whether Sousa and his publishers updated older marches for more contemporary performance habits.

Such confusion, along with the large number of unpublished and lost works, makes it unwise to search for a single line of development in Sousa's music. It is possible, however, to place his marches into broad categories and thus reveal several distinct march genres, a slow transplantation of the march from parade ground to concert hall, and a growing interest in transforming the march from a functional genre into a storytelling entertainment.

Fig. 33. The cover of the piano edition of "The Stars and Stripes Forever" showing the many arrangements available for purchase. Library of Congress, Washington, D.C.

FIELD AND GRAND MARCHES

Sousa published *Four Marches for Regimental Drums and Trumpets* in 1884. The individual works do not carry titles, and all were brief enough to be gathered together onto a single page. Three are scored for two trumpets and drums, while the fourth contains only a single trumpet part with percussion. In every case the march consists of just two eight-bar strains, with brass melodies designed for valveless trumpets and a percussion part of regimental patterns. As a rule, the trumpets play in unison for the first two measures and then break into thirds to finish the first strain. The second period then alternates between the two brass players, with the drum part reinforcing the melodic rhythms.

Two years later Sousa published his manual *The Trumpet and Drum* (1886), which included seven additional field marches: "Gallant and Gay We'll March Away," "Good Bye, Sweet Nannie Magee," "Let's Hurrah! We Are Almost There," "Hannah, My Own True Love," "Here's Your Health, Sir!," "With Steady Step," and "Funeral March" (the book also includes an original waltz). These pieces follow a pattern similar to that found in *Four Marches* but contain considerably more musical material and a far greater degree of independence between the brass and percussion. Taken together these works constitute Sousa's published output for the field music.

Prior to 1891, field manuals used in the United States differentiated between a common step and a quick step for the movement of troops. Both naturally required music with two beats per measure. Between 1815 and 1891, common step marches were taken at a tempo of 90 beats per minute to accompany a 28-inch step. When scored for band or piano, such works were often referred to as grand marches. With their slower tempi and stately mood, they were particularly appropriate for somber occasions such as inaugurations and funerals. Sousa wrote three independent grand marches while leader of the Marine Band: "President Garfield's Inauguration March" (1881)," "In Memoriam" (1881), and "The Honored Dead" (1885).

As a rule, marches consist of a march proper followed by a trio in the subdominant. Each of these sections consists of a series of strains, and the trio often includes a brief contrasting period known as the break. The Garfield inaugural piece was Sousa's first grand march, and the influence of contemporary Italian opera is quite clear, as it is in the genre as a whole (ex. 10). The work begins with a single-pitch fanfare that leads into an eight-bar strain full of Italianate vocal turns. A brief connecting passage introduces the second strain, which acts as an instrumental tutti in the midst of Sousa's aria. The third strain, featuring a rolling triplet accompaniment, returns the march

Ex. 10. "President Garfield's Inauguration March," introduction through the beginning of the third strain

Ex. 10. (*continued*)

Ex. 10. (*continued*)

to its earlier *bel canto* style. A modulation to the subdominant signals the trio, which again invokes an orchestral tutti with repeated chords and dotted rhythms. Following a brief break, the trio is repeated and the piece as a whole is marked with a *da capo* repeat. Sousa passes through a wide range of textures over the course of the work, and such variety was no doubt useful in accompanying the new president's slow-moving reception line.

For some reason Sousa does not seem to have composed similar works for the three other presidents to take office during his time as leader of the Marine Band. He did, however, write another grand march for James Garfield: "In Memoriam." A predictably more somber work, this funeral piece features a minor-key ritornello. "The Honored Dead," for Ulysses S. Grant's 1885 funeral, is similar with its alternation between dotted rhythms and lyrical passages.

Both works written for Garfield, though performed by the Marine Band, were published only for piano. Given their ties to specific events, it is not surprising that neither march became a regular part of the Sousa Band's repertoire. "The Honored Dead," on the other hand, was published for piano and for band and performed with some frequency by Sousa's ensemble (indeed, it was played at Sousa's own memorial service in 1932). Because of the new preference for quickstep marches in the late nineteenth century, such slow works stand as exceptions in Sousa's output. He did, however, return to the genre once in 1919 for "The Golden Star," written in memory of Quentin Roosevelt, the youngest son of Theodore Roosevelt, who was killed in aerial combat over France in July 1918.

THE SHORT-TRIO QUICKSTEP

The quickstep, requiring a tempo of between 110 and 120 beats per minute, has long appeared in military field manuals. The faster step had completely overtaken common step maneuvers by 1891, but military preference was much less important than its social appeal. Like other stylizations, quickstep marches were used not only to move troops but also to accompany social dances and to please seated concert audiences. It is thus not particularly surprising that quicksteps far outnumbered their slower cousins by mid-century; such pieces form the bulk of the March King's published output.

The quickstep genre, as inherited by Sousa, required a certain flexibility: music for marching had to be adaptable to various parade routes, and music for the ballroom needed to last until dancers tired of the step. It was only natural, then, that quicksteps—while still consisting of a march and trio—were really little more than strings of equal-length units. Each of these units was typically marked with a repeat, to be taken or ignored depending on the fancy of the dancers or the parade route's length. In addition to their repeated strains, the quicksteps of Sousa's youth provided another option for varying the work's duration: many were marked with a *da capo* repeat, often without any accompanying *fine*. Because each section was of equal weight, a stationary listener watching a band pass by could hear any strain as the beginning, middle, or end of a march. Such pieces could be repeated indefinitely and conclude with whichever section was nearest at hand. The quickstep march with *da capo* repeat was, in short, ideal for the parade ground or dance floor.

Sousa's 1879 march "Resumption" is typical of this flexible form (fig. 34 and table 6). The piece is in two big sections, a march in the tonic and a trio in the subdominant, each consisting of two repeated strains. This structure, which appeared in several of Sousa's earliest works, allowed for a great deal of variation. His first published march, "Review" (1873), includes a common variant: multiple introductions (in this case, four-bar units added to the second strain and the trio).

Fig. 34. "Resumption March," solo B♭ cornet part. Library of Congress, Washington, D.C.

Table 6. Da capo march structure ("Resumption")

MARCH			TRIO	
Introduction	**1st strain**	**2d strain**	**3d strain**	**4th strain**
|| 4 ||	||: 16 :||	||: 16 :||	||: 16 :||	||: 16 :||
A♭			D♭	
		fine		*d.c.*

While such pieces were useful for marching and dancing, Sousa was a product of the theater, and an unembellished *da capo* structure was hardly theatrical. Sousa rarely spoke about his own music, but on several occasions he made clear his desire to infuse the quickstep march with a sense of drama. In 1918 he explained how he hoped to create works of "cumulative force and interest." In his autobiography he described how "the chief aim of the composer is to produce color, dynamics, nuances and to emphasize the story-telling quality" of his music. With its rounded, A-B-A structure, the *da capo* march was neither cumulative nor storytelling in nature.[3]

The first step in creating a dramatic march was obvious: delete the *da capo* repeat and thus straighten a circular piece into a linear event. Sousa was hardly the first musician to make this change, and while the rounded form did return a march from the trio's subdominant to the opening tonic, its function was more practical than tonal. In 1898 Sousa recalled that even during his childhood, bandleaders would often skip the *da capo* if it failed to serve their needs:

> In my childhood in Washington I noticed that the bands parading with the regiments in nearly every instance, although the composition called for *da capo*, would finish playing on the last strain of the march; therefore, if it was done practically in the use of the march I could not understand why it should not be done theoretically in the writing of the march. Accordingly, in composing my marches I ignored the old established rule and wrote with the idea of making the last strain of the march the musical climax, regardless of the tonality.[4]

In several of his early marches Sousa retains the traditional structure but does away with the *da capo* repeat. This subtle change makes the march's fourth strain, which often includes broader rhythmic values and a higher tessitura, the work's musical climax. Jonathan Elkus has termed this form the short-trio structure, and it is found in many of the marches Sousa wrote while leader of the Marine Band, marches that would have been useful both on parade and in concert.[5]

The presence or absence of a *da capo* repeat is not always a defining formal feature, however. "Resumption," for example, which first appeared as part of Sousa's 1879 collection *Evening Pastime*, for violin or flute with piano accompaniment, lacks any *da capo* indication. A piano version of the march appeared the same year with a *da capo* marking but lacked any concluding *fine*. A band arrangement was finally published in 1882, complete with a fermata at the end of the march proper to indicate the repeat's conclusion. Such variations are common throughout the band repertoire, since pieces were often rushed to publication with little concern for the niceties of editorial detail.

By the 1880s Sousa had largely done away with the *da capo* repeat, and "The Wolverine March" (1881) even adds a fermata at the end of the trio as if to declare the work over. "Right Forward," from the same year, also lacks a *da capo* indication. These four marches—"Resumption," "Review," "Right Forward," and "The Wolverine March"—are the clearest examples of Sousa's short-trio form. Similar pieces, with greater or lesser degrees of variation, also appeared in the 1870s and 1880s. "Triumph of Time" (1885) is interesting for its introduction, which produces a false start by foreshadowing the first strain's melody. "Esprit de Corps" (1878) is unusual for its opening minor mode and lack of a repeat of the first strain. These two abnormalities are later corrected when the second strain moves to major, modulates down a whole step, and is followed by an added strain in the relative major of the opening key. Such modulations seem to have almost required the addition of a third march strain. In "Globe and Eagle" (1879), for example, the second strain moves to the dominant, and a third strain is added to return the march to its opening tonic. As if to make up for this extra length, the piece ends with a shortened strain of a mere eight bars.

A few other early marches are more distant variants of the form. An unusual repeat structure gives "Across the Danube" (1877) an opening march that effectively consists of three strains and a trio best heard as one large thirty-two-bar unit. "Guide Right" (1881) lacks an introduction and has a trio consisting of a single twenty-bar strain.

Most of Sousa's short-trio marches date from early in his career, but he did sometimes return to the form, especially when he needed pieces suitable for actual marching. "The High School Cadets" (1890), written for one of Washington's militia organizations, follows the short-trio model quite closely (with the exception of a twenty-four-bar first strain). "The Belle of Chicago," which may have been used as part of the 1892 dedication parade at the World's Columbian Exposition, uses the form as well. The structure was, of course, also useful for incidental music. When Sousa provided materials for Francis

Wilson's *The Lion Tamer* in 1891, he included an original march (published under the play's title and as "On Parade"). For this piece, which likely needed a flexible duration, Sousa reverted to the *da capo* repeat.

The publication history of these marches follows Sousa's rise to fame. "Review" (1873) appeared only in a piano edition. "Resumption" (1879) was printed for piano and did not appear in a band arrangement until 1882. "Globe and Eagle" (1879) is unusual among Sousa's earliest works in that it appeared only in a band edition, probably as part of Sousa's effort to gain the attention of the Marine Corps. "Right Forward," "The Wolverine March," and "Guide Right," all issued for piano in 1881, were included in a series of marches printed for band by Harry Coleman in 1885. By this point demand for Sousa's work made raiding his earlier catalog profitable, and Coleman also reached back to print "Across the Danube" (1877) and issued "Triumph of Time" (1885) for band. "Esprit de Corps" (1878), published for piano, had to wait until 1893 for a band edition.

The Sousa Band, of course, was a concert ensemble, not a parade organization. The group played about 15,623 concerts but is known to have marched on only eight occasions. Even without its *da capo* repeat, the short-trio structure still consisted of undifferentiated strains and thus was not particularly effective on the concert stage. It is not surprising, therefore, that none of the short-trio marches from the 1870s and 1880s found a regular position on the band's programs. With his rising fame of the early 1890s, however, a handful of the newer short-trio pieces did make it into the band's repertoire, including "The High School Cadets," (1890), "On Parade" (1891), and "The Belle of Chicago (1892).[6]

The mature March King did sometimes look backward to this older form, most famously in "Manhattan Beach" (1893), "The Directorate" (1894), and "El Capitan" (1896). As he sought to add drama to the march, however, Sousa turned away from this inherited structure. His transformation of the march from a parade work into a thing of cumulative force and interest did not occur overnight, however. Rather, it began with the use of borrowed material. So before turning to the concert march itself, it is worth examining how some of Sousa's earliest marches made use of preexisting melodies.

BORROWING IN THE MARCH

Sousa's most successful marches are all based on original material, but the use of borrowed tunes has a long history in march composition. In 1875, G. F. Patton advised amateur composers that they might find composing original melodies and arranging them for band too daunting a task. The process could be simplified by borrowing at least some of the material. If such borrowing was done by putting popular tunes to new use, this technique had the pleasant side effect of making a new march instantly recognizable:

> As it is hardly probable that a beginner in the art of arrangement will be able to compose original marching pieces, we shall speak principally of the plan of getting up "Medley" Quicksteps, that is to say, taking some two or three suitable airs and combining them so as to form a single piece. Many of the most popular Quicksteps of the day are made up in this way, and the plan is particularly convenient for Amateur arrangers, who are often incapable of composing an original Quickstep, but can generally get up quite a credible medley composed of popular airs in the Quickstep style.

Patton is writing of medley marches, pieces that are little more than a stringing together of popular tunes. Sousa wrote several such works, mostly in the 1880s, and because they often throw together borrowed melodies of varying lengths, such marches do not readily fit into the usual quickstep structures.[7]

Sousa's first medley march was "Mother Goose" (1880). The opening march contains three repeated eight-bar strains based on "Come All Ye Young Maids," "I'se Come to See Miss Jennie Jones," and "Little Jack Horner." A transition leads to the trio, which contains both the expected modulation and a change of meter from 6/8 to 2/4. Sousa begins the trio by borrowing from "There Is a Man in Our Town." The march then in effect returns to the opening key, and Sousa borrows the melodies of "Oh, Dear Doctor" and "Down in the Meadow." An eight-bar break returns the march to the subdominant and introduces a final strain that reprises "There Is a Man in Our Town." The result is a rounded trio, both in terms of borrowed material and key area (table 7). In the piano edition, the march ends with a *da capo* repeat. A companion piece to this march was the medley "Mother Hubbard March" (1885). This time Sousa uses "Three Blind Mice," "Thus the Farmer Sows His Seed," "Little Jack Horner," and "Hey Diddle Diddle" in the march proper, while the trio states "London Bridge" and "Minstrel Boy" in a rounded form similar to that used in "Mother Goose." Both marches appeared in piano and band arrangements, and both were periodically heard during Sousa Band concerts.

Table 7. Medley march ("Mother Goose," trio only)

TRIO				
"There Is a Man"	**"Oh, Dear Doctor"**	**"Down in the Meadow"**	**Break**	**"There Is a Man"**
|| 4+16 ||	||: 8 :||	16	8	16
C	[G]		[C]	
				da capo

Sousa wrote several other medley works. "Mikado March" (1885) uses a number of themes from Gilbert and Sullivan's operetta. "The Blending of the Blue and the Gray" (1887), which Sousa called "A Medley in March-Form," is based on Civil War and other regional and military tunes, including "Reveille," "Maryland, My Maryland," "Carry Me Back to Old Virginny," "Gay and Happy," "The Star-Spangled Banner," "Dixie," and "Yankee Doodle." "Ben Bolt" (1888) borrows material from "The Daisy," "Go Down, Moses," "Sally in Our Alley," "Ben Bolt," and "O Fair Dove, O Fond Dove." Finally, Sousa used J. L. Molloy's "The Song of the Triton" for several related works. He included an arrangement of the piece in his 1879 collection *Evening Pastime*, and in 1892 he added some extra material to create "The Triton Medley March." This piece was also published as "Triton March," "Souvenir," "Paris Exposition," and "The Triton Two-Step." None of these medley marches were regularly used in Sousa Band programs.

Creating medleys was not the only way to use borrowed material, however. In 1876, while working in Philadelphia, Sousa published several pieces based on Joseph P. Webster's hymn "The Sweet By-and-By," which was enjoying a certain vogue thanks to local performances by Lotta Crabtree. Sousa probably saw an opportunity to benefit from a popular song, and one of his efforts resulted in "Revival March" (1876), the piano sheet music of which proudly announces the use of Webster's hymn.

Sousa's piece is in the familiar *da capo* form but with several significant changes. As in most marches, each of Sousa's strains is sixteen bars long. The march proper contains three such strains, each marked to be repeated. The two trio strains, however, are left unrepeated (fig. 35). The reason is clear: Webster's hymn contains a sixteen-bar verse and a sixteen-bar chorus. In order to present the entire hymn, Sousa requires an unbroken thirty-two-bar unit. The trio is in effect one strain, twice as long as each of the preceding sections.

Increasing the length of the trio gives that section further weight, but the real attraction is the borrowed material itself. Presenting a vernacular tune, popular song, or hymn as the theme for a series of variations can lead to new pieces in which the emotional impact of the borrowed material is spent even as the work begins. Using the music of Charles Ives, J. Peter Burkholder has shown how reversing the process and hinting at well-known material before stating it outright can create a more effective dramatic arc. In "Revival March," the unsuspecting listener sits through three strains before hearing the familiar hymn. On the first listen the opening sections appear to be made up entirely of original material, but in fact they contain hints of the hymn to come. Webster's melody is dominated by a dotted rhythmic pattern, and although Sousa

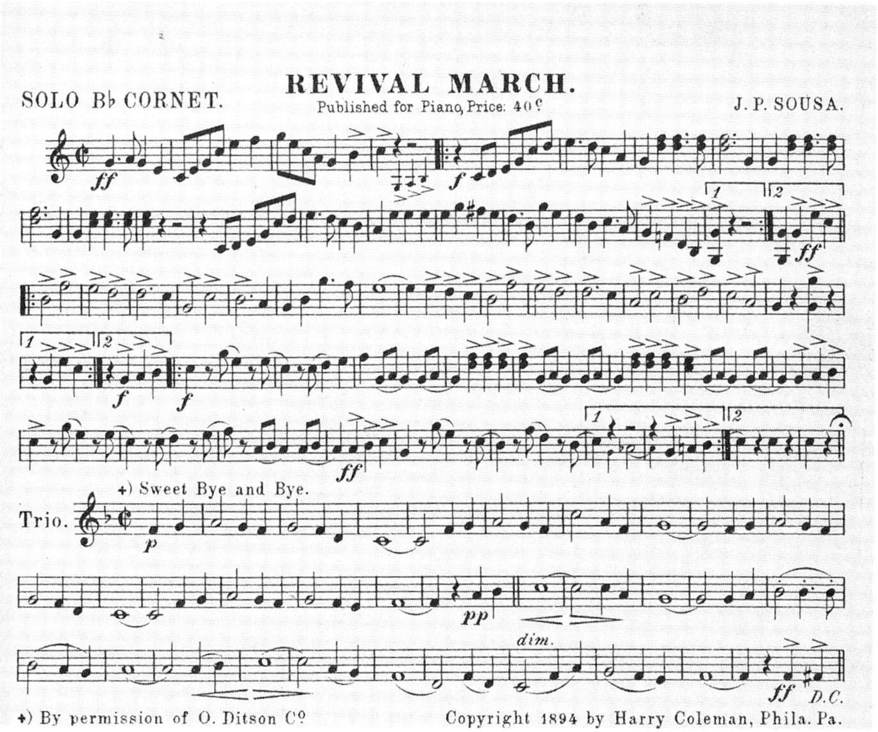

Fig. 35. "Revival March," solo B♭ cornet part. Library of Congress, Washington, D.C.

ignores this rhythm in the trio, it plays an important role in the march's first strain. This surface rhythm is hardly Sousa's only gesture toward the hymn, however. In the first measures of his first strain he paraphrases the hymn's opening material, and several bars later he hints at the second and fourth phrases of the hymn (exs. 11a and 11b). Such subtle paraphrasing is easily missed the first time through the opening march, but on the repeat—once the full hymn has been heard—Sousa's earlier paraphrase is made explicit.[8]

We might call pieces in which a single familiar tune impacts the structure of the work as a whole song marches. There are relatively few such pieces in Sousa's output, and most of them date from the early part of his career. "Bonnie Annie Laurie" (1883) is based on a Scottish tune that Sousa called "the most beautiful of all folk songs." As in "Revival March," it is the trio that accommodates the borrowed material. Here a wobbling eighth-note figure and a series of trills suggest something of the song's pastoral setting, and two additional strains work together to present the entire thirty-two bars of the borrowed tune, with

Ex. 11a. Comparison of "Revival March" (mm. 5–6) with the hymn tune

the pastoral material now acting as a countermelody. This piece is also marked with a *da capo*, and only on the repeat might an attentive listener pick up Sousa's subtle references to the borrowed tune, which include a characteristic octave leap and an articulated downward step in his introduction.[9]

Two other song marches are somewhat more direct. Surviving materials for the unpublished "The Quilting Party" (1889) show that its first strain borrows from Gilbert and Sullivan's *The Yeomen of the Guard*, while the trio is taken from "Aunt Dinah's Quilting Party." "The White Plume" (1884) is an example of self-borrowing. The march's trio is expanded to thirty-two bars to accommodate the entirety of Sousa's campaign song "We'll Follow Where the White Plume Leads." In the piano and the band arrangements the trio includes fanfares, perhaps meant to endow the presidential candidate James G. Blaine, who had not served in the Civil War, with the military bearing he otherwise lacked. Of these early song marches, only "The White Plume" was performed with any regularity by the Sousa Band.

The most famous example of Sousa's self-borrowing occurs in "Semper Fidelis" (1888), and once again it is the trio that is most directly impacted. The trios of many of Sousa's most famous marches make use of a layering effect, which Frederick Fennell has called a "four-layer musical cake." In the band edition of "Semper Fidelis" the trio begins with an eight-bar regimental

Ex. 11b. Comparison of "Revival March" (mm. 15–18) with the hymn tune

drum solo, followed by a sixteen-bar strain that is heard three times. In the first statement we hear only cornets and a simple accompaniment as Sousa states his own "With Steady Step," borrowed from *The Trumpet and Drum*. In the second statement this melody is decorated by woodwind flourishes, and these two elements are finally joined by a trombone countermelody (ex. 12). In later marches this layering would have served as the piece's climax, but in

Ex. 12. The layering effect in the trio of "Semper Fidelis"

"Semper Fidelis" Sousa is still using the older short-trio structure, and so he ends the march with a final repeated strain. "Semper Fidelis" was regularly played by the Sousa Band on tour, and as the traditional march of the United States Marine Corps, it is one of the earliest of Sousa's works to have secured a permanent place in the wind band repertoire.[10]

A number of later marches also make use of preexisting material, either in medley or song march form. "Columbia's Pride" (1914) borrows from Sousa's song "Nail the Flag to the Mast," "March of the Pan-Americans" (1915) uses several national anthems, "America First" (1916) makes use of political tunes, "The Naval Reserve" (1917) borrows from Sousa's song "Blue Ridge, I'm Coming Back to You," "The Chantyman's March" (1918) uses several sea chanteys, "Ancient and Honorable Artillery" (1924) borrows from "Auld Lang Syne," "The Minnesota March" (1927) uses several Native American melodies, "New Mexico" (1928) draws on Spanish songs, and "Salvation Army" (1930) uses the hymn tune "O Boundless Salvation." Sousa, of course, also wrote marches based on material from his operettas: "El Capitan" (1896), "The Bride Elect" (1897), "The Charlatan" (1898), "The Free Lance" (1906), and "From Maine to Oregon" (1913), the last of which was based on *The American Maid*.

In medley and song marches, Sousa was forced to rethink his trio. In the latter, this section was often lengthened to accommodate a thirty-two-bar borrowed tune. In the former, a series of trio strains was broken up by brief musical breaks. These two elements, the short break and the lengthened trio, would become the hallmarks of Sousa's most successful marches as he transplanted the genre from the parade ground to the concert hall.

THE CONCERT MARCH

Sousa recognized the older *da capo* march as a circular structure: "As a child I was brought up on band music. As I grew I noticed something about the marches of that day—they did not climax. Speaking gastronomically, when they got through with the ice cream they went back to the roast beef. And the beef had no new sauce on it, no new flavor." In working to make his concert marches theatrical, Sousa endeavored to create pieces consisting of distinct musical courses contained within a clear dramatic shape. Creating this culinary drama would require more radical changes to the short-trio structure than merely deleting its *da capo* repeat.[11]

Over the course of the 1880s, Sousa aimed to construct a trio that could serve as a march's climax. The first step was to make the piece's key change

Table 8. Short-trio structure ("Congress Hall")

MARCH			TRIO		
Intro.	**1st strain**	**2d strain**	**trio 1**	**break**	**trio 2**
|| 4 ||	||: 16 :||	||: 16 :||	|| 4+16 ||	|| 16 ||	|| 16 ||
B♭			E♭		
		fine			*d.c.*

correspond with its final material and thus do away with the trio's second strain. In order to maintain the section's length, he inserted a brief interlude between repeated statements of the principal trio melody. The result was very much like the rounded trio structure found in some medley marches, only instead of a key change, the break would be differentiated by heightened chromaticism, low brass melodies, or sharply articulated woodwind punctuation. An early example of this structure is "Congress Hall" (1882). While the use of a break strain is new, this march also has several older formal elements, including an introduction to the trio and a *da capo* repeat (table 8).

In the early and mid-1880s Sousa experimented with this new trio-break arrangement. In the band version, "Pet of the Petticoats" (1883) has two trio statements separated by an eight-bar break. The trio of "Transit of Venus" (1883) is heard three times, and though it has no distinct break, the middle trio statement is transposed by a half-step and reharmonized, thus clearly separating its material from the principal trio melody. In "Right-Left" (1883), Sousa creates the effect of a break not only in the trio but also in the opening march by repeating the first strain after the second. "The Rifle Regiment" (1886) includes a break along with an unusual twenty-one-bar introduction that is incorporated into the repeat of the opening strain. Of all these proto-break marches, only the last found a regular place on Sousa Band programs.

Two marches demonstrate how these various forms could overlap. "On the Tramp" (1879) is a song march based on Septimus Winner's "Out of Work." The borrowed song consists of a sixteen-bar verse and eight-bar chorus, both of which use the same melodic material. Winner's tune became the basis for Sousa's sixteen-bar trio, two statements of which are interrupted by a break. For the modern listener unfamiliar with the melody, this march's trio seems to be stated twice with an interrupting break strain. To a listener who knows Winner's melody, it is the borrowed tune's verse and chorus that are interrupted. "Yorktown Centennial" followed the old short-trio form when it was published for piano in 1881 (complete with a second trio strain that bears an unusual melodic relationship to the march's second strain). In 1885, when the piece was published for band, it included an eight-bar percussion introduction to the trio and a cornet break. "Yorktown Centennial" was occasionally performed by the Sousa Band, while "On the Tramp" made only rare appearances.

Sousa had committed to the break strain by the mid-1880s, and to better highlight this new cumulative form he began to repeat both trio and break together. The result is a structure in which the principal trio strain is heard a total of four times: twice on its own repeat, and twice repeated with the break. In order to vary this repetition, Sousa often decorated the trio repeats with additive countermelodies as he had in "Semper Fidelis." With the break now playing such a large role in the march, Sousa often foreshadows its typically dark mood by opening the piece in the minor mode and modulating to the major in the second strain. This long-trio form is seen most clearly in "Sound Off" (1885), in which a skipping trio melody is later decorated with a florid clarinet obbligato (table 9). This form had been tried out in one earlier work, the theater march "Our Flirtation" (1880); both pieces were periodically played by the Sousa Band.

With the long-trio form, Sousa had found a satisfying structure that allowed him to create the type of musical event he had been seeking. It was clearly the trio, heard four times, that functioned as the march's climax. By separating trio statements with a significant break strain and varying their repetitions with additive countermelodies, he avoided any sense of monotony. Something had also changed about the march's key structure. In the older *da capo* form, the piece as a whole moved from the opening tonic to the subdominant, and back again on the repeat. When the *da capo* was dismissed, Sousa's marches seemed to end in the subdominant. But with its multiple statements, the trio was now the meat of the march, and as Jonathan Elkus has suggested, Sousa's mature marches modulate not from tonic to subdominant but from an introductory area to a concluding tonic at the trio.[12]

Further undermining the opening strain's claim to the tonic is Sousa's frequent practice of beginning long-trio marches in the minor mode. The result is a three-key structure: a march beginning in minor, modulating to the relative major in the second strain, and shifting to a final tonic at the

Table 9. Long-trio structure ("Sound Off")

MARCH			**TRIO**		
Intro.	**1st strain**	**2d strain**	**trio 1**	**break**	**additive trio**
|| 4 ||	||: 16 :||	|| 32 ||	||: 16 :||	||: 16	16 :||
d		F	B♭	g	B♭

trio. This form first appeared in "Sound Off" and would reappear in "The Gladiator" (1886), "The Picadore" (1889), and "The Loyal Legion" (1890). Of course, not all long-trio marches begin in the minor. "The Occidental" (1887), "National Fencibles" (1888), "The Crusader" (1888), "The Washington Post" (1889), and "The Thunderer" (1889) all begin in major, as does the unpublished "Homeward Bound." "The Beau Ideal" (1893) hints at minor in its introduction before quickly moving to the major mode.

With his long-trio marches of the late 1880s, Sousa had settled into a standardized form, and very few of these works vary the structure in any significant way. "The Loyal Legion" is notable for its use of materials from *The Queen of Hearts*, "National Fencibles" for its trio with text, and "The Thunderer" for its unusual layering of a regimental melody in the second strain (borrowed from Sousa's "Here's Your Health, Sir!"). These outliers notwithstanding, the long-trio structure seems to have satisfied Sousa's needs: the trio-break repeats—often with additive countermelodies—could fulfill the dramatic desires of an attentive audience. That all of these pieces were better suited to the concert hall than to the parade ground or dance floor is confirmed by the fact that most were immediately published in both piano and band arrangements, and all found a regular place in Sousa Band programs. Several of Sousa's quite popular later marches would also use the long-trio structure, including "King Cotton" (1895) and "Hands Across the Sea" (1899).

Despite the success of the long-trio march, Sousa was still not completely satisfied in his efforts. In 1890 he wrote "Corcoran Cadets," the trio of which includes an original texted song. The tune's thirty-two-bar A-A-B-A structure created a trio of twice the usual length, and there was now little reason to repeat it before moving on to the break strain. In a sense it is a song march, but it is also a long-trio structure whose trio had been doubled in length by the sung material. In "Corcoran Cadets" we find the prototype of a new extended-trio form, which would come to fruition late in 1893 with "The Liberty Bell." Here Sousa includes a thirty-two-bar trio that is heard three times in its entirety, each statement separated by the break strain (table 10). "Corcoran Cadets" foreshadowed this new form, but in this march Sousa was not yet quite ready to commit, and the trio repeats include only the section's first sixteen bars. There is little doubt as to where the climax of an extended-trio march lies: the final section is twice the length of all earlier strains and is heard three times. It was this form that Sousa used in his most successful post-1893 marches: "The Stars and Stripes Forever" (1896), "The Invincible Eagle" (1901), "The Glory of the Yankee Navy" (1909), "The Black Horse Troop" (1924), and "George Washington Bicentennial" (1930).

Table 10. Extended-trio structure ("The Liberty Bell")

MARCH			**TRIO**		
Intro.	**1st strain**	**2d strain**	**trio**	**break**	**trio**
|| 4 ||	||: 16 :||	||: 16 :||	|| 32 ||	||: 24	32 :||
F			B♭		

This overview of the march forms used by Sousa between 1876 and 1893 demonstrates several things. First, the composer had at his disposal an extraordinary variety of choices for such a deceptively simple genre. There were marches for the field music, for the parlor piano, for the parade band, and for the concert ensemble (along with a host of other small instrumental combinations). There were grand marches, medley marches, and song marches. There were *da capo* quicksteps and dramatic concert pieces. Second, Sousa dabbled in the full range of possibilities, and he clearly felt free to vary and combine structures. As he matured and his fame grew, however, he settled on just a handful of march types, most notably the long and extended-trio structures. The reasons for this narrowing are obvious: his new position as leader of a constantly touring commercial concert band meant that he had little use for the earlier parade forms and little time for experimentation. Finally, during the late 1880s Sousa was making a gradual move away from the circular structures of the parade ground and toward the dramatic forms needed to please concert audiences. The key to this drama was in the trio. But Sousa, once called "the best actor America has ever produced," did not limit his concern for the dramatic merely to the invention of new forms. Rather, he infused every element of his mature marches with drama.[13]

BEYOND STRUCTURE

Most audiences were, of course, blissfully unaware of the structures passing before them. For these listeners it was the ever-changing moods of a Sousa march that caught their attention, moods bound together with melody, rhythm, and texture. Sousa's own words suggest that his melodies came from a pairing of inspiration and craft: "I do not, of course, manufacture my themes deliberately; the process isn't direct or arbitrary enough for that. It is not a nonchalant morning's work. I often dig for my themes. I practice a sort of self-hypnotism, by penetrating the inner chambers of my brain and *receiving* the themes. Any composer who is gloriously conscious that he *is* a composer must believe that he receives his inspiration from a source higher than himself." Earlier in his career, he had described the way melodies rushed at him:

Ex. 13. The lilting of the dance floor in the first strain of "Resumption March" (melody only)

"Great ideas come often as surprises, and a musician is awestruck when he gives birth to a melody that he feels is all his own. There have been such times when I have been almost overpowered by a feeling of fright."[14]

Sousa's melodies, of course, vary widely. A great many (especially in the first strain) betray the lilt of the dance floor with their predictable 6/8 patterns and full stops at mid-period (ex. 13). The parade ground is also well represented by the melodies consisting of foursquare rhythms, accented downbeats, and octave doublings (ex. 14). Trios, of course, are often graceful songs broken up by violent break strains. But these descriptions simply reinforce the words of Deems Taylor, who like many critics found Sousa's charm difficult to explain: "They have a deceptive simplicity, those Sousa marches. Their tunes are so uncomplicated, so easy to catch, so essentially spontaneous and diatonic, that one can easily underrate them." In the Sousa march, form, melody, and mood work together. It is the change in tune that defines movement from one strain to the next, and it is the sharp contrast—most notably between trio and break strain—that lends these miniature pieces their drama. "The Washington Post," a model long-trio march, serves as an excellent example of Sousa's unfolding theatricality.[15]

Like virtually all Sousa marches, "The Washington Post" begins with an introduction. This one, like many, is left unharmonized as the parts move chromatically in glorious octaves (ex. 15a). There are many ways to introduce harmony, and in some marches Sousa allows it to unfold naturally. In "The Washington Post," however, the contrast is sudden, as the first triad appears on the introduction's last beat. As if to make this gesture even more forceful, this first chord is set off by rests, articulated, and accented. A lack of harmony might be taken as a defect, but Sousa has a trick up his sleeve. The ringing octaves and rocking chromatic motion focus attention on meter and rhythm: this is a march,

Ex. 14. The parade ground in the second strain of "The Gladiator"

after all. Or is it? The first seven bars are dominated by a lilting quarter-note, eighth-note pattern, but the long ties at the end of the first and third measures displace the basic pulse. To the unsuspecting listener, the first dotted quarter note just might be the downbeat, and perhaps the marching band has stepped off on the wrong foot. If this is the case, then that first triad is on the downbeat: from its very start, Sousa has created a piece that is both march and dance.

Ex. 15a. Octaves as both march and dance in the introduction of "The Washington Post"

The rhythmic displacement of the introduction is only heightened by the opening of the first strain, in which Sousa continues to accent the second beat while avoiding any clear statement of the opening tonic. This strain does, however, introduce two elements that will become vital to the remainder of the work: a chromatic lower neighbor and a pulsating rhythmic accompaniment, both of which work to propel the march forward into a two-step (ex. 15b). By the end of the first strain the lower neighbor—earlier a mere pickup—has been transformed to decorate the cadence's repeated pitches. The Johann Strauss biographer H. E. Jacob calls this trick Sousa's "sailor's knot," a term Jonathan Elkus borrows to describe a moment that cinches

Ex. 15b. Rhythmic propulsion in the first strain of "The Washington Post"

"an important half-cadence only to hurl it forward to the return of the tune, rather than merely to decorate an already obvious close."[16]

If meter had been a problem at the beginning of this march, all is well in the second strain. Here bold octaves articulate each beat, and ties over the bar line allow for pickups to boost momentum into the following measure (ex. 15c). The key, however, remains unsettled: the opening tune arpeggiates D major, and a repeated high E rings out defiantly, further complicating tonal stability. Only as the trio begins will the opening key of G be firmly planted in the melody, but of course by that point Sousa has modulated. While the

Ex. 15c. Melodic clarity in the second strain of "The Washington Post"

accompaniment provides full chords, a listener might expect the soothing melodic thirds and sixths found in so many second strains. Sousa, however, maintains the clarity of octaves in his melodic line. As the strain comes to an end, he does, however, introduce an altered chord, a trick that Edward Berlin has called the measure-13 convention common to both the march and the ragtime repertoire.[17]

Following these strains, Sousa modulates and dissolves his chaotic and rhythmically confused opening into a singing trio. It is here that the march most clearly becomes a concert work, and Jacob notes that this shift in mood was a "typical 'Sousa-effect' when the depths of a lyrical monologue replace the bluster of the parade-ground." The magic of Sousa's trio is obvious from the start. Here two ideas—four slurred dotted-quarter notes and a faster, staccato arpeggiation—stand in stark contrast (ex. 15d). The lower neighbor dip from the first strain is also present, now in an accented position and with a comparatively long rhythmic value that propels the melody forward into both the lyric and the articulated passages. The dance's dip, present from the beginning, serves as a sort of mini-ritornello, unifying the trio's two contrasting moods. At the start of the trio, the two legato bars had reached downward while the staccato eighth notes ascended. But just as the listener becomes aware of this contrast, Sousa achieves resolution. Suddenly, in the trio's eleventh bar, a slurred leap breaks the descending pattern, jumps to the trio's apex, and reintroduces the march's opening quarter-eighth rhythmic pattern. As in all long-trio marches, this section will be heard two more times, each interrupted by a break strain.[18]

Such writing—so seemingly simple—has caught many critics off-guard, as when one unhelpfully declared: "There is little doubt that the favorite chords of Sousa were the tonic, dominant and the dominant seventh." But the genius of Sousa is in his brevity and boldness. Ideas never last too long, nor are they overly complicated or self-conscious. As the bandmaster once explained, a march "must be as free from padding as a marble statue. Every line must be carved with unerring skill. Once padded, it ceases to be a march. There is no form of musical composition where the harmonic structure must be more clean-cut. . . . There must be a melody which appeals to the musical and unmusical alike. There must be no confusion in counterpoints." Or as H. E. Jacob described the spirit of the trio in "The Washington Post": "Without altering a note, simply writing it in octaves, in an absolutely inartistic parallel, he achieves indescribable effect." For Jacob this was Sousa at his most accessible, and this march served as "the great democratic total survey of America."[19]

Ex. 15d. The pervasive lower neighbor dip in the trio of "The Washington Post"

SOUNDING SOUSA: THE MARCH IN PERFORMANCE

By the late 1890s, Sousa's reputation as leader of America's most important touring ensemble had spread well beyond the United States. The end of the Spanish-American War allowed for the ensemble's first European tour, and in April 1900 it set sail for the Paris Exposition and concerts across Europe. In 1901 it made a tour of Great Britain, and in 1903 it traveled as far east as St. Petersburg. Another British tour was undertaken in 1905. On the heels of these international successes, the Sousa Band sailed from New York on December 24, 1910, for a world tour that would last a full year and allow the ensemble to play before English-speaking audiences in the United Kingdom, South Africa, Australia, New Zealand, and Hawaii. These listeners had, of course, heard Sousa's music before—performed by local bands, played in parlors, and etched into recordings—but they had never seen the March King himself, and much of Sousa's dramatic appeal could be witnessed only in performance.

Reviews make clear that the Sousa march as performed by the Sousa Band was quite different from the Sousa march as published. One South African writer, who was not particularly interested in hearing *El Capitan* yet again, found himself pleasantly surprised:

> Sousa's marches have been done to death by German bands, have been mangled by barrel organs, hashed up by gramophones, and whistled fiendishly by street urchins, and perhaps one did not look forward . . . to hearing them again. . . . But as soon as the band struck up *El Capitan*, one realised that one had never heard a Sousa march played before. There is a vim about the Sousa march as played by the Sousa Band that sets the blood a-tingling, and you feel that you could march anywhere to such virile music.[20]

At the height of Sousa's fame, his marches were sold as sheet music and played by ensembles all across the country. Under the March King's own baton, however, they led a second life as composer-conducted works. These two existences—as printed music and as performed entertainment—reinforced one an other: after a concert any audience member might be inspired to obtain sheet music, and after mastering a march at home the amateur pianist might desire to hear the composer in person. In either case, money changed hands.

Sousa's publishers worked quickly to take advantage of this situation. New marches were churned out each season, and Sousa often worked to connect his pieces to events of local or national importance: "The Fairest of the Fair" for a 1908 Boston exhibition, "Liberty Loan" to aid in fundraising for World War I, "A Century of Progress" for the 1933 World's Fair in Chicago. Such timely titling was a sure way to drum up interest, improve ticket sales, and guarantee the success of sheet music, which was often decorated with lavish images designed to make the connection all the more obvious. Once written, Sousa's newest marches were adapted to nearly every performance situation. Multiple arrangements were available for various combinations of parlor instruments, and band editions were printed with a wide range of redundant parts, allowing players to choose from treble or bass clef, C or B♭ transposition. Parts were doubled, cues printed, and everything done to make a piece as accessible as possible to ensembles of any size, instrumentation, or skill.

These published editions, along with the band's many hundreds of recordings, made it all the more important that a Sousa concert stand apart as a unique dramatic event; the Sousa purchased with a ticket must have value distinct from the Sousa purchased in the form of sheet music or recordings. The flutist Joseph Lefter hinted that the changes Sousa made to his marches from the podium were done, at least in part, to protect the brand: "I asked him one time why he changed his music when he played it in the marches. When it's marked loud, why he didn't play it loud. He told me, he says, 'Mr. Lefter, if everybody played it the way it's written, then everybody's band would sound like Sousa's Band so we make some changes now and then just to make it a little bit different.'" The bass drum player August Helmecke was even more blunt: "He didn't want any other band to play his marches the way he did. You may recall that on all the billings for the band was the statement, 'There is only one Sousa,' and I second the motion!"[21]

After Sousa's death in 1932 much of his performance practice lay forgotten, and Helmecke could lament that "people have no idea how Sousa wanted his marches played, because the tricks and effects that brought them to such vivid life under the Big Boss' own direction never got marked into the scores." As the music entered the school band repertoire it was further edited, revised, and simplified, making it even more difficult to assess the original compositions, let alone Sousa's performance practice. This situation began to improve in 1944 when some of his former players came together to form the Sousa Band Fraternal Society, publish a newsletter, and promote Sousa's legacy. In 1953 the organization's president, William C. Gens, told his former colleagues, "[We should] do everything in our power to stop publishers from murdering Sousa marches. It is a crime what they are doing to make a sale. We should all refuse to buy, play, or handle anything but those from the original publishers. Be careful when you buy that you get the copies you know are genuine."[22]

In January 1951 the University of New Hampshire hosted a Sousa conference at which Helmecke, along with the former bandsmen Frank Simon and Samuel Harris, demonstrated aspects of Sousa's performance style. This activity prompted the Theodore Presser Company, which had purchased John Church's catalog, to publish new editions of Sousa's marches. In 1962, Frank Simon—one of Sousa's star cornet players and assistant conductor—initiated a project to record the pieces in their original performance style. Two volumes were released by the American School Band Directors Association as *The Sounds of John Philip Sousa*, and they contain the composer's most famous marches along with commentary on their performance practice.[23]

While the details vary from piece to piece, most marches seem to have followed a similar pattern under the composer's baton. The introduction and first strain were played as written. On its first hearing the second strain was played at a lowered dynamic level and in a reduced scoring (in which cornets and trombones were absent, and clarinets dropped an octave). Only on its repeat was the second strain played as notated. The trio was also first heard with this reduced dynamic and scoring, and on its second statement (when the first countermelody was introduced), the dynamic was dropped even further. On each of its appearances, the break strain was played as written. The last break led to the only statement of the trio to be heard with the entire band playing at full volume, what Simon called "fire and tongs."[24]

These changes may seem trivial, but their effect is significant. On the printed page even the long- and extended-trio structures are full of literal repeats. But as a man of the theater, Sousa's interest lay in the dramatic. In writing his song marches he had learned that excitement and anticipation could be built by first hinting at the borrowed material and only later revealing it. Something similar happens when Sousa's performance adaptations are applied to his concert marches. By first presenting each strain at a lowered dynamic and in a reduced scoring, Sousa created a sense of anticipation that slowly gave way to heightened volume and density. The result is a musical miniature full of dramatic effect. When combined with Sousa's penchant for adding countermelodies, long- and extended-trio works became exciting crescendos, finally cementing the march as "a thing of cumulative force and interest."

THE SPECTACLE OF SOUSA

By imbuing his concert marches with a cumulatively dramatic performance practice, Sousa created an exciting and storytelling aural product. Without mentioning the March King, one writer for *Metronome* noted just how much the genre had changed by the late 1880s:

> Many years ago the march was quite a different thing from what it is at present; all that was required was a good E♭ cornet player to carry the melody along, while the rest of the band could tumble in almost any way so long as they kept on blowing. Not so at the present time, however. The march of to-day is, as any one can see, much more artistic in form, and calls for many varieties of effect, which a few years ago were not dreamed of.[25]

Sousa's dramatic skills were not, however, limited to the sounds of a march. When the Marine Band had gone on tour in 1891, critics again and again had noted the visual appeal of their bright uniforms and military bearing, traits that would be continued by Sousa's civilian ensemble. For his part, the March King was nearly obsessive in his appearance and renowned for his use of immaculate white kid gloves. Sousa the conductor was often described as restrained, but he was also fully capable of satisfying an audience. One Australian reporter was shocked by the visual antics:

> I've just been Sousa-ed. . . . But, big as my admiration is for the Toot-toot-two Step King, I've always felt that his audiences over-estimated the value of his left hooks and uppercuts. Don't you think the piccolo would be just as tremulous without the fingers twiddling at him? Don't you reckon the

> big drum would butt in just as accurately in the dead centre without that jerk of an imaginary string? Doesn't it strike you that the cornet and the trombones and the triple-barrelled brass instruments would be just as ferocious without that frantic baton sawing off the atmosphere and flinging the pieces to the dogs?

This reporter may have begun by questioning the value of Sousa's flamboyant showmanship, but he soon came to realize its worth: "I've got a suspicion that he might start the item and then sit down and read the newspaper comfortably, and his band would get along just as well as it does now. . . . Yet, as a matter of business, I suppose he's right. The people pay just as much to see him and his energetic counters and right-crosses and double-handed punch, his hypnotic passes, cut-and-thrust-exercises, wood-chopping contests and flag-wagging gesticulations as they do to hear his band. So he gives them the goods they come for."[26]

Time and again, it was not only Sousa's music that tapped into this sense of drama but also his means of employing it. In 1901, for example, the ensemble appeared at the Pan-American Exposition in Buffalo, where one of the wonders on display was a lighting device that gradually increased "from a glow that is scarcely perceptible" to "the extreme of brilliancy." Sousa noticed the effect at the band's first concert in early June: "The lights were suddenly dimmed until the grounds were shrouded in darkness; then a little light appeared, the illumination grew steadily, till, brightening and brightening, the full blaze was restored." Seeing the impact on fairgoers, Sousa decided that a hymn would be more appropriate than a march, and so the next day he adjusted his program and had the band "softly begin, 'Nearer my God to Thee,' [and] as the lights grew the band crescendoed and swelled out its power to the utmost. The effect was thrilling!"[27]

Sousa's success was due, in no small part, to his marches and other programmed works, but it was also the result of a carefully constructed relationship with his audience, a relationship built via the press. Throughout the course of his long career he made a handful of promotional missteps, but more often than not Sousa used his megaphone to reinforce and amplify public opinion. The tutelage of David Blakely, well versed in the world of journalism, naturally aided in Sousa's rise to celebrity status. The secret to the March King's success was that individuals in his audience could find in their bandmaster an extension of their own national pride, artistic sophistication, and economic ambition. As Constant Lambert once noted, Sousa's music embodied the optimism, surefootedness, and financial success that were the hallmarks of the American self-image: "'What fine fellows we all are' is the predominant sentiment of *Liberty Bell, On to Victory* and the other magnificently extrovert marches of John Philip Sousa. A general air of physical attractiveness, sexual bounce and financial independence is naturally assumed."[28]

Sousa's process of connecting to his public started even before a concert began. Arriving in New Jersey for his band's very first performance, for instance, Sousa told reporters that he had been warned about local taste: "You will find the intelligence of a Plainfield audience far above the average—in fact as good as you will find anywhere. They're no country hayseeds out there, but they are as good as the best critics in this country." Such statements were not simple pandering. By flattering his audience's taste, Sousa humbled himself; he became, in their view, not a celebrity artist but an entertainer willing to both listen and respond. As would become the pattern for the next forty years, the Plainfield press accepted and amplified Sousa's sentiment: "That the public taste is not so depraved or vapid is evidenced by the marked contrast in the make up of the audiences which the trashy performances attract and the fine one that was attracted to Music Hall last evening." Those in attendance were "all good patrons of the better class of entertainments, and all able to appreciate true merit."[29]

Such exchanges became a regular part of Sousa's strategy, and they make frequent appearances in his writings. He used a visit to North Dakota to show that his audiences were cultured enough to demand not only the best music but the best circumstances for hearing it. He, of course, proudly complied. As he recounted: "I got a telegram saying: 'In the name of a hundred citizens of Fargo, will you kindly put the *Tannhaeuser* on your program?' Don't put it No. 1, because we want the house to be quiet.' I put it No. 6 on the program. Every one wanted to hear *Tannhaeuser*, not because it was *Tannhaeuser*, but because they loved it; it appealed to them."[30]

By means of such statements, Sousa built a bridge to his audience across the footlights. Much has been made of the March King's willingness to mix serious music with popular favorites, but this was the type of programming he had experienced as a boy in the Navy Yard, had participated in during the nation's centennial celebrations, and had used to advantage at the Columbian Exposition. In other words, Sousa's mixed programming was not an innovation but a continuation of past traditions. It is telling that he justified the mixture by appealing to both history and the theater: "It is not incongruous," he wrote, "to see a comedy scene immediately follow a tragic one; in fact it is a favorite device of Shakespeare and many other master dramatists."[31]

By playing the most cultured music, the March King promised his audiences sophistication; in performing popular favorites, he rewarded them for their efforts. In many cases these popular favorites were not programmed works but rather Sousa marches played as encores. On the printed program the bandleader's name was thus largely absent, because it appeared only next to his latest march (advertised as "new") and a programmatic work or suite. But virtually every programmed piece was followed by an encore, often a Sousa march. Therefore, while the printed program might list only nine numbers, the actual concert could consist of twenty or more selections, and Sousa's music, while mostly invisible in print, was in fact everywhere (table 11).

In separating his marches from the printed program, Sousa appeared not the vain composer-performer programming his own music but simply an entertainer complying with the demands of his fellow citizens. On the stage Sousa was no demanding prima donna; rather, he was a distinctly masculine, and American, everyman. His programming humbled the March King before his audiences and countered any perception of the conceited—or foreign—entertainer. Just as he had given Wagner to Fargo, Sousa now gave his own

Table 11. A Sousa concert program with encores, 1894 (from Bierley, *The Incredible Band of John Philip Sousa,* 2006)

Selection	Composer
1. *Tannhäuser*: Overture	Wagner
encore: "Plantation Chimes"	Hall
encore: "The Washington Post," march	Sousa
encore: "Jesus, Lover of My Soul"	Marsh
2. *Hungarian Rhapsody No. 2*	Liszt
encore: "Minuet l'Antique"	Paderewski
encore: "The Directorate," march	Sousa
3. "Annie Laurie," *air varie*	Pryor
encore: "Love's Old Sweet Song"	Molloy
Arthur Pryor, trombone	
4. *Scenes at a Masquerade*	Lacombe
encore: "Crack Regiment"	Haimann
encore: "Corncracker"	Meacham
5a. "Serenade Enfantine"	Bonnaud
5b. "The Liberty Bell," march	Sousa
encore: "Manhattan Beach," march	Sousa
6. "O Hall I Greet Thee," from *Tannhäuser*	Wagner
encore: "Old Folks at Home"	Foster
Francesca Guthrie-Moyer, soprano	
7a. *Intermezzo Russe*	Franke
7b. *Pasquinade*	Gottschalk
encore: "At the Circus"	Dunewaller
encore: "Bamboula"	Urich
8. "Good-bye," humoresque	Sousa
encore: "The High School Cadets," march	Sousa
9. Prelude to Act I of *Lohengrin*	Wagner

marches to a public that called for them: "Marches are only a small part of my programmes," he wrote. "There is rarely more than one listed. If the audience gets others, it is because they are demanded as encores."[32]

Like many of Sousa's autobiographical statements, this notion that the marches were spontaneously demanded is an example of what he might have called a polite fiction. The band's advertised programs would have been unacceptably short without encores, and by all accounts Sousa's marches appeared far too quickly not to have been planned. But most important, they were what drew audiences to the theater in the first place: each encore was an integral part of any Sousa performance, and their absence would surely have resulted in a revolt. In camouflaging his own fantastically popular marches as mere encores, Sousa fictitiously invited his public to take part in the evening's programming and engage with their bandmaster in an illusionary dialogue. Sousa's character in this story happily responded with an endearing generosity, and as a result each concert became as predictable in format and as surprising in content as were the marches themselves; the music acted as a ritornello, expected in principle and variable in identity.

The flattery, humility, and pseudo-consultative programming of a Sousa concert allowed the March King to appear a regular American, one whose hard work and perseverance had led to critical and financial success. By presenting this persona to audiences, he reflected back a late nineteenth-century American notion of striving masculinity. In a myriad of ways, audiences could see in Sousa—the entertainer, composer, conductor, intellectual, entrepreneur, and athlete—a reflection of their own desires and ambitions. Like a Sousa march, a Sousa concert thus became a drama, one in which every member of the audience could play a leading role.

It was this March King—a composer who created dramatic structures, a conductor in possession of an exciting performance practice, and an entertainer who invited audiences to become successful entrepreneurs themselves—who achieved national fame in the early 1890s. He did so with the help of David Blakely and the good fortune of Patrick Gilmore's death. But the March King was also John Philip Sousa, a musician born in the Washington Navy Yard, a performer who apprenticed in the capital's most important musical organization, a conductor who trained in the city's theater pits, and an entertainer who modeled the skills and ambitions of working-class musicians and audiences along the Potomac. Sousa would return to Washington often, but after 1893 he belonged to the nation, and over the next forty years he would travel it, east to west and north to south.

Epilogue

Marching Along

ON MAY 14, 1897, JOHN PHILIP SOUSA and his band of fifty musicians arrived in Philadelphia, where they were scheduled to begin a series of three concerts at the Academy of Music. The arrival of the celebrated ensemble coincided with that of William McKinley, and both the president and the March King were in town to celebrate the dedication of Rudolf Siemering's statue of George Washington in Fairmount Park. Sousa was well known to Philadelphia audiences by this time. As a young man he had played a small part in the centennial celebrations, performed in the city's theaters, and written for local publishers. He had returned in the late 1880s as leader of the United States Marine Band for concerts at the Academy of Music. Most recently, he had conducted his own ensemble in Philadelphia, and, indeed, the concert series marked his third visit of the season. This time, however, Sousa had something special in mind; he had promised the city a new piece, one whose title would be kept a secret. The *Inquirer* wrote: "Mr. Sousa's latest march will be given, the name of which, by arrangement with his publisher, cannot be announced until the 14th inst. Of this, Mr. Sousa writes that it is the greatest of his career."[1]

The five years since Sousa had formed his commercial ensemble had brought him some remarkable—and quite surprising—rewards. Following its inaugural season, the band had given concerts every month in 1894, closing the year with more than 650 performances under its belt. Blakely had found the venture so satisfying that in May 1895 he had written to his bandmaster and informally amended their contract. No longer would Sousa be entitled to just 20 percent of the profits; now the two men would "share alike in all the revenues which are derived from the enterprise which we undertook together," an enterprise that Blakely had found a most "unexpected and gratifying success."[2]

Just as it had each summer, the band had spent July 1896 at Manhattan Beach, and Sousa and his wife had then returned to Europe for a much-needed vacation. The couple's excursion had been cut tragically short, however. On the afternoon of November 7, David Blakely's secretary had returned to the office and found the manager dead at sixty-two years of age. A cable had been sent to Sousa, who immediately began the long journey home. He later recalled his thoughts aboard the *Teutonic*:

> As the vessel steamed out of the harbor I was pacing the deck, absorbed in thoughts of my manager's death and the many duties and decisions which awaited me in New York. Suddenly, I began to sense the rhythmic beat of a band playing within my brain. It kept on ceaselessly, playing, playing, playing. Throughout the whole tense voyage, that imaginary band continued to unfold the same themes, echoing and re-echoing the most distinct melody. I did not transfer a note of that music to paper while I was on the steamer, but when we reached shore, I set down the measures that my brain-band had been playing for me.[3]

The bandleader had begun his normal process of composition on returning home. A pencil draft had been completed shortly after his arrival, and an ink version was dated Christmas Day, 1896. Sousa normally would have moved quickly to orchestration, but without his manager his time was stretched thin. The band began concerts on December 27, and it was not until April 26, 1897, that Sousa had a chance to complete a full score. There were now just three weeks remaining until the promised Philadelphia premiere.

Over the course of these nineteen days the Sousa Band would play thirty concerts in nearly as many different cities; not a single evening was left dark, and only a handful of afternoons lacked matinees. As they traveled, Sousa must have worried: his band was certainly impressive, but he had just composed a remarkable extended-trio march, complete with layering effects. This piece would require at least some rehearsal.

It seems clear that when Sousa presented "The Stars and Stripes Forever" in Philadelphia on May 14, 1897, the piece had already been heard in public at least once. James Smart's careful reading of the press reports reveals that when the band played in Augusta, Maine, on May 1, the first programmed work was encored with "a march that has not been named," surely the new piece. Like many of Sousa's mature marches, the work was rushed to publication. It was registered for copyright the very day of its Philadelphia premiere and quickly made available in versions for piano, banjo, guitar, zither, mandolin, and various combinations thereof. In order to capitalize on the piece's success, a band edition followed on June 5. By the end of the year, the march had been recorded by Sousa's ensemble at least twice and also by several anonymous bands, the Metropolitan Orchestra, and at least two banjo soloists.[4]

This march, easily Sousa's most successful work, is in fact a summation of his career, and in it the character of the March King is made manifest. Like many of Sousa's pieces, it had been written for a specific event in a specific city. After the Philadelphia concert it found a featured place on Sousa's programs, but it almost certainly began its concert life as an encore, a generous gift from the March King to his grateful public. It also contains within itself more than one polite fiction. On one hand, it had an official premiere, but on the other, the practicalities of touring likely prevented Philadelphia from being the first to hear it. Sousa's own comments about the work seem suspect, calculated to elicit an emotional response rather than elucidate the march's actual material: "My idea was to climax the march with three themes—one representing the North, a broad sweeping theme; the South with its languorous beauty and romance, and the West, a strong, pushing melody carrying all before it." Such a description, while moving, is difficult to reconcile with the three layered themes, and it seems clear that Sousa was most interested in crafting a patriotic reply to a reporter on the eve of the Spanish-American War.[5]

The March King's public image may have been helpful in winning critical and financial success, but polite fictions aside, Sousa was, quite simply, a remarkable composer. No piece demonstrates his craft so well as "The Stars and Stripes Forever." As in many of his marches, the band steps off in unison, boldly singing out the tonic pitch from the first beat (ex. 16a). The ensemble then dips a half step, only to return upwards and propel the march forward with a glorious dotted rhythm. Always the trickster, Sousa then instructs the band to skip with a light syncopation. Only in the second bar is harmony introduced, as horns and trombones move in thirds. The ensemble then pulls apart, with the melodic instruments chromatically ascending while the basses move downward. Lest anyone forget that Sousa had been trained in the theater, this introduction bears a striking resemblance to the motive

Ex. 16a. "The Stars and Stripes Forever," introduction

Arthur Sullivan wrote to accompany "Bow, bow, ye lower middle classes!" in *Iolanthe*'s "Entrance and March of the Peers," a work Sousa knew well, since he had once been named in a lawsuit regarding its performance in the United States.

As the first strain begins, Sousa continues the swagger of his introduction (ex. 16b). Short, accented downbeats paired with rapidly changing harmonies thrust the listener's internal parade forward. But after eight bars of ascent the mood changes with a sudden drop in dynamic. Widely spaced eighth notes cause the band to dance rather than march, but their lilting is interrupted by powerful *forte* blasts, which bring the first strain to a close. Its repeat is followed by a second sixteen-bar strain, at the start of which the conductor

Ex. 16b. "The Stars and Stripes Forever," first strain

would have hushed his ensemble by waving out the upper brass and woodwinds. Military brashness is traded for a gracefully optimistic tune, decorated by melodic leaps. A repeat allows the full band to sing.

Sousa's trio borrows the dip of the introduction, and the accented, chromatic lower neighbor is everywhere, creating a gravitational pull from which the band cannot break free (ex. 16c). For twenty-four bars Sousa avoids any strong indication of the new tonic, but then, just as the trio is coming to an end, he leaps upward an octave and gloriously announces the keynote. A rushing, thrice-heard figure closes the section and pounds home the new tonic.

As in most extended-trio marches, this one contains a break strain that is very much in debt to the late nineteenth-century Italian opera Sousa heard so often in Washington: unison writing, virtuosity, and call-and-response patterns are everywhere. After a sweeping gesture the trio returns, now at the march's lowest dynamic level, which allows the piccolo to sparkle. After another interruption, Sousa concludes the march with the third statement of the trio, now with a countermelody in the low brass. Only in the final passage is the trio's layered cake complete, and the full band finally plays with fire and tongs.

Critics at those first Philadelphia performances may not have known that the march had been heard before, but they did not miss the wonder of "The Stars and Stripes Forever." One, with a zealous joy often found in the reviews of Sousa's newest works, exclaimed that it was "stirring enough to rouse the American eagle from his crag and set him to shriek exultantly while he hurls his arrows at the aurora borealis." Sousa also recognized the promise of this march, and at the outbreak of war in 1898 he included it as part of a "Grand International Spectacle" titled *The Trooping of the Colors*. To further heighten the piece's patriotic connection, he added his own text. With new interest shown in Sousa's music during the 1950s, the work became synonymous with the March King himself, and it provided the title for his 1952 biographical film. In December 1987, nearly a century after its premiere, "The Stars and Stripes Forever" officially became the national march of the United States.[6]

While not all of Sousa's works would be quite so successful, after the mid-1890s he enjoyed one triumph after another. Annual tours, festival appearances, and lengthy stays at summer resorts led to more than fifteen thousand concerts over the course of the band's forty-year existence. Almost every year saw at least one new march. Songs and dances may have come to play a less important role in Sousa's output, but new suites, fantasies, and humoresques continued to delight American audiences as he crisscrossed the nation. Sousa

Ex. 16c. Layered melodies in the trio of "The Stars and Stripes Forever"

Ex. 16c (*continued*)

was, at heart, a theater musician, and he continued to search for a success on the operetta stage. The year 1896 saw the premiere of his most popular stage work—one that benefited from both its star, DeWolf Hopper, and the war with Spain—*El Capitan*. Other stage works would quickly follow, and in them Sousa continued to depict the images of self-made American manhood that had come to define his persona as the March King.[7]

The mid-1890s were tainted by the fallout from David Blakely's death. The manager's business interests had been transferred to his wife, but as the entire Sousa Band enterprise had been Blakely's creation, Sousa had little interest in touring under the guidance of an inexperienced widow; as far as he was concerned, his legal obligations to the Blakely family had died with the manager. For her part, Ada Blakely believed that the original agreement remained in force for its full five-year term. Frustrated, Sousa unilaterally dissolved the contract on April 6, 1897, hired the band under his own name, and continued to give concerts without regard to the Blakely estate. Four days later, Ada Blakely filed suit in Philadelphia. In addition to compensation for the losses incurred when Sousa failed to appear at concerts Blakely had booked, she asked for the full force of the original contract and insisted that the bandleader turn over half of his royalty earnings, the band's entire music library, and control of his name for advertising purposes.

The ensuing battle was not resolved until 1900, when the Supreme Court of Pennsylvania determined that the original contract had indeed relied on the two men's unique abilities: the manager's estate could no more expect Sousa to tour under its care than the Sousa Band could exist without the March King. Ada Blakely, however, was correct in her interpretation of property rights, and Sousa was forced to turn over his valuable library and an interest in his compositions.

No small part of the March King's appeal was due to his remarkable achievements in that most American of enterprises: business. The legal skirmish with Blakely tarnished Sousa's reputation, and one Wilkes-Barre reporter wondered how anyone could have been taken in by such a "gigantic swindle" that "had practically given the Blakeley [*sic*] people something like an independent fortune." Even the referee who decided the case noted that the original contract "evidently was not written by a lawyer, but by a layman." After this embarrassment, Sousa would never again be so cavalier when it came to business, contracts, or money. David Blakely had taught him much about finance, and the conflict with Blakely's widow completed Sousa's education.[8]

In 1901 the band began a series of annual appearances at Willow Grove Park, just outside Philadelphia. If Manhattan Beach had been its first home, Willow Grove would become its long-term residence, and it played nearly 3,000 concerts there before the end of 1926. The year 1902 was the band's busiest, with 730 concerts and not a single month of rest. Thriving on the hectic schedule, Sousa found time to work on his literary endeavors. He had considerable success with his first novel, *The Fifth String* (1902), and with the semiautobiographical *Pipetown Sandy* (1905). A musical almanac, *Through the Year with Sousa* (1910), and another novel, *The Transit of Venus* (1920), would follow.

With the world tour followed by regular trips across the country, the decade 1910–20 remained remarkably busy. A six-month tour in 1915 included lengthy engagements at the Panama-Pacific Exposition, Willow Grove, and the Pittsburgh Exposition. The band settled into New York on September 30 to perform at the Hippodrome in the extravaganza *Hip! Hip! Hooray!* and remained there for thirty weeks before taking the production on tour through mid-March 1917. On May 31, with the outbreak of war, the sixty-two-year-old Sousa returned to the military and joined the United States Navy. Commissioned as a lieutenant and receiving a self-imposed salary of just $1 per month, Sousa reported to the Great Lakes Naval Training Station, where he organized bands, aided in recruiting, and took part in brief Liberty Loan tours. Shortly after being relieved from active duty in 1919, he was promoted to the rank of lieutenant commander.

As leader of the Marine Band, Sousa's pay grade had fluctuated between that of private and that of warrant officer. His World War I service brought his only commissioning as an officer, and he would proudly wear his naval uniform at concerts throughout the 1920s. But Sousa had scaled back his private band's activities during the war, and it was impossible to return to touring as usual. Many of the most experienced players had moved on to other work, and in 1920 a series of poorly planned rail connections and hotel arrangements prompted thirty-eight of Sousa's musicians to go on strike. The infuriated conductor dismissed many of his players, including several longtime soloists. Matters were made worse when Sousa was thrown while horseback riding in September 1921. The resulting cracked vertebrae severely limited his range of motion on the podium, and he was quickly becoming less a model of masculine health than a relic of nineteenth-century entertainment. The Willow Grove engagements were dropped in 1926, and even before the crash of 1929, tours were dramatically curtailed: the band traveled for only thirty-four days in 1930 and a mere eleven in 1931.

By the late 1920s Sousa's active composing career was slowing down. Marches now almost completely dominated his output, and few Americans seemed to remember the old Sousa of the stage. More and more he became associated with bands and was happy to act as their spokesperson. In 1927 and 1928 he appeared before Congress to encourage the commissioning of military bandmasters, in 1930 and 1931 he conducted at the National High School Orchestra Camp at Interlochen, and in 1930 he was named honorary life president of the newly formed American Bandmasters Association.

Sousa had often been asked to reflect on his career, and in 1925 he published a series of autobiographical articles as "Keeping Time" in the *Saturday Evening Post*. In 1928 they were revised and published as *Marching Along: Recollections of Men, Women, and Music*. He closed the work with a hope for his reputation: "If, out of the cadences of Time, I have evoked one note that, clear and true, vibrates gratefully on the heartstrings of my public—I am well content."[9]

After forty years as America's most successful bandmaster, the end came for John Philip Sousa in 1932. He had been invited to conduct a concert for the Ringgold Band in Reading, Pennsylvania. Sousa returned to his room at the Abraham Lincoln Hotel after a rehearsal and dinner, and sometime early in the morning on March 6, he suffered a fatal heart attack at the age of seventy-seven. The last piece to be heard under the March King's baton was, fittingly, "The Stars and Stripes Forever."

Sousa was a bandmaster, and it would be hard to argue that he has not been well honored as one. In addition to endless medals and citations, he received two honorary doctorates and was feted by Native American tribes. Sousa was also buried a bandmaster. His body lay in honor at the Marine Band Auditorium, and a black caisson carried it to Washington's Congressional Cemetery—just blocks away from his birthplace in the Navy Yard—where he now lies surrounded by his former marine colleagues. His tombstone is engraved with the first measures of his most famous march.

Sousa, however, came of age neither as a bandmaster nor as the March King. As a young man he was a theater musician training at Ford's Opera House, apprenticing on the road, and earning a place in the trade of music in Philadelphia's playhouses. Given his current fame, all of these experiences seem to pale in comparison to Sousa's Marine Corps apprenticeship and the foreshadowing example of his father's career. But in the March King's success, it is the theater that resounds most strongly. His greatest ambitions were for the stage, his greatest successes in dramatically inspired marches, and his greatest fame as a theatrical persona. From John Esputa, George Felix Benkert, and the musicians in the Navy Yard, Sousa learned the breadth of a musical career, and this breadth allowed him to transcend the theater and find success when opportunity appeared. In short, to limit our modern understanding of the March King to a composer of repeated strains for ensembles of winds alone would be to ignore both the realities of nineteenth-century American musical life and to misunderstand Sousa's career and ambition. In the end, John Philip Sousa was not born the March King. He was, however, a born musician.

Notes

The following abbreviations are used in the notes.

BP	David Blakely Papers, New York Public Library
DMB	United States Marine Band Library, Washington, D.C.
HJ	Sousa Band Press Books (cited by Herbert Johnston number), United States Marine Band Library
LCSC	John Philip Sousa Collection, Music Division, Library of Congress
MA	Sousa, *Marching Along* (1928/1994)
MC	*Musical Courier*
MLK	Martin Luther King Jr. Public Library, Washington, D.C.
NARA	National Archives and Records Administration, Washington, D.C.
NYPL	New York Public Library
NYT	*Times* (New York)
PI	*Inquirer* (Philadelphia)
RG	Record Group
SACAM	Sousa Archives: A Center for American Music, University of Illinois
SSA	Sumner School Archives, Washington, D.C.
WP	*Post* (Washington, D.C.)
WS	*Star* (Washington, D.C.)

Prelude: A Triumph on the Waves

1. Dreiser, *Color* (1923/1987), 122. Despite an outward generosity toward mixed social classes, Corbin did not welcome everyone, and in 1879 he gained some undesirable attention by banning Jewish Americans from his property.

2. "Determined not" and "raised his": "Where the Surf Roars," clipping labeled *Commercial Advertiser* (New York), July 3, 1893; "only a": clipping labeled *Citizen* (Brooklyn), July 2, 1893 both in HJ 2, p. 43, DMB.

3. "In the Theaters," clipping labeled *Post Express* (Rochester), Apr. 3, 1906, HJ 26, p. 3, DMB.

4. This book contains a number of musical examples, but further samples of Sousa's output can be found at the Library of Congress's Sousa webpages: http://lcweb2.loc.gov/diglib/ihas/html/sousa/sousa-home.html. Whenever manuscript materials are known to exist, their location is indicated in the notes.

5. "Where the Surf Roars," HJ 2, p. 43, DMB.

6. "Mantle had": "Charmed by Sousa," clipping labeled *Recorder* (New York), July 16, 1893, p. 51; "new era": "Sousa's New Band," clipping labeled *Advertiser* (New York), p. 53; "the old": "The Manhattan Beach Jubilee," clipping labeled *Mail and Express* (New York), ca. Aug. 17, 1893, p. 69; "as the": "Where the Surf Roars," p. 43, all in HJ 2, DMB.

One. A Capital Boyhood

1. *MA*, 307. Sousa's autobiography was a revision of six articles the bandmaster dictated to his personal secretary Fred Campbell and published in the *Saturday Evening Post* under the title "Keeping Time" (1925). In several cases Sousa added lengthy quotations from his other published articles, and in this case he is reprinting from Sousa, "Mr. John" (1908), 224. The story about S. O., U.S.A. persisted long enough that it had to be denied even after Sousa's death; see, e.g., "The Origin" (1936).

2. Letter by Mills, Dec. 12, 1815, in Lodge, "Extracts" (1881–82), 14.

3. In 1870 the City of Alexandria became independent of the county, and in 1920 the resulting confusion in names led Alexandria County to become Arlington County.

4. "Never let": *MA*, 24; "illustrious line": Sousa, *Through the Year* (1910), entry for Nov. 8. One example of Sousa's reflecting on his name and potential ancestors can be found in *Telegraph* (Macon), Feb. 11, 1906.

5. Sousa reported that his father was born on Sept. 14, 1824, but various military documents suggest birth years between 1820 and 1827. The family name was variously spelled Sousa, Soussa, Sioucca, Soucca, Souca, Souza, and Saucca. See *MA*, 23; and RG 127, Entry 76, File of Antonio Sousa, NARA.

6. For details on the Trinkaus (sometimes Trinkhaus) family, see photocopied materials in the Paul E. Bierley Papers, SACAM. A letter from Catherine Margaret to Sousa's daughter Jane Priscilla explains that Sousa's maternal grandparents were Peter Trinkaus (1804–72) and Catherine Schafer (1808–70). See John Philip Sousa Collection, Correspondence, Individuals, "Sousa, Catherine Margaret," DMB.

7. "My mother": "Sousa has Realized His Father's Ambition," clipping labeled *Chronicle* (Spokane), Dec. 22, 1923, HJ 61, p. 235a, DMB; "by chance": Sousa, "In the Days of My Youth" (1901), 388; the commandant's letter can be found as Henderson to Reynolds, March 4, 1854, RG 127, Entry 76, File of Antonio Sousa, NARA.

8. *WS*, July 19, 1925.

9. "Interview" (1898), 171. Antonio declared his intention of becoming of U.S. citizen in October 1857 and succeeded in June 1864. See his citizenship papers, John Philip Sousa Family Collection, DMB. In 1975 the Concordia German Evangelical Church joined with the Union Methodist Episcopal Church to form the Concordia United Church of Christ. The church's records are now held by the Historical Society of Washington, D.C.

10. Sousa, *Through the Year* (1910), entry for Nov. 8. None of the other Sousa children found the popular fame of their eldest brother. Catherine married Alexander C. Varela. George Williams served as a percussionist in the Marine Band under his brother. Mary

Elisabeth married the Washington musician Robert Camp Bernays and later James McKesson Bower. Antonio Augustus became a popular sports writer in Washington. Louis Marion spent most of his life working as a machinist in the Navy Yard.

11. "No buried": Harris, "John Philip Sousa" (1983), 11; "one trying": Schneider; paraphrased in Bierley, *Phenomenon* (1973/1998), 101; "toted a": *MA*, 20–21.

12. Sousa, "Then and Now" (1921), 306.

13. "I was": Sousa, "Keeping Time" (Oct. 31, 1925), 3; "I moved": *MA*, 5; "one of": *MA*, 22–24. Sousa's doughnut story may be another polite fiction because a press release from the 1890s contains a similar account of how the young musician nearly froze to death returning home from a boyhood performance in Alexandria. Printed Ephemera, BP, NYPL.

14. "Such a": "The Era of Sousa" (1898); "man with": "Sousa and His Mission" (1899), 272; "there are": W. S. B. Mathews, "An Interview" (1896), 487. Much of Sousa's personal library is preserved at DMB.

15. *MA*, 6.

16. For details about Washington's early educational system, see J. Wilson, "Eighty Years" (1896). Sousa's award can be found in *WS*, July 12, 1865, and in the schools' twenty-first report (1864–65). Annual reports for the public schools, whose numbering system restarts in 1874, can be found at SSA.

17. First report (1844–45), reprinted in the seventeenth report (1860–61), SSA. For biographical information on Daniel (1816–97) see *WP*, Feb. 5, 1897, and *WS*, Jan. 4, 1931.

18. "The science": twenty-second report (1865–66), 121, SSA; "the very": *MA*, 83–84. Sousa recalled singing in the schools in "In the Days of My Youth" (1901), 388. For details about musical activities in the schools see the summaries of vocal music in the various annual reports, and also Elward, "History" (1975).

19. *WS*, May 23, 1865. This scene is also recounted in the school's twenty-first report (1864–65), SSA.

20. Sousa, *Pipetown* (1905), 197–99, reproduced with minor changes in *MA*, 13–20.

21. "Washington was": *MA*, 6; "a day": Sousa, "Parks" (1920), 163.

22. After Sousa's father purchased the lot at the corner of Seventh and E Streets, he sold a portion of it to Salvador Accardi, and it was with Accardi's son Edward that Sousa shared his good fortune.

23. The idea that Sousa was predestined for bands and patriotic music remains strong, and it can be seen in the several Sousa biographies written for children and young adults: Lingg, *John Philip Sousa* (1954); Weil, *John Philip Sousa* (1959); Greene, *John Philip Sousa* (1992); Lutz, *Marching with Sousa* (1998); and Venezia, *John Philip Sousa* (1998).

24. Parental permission document, RG 127, Entry 76, File of John Philip Sousa (Re-enlisted Oct. 2, 1890), NARA. Although thirteen may seem a young age for a marine enlistment, it was the minimum age set by regulations from 1837 (new rules from 1859 further lowered the cutoff age to eleven). Even these guidelines were not always followed, as when Sousa's seven-year-old neighbor, John Prosperi, joined the Corps in 1847.

25. "An Act for the Establishing and Organizing a Marine Corps," Fifth Congress, Session II, 1789, in Peters, *Public Statutes* (1848), 595.

26. Carusi in Heintze, "Gaetano Carusi" (1994), 83. The story of the Sicilian musicians has often been exaggerated, as when one reporter claimed: "When the Yankee navy wanted a band, one of our sea captains kidnapped a strolling band of musicians on the shore of the bay of Naples. From this handful of Italians was developed the Marine band. . . . The descendants of many of these kidnapped Italians are among the wealthiest people in Washington." "Mr. Sousa's Book," unlabeled clipping, ca. Dec. 24, 1890, Fowles Scrapbook, p. 47, DMB. Some members of the foreign band did go on to successful musical careers in Washington. Venerando Pulizzi served briefly as leader of the Marine Band, whereas Carusi found the adjustment more difficult and spent much of the rest of his life unsuccessfully seeking reparations for the fraudulent claims made during his recruitment.

27. Scala in *Washington Times*, Apr. 26, 1903.

28. "The only": Henderson to Paulding, Apr. 13, 1839, RG 127, Entry 4; "all vacancies": McCawley to Thurman, Feb. 9, 1885, RG 127, Entry 5, both in NARA.

29. "Son's faults": McCawley to Bolling, Aug. 13, 1881, RG 127, Entry 4; "a reformatory": Hebb to Travis, Sept. 27, 1890, RG 127, Entry 5; "so incorrigibly": Harris to Wells, Dec. 31, 1861, RG 127, Entry 4, all in NARA.

30. The Esputas and the Prosperis owned lots on the same square as did the Sousas. See *WS*, Aug. 23, 1925. The Prosperi family is the subject of Preston, *Music for Hire* (1992).

31. For more on Roach see Sullivan, *United States Marine Corps* (1997), 314–15.

32. Elliott in Reisinger, "Andrew Mealey" (1931), 41. The teacher's report of Clarence M. Barton can be found in RG 127, Entry 112, NARA.

33. *MA*, 27.

34. "Although Snobs": *Sunday Morning Chronicle* (Washington, D.C.), June 15, 1862; "it is": Orabona to Robeson, May 8, 1870, RG 45, Entry 464, NARA. See Sullivan, *United States Marine Corps* (1997), 305–6, for a complete discussion of the criticism of Scala's repertoire.

35. For Sousa's condensed recollection, see Sousa, "In the Days of My Youth" (1901), 388. For Sousa's leave see T1118, NARA.

36. Sousa, "Then and Now" (1921), 306. Sousa may be referring to either the lost "Salutation" or to his first published march, "Review." He explains that *Moonlight on the Potomac Waltzes* was performed by the band in "Parks" (1920), 163. Schneider's reaction to "Salutation" is described in *MA*, 29–30.

37. "Loved all": *MA*, 6–7; "held forth": Sousa, "Parks" (1920), 163.

38. Sousa, "How I" (1908), 696.

Two. Into the Pit

1. Whitney to Yates, May 28, 1885, reprinted in "Justice Triumphant" (1885), 4.

2. Preston, *Music for Hire* (1992), 72–104.

3. Case to Zeilin, Oct. 15, 1872, RG 127, Entry 42, NARA.

4. Ford's Theatre would not function as a playhouse again until 1968. Ford's Opera House, which would change names several times before its demolition in 1931, was known variously as the Bijou, the Majestic, and the Gayety. See *WS*, July 18, 1943.

5. *WS*, Feb. 3, 1874. See also *MA*, 37–38.

6. Like Ford's Opera House, this building would also change names, and it was later known as the Lyceum, the Capitol, and the President before being razed in 1931. By the 1890s Kernan had financial interests in theaters in Washington, Buffalo, Philadelphia, and Chicago. He soon became involved with Baltimore's Hospital for Crippled and Inadequate Children, which in 1911 was renamed the James Lawrence Kernan Hospital and Industrial School of Maryland for Crippled Children. The most complete source on Kernan is Cammack, "James Lawrence Kernan."

7. Janvier, *Baltimore* (1933), 51.

8. *MA*, 32–34. The absent leader was likely John Pistorio, who often spent the summers playing at Orkney Springs, Virginia. See *WS*, July 19, 1925.

9. The recollection of an early theatrical start appears in Sousa, "Then and Now" (1921), 306.

10. J. Mathews, "*El Capitan*" (1896), 167. This early scrapbook, the contents of which date from between April 1873 and May 1884, is preserved as LCSC 20.

11. Sousa, "In the Days of My Youth" (1901), 388. *An Album Leaf* is mentioned in *MA*, 36. The song "Fall Tenderly, Roses" can be found as LCSC 37.

12. *MA*, 28. Sousa recalled that the group published a journal for which he wrote, but no copies seem to have survived.

13. W. S. B. Mathews, *Hundred Years* (1889/1970), 102.

14. *MA*, 38. It is not possible to account for all of Sousa's opus numbers, and he stopped using them completely in 1881 with the march "Yorktown Centennial," op. 135.

15. T. B. M., "Illiterate Music" (1858), 149. The statistics of piano sales are from Loesser, *Men*, (1954/1990), 511–12.

16. Both works can be found in LCSC 20.

17. *MA*, 38. Bierley has suggested that "Salutation" may have become the unpublished march "Recognition." See Bierley, *Works*, (1984), 79.

18. *MA*, 40. The song can be found in LCSC 20. The waltzes appear as LCSC 57. The dedicatee was the local singer Charlotte Jane Cawthorne Swallow. See *WP*, Oct. 31, 1879.

19. "Wilt Thou Be True?" can be found in LCSC 20. Sousa discovered the text in *Graham's Magazine* (Aug. 1853), 202.

20. On Swallow as lyricist see Bierley, *Works* (1984), 114. "Valse" can be found in LCSC 20. The Rev. Swallow often appeared on Washington programs. He delivered an oration at Congressional Cemetery for Decoration Day in 1879 and served as chaplain for the dedication of the Grand Army of the Republic's new building on May 10, 1887. See programs in the Saxton Scrapbooks, MLK; *WS*, May 30, 1879.

21. For more on Sousa's songs see Whisler, "Songs" (1975); and Graziano, "John Philip Sousa" (2007).

22. *MA*, 29–30.

23. "Though Mr.": *MA*, 31; "is an": "Marine Band Concert," clipping labeled *Daily News* (Chicago), Mar. 22, 1892, Fowles, pp. 52–53, DMB.

24. "To be": "Sousa's Band Plays Twice Sunday," clipping labeled *Tribune* (Detroit), Apr. 6, 1899, HJ 8, p. 243, DMB; "that is": *MA*, 340.

25. "The organizing": Sousa, "The Business of the Bandmaster," clipping labeled *Criterion* (Aug. 1900), HJ 12, p. 47, DMB. This article was reprinted in two parts in *Band International* (2000). "If a": Sousa, "No State Aid for Art." This letter to the editor can be found in *MA*, 187–92, where the bandleader explains that it appeared in the French press. It also appears in a clipping labeled *Herald* (New York), ca. Sept. 1900, HJ 12, p. 120, DMB. Remembering that he had but a short time earlier been employed by the federal government, Sousa added: "I have been converted completely by a comparison of the superior results produced by individual effort with those due to a governmentally-subsidized art."

26. *MA*, 31 (emphasis in original).

27. Ibid., 42.

28. Ibid., 50.

29. Ibid., 52–53.

30. "That devastating": Odell, *Annals* (1938), 28; "draping the," "tableaux are," and "a narrow": *New York Dramatic News*, Dec. 11, 1875, Jan. 29, 1876, and Dec. 25, 1875, respectively, in McCullough, *Living Pictures* (1983), 76–80.

31. *Daily Dispatch* (Pittsburgh), Apr. 11, 1876.

32. *Daily Dispatch* (Pittsburgh), Apr. 13, 1876.

33. *Daily Dispatch* (Pittsburgh), Apr. 14 and 17, 1876.

34. *Daily Dispatch* (Pittsburgh), Apr. 19, 1876. Sousa's account of the trial differs somewhat, and he claims that the judge dismissed the case. See *MA*, 53.

35. The "Bludso" march corresponds to the only portion of "The Phoenix March" ever to appear in print, as part of the May 10 entry in Sousa, *Through the Year* (1910). Sousa later claimed that this early march served as the basis for "Manhattan Beach," but a comparison of the works reveals no borrowed material. For an example of the claim see "Sousa Admits He Can't Write March," clipping labeled *Daily Independent* (Grand Island), Oct. 31, 1927, HJ 72, p. 137, DMB.

36. Some of Sousa's music for the Living Statues (sometimes called Living Pictures) survives at SACAM, including parts for "Cleopatra Before Caesar," "Coral Gatherers," "Christian Martyr," "The New Slave," "Judgment of Paris," "Diana Surprised," "The Slave Market," and "Phryne Before the Tribunal." A flute part titled "Old Age" is also with the show's surviving materials, but since a similarly titled cornet part is housed at LCSC, along with music for Sousa's later *Our Flirtations*, it is possible that some numbers were reused.

37. Nobles, *Shop Talk* (1889), 143–45.

38. "It is": Sousa, "How to Make Programs" (1893), 15; "my theory": Sousa, "Bandmaster Sousa" (1910), 28.

39. *WS*, Apr. 3, 1876.

40. "Could not": Sousa, paraphrased in "Sousa's Band," clipping labeled *Evening Mail* (Bendigo), July 5, [1911], HJ 34, p. 57; "from a": "Sousa and his Band," clipping labeled "Melbourne," ca. June 22, 1911, HJ 34, p. 48, both in DMB.

41. "Sousa as a Composer," clipping labeled *Advertiser* (New York), Aug. 27, 1893, HJ 2, p. 76, DMB.

Three. A Nineteenth-Century Musical Career

1. For details on Sousa's programming see Brion, "Master" (2004). For a selection of sample programs see Bierley, *Incredible Band* (2006), 270–320.

2. Sousa in "Sousa on Classical Music," clipping labeled *New York World*, Aug. 6, 1893, HJ 2, p. 65, DMB.

3. *PI*, March 28, 1889.

4. *MA*, 25.

5. The manuscript of Benkert's *The Indian Girl* (1859) is housed at SACAM, and a string quartet from 1849 can be found in the Musical Fund Society of Philadelphia Collection of Music, University of Pennsylvania.

6. "G. F. Benkert and His Works" (1856), 99. *Dwight's* also covered Benkert in "Musical Intelligence" (1856) and "George F. Benkert" (1856). A less flattering review can be found in "American-Music Association" (1858). See also Taper, *Mark Twain's San Francisco* (1963/2003), 133. On Benkert's songs see W. Upton, *Art-Song* (1930/1969), 53–54.

7. On the Orchestral Union see "More Beethoven Celebrations" (1871), 384. The notebooks can be found as LCSC 137 and 149. Sousa's exercises are found in LCSC 20.

8. Brion and Schissel, *Stars and Stripes Forever* (1996). On Benkert's encouragement, see *MA*, 38.

9. On Benkert's death see *National Republican* (Washington, D.C.), Jan. 31, 1876. For the inaugural music see a program from 1889 in Fowles, p. 58, DMB.

10. See the advertisement for Benkert's "First Classical Chamber Concert," *WS*, Feb. 10, 1874.

11. *MA*, 7. Francis Esputa (ca. 1797–1866) served on U.S.S. *Constitution* (1835–38) and perhaps on U.S.S. *Ohio* and *North Carolina*. See *WS*, June 21 and 28, 1925. For his work at Georgetown see a house ledger and commencement files, Georgetown University, Washington, D.C. Susan (Anna) Adelle Esputa was also an accomplished craftsperson, and one of her counterpanes is in the Smithsonian's National Museum of American History, Washington, D.C.

12. *MA*, 36 and 27, respectively. Esputa (ca. 1831–82) is discussed more fully in Warfield, "John Esputa" (2009). Sousa's award is mentioned in *WS*, July 7, 1869. Another award was reported in the *National Republican* (Washington, D.C.), March 2, 1870.

13. For Esputa's enlistment in the Marines see RG 127, Entry 76, File of John Espiuta (Re-enlisted July 19, 1858), NARA.

14. "Our Washington Letter" (Oct. 11, 1873), 1.

15. "Our Washington Letter" (Feb. 1, 1873), 1.

16. "We hope": *National Republican* (Washington, D.C.), Feb. 1, 1873; "nearly all": *WS*, Feb. 4, 1873; "among them": *Morning Chronicle* (Washington, D.C.), Feb. 4, 1873.

17. "It would": "Our Washington Letter" (Feb. 15, 1873), 1; "of the": *National Republican* (Washington, D.C.), Feb. 5, 1873; "would be": *Evening Bulletin* (Philadelphia), Feb. 22, 1873.

18. "By request": "Our Washington Letter" (May 10, 1873), 1; "Prof. Esputa": *WS*, May 10, 1873.

19. *National Republican* (Washington, D.C.), Feb. 5, 1873.

20. *New National Era* (Washington, D.C.), Feb. 6 and May 15, 1873, respectively.

21. "With arrangements": "Our Washington Letter" (June 17, 1876), 5; "perhaps the": *Fair Gazette* (Feb. 13, 1882), in MacGregor, *Emergence* (1999), 490. For additional reviews of the opera company see Trotter, *Music* (1878). The original St. Augustine's building was sold in 1946, and the congregation now uses the structure once known as St. Paul's at 1419 V Street, NW.

22. "The National Capital" (Mar. 31, 1888), 1. Sousa's partial arrangement of Giorza's Kyrie can be found as LCSC 63. Sousa places his *Te Deum* during the time he spent in Philadelphia, and it may have been written for a church in that city; see *MA*, 58. The manuscript can be found as LCSC 237.

23. "Washington Letter" (Feb. 2, 1878), 5, emphasis in original.

24. "I examined": Esputa in the schools' third report (1876–77), 255; "in no": Cook in the first report (1874–75), 251, both in SSA.

25. "Through a": Cook in the second report (1876–77), 180, SSA; "an educator": "St. Augustine's Parish" (1900): 5.

26. See *WP*, Jan. 6 and Feb. 17, 1882.

27. *Fair Gazette* (Feb. 10, 1882) in MacGregor, *Emergence* (1999), 492.

28. On the "Jakey Polka" see a letter from Josephine Esputa-Daly dated May 3, 1901, that accompanies the quilt given to the Smithsonian.

29. *WS*, June 28, 1925.

30. In 1894 Josephine Esputa-Daly would also write a music textbook, *The Note Chain System*.

31. Sousa in G. C. T., "Sousa's Birthday" (1915), 2.

Four. The Centennial City

1. Sousa, "Commander John Philip Sousa" (1930), 470.

2. Walker, *International Exhibition* (1880), 354.

3. "Music at the Centennial" (1875), 43.

4. Gilmore to Watson, Nov. 13, 1875, reprinted in ibid. (emphasis in original).

5. "Exceedingly tranquil": *NYT*, May 11, 1876; "world of": "Inauguration," *Press* (Philadelphia), May 11, 1876, in Schabas, *Theodore Thomas* (1989), 74; Wagner's thoughts about his march are referenced in Newman, *Life* (1946), 475 n. 20.

6. Offenbach, trans. MacClintock, *Orpheus* (1957), 191.

7. Thomas, *Musical Autobiography* (1905/1964), 67.

8. "Amusements," *PI*, June 19, 1876.

9. For details on the Hasslers see Gerson, *Music in Philadelphia* (1940), 153–55. Obituaries for Simon (1832–1901) and Mark (1834–1906) can be found in *PI*, Jan. 26, 1901, and Dec. 2, 1906, respectively.

10. For Offenbach's opening program see a classified advertisement, *PI*, June 19, 1876.

11. "People go": Thomas, *Musical Autobiography* (1905/1964), 67; "gave Wagner": *MA*, 132.

12. Sousa in *Musical Leader*, March 21, 1918, HJ 48, p. 1, DMB. On the orchestra's demise see *PI*, July 12, 1876; and "Music at the Centennial" (1876), 272.

13. The productions are mentioned in *MA*, 56–57, and Sousa, "Keeping Time," (Nov. 7, 1925): 96.

14. Manuscript materials for "Myrrha Gavotte" can be found as LCSC 134.

15. Sketch materials for "Ah Me!" and "Only a Dream" can be found in LCSC 20. During the week of November 19, 1877, the Hess Company presented Philadelphia audiences with Robert Planquette's *The Chimes of Normandy*, Ambroise Thomas's *Summer Night's Dream*, Michael Balfe's *The Bohemian Girl*, and Daniel Auber's *Fra Diavolo*.

16. Nobles took credit for introducing Sousa to Hassler in "Sousa's First March," *Philadelphia Times*, ca. Feb. 1898, HJ 5a, p. 204, DMB. Manuscript materials for *Sounds from the Revivals* can be found at SACAM.

17. Esputa, *Musical Monitor*, Sept. 30, 1876, in Bierley, *Works of John Philip Sousa* (1984), 80.

18. Manuscript materials for "Recognition" can be found as LCSC 69. The march, as well as *Sounds from the Revivals*, is mentioned in a classified advertisement in *PI*, May 14, 1877. Sousa's "Grand selection from Sullivan's opera, *Trial by Jury*" is similarly mentioned on May 21 and June 8, 1877. Manuscript materials for the 1887 version of "The International Congress" can be found as LCSC 316. Always the economical composer, Sousa reused some of its material in his suite *Cubaland* (1925).

19. Manuscript materials for *In Parlor and Street* can be found as LCSC 196 and at SACAM. Materials for the *Phoenix Medley* can be found as LCSC 43.

20. See programs from the Chestnut Street Theatre published as *The Play-bill*, July 31, 1876, Nov. 16, 1876, and Feb. 5, 1877; and a program labeled Sept. 20, 1878, Scrapbook of Programs, all in the Theatre Collection, Free Library of Philadelphia.

21. Manuscript materials for *Sandalphon Waltzes* can be found as LCSC 39, those labeled *Sardanapolis* as LCSC 234. Bierley, *Works of John Philip Sousa* (1984), mentions a gavotte titled "Alexander" that may also have been performed at the Chestnut Street Theatre.

22. On Cape May Point see Sousa, "Keeping Time" (Nov. 7, 1925), 98. It was likely for this resort that he arranged Simon Hassler's *Greeting to Cape May* (LCSC 9).

23. Swallow's marriage announcement appeared in *WS*, Oct. 6, 1877.

24. Unlabeled clipping, Sousa Scrapbook, BP, NYPL. Vance's obituary can be found in "Late Wilson Vance as Warrior and Author," clipping labeled *Evening*

News (Newark), Nov. 18, 1911, HJ 35, p. 102, DMB. There is also a small collection of Vance's letter books at the Ohio Historical Society in Columbus. Manuscript materials for *Katherine* can be found as LCSC 19.

25. *Laura Keene v. Moses Kimball.*

26. *PI*, Feb. 25, 1879.

27. "Never was": Odell, *Annals* (1938), 605; "it seemed": Sullivan in Lawrence, *Sir Arthur Sullivan* (1900), 142.

28. There are two surviving copies of Sousa's orchestration of *H.M.S. Pinafore.* The first is the incomplete orchestral manuscript preserved as LCSC 66. The other is a manuscript that Sousa sent to Australia with the actor James Cassius Williamson that is now housed at the State Library of New South Wales, Australia.

29. Biographical information on the company's members can be found in *PI*, Apr. 7, 1879.

30. Much of the company's tour schedule was reconstructed on the basis of Cole, "For They Are American" (1985).

31. Odell, *Annals* (1938), 604.

32. *NYT*, Apr. 26, 1879.

33. See an undated program, after Apr. 26, 1879, Program Files, Music Division, Free Library of Philadelphia.

34. "New York Amusements" (1879), 6.

35. Sullivan to Ford, March 6, 1879, in Sollers, "Theatrical Career" (1962), 423.

36. *MA*, 64.

37. *Dramatic Mirror*, Jan. 5, 1880, in Cole, "For They Are American" (1985), 43. Much of Sousa's orchestration for *The Smugglers*, based on *The Contrabandista*, survives as LCSC 12 and 70, with a few orchestral parts at SACAM. It appears that the young composer both orchestrated Sullivan's music and added some of his own. Because Sousa reused much of his arrangement for a later operetta of the same name, it is impossible to fully reconstruct the 1879 version.

38. *MA*, 343. Sousa's eldest daughter, Jane Priscilla, provided details about the wedding in "The Origin" (1936), 589. There is some uncertainty regarding Bellis's age because her birth year is given variously as being between 1860 and 1866. See Bierley, *Works of John Philip Sousa* (1973/1998), 245–46.

39. Clipping labeled *Standard* (Syracuse), May 9, 1893, HJ 2, p. 17, DMB. For a discussion of turn-of-the-century antimodernism see Lears, *No Place of Grace* (1981).

40. Sousa in "Sousa on the Mongrels," clipping labeled *Post* (Houston), May 17, 1903, HJ 19, p. 97, DMB.

41. "Hypocrisy in": Sousa in "Sousa as a Composer," clipping labeled *Advertiser* (New York), Aug. 27, 1893, HJ 2, p. 76, DMB; "affect any" and "a tall": "The President's Band," clipping labeled *Telegram* (Worcester, Mass.), ca. Apr. 3, 1891, Printed Ephemera, BP, NYPL.

42. "Sousa as a Boxer," clipping labeled *Morning World* (New York), Aug. 13, 1899, HJ 9, p. 28, DMB.

43. Unlabeled clipping, Sousa Scrapbook, BP, NYPL.

44. Manuscript materials for Sousa's medley march "The Triton" can be found as LCSC 177.

45. "Only just": *PI*, Aug. 31, 1880; "the music": "Our Flirtations," unlabeled clipping, Sousa Scrapbook, BP, NYPL.

46. For details on Cox see *MA*, 65–66; a classified advertisement in *PI*, Aug. 28, 1877; a program dated Aug. 29, 1877, Music Folder, Centennial Bureaus of Administration, Centennial Collection, Historical Society of Pennsylvania; and an 1866 playbill in the Minstrel Show Collection, Harry Ransom Center, the University of Texas at Austin. The manuscript for Sousa's incidental music can be found as LCSC 10.

Five. A Presidential Musician

1. McCawley to Durand, Oct. 1, 1880, RG 127, Entry 4, NARA, emphasis in original (several additional letters from between August and October 1880 discuss charges against Schneider); see also *WP*, July 1, 1878 and Sept. 22, 1880; and *NYT*, Nov. 27, 1906.

2. *WP*, Nov. 15, 1878. Both pieces are mentioned in *WP*, Nov. 8, 1878. The march was published as "Esprit du Corps."

3. Contract between Sousa and Vance, Sept. 3, 1879, Barry Owen Furrer Collection. Manuscript materials for "Globe and Eagle" can be found as LCSC 194; those for *Paroles d'Amour Valses* are at SACAM. For the Marine Band's performance see *WP*, June 19, 1880.

4. McCawley to Sousa, Aug. 4, 1880, RG 127, Entry 4, NARA. On McCawley's attendance at *Our Flirtations* see Sousa, "How I Got That Way," clipping labeled *Brooklyn Eagle*, July 1926, Sousa Clipping File, Music Division, NYPL.

5. Manuscript materials for "Nymphalin" can be found in LCSC 15 and 181.

6. *WS*, Oct. 2, 1880. Because three earlier directors had served two terms, Sousa was the fourteenth individual to lead the ensemble. For an example of another applicant see a letter from Luciano Conterno, leader of the Brooklyn Navy Yard Band, to Nicholson, Oct. 9, 1880, RG 127, Entry 42, NARA.

7. *MA*, 363–64.

8. Many of the band's performances are documented in orders preserved in RG 127, Entry 42, NARA.

9. *MA*, 71. On the Baltimore event see Orcutt to Nicholson, Oct. 15, 1880, RG 127, Entry 42, NARA. This letter thanks Sousa by name, suggesting his presence. Given the high opus numbers assigned to "Right Forward" and "Guide Right," Sousa must have been counting the many individual arrangements he had made during his last months in Philadelphia. Manuscript materials for "Guide Right" can be found as LCSC 130.

10. "The playing": "Yesterday!"; "all at": "Scenes and Incidents," both in *Penny Press* (Cleveland), Sept. 26 and 27, 1881, respectively. A letter of thanks from the Ohio governor can be found as Forter to Hunt, Oct. 20, 1881, RG 127, Entry 42, NARA. Sousa must have remembered this event, for in 1924 he composed the march "The Black Horse Troop" in honor of the Cleveland National Guard.

11. *WP*, June 20, 1881. Manuscript materials for "Yorktown Centennial" can be found as LCSC 377. The march was later given the new title "Sen Sen" and reprinted in 1900 as part of a Sen Sen Chiclet Company promotion.

12. *MA*, 78–79. The incident was reported in "The Marine Band Trouble," *WP*, Feb. 18, 1882. McCawley made clear the need for a consistent chain of command in a letter to Wilson, July 31, 1885, RG 127, Entry 5, NARA. Manuscript materials for *Intaglio Waltzes* can be found as LCSC 204. The piece's premiere is mentioned in *WP*, Sept. 27, 1884. The work was later revised as *The Lady of the White House*, dedicated to First Lady Ida Saxton McKinley, and published in the January 1898 issue of the *Ladies' Home Journal*.

13. For more on the events at Cape May see Alexander, "Congress Hall March" (1961). Sousa would return to the transit of Venus in 1920 for his novel of the same name. On the later statue dedications see *WP*, Dec. 21, 1884; and *WP*, May 13, 1887.

14. Manuscript materials for "Triumph of Time" can be found as LCSC 107; materials for "Right-Left" are at SACAM. For the performance of "Pet of the Petticoats," "Triumph of Time," and the pharmaceutical meeting see *WP*, May 26, June 2, and Sept. 12, 1883, respectively.

15. *MA*, 86. On the ceremonies see *WP*, Dec. 27, 1884; the continuous concert is described in an advertisement in *WP*, March 6, 1885.

16. Manuscript materials for "The Honored Dead" can be found as LCSC 354. A later piano arrangement of the march has been labeled with the date June 7, 1876, prompting speculation that Sousa may have recycled the piece for Grant. Sheridan's funeral is described in "At Rest in Arlington," *WP*, Aug. 12, 1888.

17. *Washington Weekly Star*, June 11, 1886, in Kirk, *Music at the White House* (1986), 139–40.

18. Manuscript materials for "Sound Off" can be found as LCSC 123. Those for *La Reine de la Mer Valses* are preserved as LCSC 57. "Tyrolien" exists only in later copyist's parts at DMB.

19. "The Marine Band," unlabeled clipping, Sousa Scrapbook, Blakely Papers, NYPL.

20. *MA*, 68. According to a letter from 1877, even the bandleader Louis Schneider had not spoken satisfactory English. See McCawley to Thompson, June 23, 1877, RG 80, Entry 14, NARA.

21. "For the": Sousa to Williams, July 11, 1881, RG 127, Entry 42; "of no": McCawley to secretary of the navy, Nov. 11, 1881, RG 127, Entry 4, both in NARA.

22. "Perpetual grouch": *MA*, 68. "Continuous insubordination": Sousa to Bartlett, Sept. 2, 1881; "ever since": Manco to McCawley, Sept. 8, 1881, both in RG 127, Entry 42, NARA.

23. "Insubordinate and" and "false and": Bartlett to McCawley, Sept. 10 and 14, 1881, respectively, RG 127, Entry 42, NARA. Manco's statements are from *Evening Critic* (Washington, D.C.), Sept. 13, 1881. See also *WP*, Sept. 10 and 11, 1881.

24. "By the": *MA*, 69; "musicians required": document by Sousa dated June 15, 1882, RG 127, Entry 42, NARA. The sentiments were echoed in McCawley to Cochrane, June 26, 1882, RG 127, Entry 4, NARA.

25. McCawley to Chandler, June 14, 1882, RG 127, Entry 4, NARA.

26. *WS*, June 14, 1890.

27. Sousa to McCawley, Nov. 11, 1882, RG 80, Entry 14, NARA.

28. *MA*, 70. On the requested discharges see RG 80, Entry 14, NARA.

29. Sousa to Heywood, May 20, 1890; the secretary's order can be found as Soley to the commandant, Aug. 20, 1891, both filed with correspondence from 1892, RG 127, Entry 42, NARA.

30. Sousa, communication to the Navy Department, Dec. 17, 1890, included in the testimony related to House Resolution 12788, "Reorganization of the Marine Band" (1891).

31. Clipping labeled *Republic* (Washington, D.C.), Jan. 25, 1891, Fowles Scrapbook, p. 54, DMB.

32. Sousa in *WP*, Feb. 6, 1893. The band was finally reorganized in 1899, and the naval appropriations bill of that year provided for one leader paid as a first lieutenant, one second leader paid $75 per month as a sergeant major, thirty first-class musicians paid $60, and thirty second-class musicians paid $50.

33. *MA*, 70.

34. See letters dated May 18, 1881, and May 9 and 13, 1882, RG 127, Entry 4; May 24, 1886; Apr. 19, 1887; Apr. 17, 1888; and May 6, 1890, RG 127, Entry 42, all in NARA. A program for the service of 1889 can be found in Fowles, p. 12, DMB.

35. McCawley to Chandler, Nov. 14, 1882, RG 127, Entry 4, NARA.

36. Nichols to McCawley, May 14, 1883, RG 127, Entry 42, NARA.

37. On the normal school see McCawley to Maton, May 12, 1884; on the Philadelphia event see McCawley to Thompson, Sept. 3, 1887, both RG 127, Entry 5; on Morton's request see a letter dated March 28, 1889, RG 127, Entry 42, all in NARA.

38. The governance document can be found as "Regulations for the Government of the U.S. Marine Band," July 15, 1872; "having appropriated": Manco to McCawley, Sept. 8, 1881, both in RG 127, Entry 42, NARA.

39. Bartlett to McCawley, Sept. 10, 1881, RG 127, Entry 42, NARA. Programs from these and other events can be found in Fowles, DMB, the Georgetown College Commencement Files, and in the Theatre Collection, Historical Society of Washington, D.C. On "The Wheelmen" see Preston, *Music for Hire* (1992), 199.

40. *MA*, 68, 70.

41. The complete catalog is reproduced in Carpenter, "History" (1970), 237–54.

42. "The Famous Marine Band: A Talk with Walter Smith," *Daily Telegraph* (Kalamazoo), Nov. 10, 1886, in Kirk, *Music at the White House* (1986), 131.

43. *WS*, May 8, 1932.

Six. Civilian Music in Washington

1. "The exquisite": *WP*, Dec. 3, 1880; "my first": Saxton's program, contained in her scrapbooks, MLK.

2. Program dated Nov. 10, 1884, Saxton scrapbooks, MLK.

3. On Speyer's Washington career see *WS*, March 12, 1892. For more on Kaspar (1858–1936) see *WP*, May 4, 1890, and March 20, 1936.

4. *WS*, Apr. 25, 1885. See also *WP*, Dec. 6, 1937.

5. "The enjoyment": *WS*, Apr. 25, 1885; "with a": *WS*, Jan. 20, 1882.

6. "On its": *WP*, Jan. 31, 1891; "few musical": *WP*, Nov. 15, 1891.

7. "Rendered entirely": *WP*, Mar. 29, 1885; "it is": *WP*, Jan. 31, 1891.

8. *WP*, Nov. 21, 1886.

9. *WP*, Nov. 22, 1891.

10. *WP*, Apr. 12, 1890. Manuscript materials for "The Coquette" can be found as LCSC 60A.

11. "Oratorio and": "The Musical Festival," unlabeled clipping, Sousa Scrapbook, BP, NYPL; "one could": *WP*, May 15, 1881. A roster of Bernays's orchestra was printed in *WP*, Nov. 28, 1886. A program for the *Ancient Mariner* performance can be found in Fowles, p. 11, DMB.

12. *WP*, March 11, 1888. For more detailed looks at Washington orchestras during this period see Krasner, "A Capital Idea" (2011); and Warfield, "Amateur and Professional" (2012).

13. *Sullivan et al. v. Goullaud*, Equity Case No. 1391 (C.C. MA 1879).

14. "A more": Browne, "Sir Arthur Sullivan and Piracy" (1889), 753; "an orchestral": *Carte v. Ford*.

15. *Carte v. Ford*.

16. Ibid.

17. "A Grand Success," unlabeled clipping, Sousa Scrapbook, BP, NYPL.

18. "Two ladies": *WP*, Feb. 3, 1882; "somewhat defective": "*The Smugglers* at Lincoln Hall," *WP*, Feb. 18, 1882; "desirous of": typescript letter to Vance and Sousa, Mar. 4, 1882, Printed Ephemera, BP, NYPL. On Sousa's arrangement with Vance, see a contract dated Feb. 8, 1881, Barry Owen Furrer Collection. For information on rehearsals of the work see *WP*, Feb. 2, 1882. Manuscript materials for *The Smugglers* can be found as LCSC 12 and 70.

19. "Either vapid": "A Variety of Musical and Dramatic Entertainments of Various Merit"; "more prone": "Sousa's Opera"; "the worst": "*The Smugglers*," all unlabeled clippings in the Sousa Scrapbook, BP, NYPL; "painful paucity": *Intelligencer* (Lancaster, Pa.), March 29, 1882; "I examined": *MA*, 82.

20. "I think": *WP*, Feb. 15, 1885; "buried in": *MA*, 82. On Sousa's trip to New York and the actors he hired see *WP*, March 11, 1883.

21. On Sousa's self-borrowing from *The Smugglers* see Bierley, *Works of John Philip Sousa* (1984), 32.

22. *PI*, Nov. 11, 1884. Manuscript materials for *Désirée* can be found as LCSC 71.

23. "Very sweet": *PI*, Nov. 11, 1884; "undeniably dull": *Globe* (Boston), Dec. 16, 1884.

24. "May, in": *Globe* (Boston), Dec. 16, 1884; "able to": Hopper and Stout, *Once a Clown* (1927), 49.

25. "American Comic": advertisement in *WP*, Apr. 28, 1884; "can *Désirée*": *WP*, May 7, 1884; "in your": "*Desiree*," *WP*, May 11, 1884.

26. "The lobby": *PI*, Nov. 11, 1884; "a patriotic": *WP*, Nov. 16, 1884.

27. "It is": *MA*, 355; "that is": "Boston" (1884).

28. *WP*, March 8, 1885.

29. The operetta's plot is detailed in *WP*, May 17, 1885. On Sousa's self-borrowing see Bierley, *Works of John Philip Sousa* (1984), 30. Manuscript materials for *The Queen of Hearts* can be found as LCSC 6 and at SACAM; those for "Mother Hubbard March" can be found as LCSC 119 and 235.

30. On the Bernays-Sousa wedding see *WP*, Jan. 8, 1890. A program for *The Queen of Hearts* can be found in Fowles, p. 6, DMB.

31. Clipping labeled *Telegraph* (New York), March 30, 1898, Sousa Clipping File, NYPL. Information on performance rights for *The Wolf* can be found in "Sousa as a Composer," clipping labeled *Advertiser* (New York), Aug. 27, 1893, HJ 2, p. 76, DMB. On Sousa's self-borrowing, see Bierley, *Works of John Philip Sousa* (1984), 33. Manuscript materials for *The Wolf* can be found as LCSC 68.

32. Manuscript materials for the *Tally-Ho!* overture can be found as LCSC 175, those for the song as LCSC 51, and those for *Vautour* as LCSC 228.

33. "*The Merry Monarch*," clipping labeled *Herald* (New York), Jan. 3, 1892, Fowles, p. 78, DMB. Manuscript materials for *The Lion Tamer* can be found as LCSC 359, those for *The Devil's Deputy* as LCSC 18 and 238. On *The Oolah* see "Sousa's Rare Treat," clipping labeled *Press* (Plainfield, N.J.), ca. September 27, 1892, HJ 1, p. 1, DMB.

34. Manuscript materials for "The Window Blind" can be found as LCSC 198; those for "O'Reilly's Kettledrum" can be found as LCSC 53; and those for "You'll Miss Lots of Fun When You're Married" can be found as LCSC 54.

35. "Sousa as a Composer," clipping labeled *Advertiser* (New York), Aug. 27, 1893, HJ 2, p. 76, DMB. Manuscript materials for "I Wonder" can be found as LCSC 329.

36. Manuscript materials for "My Own, My Geraldine" can be found at SACAM.

37. Manuscript materials for "Love That Comes When May-Roses Blow" can be found as LCSC 191. A revised version of "Wissahickon Waltz" was published as *The Colonial Dames Waltzes* in 1896. On the MacCulloch song see *PI*, June 6, 1889. A complete version of the poem, now titled "June Days," appeared in MacCulloch, *From Dawn to Dusk* (1887).

Seven. America's Court Composer

1. "The Era of Sousa" (1898).

2. Sousa, *The Trumpet* (1886/1985), 2. For comparison see E. Upton, *Infantry Tactics* (1875), 397–434.

3. *MA*, 84–85.

4. For the likely premiere of "In Echelon Polonaise" see *WP*, July 9, 1887. The piano sheet music for "Presidential Polonaise" advertises its performance at the inaugural ball. Manuscript materials for the work can be found as LCSC 11 and 365.

5. *American* (Baltimore) in "The Marine Band" (1889), 287. Sousa also discussed timing the piece so that the strain for drum and trumpet would greet the president

in "Sidelights" (1910), 31. Manuscript materials for "Semper Fidelis" can be found at SACAM and DMB.

6. Tracy in Sousa, *National, Patriotic, and Typical Airs* (1890/1977), xi.

7. Ibid., preface.

8. "Airs of All Lands," unlabeled clipping, Fowles, p. 50, DMB.

9. Sousa in *NYT*, Aug. 25, 1889.

10. Ibid.

11. *MA*, 112–13.

12. *MA*, 114. On a unifying crisis see a clipping labeled *American Musician* (New York), Aug. 31, 1889, Fowles, p. 40, DMB.

13. For examples of Sousa's generational racism see *MA*, 33–34, 73, and 256. His novels are also filled with problematic language.

14. Sousa, *National, Patriotic, and Typical Airs* (1890/1977), preface.

15. *NYT*, Aug. 25, 1889. On San Marino see *PI*, Oct. 24, 1889.

16. "Mr. Sousa": clipping labeled *Telegraph* (Philadelphia), Fowles, p. 46a; "must not": clipping labeled *Globe* (Chicago), Fowles, p. 48, both in DMB; "a capable": *Eagle* (Brooklyn), quoted in *WP*, Sept. 1, 1889.

17. On Walker's story see *WP*, Oct. 25, 1889, and a clipping labeled *Eagle* (Brooklyn), Oct. 20, 1889, Fowles, p. 46a, DMB.

18. "Modern conceptions": *NYT*, Aug. 26, 1928; "the only": "The Opinion of John Philip Sousa Concerning 'The Star-Spangled Banner' as the National Anthem of the United States" in Delaplaine, *John Philip Sousa* (1983/2001), n.p.

19. Columbia brochure, Feb. 1890, in Brooks, "Columbia Records" (1978), 7.

20. Sousa in a clipping labeled *Traveller* (Boston), Sept. 11, 1890, Fowles, p. 67, DMB.

21. Copies of Columbia catalogs can be found at DMB, as can many of the recordings. A more or less complete list of early Marine Band recordings is included in Smart, *Sousa Band* (1970), 83–85.

22. "Bottled Music," unlabeled clipping, Fowles, p. 67, DMB.

23. Sousa, "The Menace" (1906), 278–80.

24. In Brylawski and Goldman, *Legislative History* (1976): vol. 4, pt. H, p. 3 and p. v.

25. Sousa, June 6, 1906, in ibid., p. 23.

26. Ibid., p. 24.

27. Ibid.

28. "The talking": *Chronicle* (San Francisco), June 17, 1906; "in reality": "Sousa a Prophet of Evil," clipping labeled June 12, 1906, HJ 21, p. 126, DMB.

29. Sousa, *Times* (London), Jan. 16, 1903.

30. *MA*, 246.

31. Sousa, *Times* (London), Feb. 27, 1905. The piece is reproduced in *MA*, 246–48. Another "dignified" letter appeared in the *Telegraph* (London), Apr. 27, 1905.

32. Sousa, "Mr. Sousa on Musical Pirates," clipping labeled *Daily Mail*, Apr. 22, 1905, HJ 22, p. 104, DMB. A portion of this letter is reproduced in *MA*, 248–49.

33. Sousa, "The Menace" (1906), 278–84.

34. Sousa, June 6, 1906, in Brylawski and Goldman, *Legislative History* (1976), vol. 4, pt. H, p. 24.

35. Sousa, "The Menace" (1906), 281–82.

36. Sousa, "The Year in Music," clipping labeled *Town Topics*, Dec. 6, 1906, pp. 178–79; another serious article appeared as Sousa, "My Contention," *Music Trades* (Christmas 1906), p. 183, both in HJ 21, DMB.

37. "Mr. Sousa": Cameron, June 8, 1906; "we started": Cromelin, Dec. 10, 1906, both in Brylawski and Goldman, *Legislative History* (1976), vol. 4, pt. H, p. 141 and pt. J, p. 312.

38. "An organization": Sousa, June 8, 1906; "I will": Sousa, Dec. 10, 1906, both in ibid., pt. H, pp. 143–44 and pt. J, p. 312.

39. "The music": Columbia advertisement, *Phonogram* (Oct. 1891); "you and": *Phonogram* (May 1891), both in Brooks, "Columbia Records" (1978), 14 (emphasis in originals).

40. *World Herald* (Omaha), Dec. 28, 1890.

41. Sousa in "Chats with Big Americans for Young Americans," *American Boy* (ca. Apr. 1907), HJ 21b, p. 211, DMB. On the *Mother Hubbard* performance see *PI*, Sept. 9, 1885.

42. Manuscript materials for "The Crusader" can be found as LCSC 86, those for "The Occidental" as LCSC 121.

43. *WP*, Apr. 7, 1889.

44. On the sale of Sousa's marches see *MA*, 144. Manuscript materials for "The Washington Post" can be found as LCSC 373.

45. "Perpetuated in Bronze," *WP*, May 11, 1884.

46. "To introduce": *MA*, 117; "the Venetian": Sousa, "How John Philip Sousa Wrote the *Washington Post*," clipping labeled *Truth* (Buffalo), March 4, 1911, HJ 36, p. 133, DMB.

47. For notices of "Do We? We Do?" see *WP*, Jan. 27 and 28, 1889.

48. On the premiere see *WP*, July 21, 1888.

49. Sousa in *WS*, Apr. 1, 1934. On early performances of "The High School Cadets" see *WP*, Aug. 17 and Sept. 13, 1890. Manuscript materials for this march can be found as LCSC 229 and 353, those for "The Corcoran Cadets" as LCSC 92 and 341.

50. Manuscript materials for "The Rifle Regiment" can be found as LCSC 124 and at SACAM, those for "Nail the Flag to the Mast" as LCSC 23. Frisbie's stepson remembered the song in *WP*, Nov. 25, 1917.

51. Manuscript materials for "Ben Bolt" can be found as LCSC 109, those for "The Quilting Party" as LCSC 236.

52. "In the": *WP*, March 27, 1890; "it behooves": Sousa, *WP*, March 28, 1890. Sousa recounts the story in *MA*, 96–97.

53. *WS*, June 14, 1890.

54. *MA*, 111.

55. "I think": Whitney to McCawley, Dec. 27, 1888, RG 127, Entry 42; "without cost": McCawley to Chandler, Nov. 17, 1882, RG 127, Entry 4, both in NARA (emphasis in original).

56. Sousa, *PI*, March 28, 1889; for the original complaint see *PI*, March 21, 1889.

57. "A good": *PI*, Oct. 21, 1889; "noisy and": *PI*, Dec. 18, 1889.

58. "A surprise": *PI*, Apr. 14, 1890; "indicated all": *PI*, Apr. 19, 1890. Manuscript materials for "The Loyal Legion" can be found as LCSC 176.

59. "The great": "The Great Band Here"; "accorded a": "The Marine Band Concert," both in Fowles, p. 61, DMB.

60. "Strong men": *MA*, 110; "hears it": clipping labeled Pittsburgh, June 15, 1890, Fowles, p. 60, DMB. A clipping that even more closely resembles Sousa's story can be found as "Pittsburgh as a Musical Centre," Fowles, p. 61, DMB.

61. Program labeled Oct. 1890, Fowles, p. 26, DMB. Manuscript materials for "The Stag Party" can be found at SACAM.

62. "The sole": *PI*, Oct. 19, 1890; "I know": Harris to Sousa in *MA*, 178. Manuscript materials for "The Chariot Race" can be found as LCSC 324.

63. Program labeled Dec. 13, 1890, Fowles, pp. 26–27, DMB.

64. "The late": "Entertainments," clipping labeled *Ledger* (Philadelphia), Dec. 15, 1890, Fowles, p. 63; "would not": "The Marine Band Concert," clipping labeled *American* (Philadelphia), Fowles, p. 61, both in DMB.

65. *PI*, March 15, 1891.

Eight. Making the Sousa Band

1. Blakely to Sousa, Apr. 19, 1890, Thomas/Strauss Letter Book, p. 323, BP, NYPL. Summaries of some of Blakely's endorsements can be found in *NYT*, March 2, 1890.

2. Levy to Blakely, Aug. 13, 1891, General Business Correspondence, BP, NYPL (emphasis in original). Additional letters from Levy, as well as from Liberati and Hecker, can be found in the same location.

3. Blakely to Sousa, Apr. 19, 1890, Thomas/Strauss Letter Book, p. 323, BP, NYPL.

4. Blakely to Sousa, Dec. 9, 1890, pp. 19–20; after getting Sousa's approval, the letter was forwarded to Tracy on Dec. 16 (p. 36). Both letters are in Personal Letter Book 1, BP, NYPL.

5. Blakely to Nettleton, ca. Jan. 13, 1891, Personal Letter Book 1, p. 71; Nettleton's endorsement appears as Nettleton to Soley, Jan. 20, 1891, General Business Correspondence; both in BP, NYPL.

6. Quoted in *MA*, 98.

7. Blakely to Johnson, ca. Feb. 4, 1891, Marine Band Letter Book, p. 21, BP, NYPL.

8. "Has not": Pew to Johnson, Feb. 3, 1891, p. 11; "enclosed is": Blakely to Sousa, Feb. 7, 1891, p. 36; both in the Marine Band Letter Book, BP, NYPL.

9. "Has not": Phinney to Blakely, March 16, 1891, General Business Correspondence; "Washington views": Pew to Atwell, March 13, 1891, Marine Band Letter Book, p. 173; both in BP, NYPL; "the pet": Marine Band Program, Apr. 11, 1891, Barry Owen Furrer Collection.

10. Pew to Sousa, ca. Jan. 29, 1891, Marine Band Letter Book, p. 2, BP, NYPL.

11. "The playing": *Tribune* (Chicago), Apr. 18, 1891; "excruciatingly funny": "The Marine Band's Inaugural," clipping labeled *Herald* (Chicago), Apr. 18, 1891, Printed Ephemera, BP, NYPL.

12. "Are subjected": clipping labeled *Times* (Chicago), Apr. 12, 1891; "the audience": "Grand Concert by the Marine Band and Mlle. Decca," clipping labeled *Beacon and Republican* (Akron), Apr. 11, 1891; both in Printed Ephemera, BP, NYPL.

13. Letter to Sousa, probably from Pew, Apr. 29, 1891, Thomas Letter Book, p. 998, BP, NYPL.

14. "Why?" (1891), 486.

15. Laine to Blakely, Apr. 13, 1891, General Business Correspondence, BP, NYPL (emphasis in original).

16. Blakely to Sousa, May 6, 1891, Thomas Letter Book, p. 980, BP, NYPL.

17. *MA*, 99. Sousa's illness was reported in *WP*, May 16 and July 12, 1891.

18. Sousa's account of his Atlantic crossing essentially agrees with that in *NYT*, June 15, 1891.

19. *WP*, Sept. 3, 1891.

20. Blakely to Heywood, Oct. 8, 1891, Sousa Band Letter Book 1, pp. 15–16, BP, NYPL.

21. "Would come": Pew to Sousa, Oct. 27, 1891, p. 18; "the grandest": Blakely to Sousa, Nov. 28, 1891, p. 21, both in Sousa Band Letter Book 1, BP, NYPL.

22. "pictur tuk": Christianer to Sousa, ca. Jan. 11, 1892, Sousa Band Letter Book 1, p. 76, BP, NYPL; "with such": letter from Gilmore, March 1, 1892, in an 1892 Columbia catalog, DMB (emphasis in original).

23. "He is": "Marine Band's Concert," clipping labeled *Daily News* (Chicago), March 22, 1892, p. 53; "Mr. Sousa": clipping labeled *Express* (Los Angeles), Apr. 11, 1892, p. 52; both in Fowles, DMB.

24. *WP*, Feb. 26, 1892. Manuscript materials for "Sheridan's Ride" can be found as LCSC 319 and 369.

25. "A thrilling": *WP*, Feb. 23, 1892; "roused perhaps": *Times* (Los Angeles), Apr. 14, 1892. For the musical examples see a classified advertisement in *Express* (Los Angeles), Apr. 9, 1892; a program with poetry can be found in Fowles, p. 32b, DMB.

26. Undated program, ca. Dec. 6, 1892, HJ 3, p. 5, DMB. On a possible earlier version of the piece see "The Marine Band Concert," clipping labeled *Journal* (Boston), Apr. 4, 1891, Printed Ephemera, BP, NYPL. Manuscript materials for the work can be found as LCSC 323.

27. Sousa in "Music for the People," unlabeled clipping, c. 1890, Fowles, p. 69, DMB.

28. *Times* (Los Angeles), Apr. 13, 1892.

29. *MA*, 292. Manuscript materials for "Homeward Bound," found as LCSC 203, contain only later dates, and it is impossible to definitively place the work.

30. "One of": Blakely to Sousa, Feb. 11, 1892, Sousa Band Letter Book 1, p. 178, BP, NYPL; "if the": *Tribune* (Chicago), Apr. 8, 1892.

31. *WP*, Apr. 13, 1892.

32. Heywood to Lt. Col. William H. Powell, May 16, 1892, RG 127, Entry 5, NARA.

Applications can be found in RG 127, Entry 42, the commandant's replies in RG 127, Entry 5, both in NARA.

33. Heywood to Sousa, reprinted in *WP*, Aug. 1, 1892.

34. "For an": Blakely to Lyman, June 18, 1892, General Business Correspondence; "it is": Blakely to Smith, Aug. 16, 1892, Sousa Band Letter Book 1, p. 382; both in BP, NYPL.

35. Nettleton to Blakely, July 22, 1892, General Business Correspondence, BP, NYPL. A letter from Secretary of the Navy Tracy dated July 29, 1892, can be found in the same location (and was printed in "A Tribute," *WP*, July 30, 1892).

36. "If I": Sousa in "The Band's," July 30, 1892; "Sousa has": July 31, 1892, both in *WP*. The request for the performance can be found in a letter to Sousa, July 7, 1892, General Business Correspondence, BP, NYPL. Manuscript materials for "The Belle of Chicago" can be found as LCSC 336.

37. On June 28 Sousa wrote to Francis Wilson's wife seeking advice on finding a home for himself, his family, and a "colored nurse" in New Rochelle. His letter is in the Francis Wilson Papers, Billy Rose Theatre Division, NYPL. Fanciulli was tried by summary court martial and ordered to be dishonorably discharged. His sentence was lifted by Acting Secretary of the Navy Theodore Roosevelt, but Fanciulli would not reenlist. See RG 127, Entry 76, File of Francisco Fanciulli (Re-enlisted Nov. 1, 1892), NARA.

38. Johnston to Blakely, June 29, 1892, General Business Correspondence, BP, NYPL (emphasis in original).

39. "A Curious Engagement" (1892), 13.

40. Sousa in "Master of the Art," clipping labeled *Herald* (Grand Rapids), ca. Oct. 10, 1892, HJ 1, p. 8, DMB. On the commandant's complaint see *WP*, Oct. 8, 1892.

41. "Restricted in": Blakely in "Sousa's New" (Nov. 9, 1892), 11; "we are": Blakely to Sousa, July 6, 1892, Sousa Band Letter Book 1, p. 289, BP, NYPL.

42. "I got" and "in Italian": "Band Leader Sousa Tells What Music the Presidents and Their Wives Preferred," clipping labeled *Daily News* (Chicago), ca. Oct. 12, 1892, HJ 1, p. 13, DMB; "the first": Blakely in "Sousa's New" (Nov. 9, 1892), 11; on the New York claim see "In Existence a Year," clipping, ca. July 26, 1893, HJ 2, p. 59, DMB.

43. Sousa to Smith, Aug. 18, 1892, Sousa Band Letter Book 1, p. 385, BP, NYPL.

44. Manuscript materials for "March of the Royal Trumpets" can be found as LCSC 110. Sousa later incorporated portions of this piece into his suite *At the King's Court* (1904). For program details in Plainfield see clippings in HJ 1, pp. 1–3, DMB.

45. "Not catering": "The Marine Band Concert," clipping labeled *Star* (Elmira), ca. Sept. 30, 1892, p. 2; "covered a": "Amusements," clipping labeled *Democrat* (Grand Rapids), ca. Oct. 9, 1892, p. 9; "no such": "The Drama," clipping labeled *News* (Williamsport), ca. Sept. 29, 1892, p. 2; "the greatest": "Sousa's New Marine Band," clipping labeled *Evening News* (Muskegon), ca. Oct. 8, 1892, p. 10; all in HJ 1, DMB.

46. "Unlike the": clipping labeled *Globe* (Saginaw), ca. Oct. 6, 1892, p. 11; "if there": "Master of the Art," clipping labeled *Herald* (Grand Rapids), ca. Oct. 10, 1892, p. 8; "not suffer": "The Marine Band Concert," clipping labeled *Star* (Elmira), ca. Oct. 1, 1892, p. 2; all in HJ 1, DMB.

47. For samples of the enthusiastic reviews received by the band during their initial engagement in Chicago see clippings in HJ 2, pp. 11–14, DMB.

48. *MA*, 130.

49. *Herald* (Chicago), Oct. 22, 1892.

50. "Sousa has": "Maj. Sousa's New Band," clipping labeled *Record* (Chicago), ca. Oct. 11, 1892, HJ 1, p. 12, DMB; "if they": clipping labeled *Herald* (Chicago), ca. Oct. 11, 1892, HJ 1, p. 11, DMB.

51. *WP*, Oct. 30, 1892.

52. "In the": "Last Night's Music," clipping labeled "Philadelphia Press," ca. Oct. 30, 1892, p. 16; "should let": clipping labeled *Record* (New York), ca. Oct. 31, 1892, p. 12, both in HJ 1, DMB; "there is": "Sousa's New," (Nov. 2, 1892): 13.

53. "Sousa's New" (Nov. 9, 1892): 11.

54. *MA*, 127.

55. "Sousa's Band," clipping labeled *Journal* (Lowell), ca. Nov. 20, 1892, HJ 1, p. 19, DMB.

56. Blakely to Thomas, Nov. 11, 1892, Sousa Band Letter Book 1, p. 455, BP, NYPL.

57. Johnston to Blakely, Jan. 5, 1893, General Business Correspondence, BP, NYPL (emphasis in original).

58. Blakely to Johnston, Jan. 10, 1893, General Business Correspondence, BP, NYPL.

59. "A Popular" (1893), 13.

60. "Sousa's Band Concert," clipping labeled *Commercial* (Buffalo), ca. Oct. 3, 1892, HJ 1, p. 3, DMB. Manuscript materials for *Songs of Grace and Songs of Glory* can be found as LCSC 320.

61. "Gilmore and Sousa" (March 15, 1893), 8. For Sousa's comments see "Musical Festival," clipping labeled *Journal* (Syracuse), Dec. 6, 1892, HJ 1, p. 34, DMB.

62. "Amazed and": Ellen Gilmore to Blakely, ca. March 6, 1893; "thereby giving": Reeves to Blakely, March 31, 1893; both in General Business Correspondence, BP, NYPL.

63. "Sousa's organization": "Gilmore and Sousa" (March 15, 1893), 8; "final judgment": "Gilmore and Sousa" (March 22, 1893), 10.

64. Sousa program, 1893, Gaskill, p. 12, DMB. On Blakely's efforts to purchase the Gilmore library see *NYT*, Oct. 9, 1892. For period descriptions of Gilmore's successors see "Gilmore's Successor," clipping labeled *Telegram* (Kalamazoo), ca. Oct. 7, 1892, HJ 1, p. 7, DMB; and "Wants to Lead" (1892), 14.

65. See *MA*, 135–38.

66. For a sample program from 1893, see an unidentified Buffalo clipping, ca. May 9, HJ 2, p. 18, DMB.

67. Manuscript materials for *The Last Days of Pompeii* can be found as LCSC 318.

68. Sousa in Mathews, W.S.B., "An Interview" (1896), 491.

69. Manuscript materials for "Salute of the Nations" can be found as LCSC 262, those for "The Beau Ideal" at SACAM.

70. "An overestimate": "The Musical Festival," clipping labeled *Herald* (Boston), May 6, 1893, p. 10; "lovers of": "The Sousa Matinee Concert," clipping labeled *Pioneer Press* (St. Paul), May 21, 1893, p. 35, both in HJ 2, DMB.

71. “I tell”: Frank Gaiennie in “Manager Gaiennie Pleased with the Music of Gilmore’s Successor,” clipping labeled *Chronicle* (St. Louis), May 13, 1893, p. 22; “it can”: “Sousa’s Grand Band,” clipping labeled *Globe Democrat* (St. Louis), May 13, 1893, p. 23; “if Gilmore”: clipping labeled *Journal* (Kansas City), May 15, 1893, p. 25; all in HJ 2, DMB.

72. “Music at the Columbian Exposition” (1892), 5.

73. “Theodore Thomas”’: “Music at the World’s Fair,” (1893), 17; “for the”: Thomas to Ellsworth, Aug. 1, 1893, Felsengarten Collection, Chicago Symphony Orchestra (emphasis in original). Receipt data are from Schabas (1989), 202–8.

74. “Comprised by”: “Music by the Waves,” *Herald* (Chicago), June 26, 1893, p. 41; “one long”: “Farewell Concert of Sousa’s Band,” *Herald* (Chicago), June 28, 1893, p. 42; both in HJ 2, DMB.

75. “As ought”: “Farewell to Sousa,” *Herald* (Chicago), June 27, 1893, p. 41; “director of”: *Herald* (Chicago), June 28, 1893, p. 47; both in HJ 2, DMB. “Director Thomas”: clipping labeled *Times* (Watertown), July 3, 1893, World’s Columbian Exposition Scrapbook, Newberry Library, Chicago.

76. “Material for”: Sousa in *Tribune* (Chicago), Nov. 23, 1890; “the whole”: Sousa in “Farewell to Sousa,” *Herald* (Chicago), June 27, 1893, HJ 2, p. 42, DMB.

77. Sousa, “How to Make Programs” (1893), 15.

78. *Herald* (Chicago) in “Theodore Thomas and Sousa” (1893), 17. Some versions of the letter mention the Thomas-Liesegang-Brand trust, referring to Adolph Liesegang (of the Chicago Military Band) and Michael Brand (of the Cincinnati Military Band), both of whom were engaged at the fair.

79. “Farewell Concert of Sousa’s Band,” *Herald* (Chicago), June 28, 1893, HJ 2, p. 42, DMB.

80. “That seemed”: “Where the Surf Roars,” clipping labeled *Commercial Advertiser* (New York), July 3, 1893, HJ 2, p. 43, DMB; “Sousa and”: “Sousa at Manhattan Beach,” (1893), 17.

Nine. Theater on the Bandstand

1. “A concert”: “March King at Metropolitan,” clipping labeled *Post Intelligencer* (Seattle), Oct. 1, 1927, HJ 72, p. 104, DMB; “Sousa is”: Skinner in a Sousa press package, ca. Dec. 1896, p. 71, Printed Ephemera, BP, NYPL.

2. Helmecke, “How Sousa Played” (1950), 23.

3. “Cumulative force”: Sousa in *Post* (Boston), March 10, 1918; “the chief”: *MA*, 332.

4. Sousa, “A Letter from Sousa,” (1898), 231.

5. The structural terms used here are from Elkus, “Defining the Sousa March” (2005).

6. The only known instances of the Sousa Band on parade occurred in 1892 as part of the dedication of the World’s Columbian Exposition, in 1898 to escort a portion of the Ohio National Guard as it departed for the Spanish-American War, in 1898 to celebrate the return from war of a Pittsburgh regiment, in 1899 as part of

the victory parade for Admiral Dewey in New York, in 1900 at the Paris Exposition, in 1916 and 1917 in conjunction with the *Hip! Hip! Hooray!* show at the New York Hippodrome, and in 1929 at a procession on the Princeton campus.

7. Patton, *Practical Guide* (1875), 87.

8. On the use of borrowed material in Ives see Burkholder, *All Made of Tunes* (1995), 41.

9. *MA*, 238.

10. Fennell, "The Sousa March" (1983), 91.

11. Sousa in *Post* (Boston), March 10, 1918.

12. On Sousa's keys see Elkus, *Charles Ives* (1974), 20.

13. Two unpublished marches, "Recognition" and "March of the Royal Trumpets," are not covered in this survey because their surviving source materials leave their structures uncertain.

14. "I do": *MA*, 359–60 (emphasis in original); "great ideas": Sousa in "Next Great Composer will be an American," clipping labeled *Post* (Pittsburgh), Sept. 12, 1898, HJ 7, p. 8, DMB.

15. Taylor, *Of Men and Music* (1937), 59.

16. "Sailor's knot": Jacob, *Johann Strauss* (1940), 351; "an important": Elkus, *Charles Ives* (1974), 27.

17. The measure-13 convention is discussed in Berlin, *Ragtime* (1980), 140–46.

18. Jacob, *Johann Strauss* (1940), 352.

19. "There is": Evenson, "March Style of Sousa" (1954), 15; "must be": *MA*, 359; "without altering": Jacob, *Johann Strauss* (1940), 352.

20. "Sousa in Pretoria," clipping labeled *News* (Pretoria), Apr. 4, 1911, HJ 34, p. 8, DMB.

21. "I asked": Lefter (interviewed Aug. 1980), The Sousa Oral History Project, p. 65, DMB; "he didn't": Helmecke, "Why the Accents Weren't Written In . . ." (1951), 15.

22. "People have": Helmecke, "How Sousa Played" (1950), 23; "[we should]": Gens, "Message from the President" (1953).

23. Written versions of the New Hampshire talks were published in the *Instrumentalist* (Mar.–Apr. 1951).

24. "Fire and tongs" is used by Simon to describe the end of several marches; see *The Sounds of John Philip Sousa* (1965, 1969). For details of performance practice see Byrne, "Sousa Marches" (1994), and Warfield, *John Philip Sousa: Six Marches* (2010).

25. W. Lewis, "Stray Notes" (1887), 2. A later *Metronome* contributor placed Sousa among several composers who had "taken the front rank" in march writing, specifically, "Tobani, Sousa, Herman, Reeves, Puerner, Innes, Brooks, [and] Heed." W. H. A., "Marches and Marches" (1895), 5.

26. Clipping from a Ballarat, Australia, paper, July 7, 1911, HJ 34, p. 31, DMB.

27. "From a": Brush, "Electrical Illumination" (1901), 20943; "the lights": *MA*, 230.

28. Lambert, *Music Ho!* (1967), 182. "On to Victory" was an alternative title for Sousa's march "The Free Lance" (1906).

29. "Sousa's Rare Treat," clipping from an unnamed Plainfield newspaper, ca. Sept. 27, 1892, HJ 1, p. 1, DMB.

30. Sousa in "Sousa and His Mission" (1899), 275.

31. *MA*, 275.

32. Sousa in *Herald* (New York), Nov. 15, 1908. A portion of this conversation appears in *MA*, 294.

Epilogue. Marching Along

1. *PI*, May 9, 1897.

2. Blakely to Sousa (May 21, 1895) in *Blakely v. Sousa* (1900).

3. *MA*, 157.

4. *Kennebec Journal* (Augusta), May 3, 1897. For chronologies see Smart, "Genesis of a March" (1983); and Ward, "Augusta's Proudest Secret" (1997).

5. Sousa in "Sousa's Band" (1897), 6.

6. "Academy of Music—Sousa's Band," clipping from Philadelphia, ca. May 15, 1897, HJ 5, p. 47, DMB.

7. For details on *El Capitan* see Hess, "John Philip Sousa's *El Capitan*" (1998); on the operettas more generally see Chessum, "(Musical) Sales Pitches" (2012).

8. "Gigantic swindle": "The Sousa Dispute," clipping labeled *Evening Leader* (Wilkes-Barre), Apr. 9, 1897, HJ 5, p. 4, DMB; "evidently was": *Blakely v. Sousa* (1900).

9. *MA*, 365.

Bibliography

Archival Sources

à Becket Family Diaries and Prompt Books. Billy Rose Theatre Division, New York Public Library.

Annual Reports from the Washington Public Schools. Sumner School Archives. Washington, D.C.

Barry Owen Furrer Private Collection. Bound Brook, N.J.

Concordia United Church of Christ Records, 1833–2003. Historical Society of Washington, D.C.

David Blakely Papers. Manuscripts and Archives Division. New York Public Library.

Felsengarten Collection (Theodore and Rose Fay Thomas). Rosenthal Archives. Chicago Symphony Orchestra.

Files of clippings, articles, and photographs. United States Marine Band Library. Washington, D.C.

Fowles Scrapbook. United States Marine Band Library. Washington, D.C.

Francis Wilson Papers. Billy Rose Theatre Division. New York Public Library.

Gaskill Scrapbook. United States Marine Band Library. Washington, D.C.

George Foreman Private Collection. Athens, Ga.

Georgetown College Commencement Files. Special Collections, Lauinger Library. Georgetown University. Washington, D.C.

House Ledgers. Special Collections, Lauinger Library. Georgetown University. Washington, D.C.

J. Wilson Vance Papers. Ohio Historical Society, Columbus.

J. C. Williamson Music Manuscripts. Mitchell Library. State Library of New South Wales. Sydney, Australia.

John Philip Sousa Clipping File. Music Division. New York Public Library.

John Philip Sousa Collection. Music Division. Library of Congress. Washington, D.C. Some materials online at: http://lcweb2.loc.gov/diglib/ihas/html/sousa/sousa-home.html.

John Philip Sousa Collection. United States Marine Band Library. Washington, D.C.

John Philip Sousa Family Collection. United States Marine Band Library. Washington, D.C.

John Philip Sousa Music and Personal Papers. Sousa Archives: Center for American Music, University of Illinois, Champaign.

John Philip Sousa Oral History Project. United States Marine Band Library. Washington, D.C.
Minstrel Show Collection. Harry Ransom Center. University of Texas, Austin.
Music Folder. Centennial Bureaus of Administration, Centennial Collection. Historical Society of Pennsylvania, Philadelphia.
Musical Fund Society Collection of Music. Rare Book and Manuscript Library. University of Pennsylvania, Philadelphia.
Paul E. Bierley Papers. Sousa Archives and Center for American Music. University of Illinois, Champaign.
Program Files and Scrapbooks. Free Library of Philadelphia.
RG 45, Naval Records Collection of the Office of Naval Records and Library. National Archives and Records Administration. Washington, D.C.
 Entry 464, Old Subject File, NJ (discipline and minor delinquencies).
RG 80, General Records of the Department of the Navy. National Archives and Records Administration. Washington, D.C.
 Entry 14, Records of the Office of the Secretary of the Navy, General Records, Letters Received, Letters from the Commandant and Other Officers of the Marine Corps.
RG 127, Records of the U.S. Marine Corps. National Archives and Records Administration, Washington, D.C.
 Entry 4: Office of the Commandant, General Records, Correspondence, Letters Sent.
 Entry 5: Office of the Commandant, General Records, Correspondence, Press Copies of Letters Sent.
 Entry 42: Office of the Commandant, Historical Division, Letters Received.
 Entry 46: Office of the Commandant, Historical Division, Scrapbooks of Clippings.
 Entry 76: Case Files, Enlisted Men.
 Entry 112: Adjutant and Inspector's Department, Miscellaneous Records.
Saxton Scrapbooks. Washingtoniana Division, Martin Luther King Jr. Public Library. Washington, D.C.
Sousa Band Press Books (cited by HJ number). United States Marine Band Library. Washington, D.C.
Susan (Anna) Adelle Esputa Counterpane. Museum of American History. Smithsonian Institution. Washington, D.C.
T1118: Muster Rolls of the United States Marine Corps, 1798–1892. National Archives and Records Administration. Washington, D.C.
Theatre Collection. Kiplinger Research Library. Historical Society of Washington, D.C.
Tillman Family Private Collection. Towson, Md.
William Wilson Corcoran Papers. Manuscript Division. Library of Congress. Washington, D.C.
World's Columbian Exposition Scrapbook. Newberry Library. Chicago.

Print Sources

Alexander, Robert C. "The Congress Hall March." *Cape May County Magazine of History and Genealogy* 5 (June 1961): 296–307.

"American-Music Association." *Musical World* 19, no. 19 (May 8, 1858): 291.

Bede, Cuthbert. *The Adventures of Mr. Verdant Green.* London: Nathaniel Cooke, 1853.

Berger, Kenneth. *The March King and His Band: The Story of John Philip Sousa.* New York: Exposition, 1957.

Berlin, Edward A. *Ragtime: A Musical and Cultural History.* Berkeley: University of California Press, 1980.

Bierley, Paul Edmund. *The Incredible Band of John Philip Sousa.* Urbana: University of Illinois Press, 2006.

———. *John Philip Sousa: American Phenomenon.* Englewood Cliffs, N.J.: Prentice-Hall, 1973. Repr. and rev., Westerville, Ohio: Integrity, 1998.

———. "John Philip Sousa: America's March King." *Short Talk Bulletin* 75, no. 11 (Nov. 1997).

———. *Sousa Band Fraternal Society News Index.* Westerville, Ohio: Integrity, 1998.

———. "That Curious Sousa Voice Tape." *Journal of Band Research* 22 (fall 1986): 45–47.

———. *The Works of John Philip Sousa.* Westerville, Ohio: Integrity, 1984. Revision of *John Philip Sousa: A Descriptive Catalog of His Works.* Urbana: University of Illinois Press, 1973.

Blakely v. Sousa, no. 353, 197 Pa. 305 (S. Pa. 1900).

Bly, Leon Joseph. "The March in American Society." Ph.D. diss., University of Miami, 1977.

———. "The March in the United States of America." In *Bläserklang und Blasinstrumente im Schaffen Richard Wagners Kongreßbericht Seggau/Österreich 1983.* Alta Musica 8, ed. Wolfgang Suppau, 245–61. Tutzing, Germany: Schneider, 1985.

Boosey, William. *Fifty Years of Music.* London: E. Benn, 1931.

"Boston." *Dramatic Mirror* (Dec. 27, 1884).

Brion, Keith. "A Master of Programming." *Instrumentalist* 59, no. 4 (Nov. 2004): 50–53.

——— and Loras Schissel, arrs. *The Stars and Stripes Forever.* Oskaloosa, Iowa: Willow-Blossom Music, 1996.

Brooks, Tim. "Columbia Records in the 1890's: Founding the Record Industry." *Association for Recorded Sound Collections Journal* 10 (1978): 4–36.

———. "A Directory to Columbia Recording Artists of the 1890s." *Journal of the Association for Recorded Sound Collections* 11 (1979): 102–38.

Brown, Margaret L. "David Blakely, Manager of Sousa's Band." In Newsom (1983), 121–33.

Browne, Alexander P. "Sir Arthur Sullivan and Piracy." *North American Review* 148, no. 391 (June 1889): 750–60.

Brush, Edward Hale. "Electrical Illumination at the Pan-American Exposition." *Scientific American Supplement* 51, no. 1307 (Jan. 19, 1901), 20943.

Bryant, Carolyn. "Sousa and the Marine Band: New Sousa Scrapbooks at the Marine Band Library." *Sonneck Society for American Music Bulletin* 22 (summer 1996): 5–7.

Brylawski, E. Fulton, and Abe Goldman, eds. *Legislative History of the 1909 Copyright Act.* South Hackensack, N.J.: Rothman, 1976.

Bulwer-Lytton, Edward. *The Last Days of Pompeii.* London: Richard Bentley, 1834.

———. *The Pilgrims of the Rhine.* London: Saunder and Otley, 1834.

Burdette, Robert Jones. *The Drums of the 47th.* Indianapolis: Bobbs-Merrill, 1914.

Burkholder, J. Peter. *All Made of Tunes: Charles Ives and the Uses of Musical Borrowing.* New Haven: Yale University Press, 1995.

Burroughs, Edgar Rice. *Tarzan of the Apes.* Chicago: McClurg, 1914.

Byrne, Frank. "Patriotism and Marketing Built the Sousa Legend." *Instrumentalist* 59, no. 4 (Nov. 2004): 20–32, 68–69.

———. "Sousa Marches: Principles for Historically Informed Performance." In *The Wind Ensemble and Its Repertoire: Essays on the Fortieth Anniversary of the Eastman Wind Ensemble,* ed. Frank J. Cipolla and Donald Hunsberger, 141–67. Rochester: University of Rochester Press, 1994.

Cammack, Shirley. "James Lawrence Kernan, 1838–1912." Unpublished paper, author's collection, n.d.

Camus, Raoul F. *Military Music of the American Revolution.* Chapel Hill: University of North Carolina Press, 1975. Repr., Westerville, Ohio: Integrity, 1993.

———. "On the Cadence of the March." *Journal of Band Research* 16 (spring 1981): 13–23.

Carpenter, Kenneth William. "A History of the United States Marine Band." Ph.D. diss., University of Iowa, 1970.

Carte v. Ford (The *Iolanthe* Case), 15 F. 439, 447 (C.C.D. Md. 1883).

Catalogue of Music, Band, U.S. Marine Corps. Washington, D.C.: Government Printing Office, 1885.

Chapman, Mary Megan. "'Living Pictures': Women and *tableaux vivants* in Nineteenth-Century American Fiction and Culture." Ph.D. diss., Cornell University, 1992.

Chesebrough, James. "Harmonic Content in the Marches of John Philip Sousa." *Journal of Band Research* 39 (spring 2004): 45–64.

Chessum, Tracey Elaine. "(Musical) Sales Pitches from the 'Salesman of Americanism': The Comic Operas of John Philip Sousa." Ph.D. diss., University of Maryland, 2012.

Church, Charles Fremont, Jr. "The Life and Influence of John Philip Sousa." Ph.D. diss., Ohio State University, 1942.

Cipolla, Frank J. "The Business Papers of David Blakely, Manager of the Gilmore and Sousa Bands." *Journal of Band Research* 13 (spring 1978): 2–7.

———. "Francesco Fanciulli: Turn-of-the-Century American Bandmaster." *Instrumentalist* 33, no. 7 (Feb. 1979): 34–36.

———. "Patrick S. Gilmore: The Boston Years and Beyond." In *Kongreßbericht Abony/Ungarn 1994.* Alta Musica 18, ed. Wolfgang Suppan, 183–87. Tutzing, Germany: Schneider, 1996.

———. "Patrick S. Gilmore: The New York Years." In *European Music and Musicians in New York City, 1840–1900*, ed. John Graziano, 182–97. Rochester: University of Rochester Press, 2006.

Clark, Allen C. "Francis Maria Scala." *Records of the Columbia Historical Society* 35–36 (1933): 222–34.

Click, Patricia C. *The Spirit of the Times: Amusements in Nineteenth-Century Baltimore, Norfolk, and Richmond*. Charlottesville: University Press of Virginia, 1989.

Cole, Sarah. "For They Are American: The Gorman's Philadelphia Church Choir's Production of *H.M.S. Pinafore*." Unpublished paper, author's collection, 1985.

Cook, Eliza. "Wilt Thou Be True?" *Graham's Magazine* 43, no. 2 (Aug. 1853), 202.

Cowherd, Ron. "Sousa Marches: The Arranged Versions." *Instrumentalist* 32, no. 5 (Dec. 1977): 44–47.

"A Curious Engagement." *Musical Courier* 25, no. 4 (July 27, 1892): 13.

Danner, Phyllis. "John Philip Sousa: The Illinois Collection." *Notes* 55 (Sept. 1998): 9–25.

———. *Sousa at Illinois: The John Philip Sousa and Herbert L. Clarke Manuscript Collections at the University of Illinois at Urbana-Champaign; A Catalogue of the Collections*. Warren, Mich.: Harmonie Park, 2005.

———, David Peter Coppen, and Ann Marie Werner. "Anatomy of a Preservation Project: The Sousa and Clarke Archives at UIUC." *Sonneck Society for American Music Bulletin* 24 (summer 1998): 33, 39–40; and 24 (fall 1998): 71.

"David Wallis Reeves." *Musical Courier* 26, no. 10 (Mar. 8, 1893): 13.

Delaplaine, Edward S. *John Philip Sousa and the National Anthem*. Frederick, Md.: Great Southern, 1983. Repr., Westminster, Md.: Willow Bend, 2001.

Dorian, Frank. "Reminiscences of the Columbia Cylinder Records." *Phonograph Monthly Review* 4, no. 4 (Jan. 1930): 114–15.

Dreiser, Theodore. *The Color of a Great City*. New York: Boni and Liveright, 1923. Repr., New York: Fertig, 1987.

Dvorak, Raymond F. "Recollections of Sousa's March Performances." *School Musician and Teacher* 41 (Dec. 1969): 58–59, 65.

Eiland, Dianna. "The 1891 Tour of John Philip Sousa and the United States Marine Band." In *Kongreßbericht Feldkirch/Vorarlberg 1992*. Alta Musica 16, ed. Wolfgang Suppan, 169–80. Tutzing, Germany: Schneider, 1994.

Elkus, Jonathan. *Charles Ives and the American Band Tradition: A Centennial Tribute*. Exeter, U.K.: American Arts Documentation Centre, 1974.

———. "Defining the Sousa March: Its Formal and Stylistic Constants." *American Music Research Center Journal* 15 (2005): 41–53.

Elward, Thomas Joseph. "A History of Music Education in the District of Columbia Public Schools from 1845 to 1945." D.M.A. diss., Catholic University of America, 1975.

———. "Pioneer Music Educators in the Nation's Capitol: They Made Black History." *Music Educators Journal* (Feb. 1981): 35–38.

"The Era of Sousa." *Musical Courier* 37, no. 1 (July 4, 1898), n.p.

Esputa, John. *Esputa's Music Instructor*. Washington, D.C.: John Esputa, 1870.

Esputa-Daly, Josephine. *The Note Chain System*. Washington, D.C.: Henry White, 1894.
Evenson, E. Orville. "The March Style of Sousa." *Instrumentalist* 9, no. 3 (Nov. 1954): 13–15, 48–50.
Fennell, Frederick. "The Sousa March: A Personal View." In Newsom (1983), 81–102 (http://lcweb2.loc.gov/diglib/ihas/loc.natlib.ihas.200152754/default.html).
Foreman, George C. "A War of Blasters: The Great Coney Island Cornet/Trombone Confrontation of 1880." In *On Bunker's Hill: Essays in Honor of J. Bunker Clark*, ed. William A. Everett and Paul R. Laird, 53–70. Sterling Heights, Mich.: Harmonie Park, 2007.
Foster, S. Conant. "Sweet Miss Industry." *St. Nicholas* 12, no. 2 (Dec. 1884): 104–8.
G. C. T. "Sousa's Birthday Made a National Event." *Musical America* 23, no. 2 (Nov. 13, 1915): 2.
Gens, William C. "A Message from the President." *Sousa Band Fraternal Society News* (Jan. 1953).
"George F. Benkert." *Dwight's Journal of Music* 10, no. 11 (Dec. 13, 1856): 83.
Gerson, Robert A. *Music in Philadelphia: A History of Philadelphia Music*. Philadelphia: Theodore Presser, 1940.
"G. F. Benkert and His Works." *Dwight's Journal of Music* 10, no. 13 (Dec. 27, 1856): 99–100.
Gifford, Robert M. "The American March: The Development of a Genre from the Eighteenth Century to the Present." In *Kongreßbericht Abony, Ungarn 1994*. Alta Musica 18, ed. Wolfgang Suppan, 189–203. Tutzing, Germany: Schneider, 1996.
"Gilmore and Sousa." *Musical Courier* 26, no. 11 (Mar. 15, 1893): 8.
"Gilmore and Sousa." *Musical Courier* 26, no. 12 (Mar. 22, 1893): 10.
Gilmore, Stephen P. "Patrick Sarsfield Gilmore: America's Prototypical Impresario." *Journal of Band Research* 34 (fall 1998): 69–100.
Grau, Robert. *Forty Years' Observation of Music and the Drama*. New York: Broadway, 1909.
———. "When Offenbach Came to Town." *Musical America* 18, no. 20 (Sept. 20, 1913): 29.
Graziano, John. "John Philip Sousa and the American Art Song." In *On Bunker's Hill: Essays in Honor of J. Bunker Clark*, ed. William A. Everett and Paul R. Laird, 71–88. Sterling Heights, Mich.: Harmonie Park, 2007.
Green, Constance McLaughlin. *The Secret City: A History of Race Relations in the Nation's Capital*. Princeton: Princeton University Press, 1967.
———. *Washington*. Princeton: Princeton University Press, 1962–63.
Greene, Carol. *John Philip Sousa: The March King*. Chicago: Children's, 1992.
Guion, David M. "From Yankee Doodle thro' to Handel's Largo: Music at the World's Columbian Exposition." *College Music Symposium* 24 (spring 1984): 81–96.
Harris, Neil. "John Philip Sousa and the Culture of Reassurance." In Newsom (1983), 11–40 (http://lcweb2.loc.gov/diglib/ihas/loc.natlib.ihas.200152753/default.html).
Heintze, James R. "Gaetano Carusi: From Sicily to the Halls of Congress." In *American Musical Life in Context and Practice to 1865*, ed. James R. Heintze, 75–131. New York: Garland, 1994.

Helmecke, August. "How Sousa Played His Marches," as told to Rose Heylbut. *Etude* 68 (Aug. 1950): 23, 63.

———. "Why the Accents Weren't Written In . . ." *Instrumentalist* 5, no. 5 (Mar.–Apr. 1951): 15. Repr., *Instrumentalist* 9, no. 3 (Nov. 1954): 51.

Hemberger, Glen James. "Selected Songs for Chamber Winds and Soprano: Rediscovering a Forgotten Repertoire of John Philip Sousa." D.M.A. diss., University of North Texas, 2001.

Heney, John J. *The Correct Way to Drum.* St. Augustine, Fla.: Heney School of Percussion, 1934.

Heslip, Malcolm. *Nostalgic Happenings in the Three Bands of John Philip Sousa.* Laguna Hills, Calif.: M. Heslip, 1982. Repr., Westerville, Ohio: Integrity, 1992.

Hess, Carol A. "John Philip Sousa's *El Capitan*: Political Appropriation and the Spanish-American War." *American Music* 16 (spring 1998): 1–24.

Hester, Michael Eric. "A Study of the Saxophone Soloists Performing with the John Philip Sousa Band, 1893–1930." D.M.A. diss., University of Arizona, 1995.

Hoover, Cynthia A. "Music and Musical Instruments." In *1876: A Centennial Exhibition*, ed. Robert C. Post, 138–43. Washington, D.C.: National Museum of History and Technology, Smithsonian Institution, 1976.

Hopper, DeWolf, and Wesley Winans Stout. *Once a Clown Always a Clown: Reminiscences of DeWolf Hopper.* Boston: Little, Brown, 1927.

Ingalls, David M. "Francis Scala: Leader of the Marine Band from 1855 to 1871." Master's thesis, Catholic University of America, 1957.

"Interview with John Phillip Sousa." *Music* (June 1898): 171–73.

Jacob, H. E. *Johann Strauss, Father and Son: A Century of Light Music.* Translated by Marguerite Wolff. New York: Graystone, 1940.

Janvier, Meredith. *Baltimore in the Eighties and Nineties.* Baltimore: H. G. Roebuck, 1933.

Jorgensen, Michael R. "John Philip Sousa's Operetta *El Capitan*: A Historical, Analytical and Performance Guide." D.M.A. diss., Ball State University, 1995.

"Justice Triumphant." *American Music Journal* 1 (June 15, 1885): 4.

Kirk, Elise K. *Music at the White House: A History of the American Spirit.* Urbana: University of Illinois Press, 1986.

Korzun, Jonathan Nicholas. "The Orchestral Transcriptions for Band of John Philip Sousa: A Description and Analysis." Ed.D. diss., University of Illinois, 1994.

Krasner, Orly Leah. "A Capital Idea: Reginald de Koven and the Washington Symphony Orchestra." In *Music, American Made: Essays in Honor of John Graziano*, ed. John Koegel, 123–59. Sterling Heights, Mich.: Harmonie Park, 2011.

Kreitner, Mona Bulpitt. "'A Splendid Group of American Girls': The Women Who Sang with the Sousa Band." Ph.D. diss., University of Memphis, 2007.

Lambert, Constant. *Music Ho! A Study of Music in Decline.* New York: October House, 1967.

Laura Keene v. Moses Kimball, 82 Mass. (16 Gray) 545 (Mass. 1860).

Lawrence, Arthur. *Sir Arthur Sullivan: Life Story, Letters, and Reminiscences.* Chicago: Herbert S. Stone, 1900.

Lears, T. J. Jackson. *No Place of Grace: Antimodernism and the Transformation of American Culture, 1880–1920*. New York: Pantheon, 1981.

LeClair, Paul Joseph. "The Francis Scala Collection: Music in Washington, D.C. at the Time of the Civil War." Ph.D. diss., Catholic University of America, 1973.

Levine, Lawrence W. *Highbrow/Lowbrow: The Emergence of Cultural Hierarchy in America*. Cambridge, Mass.: Harvard University Press, 1988.

Lewis, Robert M. "*Tableaux vivants*: Parlor Theatricals in Victorian America." *Revue française d'études américaines* 36 (Apr. 1988): 280–91.

Lewis, Walt. "Stray Notes." *Metronome* 3, no. 2 (Feb. 1887): 2.

Lingg, Ann M. *John Philip Sousa*. New York: Holt, Rinehart, and Winston, 1954.

Lodge, Henry Cabot. "Extracts from the Familiar Correspondence of the Hon. E. H. Mills." *Proceedings of the Massachusetts Historical Society* 19 (1881–82): 12–53.

Loesser, Arthur. *Men, Women and Pianos: A Social History*. New York: Simon and Schuster, 1954. Repr., New York: Dover, 1990.

Loft, Abram. "Richard Wagner, Theodore Thomas, and the American Centennial." *Musical Quarterly* 37 (Apr. 1951): 184–202.

Lutz, Norma Jean. *Marching with Sousa*. Uhrichsville, Ohio: Barbour, 1998.

MacCulloch, Hunter. *From Dawn to Dusk, and Other Poems*. Philadelphia: J. B. Lippincott, 1887.

MacGregor, Morris J. *The Emergence of a Black Catholic Community: St. Augustine's in Washington*. Washington, D.C.: Catholic University of America Press, 1999.

"The Marine Band." *Musical Courier* 14, no. 14 (Oct. 2, 1889): 287.

Mathews, John Lathrop. "*El Capitan*: A Comic Opera by Sousa." *Music* (June 1896): 163–68.

Mathews, W. S. B., ed. *A Hundred Years of Music in America*. Chicago: G. L. Howe, 1889. Repr., New York: AMS, 1970.

———. "An Interview with John Phillip Sousa." *Music* (March 1896): 487–92.

Mazzola, Sandy R. "Bands and Orchestras at the World's Columbian Exposition." *American Music* 4 (winter 1986): 407–24.

McCullough, Jack W. *Living Pictures on the New York Stage*. Ann Arbor, Mich.: UMI Research Press, 1983.

McKinley, Ann. "Music for the Dedication Ceremonies of the World's Columbian Exposition in Chicago, 1892." *American Music* 3 (spring 1985): 42–51.

McKnight, Mark. "*Morceaux de Salon*, Elegant Polkas, and *Grandes Variations Brillantes*: Instrumental Forms in Nineteenth-Century American Sheet Music." In *Music Publishing & Collecting: Essays in Honor of Donald W. Krummel*, ed. David Hunter, 95–112. Urbana: University of Illinois Graduate School of Library and Information Science, 1994.

Miller, Betsy G. "James Barton's *Iolanthe*." *Sir Arthur Sullivan Society Magazine* (autumn 2003): 7–15.

———. "J. S. Crossy, Sousa, and *The Contrabandista*." *Sir Arthur Sullivan Society Magazine* (spring 2006): 3–8.

"A Modern Columbus." *Dramatic Mirror* (June 5, 1909), 2.
"More Beethoven Celebrations." *Dwight's Journal of Music* 30, no. 22 (Jan. 14, 1871): 383–84.
Morrison, Andrew Craig. *Theatres of Washington: An Illustrated Historical List*. Washington, D.C.: Theatre Historical Society, 1972.
"Mr. D. Blakely." *Musical Courier* 26, no. 5 (Feb. 1, 1893): 20.
Mudd, Aloysius I. "Early Theatres in Washington City." *Records of the Columbia Historical Society* 5 (1902): 64–86.
———. "The Theatres of Washington from 1835 to 1850." *Records of the Columbia Historical Society* 6 (1903): 222–66.
"Music at the Centennial." *Dwight's Journal of Music* 36, no. 8 (July 22, 1876): 271–72.
"Music at the Centennial." *Watson's Art Journal* (Nov. 20, 1875): 43.
"Music at the Columbian Exposition." *Musical Courier* 25, no. 2 (July 13, 1892): 5–6.
"Music at the World's Fair." *Musical Courier* 26, no. 21 (May 24, 1893): 17.
"Musical Intelligence." *Dwight's Journal of Music* 10, no. 8 (Nov. 22, 1856): 63.
"The National Capital." *Catholic Mirror* 3, no. 49 (Mar. 31, 1888): 1.
"New York Amusements." *Dramatic Mirror* (May 24, 1879): 6.
Newman, Ernest. *The Life of Richard Wagner*. Vol. 4, *1866–1883*. New York: Knopf, 1946.
Newsom, Jon, ed. *Perspectives on John Philip Sousa*. Washington, D.C.: Library of Congress, 1983.
Nobles, Milton. *The Phoenix*. Chicago: Dramatic, 1900.
———. *Shop Talk*. Milwaukee: Riverside Printing, 1889.
Norton, Pauline Elizabeth. "March Music in Nineteenth-Century America." Ph.D. diss., University of Michigan, 1983.
———. "Nineteenth-Century American March Music and John Philip Sousa." In Newsom (1983), 43–52.
Odell, George C. D. *Annals of the New York Stage*. Vol. 10, *1875–1879*. New York: Columbia University Press, 1938.
Offenbach, Jacques. *Orpheus in America: Offenbach's Diary of His Journey to the New World*. Translated by Lander MacClintock. Bloomington: Indiana University Press, 1957.
"The Origin of Sousa's Name." *Etude* 54 (Sept. 1936): 545, 589.
"Our Washington Letter." A series in *Catholic Mirror* 24, no. 5 (Feb. 1, 1873): 1; 24, no. 7 (Feb. 15, 1873): 1; 24, no. 19 (May 10, 1873): 1; 24, no. 41 (Oct. 11, 1873): 1; 27, no. 25 (June 17, 1876): 5; 29, no. 5 (Feb. 2, 1878): 5.
Patton, G. F. *A Practical Guide to the Arrangement of Band Music*. New York: John F. Stratton, 1875.
Peters, Richard, ed. *Public Statutes at Large*. Boston: Little and Brown, 1848.
"Phonogram Records by the U.S. Marine Band." *Phonogram* 1 (Oct. 1891): 226.
"A Popular Band." *Musical Courier* 26, no. 18 (May 3, 1893): 13.
Preston, Katherine K. "Music and Musicians at the Mountain Resorts of Western Virginia, 1820–1900." In *A Celebration of American Music: Words and Music in*

Honor of H. Wiley Hitchcock, ed. Richard Crawford, R. Allen Lott, and Carol J. Oja, 154–73. Ann Arbor: University of Michigan Press, 1990.

———. *Music for Hire: A Study of Professional Musicians in Washington, 1877–1900*. Stuyvesant, N.Y.: Pendragon, 1992.

Pryor, Arthur. "How to Play a March." *Musical Courier* 103, no. 13 (Sept. 26, 1931): 45, 56.

Reisinger, Harold C. "Andrew Mealey and the Mongoose," *Marine Corps Gazette* 15, no. 4 (Feb. 1931): 41, 52.

"Reorganization of the Marine Band." Reports of Committees of the House of Representatives for the Second Session of the Fifty-First Congress, 1890–1891. Washington, D.C.: Government Printing Office, 1891.

Ressler, D. Michael. *Historical Perspective on the President's Own U.S. Marine Band*. Washington, D.C.: Headquarters, U.S. Marine Corps, 1998.

Reynolds, George E. "Sousa." *Instrumentalist* 5, no. 5 (Mar.–Apr. 1951): 12–13, 34. Repr. and rev. as "John Philip Sousa." *Instrumentalist* 17, no. 7 (Mar. 1963): 66.

——— and Allan Owen. "Favorite Sousa Marches: Playing Sousa à la Sousa." *Instrumentalist* 5, no. 5 (Mar–Apr. 1951): 14, 34.

Rosen, Zvi S. "The Twilight of the Opera Pirates: A Prehistory of the Exclusive Right of Public Performance for Musical Compositions." *Cardozo Arts and Entertainment Law Journal* 24 (2007): 1157–1218.

Schabas, Ezra. *Theodore Thomas: America's Conductor and Builder of Orchestras, 1835–1905*. Urbana: University of Illinois Press, 1989.

"Sidelights on Sousa's Personality." *Musical America* 12, no. 9 (July 9, 1910): 6, 31.

Smart, James R. "Genesis of a March: *The Stars and Stripes Forever*." In Newsom (1983), 105–19. Reprinted in *The Stars and Stripes Forever* (facsimile edition), 13–21. Washington, D.C.: Library of Congress, 1998.

———. *The Sousa Band: A Discography*. Washington. D.C.: Library of Congress, 1970.

Smith, Kathryn Schneider, ed. *Washington at Home: An Illustrated History of Neighborhoods in the Nation's Capital*, 2d ed. Baltimore: Johns Hopkins University Press, 2010.

Sollers, John Ford. "The Theatrical Career of John T. Ford." Ph.D. diss., Stanford University, 1962.

The Sounds of John Philip Sousa, vols. 1 and 2. American School Band Directors Association. Vol. 1: recorded by the Northern Virginia All-ASBDA High School Band, 1965. Vol. 2: recorded by the U.S. Army Band, 1969. Both issued by the ASBDA. Notes by Frank Simon (as dictated to Mac Carr). Vol. 1 has been rerecorded by the U.S. Army Band and released by the ASBDA.

Sousa, John Philip. "Bandmaster Sousa Explains His Mission in Music." *Musical America* 11, no. 23 (Apr. 16, 1910): 28.

———. "The Business of the Bandmaster." Repr. in *Band International* 22, no. 2 (July 2000): 69–71; 22, no. 3 (Nov. 2000): 111–13.

———. "Commander John Philip Sousa Tells of His Tour with the Offenbach Orchestra." *Etude* 48 (July 1930): 470.

———. *The Fifth String*. Indianapolis: Bowen-Merrill, 1902.

———. "The Greatest Game in the World." *Baseball Magazine* (Feb. 1909): 13–16.
———. "A Horse, a Dog, a Gun and a Girl." *American Shooter* 1, no. 16 (Aug. 1916): 3.
———. "How I Earned My Musical Education." *Etude* 26 (Nov. 1908): 695–96.
———. "How to Make Programs." *Musical Record* 383 (Dec. 1893): 15.
———. "In the Days of My Youth." *Mostly About People (M.A.P.)* 7, no. 175 (Oct. 19, 1901): 388.
———. "In the Days of Their Youth: Being a Musician." *Circle* 6, no. 3 (Sept. 1909): 127–28.
———. "Keeping Time." *Saturday Evening Post* 198 (1925), a series of six articles: (Oct. 31): 3–4, 145–54; (Nov. 7): 36–37, 96–106; (Nov. 21): 37–38, 109–14; (Nov. 28): 32–35, 97–105; (Dec. 5): 48–50, 155–65; and (Dec. 12): 45–46, 66–75.
———. "The Lady of the White House." *Ladies' Home Journal* 15, no. 2 (Jan. 1898): 16–17.
———. "A Letter from Sousa." *Etude* 16 (Aug. 1898): 231.
———. *Marching Along: Recollections of Men, Women and Music.* Boston: Hale, Cushman, and Flint, 1928. Repr. and ed. Paul E. Bierley. Westerville, Ohio: Integrity, 1994.
———. "The Menace of Mechanical Music." *Appleton's Magazine* 8, no. 3 (Sept. 1906): 278–84.
———. "Mr. John Philip Sousa Denies a Popular Fiction." *Etude* 26 (Apr. 1908), 224.
———. "My Contention." *Music Trades* (Dec. 1906): 183.
———. *National, Patriotic, and Typical Airs of All Lands.* Philadelphia: Harry Coleman, 1890. Repr., New York: Da Capo, 1977.
———. "Parks, Bands and Reminiscences." *Park International* 1, no. 2 (Sept. 1920), 162–63.
———. *Pipetown Sandy.* Indianapolis: Bobbs-Merrill, 1905.
———. "Then and Now." *Etude* 39 (May 1921), 306.
———. *Through the Year with Sousa.* New York: Thomas Y. Crowell, 1910.
———. *The Transit of Venus.* Boston: Small, Maynard, 1920.
———. *The Trumpet and Drum: A Book of Instruction for the Field-Trumpet and Drum, Together with the Trumpet and Drum Signals Now in Use in the Army, Navy and Marine Corps of the United States.* Washington: n.p., 1886. Repr., Chicago: W. F. L. Drum Co., 1954; repr., Ludwig Company, 1985.
Sousa, John Philip IV, with Loras Schissel. *John Philip Sousa's America: The Patriot's Life in Images and Words.* Chicago: GIA, 2012.
"Sousa and His Mission." *Music* (July 1899): 272–76.
"Sousa at Manhattan Beach." *Musical Courier* 27, no. 3 (July 19, 1893): 17.
"Sousa Band Encore Books Found!" *Sousa Band Society News* (Nov. 1968), 1–2.
"Sousa's Band." *Musical Age* 18, no. 8 (July 1, 1897): 6.
"Sousa's New Marine Band." *Musical Courier* 25, no. 18 (Nov. 9, 1892): 10–11.
"Sousa's New Marine Band Concert." *Musical Courier* 25, no. 17 (Nov. 2, 1892): 13.
"St. Augustine's Parish," *Church News* 14, no. 18 (Jan. 20, 1900): 5.
Stacy, William Barney. "John Philip Sousa and His Band Suites: An Analytic and Cultural Study." D.M.A. diss., University of Colorado, Boulder, 1972.

Sterngass, Jon. *First Resorts: Pursuing Pleasure at Saratoga Springs, Newport and Coney Island*. Baltimore: Johns Hopkins University Press, 2001.

Sullivan, David M. *The United States Marine Corps in the Civil War: The Second Year*. Shippensburg, Pa.: White Mane, 1997.

Sullivan et al. v. Goullaud, Equity Case no. 1391 (C.C. MA 1879).

Summers, C. Oland. "The Development of Original Band Scoring from Sousa to Husa." D.M.A. diss., Ball State University, 1986.

T. B. M. "Illiterate Music." *New York Musical Review and Gazette* 9, no. 1 (Jan. 9, 1858): 149–150; 9, no. 11 (May 29, 1858): 164–65.

Taper, Bernard, ed. *Mark Twain's San Francisco*. Berkeley: Heyday, 1963. Repr., 2003.

Taylor, Deems. *Of Men and Music*. New York: Simon and Schuster, 1937.

Terwilliger, Gloria H. "'The President's Own,' The United States Marine Band, 1798–1964; Chronologically Arranged and Annotated." M.S.L.S. thesis, Catholic University of America, 1967.

"Theodore Thomas and Sousa." *Musical Courier* 27, no. 7 (Aug. 16, 1893): 17.

Thomas, Theodore. *A Musical Autobiography*. Edited by George P. Upton. Chicago: A. C. McClurg, 1905. Repr., New York: Da Capo, 1964.

Trotter, James M. *Music and Some Highly Musical People*. Boston: Lee and Shepard, 1878.

Upton, Emory. *Infantry Tactics, Double and Single Rank*. New York: D. Appleton, 1875.

Upton, William Treat. *Art-Song in America: A Study in the Development of American Music*. Boston: Oliver Ditson, 1930. Repr., New York: Johnson, 1969.

Venezia, Mike. *John Philip Sousa*. New York: Children's, 1998.

Walker, Francis A., ed. *International Exhibition, 1876, Reports and Awards*, vol. 7. Washington, D.C.: Government Printing Office, 1880.

Wallace, Lew. *Ben-Hur: A Tale of the Christ*. New York: Harper, 1880.

Ward, Ellen MacDonald. "Augusta's Proudest Secret." *Down East* 43, no. 12 (July 1997): 72, 93–94.

"Wants to Lead Gilmore's Band." *Musical Courier* 25, no. 23 (Dec. 14, 1892): 14.

Warfield, Patrick. "Amateur and Professional, Permanent and Transient: Orchestras in the District of Columbia, 1877–1905." In *American Orchestras in the Nineteenth Century*, ed. John Spitzer, 194–215. Chicago: University of Chicago Press, 2012.

———. "The Essence of Uncle Sam: John Philip Sousa's 1911 World Tour." In *Kongreßbericht Oberwölz/Steiermark 2004*. Alta Musica 25, ed. Bernhard Habla, 359–78. Tutzing, Germany: Schneider, 2006.

———. "John Esputa, John Philip Sousa and the Boundaries of a Musical Career." *Nineteenth-Century Music Review* 6, no. 1 (June 2009): 27–46.

———, ed. *John Philip Sousa: Six Marches*. Music of the United States of America 21. Recent Researches in American Music 69. Madison, WI: A-R Editions, 2010.

———. "John Philip Sousa and 'The Menace of Mechanical Music.'" *Journal of the Society for American Music* 3 (Nov. 2009): 431–64.

———. "Making the Band: The Formation of John Philip Sousa's Ensemble." *American Music* 24 (spring 2006): 30–66.

———. "The March as Musical Drama and the Spectacle of John Philip Sousa." *Journal of the American Musicological Society* 64 (2011): 289–318.

———. "'Salesman of Americanism, Globetrotter, and Musician': The Nineteenth-Century John Philip Sousa, 1854–1893." Ph.D. diss., Indiana University, 2003.

"Washington Letter." *Catholic Mirror* 29, no. 5 (Feb. 2, 1878), 5.

Weil, Ann. *John Philip Sousa: Marching Boy*. Indianapolis: Bobbs-Merrill, 1959.

W. H. A. "Marches and Marches." *Metronome* 9, no. 6 (June 1895): 5

Whisler, John A. "The Songs of John Philip Sousa." M.M. thesis, Memphis State University, 1975.

"Why?" *Musical Courier* 22, no. 19 (May 13, 1891): 486.

Wilson, Francis. *Francis Wilson's Life of Himself*. Boston: Houghton Mifflin, 1924.

Wilson, J. Ormond. "Eighty Years of the Public Schools of Washington—1805 to 1885." *Records of the Columbia Historical Society* 1 (Oct. 1896): 119–70.

Wister, Owen. *The Virginian: A Horseman of the Plains*. New York: Macmillan, 1902.

Newspaper Articles

California, Los Angeles: *Express*. Classified advertisement, Apr. 9, 1892.

California, Los Angeles: *Times*. Classified advertisement, Apr. 9, 1892. "Music and Musicians," Apr. 13, 1892. "Music and Musicians," Apr. 14, 1892.

California, San Francisco: *Chronicle*. Untitled, June 17, 1906.

Georgia, Macon: *Telegraph*. "John Philip Sousa Tells Origin of His Name and How He Composes," Feb. 11, 1906.

Illinois, Chicago: *Herald*. Untitled article, Oct. 22, 1892. "Music by the Waves," June 26, 1893. "Farewell to Sousa," June 27, 1893. "Farewell Concert of Sousa's Band," June 28, 1893.

Illinois, Chicago: *Tribune*. "Music We Must Have," Nov. 23, 1890. "Music and Drama," Apr. 18, 1891. "New Band Promised for Chicago," Apr. 8, 1892.

Maine, Augusta: *Daily Kennebec Journal*. "Sousa Is a Busy Man," May 3, 1897.

Massachusetts, Boston: *Globe*. "*Desiree*, the New Opera at the Bijou," Dec. 16, 1884.

Massachusetts, Boston: *Post*. "Sousa's New War March," March 10, 1918.

Nebraska, Omaha: *World Herald*. "Washington's Latest Fad," Dec. 28, 1890.

New York, New York: *Herald*. "Mme. Chaminade and John Philip Sousa Talk about Music," Nov. 15, 1908.

New York, New York: *Times*. "The Music," May 11, 1876. "General Mention," Apr. 26, 1879. "Not One National Song," Aug. 25, 1889. "The Coming of Strauss," March 2, 1890. "An Ocean Steamer's Peril," June 15, 1891. "To Take Gilmore's Place," Oct. 9, 1892. "Famed Bandmaster Dead," Nov. 27, 1906. Sousa, "What Our National Anthem Should Be," Aug. 26, 1928.

Ohio, Cleveland: *Penny Press*. "Yesterday!," Sept. 26, 1881. "Scenes and Incidents," Sept. 27, 1881.

Pennsylvania, Lancaster: *Intelligencer*. "Vance and Sousa's New Composition," March 29, 1882.

Pennsylvania, Philadelphia: *Evening Bulletin.* "The Colored Opera Company," Feb. 22, 1873.

Pennsylvania, Philadelphia: *Inquirer.* "Amusements, Music, Etc.," June 19, 1876. Classified advertisement, June 19, 1876. "Sunday Concerts Enjoined," July 12, 1876. Classified advertisement, May 14, 1877. Classified advertisement, May 21, 1877. Classified advertisement, June 8, 1877. Classified advertisement, Aug. 28, 1877. "The *Sorcerer* at the Arch," Feb. 25, 1879. "The Church Choir *Pinafore*," Apr. 7, 1879. "The Mackay-Sylvester Combination at the Park," Aug. 31, 1880. "*Desiree* at Haverly's," Nov. 11, 1884. "Music in the Squares," Sept. 9, 1885. "Musicians Protest," March 21, 1889. "John Philip Sousa on Bands," March 28, 1889. "There's Something Most Mysterious," June 6, 1889. "The Marine Band's Concerts," Oct. 21, 1889. "A Small Republic with a Big Song," Oct. 24, 1889. "The Marine Band," Dec. 18, 1889. "What Will Be Done," Apr. 14, 1890. "The Marine Band Concert," Apr. 19, 1890. "The Marine Band Concerts," Oct. 19, 1890. "Musical Matters," Mar. 15, 1891. "May Musical Musings," May 9, 1897. "Simon Hassler Called by Death," Jan. 26, 1901. "Death Mutes Violin of Director Hassler," Dec. 2, 1906.

Pennsylvania, Pittsburgh: *Daily Dispatch.* "Amusements," Apr. 11, 1876. "A Question of License," Apr. 13, 1876. Editorial, Apr. 14, 1876. Editorial, Apr. 17, 1876. "The Tableaux Exhibition," Apr. 19, 1876.

UK, London: *Mail.* Sousa, "Mr. Sousa on Musical Pirates," Apr. 22, 1905.

UK, London: *Telegraph.* Sousa, "Musical Piracy," Apr. 27, 1905.

UK, London: *Times.* Sousa, "Musical Copyright," Jan. 16, 1903. Sousa, "International Copyright," Feb. 27, 1905.

Washington, D.C.: *Evening Critic.* "Sousa Exonerated (?)," Sept. 13, 1881.

Washington, D.C.: *Morning Chronicle.* "The Doctor of Alcantara," Feb. 4, 1873.

Washington, D.C.: *National Republican.* "The Young Ladies and Gentlemen," March 2, 1870. "The Colored American Opera Company," Feb. 1, 1873. "The Colored Opera," Feb. 5, 1873. "Personal," Jan. 31, 1876.

Washington, D.C.: *New National Era.* "The Colored American Opera Company," Feb. 6, 1873. "The Colored American Opera Company," Feb. 27, 1873. "The Colored Opera Troupe," May 15, 1873.

Washington, D.C.: *Post.* "Schneider's Sword," July 1, 1878. "A Washingtonian Heard From," Nov. 8, 1878. "City News in Brief," Nov. 15, 1878. "Miss Lottie Swallow Married," Oct. 31, 1879. "City Talk and Chatter," June 19, 1880. "Schneider's Trouble," Sept. 22, 1880. "Wilhelmj-Sternberg-Fritsch Concert at Lincoln Hall," Dec. 3, 1880. "The May Musical Festival," May 15, 1881. "City Talk and Chatter," June 20, 1881. "Trouble in the Marine Band," Sept. 10, 1881. "The Marine Band Trouble," Sept. 11, 1881. "The Esputa Estate," Jan. 6, 1882. "The Operatic Association," Feb. 2, 1882. "The National Rifles," Feb. 3, 1882. "A Reunited Family," Feb. 17, 1882. "The Marine Band Trouble," Feb. 18, 1882. "*The Smugglers* at Lincoln Hall," Feb. 18, 1882. "The Opera of *The Smugglers*," March 11, 1883. "Marine Band Concerts," May 26, 1883. "Marine Band Concert," June 2, 1883. "Closing Up the Day," Sept. 12, 1883.

Classified advertisement, Apr. 28, 1884. Musician, "Not an American Work," May 7, 1884. A Spectator, "*Desiree*," May 11, 1884. "Perpetuated in Bronze," May 11, 1884. "City News in Brief," Sept. 27, 1884. "Amusements," Nov. 16, 1884. Sousa, "Prof. Sousa Talks About His Opera," Dec. 9, 1884. "Dupont's Statue," Dec. 21, 1884. "The Inaugural Ball," Dec. 27, 1884. "Some Musical Matters," Feb. 15, 1885. Advertisement, March 6, 1885. H. L. W., "Some Musical Matters," March 8, 1885. "A Society Event," Mar. 29, 1885. "The Queen of Hearts," May 17, 1885. "Kaspar Takes the Baton," Nov. 21, 1886. H. L. W., "A Round of Concerts," Nov. 28, 1886. "Gen. Garfield in Bronze," May 13, 1887. "The White House Grounds Concert," July 9, 1887. "A Memorable Musical Season," March 11, 1888. "The White House Concert," July 21, 1888. "At Rest in Arlington," Aug. 12, 1888. "The Gridiron's Guests," Jan. 27, 1889. "Topical Talk," Jan. 28, 1889. "Attention, Scholars!," Apr. 7, 1889. "Young Authors," June 16, 1889. "Our National Air," Sept. 1, 1889. "The Collection of National Airs," Oct. 25, 1889. "Robert C. Bernays Wedded to Miss Elizabeth Sousa," Jan. 8, 1890. "A Real Event in Music," March 27, 1890. Sousa, "Not the Marine Band," March 28, 1890. "The Amateur Orchestra," Apr. 12, 1890. "Professor Kaspar's Tenth Anniversary," May 4, 1890. Classified Advertisement, Aug. 17, 1890. "The White House Concert," Sept. 13, 1890. "Good Amateur Music," Jan. 31, 1891. "John Philip Sousa Ill," May 16, 1891. "John Philip Sousa's Condition," July 12, 1891. "Will Wield His Baton," Sept. 3, 1891. "Leads as an Amateur," Nov. 15, 1891. "Music and Patriotism," Nov. 22, 1891. "Marine Band Concert," Feb. 23, 1892. "Set to Music by Sousa," Feb. 26, 1892. "Save the Marine Band," Apr. 13, 1892. "The Band's Gift to Sousa," July 30, 1892. "A Tribute to Prof. Sousa," July 30, 1892. "Sousa's Farewell Toot," July 31, 1892. "Prof. Sousa's Retirement," Aug. 1, 1892. "Only One Marine Band," Oct. 8, 1892. "Marine Bandsmen Angry," Oct. 30, 1892. "The Vexed Music Question," Feb. 6, 1893. "Professor Daniel Dead," Feb. 5, 1897. "Fanciulli a Prisoner," June 1, 1897. "Fanciulli at Liberty," June 2, 1897. "Prof. Sheldon Buried," Dec. 16, 1904. "Sousa Turns Fine Joke," Nov. 25, 1917. "Sousa Tells of March's World-Wide Popularity," Dec. 6, 1927. "Josef Kaspar, Noted Teacher and Orchestra Director, Dies," Mar. 20, 1936. Ray C. B. Brown, "Fostering of City's Musical Growth Throughout Years No Easy Task," Dec. 6, 1937.

Washington, D.C.: *Star.* "The Review," May 23, 1865. "Local News," July 12, 1865. "Musical Academy," July 7, 1869. "The Colored Opera," Feb. 4, 1873. "Our Colored American Opera Troupe," May 10, 1873. Classified advertisement, Feb. 3, 1874. Advertisement, Feb. 10, 1874. Classified advertisement, Apr. 3, 1876. "Married," Oct. 6, 1877. "Memorial Day, 1879," May 30, 1879. "The New Leader of the Marine Band," Oct. 2, 1880. "Affairs in West Washington," Jan. 20, 1882. "The Georgetown Amateur Orchestra," Apr. 25, 1885. "Our Musical Marines," June 14, 1890. "They Play the Violin," March 12, 1892. J. Harry Shannon, "Early Life of John Philip Sousa, 'The March King,' in Washington," Aug. 7, 1921. J. Harry Shannon, "Schroeder Name in D.C. Music History," June 7, 1925. J. Harry Shannon, "Esputa and Sousa Closely Associated," June 21, 1925. J. Harry Shannon, "'Northern Liberties' in Two Cities," June 28, 1925. J. Harry Shannon, "Rambler Tells Story of a

Pistorio Believed to Have Had Post with King," July 19, 1925. J. Harry Shannon, "Migration from Spain Preceded Establishment of Sousas Here," Aug. 23, 1925. J. Harry Shannon, "The Rambler Continues His Story of the Musical Sousa Family," Aug. 30, 1925. J. Harry Shannon, "Rambler's Story of Sousa Career Takes Him to Various Communities," Sept. 6, 1925. John Clagett Proctor, "Prof. Daniel, Pioneer Teacher of Music," Jan. 4, 1931. John Clagett Proctor, "Marine Band History and Its Leaders," May 8, 1932. "*High School Cadets March* Origin Revealed in Letter," Apr. 1, 1934. John Clagett Proctor, "Old Ford's Opera House and Famous Early Performances," July 18, 1943.

Washington, D.C.: *Sunday Morning Chronicle.* "Open-Air Concerts," June 15, 1862.

Washington, D.C.: *Times.* "Francis Scala, Director of Famous Marine Band for Thirty Years," Apr. 26, 1903.

Index

Page numbers referring to illustrations are in *italics*.

PATRICK WARFIELD is an associate professor of music at the University of Maryland and the editor of *John Philip Sousa: Six Marches*.

MUSIC IN AMERICAN LIFE

Only a Miner: Studies in Recorded Coal-Mining Songs *Archie Green*
Great Day Coming: Folk Music and the American Left *R. Serge Denisoff*
John Philip Sousa: A Descriptive Catalog of His Works *Paul E. Bierley*
The Hell-Bound Train: A Cowboy Songbook *Glenn Ohrlin*
Oh, Didn't He Ramble: The Life Story of Lee Collins, as Told to Mary Collins *Edited by Frank J. Gillis and John W. Miner*
American Labor Songs of the Nineteenth Century *Philip S. Foner*
Stars of Country Music: Uncle Dave Macon to Johnny Rodriguez *Edited by Bill C. Malone and Judith McCulloh*
Git Along, Little Dogies: Songs and Songmakers of the American West *John I. White*
A Texas-Mexican *Cancionero*: Folksongs of the Lower Border *Américo Paredes*
San Antonio Rose: The Life and Music of Bob Wills *Charles R. Townsend*
Early Downhome Blues: A Musical and Cultural Analysis *Jeff Todd Titon*
An Ives Celebration: Papers and Panels of the Charles Ives Centennial Festival-Conference *Edited by H. Wiley Hitchcock and Vivian Perlis*
Sinful Tunes and Spirituals: Black Folk Music to the Civil War *Dena J. Epstein*
Joe Scott, the Woodsman-Songmaker *Edward D. Ives*
Jimmie Rodgers: The Life and Times of America's Blue Yodeler *Nolan Porterfield*
Early American Music Engraving and Printing: A History of Music Publishing in America from 1787 to 1825, with Commentary on Earlier and Later Practices *Richard J. Wolfe*
Sing a Sad Song: The Life of Hank Williams *Roger M. Williams*
Long Steel Rail: The Railroad in American Folksong *Norm Cohen*
Resources of American Music History: A Directory of Source Materials from Colonial Times to World War II *D. W. Krummel, Jean Geil, Doris J. Dyen, and Deane L. Root*
Tenement Songs: The Popular Music of the Jewish Immigrants *Mark Slobin*
Ozark Folksongs *Vance Randolph; edited and abridged by Norm Cohen*
Oscar Sonneck and American Music *Edited by William Lichtenwanger*
Bluegrass Breakdown: The Making of the Old Southern Sound *Robert Cantwell*
Bluegrass: A History *Neil V. Rosenberg*
Music at the White House: A History of the American Spirit *Elise K. Kirk*
Red River Blues: The Blues Tradition in the Southeast *Bruce Bastin*
Good Friends and Bad Enemies: Robert Winslow Gordon and the Study of American Folksong *Debora Kodish*
Fiddlin' Georgia Crazy: Fiddlin' John Carson, His Real World, and the World of His Songs *Gene Wiggins*
America's Music: From the Pilgrims to the Present (rev. 3d ed.) *Gilbert Chase*
Secular Music in Colonial Annapolis: The Tuesday Club, 1745–56 *John Barry Talley*
Bibliographical Handbook of American Music *D. W. Krummel*
Goin' to Kansas City *Nathan W. Pearson, Jr.*

"Susanna," "Jeanie," and "The Old Folks at Home": The Songs of Stephen C. Foster from His Time to Ours (2d ed.)   *William W. Austin*

Songprints: The Musical Experience of Five Shoshone Women   *Judith Vander*

"Happy in the Service of the Lord": Afro-American Gospel Quartets in Memphis   *Kip Lornell*

Paul Hindemith in the United States   *Luther Noss*

"My Song Is My Weapon": People's Songs, American Communism, and the Politics of Culture, 1930–50   *Robbie Lieberman*

Chosen Voices: The Story of the American Cantorate   *Mark Slobin*

Theodore Thomas: America's Conductor and Builder of Orchestras, 1835–1905   *Ezra Schabas*

"The Whorehouse Bells Were Ringing" and Other Songs Cowboys Sing   *Collected and Edited by Guy Logsdon*

Crazeology: The Autobiography of a Chicago Jazzman   *Bud Freeman, as Told to Robert Wolf*

Discoursing Sweet Music: Brass Bands and Community Life in Turn-of-the-Century Pennsylvania   *Kenneth Kreitner*

Mormonism and Music: A History   *Michael Hicks*

Voices of the Jazz Age: Profiles of Eight Vintage Jazzmen   *Chip Deffaa*

Pickin' on Peachtree: A History of Country Music in Atlanta, Georgia   *Wayne W. Daniel*

Bitter Music: Collected Journals, Essays, Introductions, and Librettos   *Harry Partch; edited by Thomas McGeary*

Ethnic Music on Records: A Discography of Ethnic Recordings Produced in the United States, 1893 to 1942   *Richard K. Spottswood*

Downhome Blues Lyrics: An Anthology from the Post–World War II Era   *Jeff Todd Titon*

Ellington: The Early Years   *Mark Tucker*

Chicago Soul   *Robert Pruter*

That Half-Barbaric Twang: The Banjo in American Popular Culture   *Karen Linn*

Hot Man: The Life of Art Hodes   *Art Hodes and Chadwick Hansen*

The Erotic Muse: American Bawdy Songs (2d ed.)   *Ed Cray*

Barrio Rhythm: Mexican American Music in Los Angeles   *Steven Loza*

The Creation of Jazz: Music, Race, and Culture in Urban America   *Burton W. Peretti*

Charles Martin Loeffler: A Life Apart in Music   *Ellen Knight*

Club Date Musicians: Playing the New York Party Circuit   *Bruce A. MacLeod*

Opera on the Road: Traveling Opera Troupes in the United States, 1825–60   *Katherine K. Preston*

The Stonemans: An Appalachian Family and the Music That Shaped Their Lives   *Ivan M. Tribe*

Transforming Tradition: Folk Music Revivals Examined   *Edited by Neil V. Rosenberg*

The Crooked Stovepipe: Athapaskan Fiddle Music and Square Dancing in Northeast Alaska and Northwest Canada   *Craig Mishler*

Traveling the High Way Home: Ralph Stanley and the World of Traditional Bluegrass Music   *John Wright*

Carl Ruggles: Composer, Painter, and Storyteller *Marilyn Ziffrin*
Never without a Song: The Years and Songs of Jennie Devlin, 1865–1952 *Katharine D. Newman*
The Hank Snow Story *Hank Snow, with Jack Ownbey and Bob Burris*
Milton Brown and the Founding of Western Swing *Cary Ginell, with special assistance from Roy Lee Brown*
Santiago de Murcia's "Códice Saldívar No. 4": A Treasury of Secular Guitar Music from Baroque Mexico *Craig H. Russell*
The Sound of the Dove: Singing in Appalachian Primitive Baptist Churches *Beverly Bush Patterson*
Heartland Excursions: Ethnomusicological Reflections on Schools of Music *Bruno Nettl*
Doowop: The Chicago Scene *Robert Pruter*
Blue Rhythms: Six Lives in Rhythm and Blues *Chip Deffaa*
Shoshone Ghost Dance Religion: Poetry Songs and Great Basin Context *Judith Vander*
Go Cat Go! Rockabilly Music and Its Makers *Craig Morrison*
'Twas Only an Irishman's Dream: The Image of Ireland and the Irish in American Popular Song Lyrics, 1800–1920 *William H. A. Williams*
Democracy at the Opera: Music, Theater, and Culture in New York City, 1815–60 *Karen Ahlquist*
Fred Waring and the Pennsylvanians *Virginia Waring*
Woody, Cisco, and Me: Seamen Three in the Merchant Marine *Jim Longhi*
Behind the Burnt Cork Mask: Early Blackface Minstrelsy and Antebellum American Popular Culture *William J. Mahar*
Going to Cincinnati: A History of the Blues in the Queen City *Steven C. Tracy*
Pistol Packin' Mama: Aunt Molly Jackson and the Politics of Folksong *Shelly Romalis*
Sixties Rock: Garage, Psychedelic, and Other Satisfactions *Michael Hicks*
The Late Great Johnny Ace and the Transition from R&B to Rock 'n' Roll *James M. Salem*
Tito Puente and the Making of Latin Music *Steven Loza*
Juilliard: A History *Andrea Olmstead*
Understanding Charles Seeger, Pioneer in American Musicology *Edited by Bell Yung and Helen Rees*
Mountains of Music: West Virginia Traditional Music from *Goldenseal* *Edited by John Lilly*
Alice Tully: An Intimate Portrait *Albert Fuller*
A Blues Life *Henry Townsend, as told to Bill Greensmith*
Long Steel Rail: The Railroad in American Folksong (2d ed.) *Norm Cohen*
The Golden Age of Gospel *Text by Horace Clarence Boyer; photography by Lloyd Yearwood*
Aaron Copland: The Life and Work of an Uncommon Man *Howard Pollack*
Louis Moreau Gottschalk *S. Frederick Starr*
Race, Rock, and Elvis *Michael T. Bertrand*

Theremin: Ether Music and Espionage *Albert Glinsky*
Poetry and Violence: The Ballad Tradition of Mexico's Costa Chica *John H. McDowell*
The Bill Monroe Reader *Edited by Tom Ewing*
Music in Lubavitcher Life *Ellen Koskoff*
Zarzuela: Spanish Operetta, American Stage *Janet L. Sturman*
Bluegrass Odyssey: A Documentary in Pictures and Words, 1966–86 *Carl Fleischhauer and Neil V. Rosenberg*
That Old-Time Rock & Roll: A Chronicle of an Era, 1954–63 *Richard Aquila*
Labor's Troubadour *Joe Glazer*
American Opera *Elise K. Kirk*
Don't Get above Your Raisin': Country Music and the Southern Working Class *Bill C. Malone*
John Alden Carpenter: A Chicago Composer *Howard Pollack*
Heartbeat of the People: Music and Dance of the Northern Pow-wow *Tara Browner*
My Lord, What a Morning: An Autobiography *Marian Anderson*
Marian Anderson: A Singer's Journey *Allan Keiler*
Charles Ives Remembered: An Oral History *Vivian Perlis*
Henry Cowell, Bohemian *Michael Hicks*
Rap Music and Street Consciousness *Cheryl L. Keyes*
Louis Prima *Garry Boulard*
Marian McPartland's Jazz World: All in Good Time *Marian McPartland*
Robert Johnson: Lost and Found *Barry Lee Pearson and Bill McCulloch*
Bound for America: Three British Composers *Nicholas Temperley*
Lost Sounds: Blacks and the Birth of the Recording Industry, 1890–1919 *Tim Brooks*
Burn, Baby! BURN! The Autobiography of Magnificent Montague *Magnificent Montague with Bob Baker*
Way Up North in Dixie: A Black Family's Claim to the Confederate Anthem *Howard L. Sacks and Judith Rose Sacks*
The Bluegrass Reader *Edited by Thomas Goldsmith*
Colin McPhee: Composer in Two Worlds *Carol J. Oja*
Robert Johnson, Mythmaking, and Contemporary American Culture *Patricia R. Schroeder*
Composing a World: Lou Harrison, Musical Wayfarer *Leta E. Miller and Fredric Lieberman*
Fritz Reiner, Maestro and Martinet *Kenneth Morgan*
That Toddlin' Town: Chicago's White Dance Bands and Orchestras, 1900–1950 *Charles A. Sengstock Jr.*
Dewey and Elvis: The Life and Times of a Rock 'n' Roll Deejay *Louis Cantor*
Come Hither to Go Yonder: Playing Bluegrass with Bill Monroe *Bob Black*
Chicago Blues: Portraits and Stories *David Whiteis*
The Incredible Band of John Philip Sousa *Paul E. Bierley*
"Maximum Clarity" and Other Writings on Music *Ben Johnston, edited by Bob Gilmore*
Staging Tradition: John Lair and Sarah Gertrude Knott *Michael Ann Williams*

Homegrown Music: Discovering Bluegrass *Stephanie P. Ledgin*
Tales of a Theatrical Guru *Danny Newman*
The Music of Bill Monroe *Neil V. Rosenberg and Charles K. Wolfe*
Pressing On: The Roni Stoneman Story *Roni Stoneman, as told to Ellen Wright*
Together Let Us Sweetly Live *Jonathan C. David, with photographs by Richard Holloway*
Live Fast, Love Hard: The Faron Young Story *Diane Diekman*
Air Castle of the South: WSM Radio and the Making of Music City *Craig P. Havighurst*
Traveling Home: Sacred Harp Singing and American Pluralism *Kiri Miller*
Where Did Our Love Go? The Rise and Fall of the Motown Sound *Nelson George*
Lonesome Cowgirls and Honky-Tonk Angels: The Women of Barn Dance Radio *Kristine M. McCusker*
California Polyphony: Ethnic Voices, Musical Crossroads *Mina Yang*
The Never-Ending Revival: Rounder Records and the Folk Alliance *Michael F. Scully*
Sing It Pretty: A Memoir *Bess Lomax Hawes*
Working Girl Blues: The Life and Music of Hazel Dickens *Hazel Dickens and Bill C. Malone*
Charles Ives Reconsidered *Gayle Sherwood Magee*
The Hayloft Gang: The Story of the National Barn Dance *Edited by Chad Berry*
Country Music Humorists and Comedians *Loyal Jones*
Record Makers and Breakers: Voices of the Independent Rock 'n' Roll Pioneers *John Broven*
Music of the First Nations: Tradition and Innovation in Native North America *Edited by Tara Browner*
Cafe Society: The Wrong Place for the Right People *Barney Josephson, with Terry Trilling-Josephson*
George Gershwin: An Intimate Portrait *Walter Rimler*
Life Flows On in Endless Song: Folk Songs and American History *Robert V. Wells*
I Feel a Song Coming On: The Life of Jimmy McHugh *Alyn Shipton*
King of the Queen City: The Story of King Records *Jon Hartley Fox*
Long Lost Blues: Popular Blues in America, 1850–1920 *Peter C. Muir*
Hard Luck Blues: Roots Music Photographs from the Great Depression *Rich Remsberg*
Restless Giant: The Life and Times of Jean Aberbach and Hill and Range Songs *Bar Biszick-Lockwood*
Champagne Charlie and Pretty Jemima: Variety Theater in the Nineteenth Century *Gillian M. Rodger*
Sacred Steel: Inside an African American Steel Guitar Tradition *Robert L. Stone*
Gone to the Country: The New Lost City Ramblers and the Folk Music Revival *Ray Allen*
The Makers of the Sacred Harp *David Warren Steel with Richard H. Hulan*
Woody Guthrie, American Radical *Will Kaufman*

George Szell: A Life of Music *Michael Charry*
Bean Blossom: The Brown County Jamboree and Bill Monroe's Bluegrass Festivals *Thomas A. Adler*
Crowe on the Banjo: The Music Life of J. D. Crowe *Marty Godbey*
Twentieth Century Drifter: The Life of Marty Robbins *Diane Diekman*
Henry Mancini: Reinventing Film Music *John Caps*
The Beautiful Music All Around Us: Field Recordings and the American Experience *Stephen Wade*
Then Sings My Soul: The Culture of Southern Gospel Music *Douglas Harrison*
The Accordion in the Americas: Klezmer, Polka, Tango, Zydeco, and More! *Edited by Helena Simonett*
Bluegrass Bluesman: A Memoir *Josh Graves, edited by Fred Bartenstein*
One Woman in a Hundred: Edna Phillips and the Philadelphia Orchestra *Mary Sue Welsh*
The Great Orchestrator: Arthur Judson and American Arts Management *James M. Doering*
Charles Ives in the Mirror: American Histories of an Iconic Composer *David C. Paul*
Southern Soul-Blues *David Whiteis*
Sweet Air: Modernism, Regionalism, and American Popular Song *Edward P. Comentale*
Pretty Good for a Girl: Women in Bluegrass *Murphy Hicks Henry*
Sweet Dreams: The World of Patsy Cline *Warren R. Hofstra*
William Sidney Mount and the Creolization of American Culture *Christopher J. Smith*
Bird: The Life and Music of Charlie Parker *Chuck Haddix*
Making the March King: John Philip Sousa's Washington Years, 1854–1893 *Patrick Warfield*

The University of Illinois Press
is a founding member of the
Association of American University Presses.

Composed in 10.25/13.25 Adobe Minion Pro
by Lisa Connery
at the University of Illinois Press
Manufactured by Sheridan Books, Inc.

University of Illinois Press
1325 South Oak Street
Champaign, IL 61820-6903
www.press.uillinois.edu